SUCCESSFUL EXECUTIVE'S HANDBOOK

www.personneldecisions.com

Also published by Personnel Decisions International

Successful Manager's Handbook:
Development Suggestions for Today's Managers

Successful Manager's Handbook (Japanese language version)

Suggestions de développement et ressources
à l'usage des managers d'aujourd'hui

Entwicklungsvorschläge für erfolgreiches Management

Supplement to the Successful Manager's Handbook:
Readings, Seminars and Training Courses (available in the UK)

Development FIRST: Strategies for Self-Development

Development FIRST Workbook

Leader As Coach: Strategies for Coaching & Developing Others

Leader As Coach Workbook

Presentations: How to Calm Down, Think Clearly, and
Captivate Your Audience

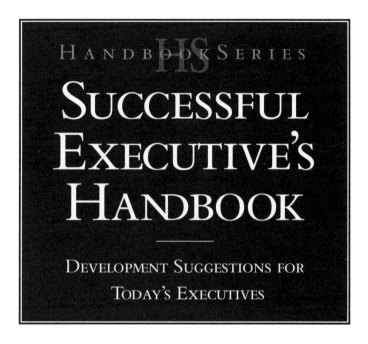

HANDBOOK SERIES

SUCCESSFUL EXECUTIVE'S HANDBOOK

DEVELOPMENT SUGGESTIONS FOR
TODAY'S EXECUTIVES

SUSAN H. GEBELEIN
DAVID G. LEE
KRISTIE J. NELSON-NEUHAUS
ELAINE B. SLOAN

PUBLISHED BY
PERSONNEL DECISIONS INTERNATIONAL CORPORATION
OFFICES THROUGHOUT
NORTH AMERICA, EUROPE, ASIA, AND AUSTRALIA

PDI | PERSONNEL DECISIONS INTERNATIONAL

www.personneldecisions.com

Book Design and Production: Barbara Redmond Design
Editorial Services: Bonnie Anderson

This book is bound by the otabind process so that it will lie flat when opened. The spine gap is a feature of the otabind method.

DevelopMentor® is a registered trademark of
Personnel Decisions International Corporation.

DevelopMentor® eAdvisor™ is a trademark of
Personnel Decisions International Corporation.

PDI Pipeline For Development™ is a trademark of
Personnel Decisions International Corporation.

www.epredix.com
www.personneldecisions.com

ISBN: 0-9725770-0-9.

CONTENTS

ACKNOWLEDGMENTS

———

We would like to recognize and thank those who helped make this book possible. The *Successful Executive's Handbook* is a result of true partnerships within and outside of PDI.

Thank you for your help.

Val Arnold	Ellen Kruser
Terri Baumgardner	Cindy Marsh
Harry Brull	LeRoy Martin
Deb Canaday	Michael McGrath
Adriana Cento	Bob Muschewske
Fred Cox	Donna Neumann
Brian Davis	Cal Oltrogge
Michael Frisch	David Peterson
Dee Gaeddert	Joanne Provo
Victor Gonzales	Lou Quast
Tami Grewenow	Pete Ramstad
JoAnn Grimes	Diane Rawlings
Kristine Habacker	Neil Sendelbach
Ken Hedberg	Carol Skube
Lowell Hellervik	Katrina Soli
Mary Dee Hicks	Jeffrey Stoner
Teresa Jensen	Dale Thompson
Kathy Kinchen	Paul Van Katwyk

INTRODUCTION

No one disputes it—people development is vital. Pick any topic—e-commerce, globalization, megamergers—and the need for new skills grows stronger.

Development is important for every position in the organization, especially executives. It's no longer the world of clear-cut career paths and a concrete set of knowledge. It is an ever-shifting, increasingly demanding, faster paced world in which knowledge is central.

The executive role is more demanding today than it was a decade ago. Executives need to display depth and breadth in more areas than their predecessors. Mindful, sustained development is the only way executives can acquire the skills they need to thrive in such an environment.

Why we wrote this handbook

Executives are busy. They rarely have time to ponder how they can develop a particular skill. They just know they have to or they will be left behind.

Development is difficult. It takes time, commitment, creativity, sustained effort, feedback, and the help of other people. It is not something that can be accomplished in one afternoon.

Finding practical, on-the-job activities and advice can be difficult. Ideas may not come easily when you're thinking of your own situation. You may not know how to get started, what is required in a certain area, whom you should ask for advice, or what it takes to reach the next level. This handbook can help.

It is filled with tips and strategies that will help you develop your competency in twenty-one areas that are vital to executive performance. It is easy to read without being simplistic. We focus on what you need to know.

However, we are not going to give you all the answers. We want you to use this book to find ideas, stimulate your thinking, and start discussions. We want you to figure out what will work for you in your role. Most of all, we want you to set some development goals and begin working on them.

Development is an adventure. Like any adventure, it requires preparation, planning, equipment, time, and the desire to reach an end goal. Consider this handbook an essential part of your gear.

What you will find in this handbook

The chapters in this book are based on the competencies of our Executive Success Profile. Each chapter contains valuable tips and strategies for action. Combined, they give you targeted suggestions, plus some context for why and how you should develop a particular competency. Books and seminars for each chapter are listed in a separate section at the end of the handbook.

Here is a capsule preview of each chapter:

Chapter 1: Seasoned Judgment

Executives are responsible for making far-reaching decisions. They need to sort through complex issues, determine which information has merit, and make tough calls. We point out how you can develop your analytical thinking skills, find the information you need, identify underlying issues, and make decisions at the right time.

Chapter 2: Visionary Thinking

Executives are responsible for thinking about the future of their organizations. What do they want to accomplish? Are they going to lead the industry or follow? We show you how to look at your organization with a fresh perspective, break through status-quo thinking and expectations, and discuss the future in a way that captures the imagination of the employees in your organization.

Chapter 3: Financial Acumen

Understanding financial information is a bottom-line skill for all executives. If you don't understand the numbers, you won't make the numbers. We outline some of the major areas you should pay attention to, and explain some key concepts.

Chapter 4: Global Perspective

As the world grows smaller, an executive's perspective must grow larger. The global marketplace continues to grow, mergers are creating more multinational organizations, and events in one area of the world have far-reaching consequences. We discuss how to broaden your outlook, anticipate how trends will affect your industry and organization, grasp your organization's market position, and operate in a global economy.

Chapter 5: Shaping Strategy

Say the word "executive" and one of the first images that comes to mind is a person who discusses strategy. What is strategy? What distinguishes your strategy from that of your competitors? What critical success factors do you need to consider? We offer our thoughts and suggestions on this key component of the executive role.

Chapter 6: Driving Execution

Executives need to achieve results; the success of the organization depends on it. However, one question must be answered: What type of results are they going to achieve? We discuss continual improvement, including how to track whether improvement is truly happening. We also tackle the thorny issues of crisis management and problem performers.

Chapter 7: Attracting and Developing Talent

It all comes down to people. If you don't have the type of people you need or want, your organization will be hobbled. We outline our cutting-edge thinking on the topics of selecting and developing talented people, including specific action steps for succession management and development planning.

Chapter 8: Empowering Others

We've all heard about empowerment, but what does it really mean? We believe it describes a place where people have the latitude and authority to do their work effectively, where they feel a sense of ownership in the business, and where they feel recognized for their efforts. You'll find suggestions on making this definition a reality.

Chapter 9: Influencing and Negotiating

How many times a day do you negotiate—about business priorities, resources, etc? How do you influence people to your point of view when you know they believe that your point of view is wrong or misdirected? We give you tips on being persuasive, winning approval for your initiatives, creating win/win results, and negotiating the best deal possible.

Chapter 10: Leadership Versatility

"If the only tool you have is a hammer, you'll treat every problem like a nail." If you only have one leadership style, you will only be effective with the type of employee that responds to that style. We discuss a number of leadership roles and when it is appropriate to use (or not use) each one.

Chapter 11: Building Organizational Relationships

Executives need to know what is happening in all areas of the organization and across their industry. They can't afford to dwell in the "upper atmosphere." They need to actively cultivate a network of relationships inside and outside the organization, and relate well to colleagues at all levels. We address networking and offer specific tips for relating well to your boss, your peers, and your direct reports.

Chapter 12: Inspiring Trust

People want leaders who are fair, trustworthy, respectful, and ethical. In other words, they want people with integrity. We discuss some of the key areas in which you need to demonstrate your integrity, such as acting with consistency and establishing open, candid relationships.

Chapter 13: Fostering Open Dialogue

How many times have you heard someone say, "I didn't hear about that in time," or "Why didn't they tell me? It would have saved hours of research!" We'll help you create an environment of fearless communication, where information flows freely through the layers of the organization.

Chapter 14: High-Impact Delivery

It seems that many people would rather walk on burning coals than give a speech. Executives need to be comfortable giving presentations, speaking to the media, addressing large audiences, and conducting high-profile meetings. We offer tried-and-true strategies for preparing your presentation, delivering it, answering tough questions, and conquering your nerves.

Chapter 15: Drive for Stakeholder Success

There may be days when it seems that every stakeholder has a different idea of how things should be done and they all contradict each other. That is the challenge for an executive—pulling stakeholder groups together to pursue aggressive goals and achieve results that will benefit everyone. We share tips on how you can do what is best for all your stakeholders, including customers, shareholders, and employees.

Chapter 16: Entrepreneurial Risk Taking

Entrepreneurialism is in the air; it seems that every day you read an article about a new start-up, an IPO, or a new venture by an established company. How can you join them? We discuss how to champion new ideas within your organization, make opportunities a reality, and foster creativity and risk taking with your employees.

Chapter 17: Mature Confidence

Confidence can be difficult to pin down—you need it to be a leader but you don't want to have so much that you come across as an egotist. We talk about genuine, mature confidence that allows people to face both their strengths and shortcomings, stand their ground on important issues, and share credit with others.

Chapter 18: Adaptability

Executives who try to do things in a traditional way often find that they are fighting a losing battle. The world is not going to wait for people to catch up. We cover some of the big topics: stress, pressure, change, ambiguity, and remaining positive.

Chapter 19: Career and Self-Direction

What is your plan? Where do you want to be in the next five years? How are you going to get there? We outline ways in which you can purposefully plan your career and align it with your deeply held values. We also talk about work/life balance and prioritizing your time so you can pursue what is important to you.

Chapter 20: Cross-Functional Capability

Executives often rise through the ranks in one area of the organization, such as operations or sales. As they advance, they realize that their knowledge of other functions must increase because their work intersects with other groups. We discuss the functions common to most organizations and give you strategies for working across functional and organizational lines.

Chapter 21: Industry Knowledge

You may be in an industry where the knowledge set seems to double every few months. How can you possibly keep up? What should you focus on? We talk about how to develop your historical sense, how to assess your competitors within the industry, and why you should learn about industries outside your realm.

Ideas for Using this Handbook

This handbook can play an important part in your development and the development of people in your organization. There are a number of ways you can use it; here are a few to get you started:

- Look for action steps for your development plan, or for someone you are coaching or mentoring.

- Search for ideas and activities for your long-term career development.

- Refer people to specific sections or chapters as you help them with their development.

- Advise others on the competency and performance expectations for executive management.

- Diagnose development needs and opportunity areas for executives.

- Consult the handbook during the development portion of performance management and succession management.

Final Thoughts

We at PDI are interested in your feedback. Please let us know what you think of this handbook:

- What was helpful?

- What would you like to see more or less of?

- What one area was the most useful for you?

- How are you using the book? Are you using it for your personal development or for development planning with the people you are coaching?

- What would you like to see in future editions of the handbook?

Send your comments directly to Kristie Nelson-Neuhaus at kristien@pdi-corp.com. We look forward to hearing from you!

EXECUTIVE SUCCESS PROFILE

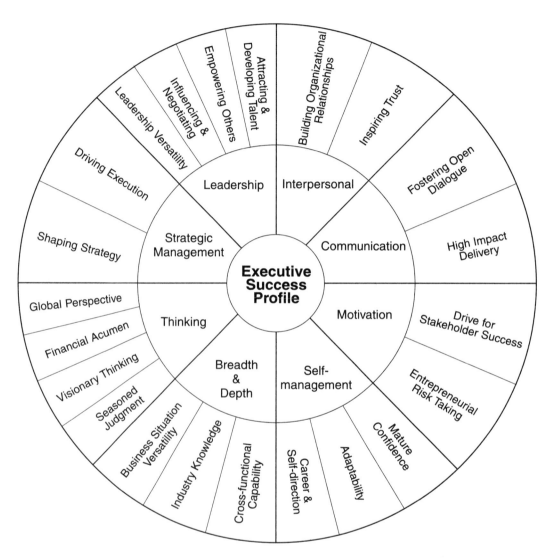

I
SEASONED JUDGMENT

———

APPLY BROAD KNOWLEDGE AND SEASONED
EXPERIENCE WHEN ADDRESSING COMPLEX ISSUES;
DEFINE STRATEGIC ISSUES CLEARLY DESPITE
AMBIGUITY; TAKE ALL CRITICAL INFORMATION
INTO ACCOUNT WHEN MAKING DECISIONS;
MAKE TIMELY, TOUGH DECISIONS.

KEY BEHAVIORS

———

1. *Apply broad knowledge and seasoned experience to address complex/critical issues.*
2. *Define issues clearly despite incomplete or ambiguous information.*
3. *Dig deeply to get the necessary information for decision making.*
4. *Link problems and symptoms to identify underlying strategic issues.*
5. *Creatively integrate different ideas and perspectives.*
6. *Take all important issues into account when making decisions.*
7. *Come to a decision at the right time.*
8. *Make tough, pragmatic decisions when necessary.*

INTRODUCTION

Seasoned judgment is a critical skill for every executive. The relative importance of other skills may vary due to the nature of an executive's responsibilities and the industry in which he or she works, but a consistent display of effective, seasoned judgment is crucial for all executives.

Seasoned judgment is a mental balancing act. Making timely, sound decisions requires a balance between analysis and decisiveness. People skilled in seasoned judgment are able to grasp the specifics of a situation and step back to see the larger picture. They can define an issue despite incomplete or ambiguous information. They know how to identify and focus on the most critical, high-impact issues and separate important issues from the merely urgent. They practice systems thinking wherein they recognize key patterns and interrelationships, and anticipate the implications of their actions on other parts of the organization.

VALUABLE TIPS

- When you encounter problems or opportunities, draw on your experience for insight and ideas. Identify similar situations and adapt that approach to the current situation.

- Learn from your direct reports; spend time with people on your team who have the expertise and skills you need.

- Involve others to provide feedback about a tentative decision. Modify your decision as appropriate.

- Surround yourself with experts in problem analysis, root cause analysis, and opportunity analysis.

- Regularly use process charts to understand flow, interdependencies, and opportunities.

- Determine what level of detail you truly need and what value it will add to your decision.

- Identify the biggest problem people do not expect to be resolved and challenge the belief that the situation is a given.

- Identify and consider the point of view of all stakeholders involved in a problem or situation.

- View problems as a process rather than an event, which will free you to explore a much broader range of possibilities.

- Predict probable consequences for your team's actions. Predict at least five consequences for each possible option.

- When you find yourself reacting emotionally to an issue, hold off on making your decision until your emotional state changes.

- Give people permission to give you feedback and tell you when they think you may have overreacted. It is essential that you get this kind of feedback.

- Challenge others to anticipate issues and determine the implications for your area.

STRATEGIES FOR ACTION

1. Apply broad knowledge and seasoned experience to address complex/critical issues.

As an executive, you are likely to have considerable experience in your organization, function, business, or industry. As such you are able to bring perspective to situations.

Draw from your knowledge bank

- When you encounter problems or opportunities, draw on your experience for insight and ideas. Identify situations that were similar to the one you face now. What worked in the past? What options did you have? How could you adapt that approach in the current situation?

- To gain perspective, seriously consider the real difference between one course of action and another. As one executive in the health care industry asked, "In the light of eternity, what difference does it make?"

- Reflect and learn from your successes and failures. Ask "What did I do well?" "What didn't work?" and "What will I do differently next time?"

- Remember your experiences by keeping a journal. Note what you learned and how you approached problems.

- Take advantage of opportunities to teach others what you know. Challenge yourself to work with high-potential people who need to combine their intelligence with seasoned judgment.

- Draw out the expertise of others by challenging them to identify patterns, trends, or themes.

Continually expand your base of knowledge and experience

- Expose yourself to new ideas. Challenge yourself to learn something of substance each quarter. Expand your knowledge beyond your job, industry, or usual interests.

- Choose an area of your organization about which you know relatively little. Over the next three months, learn all you can about that area. Ask people about their responsibilities and the types of decisions they make. Find out how they keep up with developments in their field.

- Allow your direct reports to teach you. Spend time with people on your **team who have the expertise and skills you need. Ask questions** and seek advice on important issues. Let them teach you; you will learn a great deal and they will be empowered.

- Catch yourself when you are unwilling to learn something new. Think about whether you really have the luxury of not knowing the information or concept.

- Listen to the questions others are asking and identify what they expect you to know. If you do not understand the value of the information, ask more questions to clarify its importance before you pursue it further.

- Identify the knowledge and experience you need to round out your seasoned judgment. Develop a plan to acquire that experience and knowledge.
    - Study other functions and industries. What can you learn?
    - Take care that you do not limit benchmarking to your industry. Expertise in particular business processes may be located outside your industry.

- Determine your most effective learning style. Some people prefer to learn step by step; others learn by watching others. Use what works best for you. Also, learn how to increase your rate of comprehension by taking a rapid reading or accelerated learning course.

- Sponsor learning opportunities in the community such as speakers' series.

2. Define issues clearly despite incomplete or ambiguous information.

Recognize that you will make many decisions in which you do not have enough information, the issues are not well defined, or there are no clear solutions. You will encounter many situations in which you cannot obtain enough information to be certain of your decision. You will also be in countless situations in which trusted advisors disagree about the course of action to take. Yet, you still need to make a decision.

In fact, if you are on the cutting edge and creating opportunities, you will not be able to get the information because the idea will be so new. For example, it was impossible to do research on the size of the market for 3M's Post-it® notes, because no one knew what they were, how to use them, or that they would be invaluable in office life.

Identify the kind of issue you have

- Deconstruct the problem, so that you understand its parts. Determine what needs quick action and what can wait. You may want to use some of the problem analysis tools discussed later in this section to identify the parts of the problem and the root issues.

- Plan to resolve the issues that have to be resolved quickly. Wait on those that can wait.

- Determine the criticality of a decision.

- Identify whether you have a simple or complex issue. In some situations, you can make a unilateral decision and action will occur. In other situations, the process for making a decision will be complicated and involve many people.

Identify core issues

- When you look at an issue, identify the core issues, decide what needs to be decided, and then determine what can be decided without further analysis.

- Use an analysis process which identifies key elements/critical path/root causes.

- When you are looking for root causes, focus on the system instead of specific events or people. Develop a plan to gather the necessary information that is available.

- Create a flow or process chart to understand the steps in the process or parts of the issue. This can help you trace the likely sources of the problem and focus on the system.

- Use graphs or charts to illustrate the problem or some part of it. It is often helpful to create a graph showing when the problem occurs and when it does not.

Make a decision in the face of ambiguity

- When you have gathered all the known information, make a guess about the unknown factors. Then look at the alternatives. Analyze the benefits and possible costs of each option, especially if the option could lead to a wrong decision.

- Figure out how you can recover if you make the wrong call. Selecting an option that can be changed relatively easily will give you more flexibility than an option that eliminates or limits the choices available to you.

- Determine the plan you will use to fix the situation if you have just made a wrong call. Effective executives recover well and fast!

- Involve others to provide feedback about the tentative decision. Modify your decision as appropriate.

3. Dig deeply to get the necessary information for decision making.

Executives need to sort through issues to identify the critical few in which they need to be involved. It is extremely easy to get bogged down by the huge amount of information coming through voice mail, e-mail, and other channels.

Identify and focus on the most critical, high-impact issues

- Surround yourself with people who have expertise in problem analysis, root cause analysis, and opportunity analysis. They will help you ferret out root issues to address.

- Consider using the "five whys" approach for identifying root issues. State a problem, then uncover layers of cause and effect by asking why five times. For example, why did the event occur, why did that condition exist, why was the situation affected by that condition, why did people try a certain course of action, and why was that the result?

- Trust your staff to produce analyses and recommendations. This will allow you to focus on making sure the right issues have been identified, and that enough options have been generated for you and others to have choices.

- Welcome unusual points of view or controversial ways of looking at the situation. Out-of-the-ordinary thinking may be exactly what you need, especially when working on long-standing, repetitive problems.

Focus on important information without getting bogged down in detail

- Focus your attention on the processes that were used to identify the key issues or develop the key strategies. What assumptions were made? Who was involved in gathering and analyzing the information? What are the risks?

- As people are presenting their understanding of a situation, draw pictures of what you are hearing. The analysis should be clear enough that you or someone else can draw it. Use fishbone diagrams, process maps, etc. Ask that your staff present information to you visually as well as in words.

- When you are problem solving yourself, determine the information you need. Categorize the information you gather as a way to identify patterns and trends.

- Use pictures to understand what is happening. Look at process charts to identify the current flows and processes. Check that process charting is used regularly as a way of understanding flow, interdependencies, and opportunities.

- When you find yourself buried under stacks of information, ask yourself who should be looking at this information rather than you.

- Catch yourself drilling your staff for detail. Do you really need it? What value does it add?

Evaluate the costs, risks, and benefits of alternatives

Prior to finalizing a course of action, ensure that you have looked at enough alternatives, understand the risks and costs, and can anticipate the consequences. Critically review your analysis of the problem or opportunity.

- How have the assumptions about the problem or opportunity influenced who you have involved in problem solving? How would others look at the problem or opportunity differently?

- What assumptions are you making? How do you know those assumptions are valid?

- Was a systems approach used to look at the problem?

- What, if anything, could more accurately or completely define the problem?

- Which elements of the opportunity look promising?

- What are the costs of pursuing the opportunity?

- What are the costs of not pursuing the opportunity?

- Does the opportunity bring anything to the table that might be used in other ways?

4. Link problems and symptoms to identify key strategic issues.

As you talk with your staff about their plans for the future, the challenges they face, and the marketplace they are encountering, listen for the common themes. How is the competition different? What are the underlying strategic issues? What are distributors asking for now? How have your customers' requirements changed? How have your customers changed?

Listen carefully to the patterns and themes

- Provide opportunities for sharing of information among your staff and enough time to hypothesize what it means. What are the underlying issues? What impact do these changes have on your core strategies? What impact do these changes have on your perception of where you add value to your customers?

- Determine the impact of changes on your organization's critical success factors. For example, if you have added value by providing service for your product, but a competitor now has a more reliable product, consider the impact on the value of your service.

- Use and ask your team to use the tools of systems thinking to understand the interrelationships.

- Whenever you plan a change, analyze and plan for the impact of that change on other parts of the system.

Examine current challenges and recurring problems

- Keep track of recurring problems and issues. There is a good chance that these are strategic opportunities for you and the organization. If you can find an approach to the problem that actually gets it resolved, it will save people a lot of time.

- What do the problems say about changes in the marketplace? What do they tell you about changes in customers, suppliers, distributors, etc.? Discuss this with your staff.

- What is the relationship between current challenges, recurring problems, and the organization's key strategic issues? Does your information confirm the diagnosis of the key issues or does it present a different picture?

- What do people tell you is impossible to do? What is the biggest challenge that they do not expect to be resolved? Challenge the belief that the situation is a given. If it really does impact the business in a significant way, some competitor or potential competitor is working to resolve the issue right now.

5. Creatively integrate different ideas and perspectives.

Effective problem solving requires involvement in the problem definition stage, not just the problem solution phase. The key to an effective solution is the definition of the problem.

Analyze the problem from different points of view

- Look at problems from the point of view of all the constituencies or stakeholders involved. When you encounter a problem or hear recommendations to solve a problem, ask about the stakeholder involvement in defining the problem as well as looking at alternatives.

- Put yourself in the position of your customer when you hear about a solution to a customer requirement or problem. How would you feel? Would you be satisfied with the solution? Delighted?

- What about your suppliers? Single-source or multiple-source supplying may make sense to you, but what is the impact of either strategy on your suppliers? Does it make a differences to you? When should it?

- Provide a forum for different groups to hear one another's points of view.

- Get in the habit of asking how other parts of the value chain see the situation. This sends a message to your staff that you expect them to look at views of others as part of their process.

Approach problems with curiosity and an open mind

- Acquire a positive mind-set about problems. Your view of a problem will influence how you solve it.

- Change your expectations regarding challenges, objections, and roadblocks. Disagreement shows people are thinking and that they care.

- Examine why some problems make you curious and enthusiastic and others make you retreat. Frame unappealing problems so that they invigorate rather than debilitate you.

- Look at problems as a process rather than a static event. Regarding the problem as a fluid event will free you to explore a much broader range of possibilities.

6. Take all important issues into account when making decisions.

Understand and practice systems thinking. *Systems thinking* involves understanding multiple relationships among the elements or parts. Components of the system feed and influence each other. A does not only cause B and C. A causes B, B influences A, which in turn causes C to impact B. Such techniques will help you uncover the consequences of your actions and strategies. They will address system issues and help you anticipate the reactions of your competitors.

- Ask your team to analyze interrelationships and conceptualize problems from a systems perspective. Use causal loop diagrams and models of the system or issue. Are you and your staff looking at what will happen to the rest of the system if you change one element?

- Ask a consultant or facilitator to lead process improvement initiatives. Learn to use their strategies.

- Use process charting or fishbone diagrams on a regular basis to understand flow, interdependencies, and opportunities. Where is the synergy? Where are the redundancies?

- Apply the "what will happen" technique to project probable consequences for your team's actions. Pose a hypothetical question, such as "What will happen if our organization opens a new market in X?" Pursue the question by predicting at least five consequences for each answer.

7. Come to a decision at the right time.

Whether you take overt action or do nothing, you are still taking action of some type. When you put off making a decision because you do not have enough information, you are really taking action. Therefore, when you encounter ambiguous situations in which issues are not clear, consider the price of inaction.

Make timely decisions

- Executives can make timely decisions by recognizing which problems can be solved with simple solutions.

- The ability to quickly discover the source of a problem is critical when you must solve problems under a deadline. To cut down on wasting time by pursuing unlikely options, follow these steps:
    1. List all possible causes in order of probability.
    2. Rate the probability of each cause being the main source of the problem. Use a scale of 1 to 100, with 1 being the lowest probability.
    3. Balance the probability of the cause with the amount of investigation required.
    4. Use this analysis to determine the order in which you will examine the causes. Also identify any causes you can eliminate.

Avoid emotional decisions

Emotions play an important part in the decision-making process. Your emotions and the emotions of others signal how important an issue is. They often tell you when the decision involves core values.

Since emotions can signal that something important is going on, it is important the decisions are not made in the heat of the moment or in reaction to the emotions of others. In other words, do not announce your decisions when you are furious, hurt, etc. It may be a good decision or it may not. You may only be taking emotion into account, instead of the data that you need to consider.

- When you find yourself reacting emotionally to an issue, hold off on making your decision until your emotional state changes. Then, analyze your potential decision, the available data, and the impact of the decision.

- Make decisions based on information and data, rather than on emotions or guesses. Obviously, you will not always have data to back your decisions, but make an effort to find it or use the information available.

- Test your decision with trusted others. Give people permission to give you feedback and tell you when they think you may have overreacted. The higher in the organization you are, the more difficult it will be for people to do this. But it is essential that you get this kind of feedback.

Avoid crisis management

- Do you have days when all you do is "fight fires"? Look at the broader context to see if proactive measures can prevent this type of crisis management.

- Over the next few weeks, keep a list of unforeseen problems that require your attention. Although it may seem inconvenient, it is important to compile this list while you are in the middle of the crisis. Examine the list and identify themes. Categorize them into general groups such as inadequate communication, lack of standardized procedures, resistance to change, customer service problems, or poor vendor response. Do similar situations occur on a regular basis?

- On a quarterly basis, ask your direct reports to identify trends in their departments. Compare your list to theirs and look for connections. How do these issues affect your organization's overall quality, productivity, and financial performance?

- Challenge others to anticipate issues. Provide clear feedback about their proactive or reactive approach.

Make decisions in the face of uncertainty

Every decision involves an element of risk. Calculated risk taking implies that decisions are made with a solid understanding of the potential risks and benefits involved. Common problems encountered in risk taking include:

- A need to gather too much data. Fact finding can be carried to an extreme. The important thing is to set a course; implementation can be fine-tuned with midcourse corrections.

- Lack of knowledge about the true risk level. Ask your team to clearly specify the pros and cons of each proposed solution and choose the one that provides the greatest benefit.

- Discomfort over consequences. Create a worst-case scenario and imagine how it would impact your organization, your team, and yourself. Develop a thorough plan to deal with the consequences of your decision.

- Discomfort over unknown factors. If you have a vague feeling that a solution contains unknown risks, identify go/no-go points where the implementation process can be halted. This will allow you to evaluate your plan as it unfolds. Inform your direct reports so that no one will be surprised if the process is discontinued at some point.

- Who are the organization's most effective risk managers? Talk with them about how they manage risks.

- Consider risky decisions you have made in the past. What has your track record been?
  - How have you managed risk in the past?
  - How resilient is the organization?

8. Make tough, pragmatic decisions when necessary.

Sometimes it is necessary to make a tough, unpopular decision that is in the best interest of the business. However, you may face a backlash of complaints and negative reactions. If you feel reluctant to face this type of decision, consider the following suggestions:

- If your decision or initiative will have a broad impact, work with your communication, investor relations, marketing, and human resources groups to manage the notification process. Listen carefully to their recommendations. Make yourself available to those groups and do your part in communicating the message.

- Show respect and concern for people by being straightforward and clearly communicating why the decision must be made. Explain how the changes will benefit the organization over the long term and show people how no one will gain if the change is not made. Be prepared to deal with their reactions.

- As you prepare your implementation plan, arrange time with all groups or departments that will be affected by the change. Solicit their suggestions on how to expedite the plan. Even if you do not use all of their suggestions, they will be more likely to accept your decision if you demonstrate that you considered the needs of all affected parties.

- Push yourself to make the transition first. A willing champion of a new directive may be what your organization needs.

RESOURCES

The resources for this chapter begin on page 430.

2
VISIONARY THINKING

HAVE A CLEAR VISION FOR THE BUSINESS
OR OPERATION; MAINTAIN A LONG–TERM,
BIG PICTURE VIEW; FORESEE OBSTACLES
AND OPPORTUNITIES;
GENERATE BREAKTHROUGH IDEAS.

KEY BEHAVIORS

1. *Develop a clear vision for the future of the business or organization.*
2. *Convey a clear sense of the organization's purpose and mission that captures the imagination of others.*
3. *Maintain a long-term, big-picture view of the business and identify the long-term, future needs and opportunities for the business.*
4. *Recognize when it is time to shift strategic direction and anticipate the evolution and future of the industry and how the organization must adapt to these changes in order to sustain competitive advantage.*
5. *See problems and understand issues before others do.*
6. *Challenge status-quo thinking and assumptions.*
7. *Come up with fresh perspectives, innovative, breakthrough ideas, and new paradigms that create value in the marketplace.*

INTRODUCTION

Interview successful leaders and you will find that almost all of them had a vision or picture of the future. They had an idea about new potential for the organization, an idea of how they could change the industry, or a vision for the core values and competencies of the organization.

Effective, forward-looking executives either are visionary thinkers or they stimulate others to create the future. It is likely that no single factor distinguishes the role of a successful executive as clearly as the ability to create and communicate a coherent vision of an organization's purpose and direction.

VALUABLE TIPS

- Define "vision" and explain it to one of your colleagues. Can you readily articulate it?

- Identify what makes a vision appealing to you, such as the language used to describe it, the person's enthusiasm for the vision, and your ability to see how you can contribute to achieving it. Apply that learning to your vision.

- Articulate the success factors for your organization in the next five years and ten years. What do you have to do well?

- Clarify whether you are trying to forge a new direction or if you are creating a vision based on what you think that your organization can realistically achieve.

- Don't limit your vision to what your organization can currently accomplish; you can fill in the gaps as you go.

- Write down your vision and be as descriptive as you can. For example, what do the products and services look like? Who are your customers and how do you communicate with them? What type of people work in your organization?

- Practice sharing your vision with your colleagues, friends, and family, and refine it using their feedback.

- Make sure your vision addresses what makes your organization unique.

- Recognize that people are counting on you to have a vision; if you don't, you're missing a valuable opportunity to capture people's imagination and energy.

- Ask people at all levels in the organization for their candid feedback regarding your organization's stated vision. Do they understand it? Are they excited by it?

- Consider the culture within your organization; if it is focused exclusively on the short-term, you may have to start with why a vision is necessary.

- Determine which business paradigms are going to hold your organization back and how you are going to break those paradigms.

- Analyze how your organization's long-term vision will affect your key stakeholders. How can you bring them "on board"?

- Talk to your customers about their long-term visions. How can you align your efforts?

- Constantly look for trends and indicators in your industry and other industries, in the general business environment, and in global events.

- Set aside time to develop your creativity; however, recognize that creativity will not necessarily strike according to your schedule.

STRATEGIES FOR ACTION

1. Develop a clear vision for the future of the business or organization.

Vision is a picture of the future that provides clarity and direction. Effective executives have or create the process through which the executive team envisions this future state. Historically vision was seen as the purview of the CEO, but more and more it is understood that the vision may not necessarily come from just one person. The leader may lead the organization's leadership to create its vision. Whether the vision comes from one person or a group, the vision must be embraced by people in the organization to make it real.

There can be many different visions within an organization. Although there may be an overall organizational vision, within each group there often is a vision for that particular group's or team's role in the organization and potential accomplishments. This is not a problem, as long as the multiple visions are aligned with one another.

Farsighted executives also often have a vision for the industry itself. Today, competition requires that you move beyond incremental change and improvement. Instead, you and your organization need to have an in-depth understanding of the trends and developments in your industry, so you can create a vision or a point of view about the future of your industry.

Evaluate your vision

1. If you do not have a vision for the organization or your part of it, determine the importance of having one by talking with people in your area to determine whether there is clarity about the organization's or work unit's direction, goals, and values. Do people in the organization have a clear picture or idea of where you are going?

   - Conduct one-on-one interviews to learn the answers to these questions.

   - Ask that a neutral person such as human resources person or external consultant conduct the interviews.

   - Use a survey method to determine this information.

   - If you have a vision, critique it.
     - Is it challenging?
     - Does it motivate and inspire you and your stakeholders?
     - Is it easy to understand and internalize?
     - Can it be used to guide decision making?
     - Is it stable, yet evolving over time?
     - Is it consistent or compatible with the organizational vision?

2. Make appropriate modifications based on the results of the analysis. You will find the following trends:

- There is a clear vision, but there is little buy-in or active commitment to the vision. Therefore:
  - Systematically engage leadership teams in discussing the vision, the rationale, their thoughts and ideas.
  - Ask that leadership teams identify their role in achieving the vision. Request plans and regular monitoring of their progress against the plans.

- There is no clear vision. Therefore:
  - Work with your leadership team to develop a process to create a clear vision.
  - Consult with your communications group to develop a plan to convey the vision.

- There is a clear vision but little alignment among unit visions throughout the organization. Therefore:
  - Carefully examine the similarities and differences among the visions. Note the ways in which the visions are complementary and the ways they are incompatible.
  - Share the observations, themes, and findings with your leadership team. Work with them to determine how to achieve closer alignment.
  - Determine whether it is necessary for you to communicate your expectation that your leadership team become aligned with the vision. Occasionally, it is necessary to "bring in your own team."

Create a vision for the future

How do you create a vision? There are no right answers in the visioning process. Many business leaders use a group process for creating a vision. They involve their executive or management team from the beginning, or at key junctures in the visioning process.

- Expect the process to be ongoing, chaotic, and iterative. Even the most visionary leaders continue to develop and fine-tune their visions. For example, Jack Welch, CEO of General Electric, has been refining the GE vision for fifteen years. In high tech industries, visions need to be continually emerging due to the rapid changes in technology.

- Choose whether you are going to focus first on the external environment or the internal environment. The outside-in approach, in which the external environmental and competitive scan is the first step, assumes that needed internal resources are or can be available.

  The inside-out approach focuses on the core competencies of the organization and its people. You may want to begin with this approach if the constraint on your organization's future is people. For example, organizations whose business is knowledge or expertise-based often cannot assume they have enough skilled people.

1. Analyze your current situation. Vision starts with a thorough understanding of your current status. Analyze the internal and external factors affecting your business. Potential areas for analysis include:

   External Analysis. Consider many dimensions in your external analysis, including: **Macroenvironment Analysis:** economic, demographic, ecological, technological, political, and cultural trends that affect your business; **Industry Dynamics:** industry trends, industry size and growth, and competitive analysis; **Target Market Needs and Perceptions:** usage, emerging needs, purchase criteria, perceptions, and market segments. Create a prioritized list of key opportunities and threats. Ask questions such as:
   - What keeps you up at night about the business?
   - What is your competition doing?
   - Who are the new competitors?
   - What changes would dramatically impact how you do business? Or what your business is?
   - What are your customers asking for?

   Internal Analysis. Create a prioritized list of key strengths and weaknesses.
   - What are the greatest barriers to your organization's success or greater success?
   - What are the internal factors that keep you and others awake at night?

- What are the organization's core competencies? **Core competencies** refer to a collection of skills or capabilities, which taken together, add significant value to the customer. Core competencies are what differentiates your organization from others.
  - What are the core competencies of your people?
  - What can your people do that differentiates the organization from others?
  - How replaceable are the people in your organization?
  - What are your people saying is the future for the organization?

Revenue Analysis: overall, by category/segment, and by geography

Investment Analysis: human resources, R&D, marketing, and sales

Marketing Mix Analysis: positioning, pricing, distribution, product/service mix, and promotion

Human Resources Analysis: organizational structure, staffing, training and development

2. Start envisioning the future. Create several alternative views of the future with the executives or managers with whom you work. Use the following questions as a guide:
   - What changes do you expect?
   - What changes might occur?
   - What changes, if they occurred, would fundamentally change the industry you're in?
   - What organizational vision will attract and retain the best talent in the organization's core capabilities?
   - What organizational vision excites and energizes the organization's most limited talent group?
   - Who are your customers/clients now? Who will they be in the future?
   - Who are your competitors now? Who will be your competitors in the future?
   - What is your competitive advantage now? What will it be in the future?
   - What delivery channels do you use now? Which channels will you use in the future?
   - What role does technology play in your business now? What role will it play in the future?
   - What are the organization's success factors now? What will they be in the future?

- Discuss the implications of each view of the future. Work through each alternative and determine what they could mean for the industry and your organization.

- Determine which vision of the future will provide the most added value to customers, build competitive advantage, and energize the most limited people resources. Write your vision statement, outlining your mission, goals, and values.

- Test your vision against the criteria listed in the "evaluate your vision" section on page 22. If your vision does not meet the criteria, continue refining and revising until you are comfortable with it.

- Communicate the vision throughout the broader organization.

Create a shared vision

Vision is not enough—it needs to be shared. A single executive can capture the imagination of others, but enthusiasm can only be sustained if the vision is collective. Effective executives get people personally engaged with and committed to the vision.

- To gain buy-in and ownership, involve others, including your direct reports, in the visioning process. The give-and-take exchanges involved in this process will help build understanding, consensus, and a core of committed individuals who are equipped to carry the message to others. The involvement in shaping and understanding the vision is critical to commitment.

- Involve organizational units in discussing their roles in achieving the vision.

- Engage the leadership teams of organizational units to align their direction and goals with the vision.

Understand your role as a visionary leader

An executive's ability to lead this vision process is critical for his or her organization. You have the potential to leave a legacy for the future through your leadership in creating and leading the vision for your organization. You also have the potential to build an organization that is well prepared for the future and positioned to provide healthy growth and meaningful employment for its people.

- Do not underestimate the importance of your leadership role in establishing, communicating, and managing the vision. People watch you—inside the organization and outside of it. Employees, customers, and investors know whether you have and are working on a significant strategy.

- Talk about the vision and give people information that will convince them it is right. Show your excitement about the vision and convey that you care deeply whether you and the organization achieve it.

- Write a personal leadership statement that will help you focus your attention and energy.

- Set aside a significant block of time to reflect on your personal mission as a leader. You may want to engage a guide or coach to work with you as you create your statement.

- Articulate a statement that captures your unique purpose and goals as an organizational leader and an individual. Begin with your fundamental values and beliefs, then expand your thinking to include what you want to do as a leader. The following questions will help you clarify your thoughts:
    - What is most important to you?
    - What are your deeply held values?
    - What kind of person do you want to be?
    - What do you want others to remember about you?
    - What do you want to be remembered for doing?
    - What legacy do you want to leave with your loved ones?
    - What legacy do you want to leave your organization?
    - What accomplishments would leave you satisfied that you had contributed to your part of the world?

2. Convey a clear sense of the organization's purpose and mission that captures the imagination of others.

Clearly communicating the organization's vision and exciting and energizing people behind the vision and direction is critical to the success of an organization. The vision gives people a picture of what can be, and gives them something to believe in and work for.

Communicate and manage the vision

- Use the corporate communications group to help you develop a strategy for communicating the vision on an ongoing basis. If an internal group is not available, ask an external communication resource for ideas.

- Test preliminary drafts of your vision statement with groups of employees. Solicit their thoughts and reactions and ask them what is missing. Then redraft your vision and incorporate useful suggestions.

- Repeatedly communicate your vision. Talk about it. Write about it. Everyone who needs to know your vision should hear it from you.

- Use the leadership team, supplemented by a cross-functional team, to help you communicate and manage against the vision. Make sure you have people around you who will tell you if you are not living the vision. Value this feedback, as it is necessary to stay on course.

- Periodically find out what others in the organization think of the vision and the progress made toward achieving it. The leadership team will need accurate information to make the necessary corrections in the architecture and implementation of the plan.

- When you communicate the vision and direction to others, present it with energy and conviction.
    - Explain the process used to create the vision.
    - Emphasize the driving forces behind a change in strategy. Make the rationale clear and back it up with compelling data.
    - Gear your presentation to your audience's needs. Clarify how the vision will impact and benefit them.
    - Simplify, streamline, and shape your messages. Concentrate on the essential points and make the underlying logic evident.
    - Project enthusiasm and commitment. Share personal experiences and feelings.
    - Use an animated, energetic delivery style; vary your voice and gestures.
    - Use images, illustrations, and real-life examples to make the vision come alive.
    - Allow objections, concerns, and questions to be aired.
    - Anticipate and address opposing viewpoints and counterarguments.

Disseminate your vision

- First and foremost, make every effort to "walk your talk." Actions speak louder than words; therefore, consciously behave in a manner that is consistent with your organization's vision and values.

- Integrate the spirit of your organization's vision into the messages you convey through formal communication channels, such as internal and external presentations, internal letters and memos, management conferences, marketing materials, staff meeting agendas, corporate brochures, newsletters, customer calls, and sales meetings.

- Incorporate the spirit of your organization's vision into company symbols, rituals, and celebrations; stories of corporate heroes and heroines; logos, letterhead, and tag lines; and employee achievement awards and social events.

- Use informal methods to emphasize the vision and signal change in the organization. For example, hold casual conversations with employees and make impromptu visits. Make changes in the dress code or in daily routines. Also pay attention to specific people, events, and activities.

Develop consistent messages

- Work with your direct reports to develop consistent messages and behaviors in support of the vision and strategy.

- Encourage your direct reports to begin the education process within their own groups, so people will understand the reasons for the change and why the change is necessary.

- Ask each of your direct reports to work with their teams to bring the vision and strategy to the next level.

- Evaluate your decisions for consistency with the new vision and direction.

- When and if you need to make a decision that appears inconsistent with the direction you have set, explain the rationale to others. For example, if you select someone who is not people-oriented, when you have stated it is important for executives to be people-oriented, it will be inconsistent with the message. Therefore, it will be important to communicate your reasons for the selection.

3. Maintain a long-term, big-picture view of the business.	Executives need to focus on a long-term, big-picture view of the business while dealing with the pressures for short-term results, the daily flurry of activity, and the tremendous demand for their time and attention.

Some executives find themselves mired down in the details of doing the business. Because they are doing the business, they do not have enough time to focus on the future. As a consequence, they prevent the growth of leaders below them.

Develop effective mechanisms to keep your focus on the future

- Highlight your goals for long-term work separately in your planner or to-do list. Review them regularly.

- Write or present a summary of actions for the future on a quarterly basis. Having to prepare this regularly will provide automatic deadlines for your work.

- At the end of each week determine whether you invested the necessary time working on long-term issues. Based on your analysis, determine what, if anything, you need to do differently about focusing on the long term.

- Review your work and the work of your staff. On what do you spend most of your time? How does that fit with the short- and long-term business goals? Determine whether you delegate enough responsibility to your team. If you work constantly and frequently and regret that you are not getting to the important, strategic work, you may need to reassign some of your responsibilities.

- Reserve time in your staff meeting for updates on strategic issues and long-term plans.

- Reserve time for yourself to think. Creativity and innovation require incubation time. If you are constantly booked with meetings, presentations, interviews, etc., you will not have time to stay ahead of the industry, learn about other industries, or think about the intersections between the two. It is your responsibility to carve out this time on a regular basis.

- Schedule periodic conferences and opportunities to learn and talk about the future.

- Find people who are gurus in particular areas and meet with them regularly.

- Find the mavericks in the organization and industry who question everything. Spend time listening to their questions and critiques.

- Anticipate the impact of broad future trends and forces on the business.

Create alternative scenarios

- Conduct regular and systematic environmental scans. Look for the driving forces that influence your business and create changes in the marketplace.

- Study your competitors and pay attention to their attempts to drive for advantage. How have they tried to "grab the platform" and shape the industry? Be assured that as you unroll your strategy, they will respond.

- Meet with others to brainstorm alternative scenarios. You may find it useful to:
    - Create alternative scenarios for your organization for the next five years.
    - Analyze the implications of each scenario, including the pros and cons and risks and benefits.
    - Identify the key strategies and success factors required for each scenario.

Conduct a "future search" conference

A future search conference is a useful planning tool for both large and small organizations, particularly in composing mission statements and formulating competitive strategies. This systematic process will help you and your team design the future you want for your organization and devise strategies for achieving it. The process consists of five phases:

1. Scan the environment. Produce a list of trends that have or could have an impact on the business or organization.

2. Classify trends that affect the organization. Narrow the list of trends to those that are probable and those that are desirable.

3. Determine the evolution of the organization. How did the organization begin? What is it like today? What are its strengths and weaknesses?

4. Envision the future design of the organization. Creatively design the organization around ideals that directly relate to your values.

5. Strategize how to get there. Decide on the best strategies to move the organization toward its future design. The last task of this final phase is perhaps the most important: Plan how you will integrate these strategies into your daily routines when you return to work. Also devise a follow-up program to check your progress.

Future search conferences may not provide all the answers to your concerns about the future, but they will serve to effectively:

- Bring people out of their "boxes" and into a shared context.

- Give people an opportunity to express their values within a shared context.

- Enable you and your team to engage in collective decision making and reach agreement on action plans.

Read Marvin Weisbord's *Discovering Common Ground* (Berrett-Koehler, 1993) for a more complete explanation of how to conduct future search conferences.

Hold firm to the necessary long-term investments

Creating enduring competitive advantage often requires long-term investment in the development of capabilities, such as investments in people or information technology.

- Identify the critical few that will need your ongoing support and nurturance. Find champions and supporters so you can protect this investment.

- Educate people on the importance of the long-term investment and the payoff it will have.

4. Recognize when it is time to shift strategic direction.

Competition in the future will consist of competing to create opportunities. Successful organizations can determine the future by accurately envisioning the possibilities that can be created. Benchmarking and keeping slightly ahead of competitors will not be enough, just as incremental change will not be sufficient. Instead, organizations will need to create paths. They will need to see where a path should be and make it.

Look for opportunities

- Look for signals in the marketplace that it is time for a change. Ensure that all business leaders and functional leaders are regularly reviewing the management systems that provide information about what is going on in the business.

- Periodically ask people what they are hearing and seeing. Analyze their answers to determine whether they are listening, or simply defending and explaining away unfavorable changes.

- Identify the assumptions that are being made about the information. Challenge others to challenge their own assumptions.

- Identify the assumptions made in your industry about what the business is, how it is done, and the constraints under which the industry and its organizations operate. Now figure out how those assumptions could be wrong. It is likely that right now one of your competitors is finding a way to remove a constraint of meeting customer needs.

- Find vulnerabilities and opportunities in your industry. Rather than assuming things will stay the same, assume they will be different. In fact, assume they will be very different!

- The adage "if it's not broken, don't fix it," does not fit many organizations or industries today. It has increasingly been replaced by "if it's not broken, break it," or "if it's not broken, improve it anyway." In today's environment, if you wait until your technology or business strategy is broken, it will probably be too late to respond. Make improvements and adjustments before disruptive and devastating changes are forced upon your organization.

- Identify the largest given in your business, such as "people go to stores to shop;" "people don't want to read books on a computer;" or "people prefer to have their own cars." Then challenge yourself to identify how the industry would change if this assumption were not true.

- Ask the following questions:
    - What are your best customers asking for? How do they see their businesses and customers changing? What keeps them up at night?
    - How do you anticipate that your customer base may change? What are the implications of those changes?
    - What assumptions do you make about who your customers are? What assumptions do you make about their needs?

Identify the risks to missing the need for change

Most organizations achieve an equilibrium that keeps them in balance. This equilibrium can cause them to miss important warning signs that it's time to change.

- Identify the risks in your organization, with your team, and in yourself that you may miss the signals to change. For example:
    - Executives or managers on your team are content with the status quo and do not challenge it.
    - There is a lack of visionary leadership at the top of the organization.
    - There is a lack of communication regarding, and management against, a clear vision of the future.
    - The board or the investment community focuses on strong, short-term returns on investment.

- Executives and managers must deal with frequent, fire-fighting crises.
- Executives are enamored with short-term ways of gaining competitive advantage.
- Performance and reward systems are based only on near-term, tangible results.
- The organization operates on a business unit or product line basis.
- There is a lack of internal support or expertise in visionary thinking that could reshape the business.
- The organization focuses only on benchmarking and keeping up with competitors, causing it to fall further behind strategically.
- The organization neglects to focus on the customer and does not anticipate what will be needed in the future.

- Look for signals inside your organization that it is time for a change. All organizations have visionaries who have insight into the future. Make sure you do not dismiss the messages you hear or the signs you see.
  - Are some of the best people complaining about a lack of vision in the organization, and leaving as a result?
  - Are some of the best innovators and product developers leaving because there is a lack of willingness to stretch current paradigms?
  - Are you hearing feedback about the organization's rigidity or lack of responsiveness?
  - Are alternative systems arising to meet needs because employees are frustrated by the current systems?
  - Are the best people raising fundamental issues such as "Who are our customers?" and "How can we meet their needs?" during visioning and strategic planning sessions, yet no one is listening?
  - Are people challenging the status quo, but their message is being rejected?

- Look outside your organization for important signals that things may be changing.
  - What technological developments can be applied to your industry?
  - What events within your industry web could impact your industry? For example, sensitivity about health care costs has had a dramatic impact on insurance companies, attorneys, company health plans, etc.
  - What political, social, or economic events have been most disruptive in your industry in the past? Do you see any of them developing today?
  - What are the current social issues in the countries in which your organization is located? How will they impact your industry?

- What criteria do customers currently use to make purchasing decisions? How does this impact your industry? For example, more and more people are concerned about an industry's or company's record on the environment, use of child labor, connection with political movements, etc.
- Have new competitors entered the marketplace? Are they from the same industry? If not, what changes will that cause in your industry?
- How are your customers changing? How have your customers' needs changed? What impact will that have on your industry?

Cultivate depth of knowledge in your industry

In addition to simply understanding your competitors, it is important that you have a deep understanding of your industry and the web of industries in which it operates. Few industries today operate in a vacuum; instead, they are linked to one another.

Learn about your industry's history. Read books written on the industry, and talk with industry veterans and investment experts who specialize in your area.

- What original customer need did the industry meet?

- How has this need changed over time?

- How have the solutions to the need changed?

- What breakthroughs caused past industry changes?

- Who were the change masters of the industry?

- Who moved the industry into and through periods of transition?

Know where your industry stands today.

- How has its position changed over the last five, ten, fifteen, or twenty-five years?

- What were the historical reasons for the change?

- If its position has remained stable, what factors prevented change?

- Is there agreement about the core success factors for the industry? If there is, then you may be in an industry in which there is little diversity in how the customer's need is met or how competitors make money.

5. **See problems and understand issues before others do.**

Visionary leadership that focuses on creating competitive advantage by getting to the future first requires intelligence, thoughtful analysis, deep understanding, logical thinking, and leaps of intuition. Ideally, you have these competencies. They will help you inspire others and earn their confidence and respect.

Obviously, you want to build a team of people that has these competencies. If you do not have these competencies or they are a significant stretch for you, it is even more critical that you attract, hire, and mobilize people who do, so your team can provide visionary leadership. This is not the time to be intimidated by people who are smarter than you. Leaders need all the help they can get from others.

Challenge yourself

- Understand the role visionary leadership plays in your effectiveness. Consider how important it is for you to trust the judgment of others. Other people have the same need. The need to trust you becomes stronger as you rise in the organization, because so much is riding on your judgment.

- Constantly challenge yourself to learn more at a faster rate. Catch yourself before you lose the opportunity to learn something new.

- Set personal goals regarding learning. Periodically reflect on what you have learned and how you have developed, so you can make your learning conscious.

- Acquire additional skills in problem analysis and creative thinking. Some people assume that if you have reached the executive suite, you are an effective problem solver. This is not necessarily true. You may have simply been effective at solving the same problem in different forms over and over again.

- Learn new problem-solving and process-improvement skills. Both will help you be a more effective problem solver.

- Be humble. Ask advice from the people who see issues, problems, and solutions before others do. Ask them how they do it.

Seek out new information related to your business

- Create an environmental scanning network that includes customers, suppliers, regulatory agencies, and related industries. Use this network to obtain information prior to relevant occurrences rather than after the events have happened.

- Prepare an early warning system. Encourage your staff to contribute and discuss ideas regarding potential developments and problems in technology, political and regulatory actions, the market, the competitive landscape, and the like.

- Seek out people within and outside your organization who are known for their expertise in recognizing key trends. Tap their knowledge and expertise in this area, and learn how to recognize trends that indicate a need for change.

Learn to anticipate problems

- Practice being a doomsayer on an intellectual level. Consider the status of the marketplace, your industry, or an issue within your organization that has not yet been resolved. Look for factors that could make the situation worse. Then postulate actions that would turn those factors to your favor.

- Try to identify problems and potential threats before they become crises. One way to do this is to stay alert to what is happening in other industries. Do you see developments that could eventually affect your organization and industry? Discuss your observations with colleagues to get their perspective.

6. Challenge status-quo thinking and assumptions.

The phrases "shifting paradigms" and "breaking paradigms" have often been used to refer to new ways of thinking about business. There is no doubt that new paradigms about leadership, quality, competitiveness, and strategy have emerged in recent years. Identify the paradigms that govern your assumptions, beliefs, and expectations about the world and your business.

Assess your organization's current status

- Look for internal and external forces that are driving the need for new ways of thinking about your organization, and are aligned with the idea that the organization needs to create its future competitive opportunities. Opportunities may include:
    - Customers who challenge you to do better.
    - Excellent competitors who force you to be more competitive and creative.
    - Executives who believe that competitive edge is created by redefining the industry, not through incremental change.
    - People in your organization who have great influence over the industry.
    - People who encourage others to challenge the status quo.

- Executives who are terrified by complacency and familiarity.
- Executives who are comfortable with technology.
- Employees at all levels who are passionately committed to the organization's vision.

- Recognize prevailing mind-sets. Begin to explore your organization's mind-set by following this process:
    1. Write your answer to the following question: What three rules would you tell a newcomer to follow to be successful in your organization?
    2. Ask three or four close associates and several of your nonmanagerial employees the same question. Write down their answers.
    3. How do the answers of the nonmanagerial employees differ from those of the management level associates? Make a list of the answers that are common to both groups.
    4. Once you have an understanding of what your people think, compare their answers to yours. List the views that are mutually held by you, your managers, and your employees. Short of polling every employee, this process will give you a good picture of your organization's mind-set.

- Challenge the old rules. For example, if you are a manufacturer, ask:
    - Is bigger always better?
    - Need there always be long setup or changeover times, even if the costs are amortized over a large number of units?
    - Is more lead time always better when ordering materials?
    - Is it really beneficial to have the factory laid out by function?

- Ask yourself the paradigm shift question: What impossible task would fundamentally change your business unit if, by some miracle, it could be done?

- Encourage staff members to assess their operations and look at their functions from other angles. Ask them to think of other, perhaps more efficient, ways of doing things.

Shake up your thinking

- At some point, every established mind-set produces a set of problems. Everybody wants to solve the problems, but no one can. Those problems can be catalysts for triggering a paradigm shift. Identify the problems that you always seem to be wrestling with and list the problems that you simply cannot solve.

- Watch for situations where people mess with the rules. It could be an early sign of a significant change—a new mind-set or paradigm—in the making.

- Also watch for people who seem threatened. New paradigms put those who practice the old paradigms at risk—especially those in high positions. The better people are at practicing their paradigms, the more they invest in them, and the more they have to lose from change. Help people with the change.

- Break paradigms, but show respect for the old ways. They were created for good reasons; respect people who created the past.

Use others to challenge established assumptions

Look for paradigm "shifters" or "movers and shakers" of mind-sets. More often than not, they belong to one of four types:

1. A young person who is still motivated by ideas and not yet bridled by realities.

2. An experienced person who is transitioning from one field to another.

3. A rebel or maverick.

4. A creative person with the most unconventional ideas.

- Find a person in your organization who fits one of the above descriptions and ask him or her to assess a particular problem.

- Seek out someone who represents an opposing position and someone whose frame of reference or background is different from your own. "Pick their brains" and learn how they think about problems.

- Create a personal board of advisors from whom you can solicit opinions on your most pressing decisions. Select people who come from educational, social, and work backgrounds that differ from your own. Discuss your problems on a casual, individual basis and listen carefully to their comments. Sometimes the most off-the-wall or irreverent idea is truly the most innovative.

7. Come up with fresh perspectives and innovative, breakthrough ideas.

It is important that you proactively look for steady, reliable information and new perspectives. Find people from whom you can learn. Listen to them, read their books and articles, and invite them to educate you and your staff.

Actively pursue state-of-the-art information

- When you learn a new idea or broaden your perspective through your reading or by listening to a speech, call the author or speaker. Investigate whether you want to talk more frequently with that person.

- Listen to ideas from your staff and other people in the organization. Learn to spot unconventional thinkers who have a fresh perspective.

- Keep abreast of the latest trends and scientific breakthroughs in your industry by reading technical journals, industry publications, newspapers, and news magazines.

- Actively participate in professional associations within your industry.

- Explore opportunities to develop relationships with your peers in other successful organizations. Actively network, exchange ideas, and examine innovative programs. Benchmark your practices and programs with those reputed to be the best in the business.

- Write down five to ten emerging technological advances that are most likely to impact your field. Share your ideas with your staff. Work together to determine ways your organization can capitalize on these innovations.

Expand your awareness and perspectives

- Regularly challenge yourself and your staff to look at your business from other perspectives in the value chain.
    - How do your suppliers describe their relationship with your organization?
    - How do they describe the business you are in?
    - How do they describe the value you add to your customers?
    - If your customers ran your business, what would they do differently?
    - If you were a competitor, how would you compete with your organization?
    - If your organization were based in another country, how would it be different?

- Meet with employees for open question and answer sessions. Listen to their questions. You will quickly learn that no matter how much time and effort you spend communicating messages, some of them will probably not be received as you intended. Rather than claiming that your intentions were misunderstood, ask what people saw and heard that made them draw that conclusion.

- Open a dialogue with employees, so you can learn from them. Tell the employees your intentions, then treat this issue very seriously. Many of your employees know a lot more than you do. Ask questions such as:
    - What are our biggest barriers to customer satisfaction?
    - What changes would make the customers' experience with us more favorable?
    - What changes would remove barriers to your work satisfaction?
    - What concerns you about our current strategy or business plans?
    - Do we say things that appear to be platitudes? If so, how can we "walk our talk"?
    - What was the biggest change we made this year that had a positive impact on you? On our customers?
    - If this were your business, what would you do differently?
    - What messages do you have for the executive team?

- Not all employee groups will feel comfortable answering these questions. Work up to asking these questions. When people see that you want to learn and understand, not argue, they will be more open.

- Develop the habit of looking at your plans and communication from the perspectives of different businesses and functions. Do not assume that all groups will hear the same message or even want the same message.

- Invite your vendors to educate you. Many times you may work with other organizations who are absolutely the best in their industry. Take this opportunity to learn from them. For example, ask your information systems contractors or hardware vendors to present their ideas about the future.

- Request that experts share best practices with you.

- Increase your staff's cross-functional and cross-organizational opportunities. Encourage them to serve on organization-wide committees and volunteer for task teams and temporary assignments outside their own areas. This will help them bring new perspectives into your group.

- Set up an employee forum to review policies and messages from the executive group. This structured approach will give you input from within the organization regarding policies and changes.

Exercise lateral thinking

- Guard against snap reactions and approaches to issues. Get in the habit of writing down your first solution or idea, then imagining alternatives that are "outside the box."

- Do not be satisfied with your first idea. Come up with as many options as you can regarding the cause of the problem and possible solutions.

- Keep an ideas file. Each time something related to your work catches your eye, clip it out or write it down. Also keep a file of ideas that seem unrelated to your job.

Expand your creativity

- Value creative ideas that you and others have. Challenge yourself to look beyond the obvious approaches. Ask, "If I were to handle this differently, I would … " or "If I had my way, I would…. "

- Attend creativity and innovation training seminars to learn techniques that will help you come up with more and different ideas.

- Use synergistic approaches to develop creative ideas. Apply parables, stories, or pictures to explain a situation. Recognize how viewing the situation in another context may stimulate thinking.

- Take time to be creative. If you are scheduled every hour of every day, you will lose your creativity. It requires some incubation or thinking time. Set aside unstructured time. Get enough sleep, so you will have some mental energy left.

RESOURCES

The resources for this chapter begin on page 432.

3
FINANCIAL ACUMEN

UNDERSTAND THE MEANING AND IMPLICATIONS
OF KEY FINANCIAL INDICATORS;
MANAGE OVERALL FINANCIAL PERFORMANCE;
USE FINANCIAL ANALYSIS TO CREATE AND EVALUATE
STRATEGIC OPTIONS AND OPPORTUNITIES.

KEY BEHAVIORS

1. *Become an astute consumer of financial information.*
2. *Grasp the full meaning and interrelationships of key financial indicators.*
3. *Readily identify soft spots in budgets and profit plans.*
4. *Use financial analysis to evaluate and create strategic choices and options.*
5. *Recognize profitability and revenue potential in business opportunities.*
6. *Manage the business' overall financial performance (income statement and balance sheet).*

INTRODUCTION

Executives must be capable users of financial information and have a solid understanding of how money flows in and out of the business.

Executives must meet four distinct but interrelated financial obligations. First, the organization must survive. While this may sound obvious, many start-up companies enjoy early success, then find that their frantic growth outpaces their ability to pay their employees and suppliers. Second, the organization must earn a profit. Profits are the reason for being in business, and you cannot continue to serve your stakeholders unless you have sufficient earnings. Third, the organization must earn a satisfactory return on shareholders' investments and other capital employed. In today's competitive market, an organization that fails to provide an acceptable return on investment will be unable to raise the necessary funds for financing growth and expansion. Fourth, the organization must generate sufficient cash flows to adequately finance the business.

Ultimately, an organization must grow. For publicly traded and most privately held companies, growth is a very significant financial objective. Developing your financial acumen will help you achieve this and other financial obligations.

VALUABLE TIPS

- Provide opportunities for members of the financial team to expand their knowledge of your business.

- Invite key financial staff to important meetings and give them opportunities to "shadow" you or your staff.

- Benchmarking your organization against other organizations, including competitors.

- Select a financial advisor who can tailor explanations to your level of financial acumen and the types of decisions you make.

- Use charts and graphs to track key indicators and ratios on an ongoing basis.

- Tailor financial report content, format, and frequency to your needs.

- Reduce clutter by abbreviating or discontinuing reports that have little value.

- Consider the costs and benefits of collecting extra information or creating customized reports.

- Identify and document your decision-making criteria up front to save time and frustration on your part and on the part of financial specialists.

- Ask which assumptions and estimates are "solid" and which are "soft," and consider how much the actual results could differ from your estimates.

- Continuously improve your decision-making process by conducting post-audits of previous decisions.

- Develop a consistent, logical approach for evaluating potential opportunities.

- Involve your staff and financial support people in identifying criteria for evaluating new opportunities.

- When you receive conflicting information, ask probing questions to evaluate the accuracy, underlying assumptions, and reliability of each source and set of information.

- Communicate financial goals to all managers and translate them into individual action plans.

- Understand your company's tolerance level for risk and manage to that level.

STRATEGIES FOR ACTION

1. Become an astute consumer of financial information.

Most executives see a significant quantity of financial information every day. Making the most of this information requires the ability to quickly identify important data, evaluate its reliability and relevance, and determine its implications for your organization.

Select a knowledgeable financial advisor as your mentor

- Seek out an advisor who is familiar with the typical financial decisions you make in your job. An advisor may be a member of your internal finance team, a respected colleague in another business unit, a certified public accountant, or another external financial professional who knows you and your company well.

- When you select an advisor, consider whether he or she can tailor explanations to your level of financial acumen and the types of decisions you make. Involve him or her in the assessment of your strengths and development needs and the creation of your development plan.

- As the process continues, discuss major financial decisions with your financial advisor before taking action.

Learn to read and interpret annual reports

Despite the wealth of regulations affecting the financial reporting of publicly held companies, there is plenty of room for judgment calls in the preparation of financial statements. Develop your proficiency at reading financial statements and interpreting annual reports. Be sure to focus on substantive financial information and learn to glean accurate data from the more descriptive and marketing-oriented language of the annual report.

Obtain annual reports for *your company*, going back several years. Review the financial statements, accompanying notes, and management's discussion and analysis section. Answer the following questions:

- What is your company's current financial health? Is it improving, deteriorating, or relatively stable?

- How are the results of your unit or organization reflected in the financial statements?

- What is the company's capital structure? How much and what types of debt is it carrying? How much and what kinds of equity? What are the implications of this capital structure for your organization?

- What "spin" has management put on operating results and significant events?

- How are potential investors and other stakeholders (suppliers, customers, etc.) likely to view the company?

Obtain annual reports for *key competitors*. Some questions to consider include:

- How is their financial position similar to, or different from yours?

- Are there significant differences in cost structure?

- Where are they investing?

- Considering their financial condition, are they likely to take competitive actions such as price cutting, easing or tightening credit terms, or entering new geographic markets?

Analyze annual reports for *major customers*, asking:

- What are the most pressing financial needs of our customers?

- What implications do these needs have for our organization?

- What does the investment strategy say about future directions and plans?

Study annual reports for *key suppliers*, asking:

- What is the financial condition of this supplier? How has it changed over the past year? The past two years?

- What win/win opportunities might this situation create (e.g., negotiating lower prices in exchange for faster payment)? How can we capitalize on these opportunities?

- What moves are the suppliers making to increase their vertical scope? What does this tell you about possible new competition?

Stay current on financial news

- Read key financial periodicals, such as the *Wall Street Journal, Fortune,* and the *Economist*. Consider the implications of breaking news for your company, industry, customers, and suppliers. Be sure you are watching events both inside and outside your home country. Pay particular attention to the following topics:
  - Economic trends
  - Industry and company analyses
  - Financial markets
  - Changes in the legislative and regulatory environments, such as Securities and Exchange Commission (SEC) actions and Internal Revenue Service rulings
  - Changes in monetary policy, both in the United States and abroad

- Discuss your interpretations of financial news with peers, staff, and your financial advisor. Compare and contrast your interpretations of the same news. Consider how you can capitalize on different viewpoints to become a more astute consumer of financial information.

Learn to interact effectively with financial specialists in your organization

- Understand the roles and capabilities of financial specialists. Spend time getting to know your financial support staff. Ask about their backgrounds and interests, and discuss your expectations for them. Emphasize their ability to add value by helping you make better financial decisions.

- Enlist financial specialists' support of your function or business unit. Clearly indicate the business and decision-making purposes for which you use financial information. Communicate openly about risks and opportunities regarding plans, forecasts, and budgets. Keep in mind that a strong partnership with your financial department will decrease the likelihood of unpleasant "surprises" at month- or year-end.

- Provide opportunities for members of the financial team to expand their knowledge of your business. Invite key members to important meetings. Offer opportunities for them to "shadow" you or your staff, accompany you on customer calls, and sit in on supplier negotiations. As they increase their knowledge, they will likely identify new opportunities for your company.

Obtain the financial information you need to make effective decisions

- Financial terminology can vary widely from industry to industry, company to company, and even between divisions or locations within a company. Learn the meaning of the accounting and financial terms used most frequently in your company. When you come across unfamiliar terms, ask financial specialists to explain them in everyday language.

- Determine the information you need to support your decisions. List the financial decisions you made during the past year, including routine, recurring decisions (e.g., pricing, credit terms) and onetime events. Group the decisions into major categories and list the ideal information that could support each category. Compare the information you would like to have and the information you used to make the decisions. Identify significant gaps, prioritize them, and develop a plan to close the gaps.

- Obtain industry information for purposes of benchmarking your organization against other organizations, including competitors.

- Determine what type of information is captured in internal financial records. Review the reports you currently receive and check your understanding of each report's purpose and contents.

- Determine how financial information influences your decision processes.

- Tailor report content, format, and frequency to your needs. Reduce clutter by abbreviating or discontinuing reports that have little value. Ask for "exception reports" that only flag information requiring management attention. Consider reducing the frequency of detailed reports or routing them directly to a subordinate.

- Remember to consider the costs and benefits of collecting extra information or creating customized reports. The potential benefit of additional information may or may not be worth the cost of producing it.

2. Grasp the full meaning and interrelationships of key financial indicators.

So much financial information is available from so many different sources that it is easy to get bogged down in the details. As an executive, you must combine financial information with other data to get the big picture of what is happening in your business.

Learn to interpret financial statements

Learn how the major transactions of your business unit are reflected in the financial statements. An understanding of how transactions translate to line items is an essential skill for using financial statements as a feedback and planning tool.

External financial statements, such as those contained in the annual report, 10-K, etc., are produced according to generally accepted accounting principles (GAAP). These reports are for external users, such as stockholders and creditors. Internal financial statements are created to support management decisions and can legitimately differ from the GAAP financial statements. Use the following process when you read statements:

- List the most significant (in terms of dollar value or frequency) transactions conducted by your business unit or function.

- Hypothesize how these transactions will be reflected in the financial statements.

- Check your hypotheses by talking with financial specialists or your financial advisor.

Track key indicators and ratios on an ongoing basis by using charts and graphs. Their visual nature will help you detect trends and relationships.

Become familiar with the major categories of ratios:

- *Profitability ratios* are designed to measure bottom-line earning power.

- *Liquidity ratios* are designed to measure the firm's ability to meet its short-term debt obligations.

- *Solvency ratios* measure the firm's ability to make long-term debt payments (principal and interest).

- *Leverage ratios* measure the extent to which the firm uses debt financing.

Keep an eye out for emerging alternative measures of business performance, such as Economic Value Added™ (EVA) and Market Value Added (MVA).

- *Economic Value Added* provides a measure of the economic profits of an enterprise by taking after-tax operating profits and subtracting the total cost of capital employed.

- *Market Value Added* is the difference between the market value of a firm and the economic value of the capital it employs.

Develop an early warning system to spot unusual trends

- Develop a comprehensive list of danger signs that will alert you to unusual or unfavorable trends and immediately trigger further investigation. Show the list to your staff and financial specialists and ask for their input. Also review the list with your financial advisor.

- Ask your staff and financial specialists to flag the danger signs to guarantee that they will not be overlooked. Set clear expectations for how and when these items should be communicated to you. Use the added lead time to take corrective action before problems reach crisis proportions.

- Periodically review and update the list to reflect changing circumstances.

- Integrate financial and nonfinancial indicators of business performance. Nonfinancial indicators can often foreshadow problems before they are reflected in the financial statements. Such indicators include customer satisfaction data, market share data, progress on key initiatives, customer traffic, merchandise return rates, capacity utilization statistics, employee turnover, and quality data.

3. Readily identify soft spots in budgets and profit plans. As an executive, you are often called upon to be a referee in the competition for scarce financial resources. This requires you to cast a critical eye on budgets and profit plans prepared by your team. Your ability to identify relative risks will help you deploy constrained resources to meet the business goals.

Focus on large items and those you can control

- Identify the items that truly drive your financial results. Avoid the temptation to review every budget item in detail. Spend the most time on large items and areas in which you have the most control. Discuss these key items with your staff and consider how you can leverage them to deliver business results.

- Perform ratio and trend analyses to identify items that warrant investigation. Compare budgets and plans to actual historical trends and ask for explanations of significant variances. Develop action plans to get problem areas back in line.

Identify assumptions

All plans are based on fundamental assumptions. To identify potential risk, identify the assumptions which underlie the plan. For example, common assumptions include "Our large customers will continue to buy from us," "We'll have adequate materials for manufacturing," or "The new product will be rapidly adopted."

- Challenge the team to identify the assumptions they are making.

- Then, determine the risk that the assumptions may be wrong.

- Determine the impact on the plan if the assumptions are wrong.

4. Use financial analysis to evaluate and create strategic choices and options.

Used appropriately, analytical techniques will help you make better decisions. A basic understanding of the most frequently used techniques will allow you to fully utilize their potential.

Identify and document your decision-making criteria up front

Identifying criteria, a step which is often overlooked, will save time and frustration on your part and on the part of financial specialists. Staff members and specialists will be able to avoid spending precious time analyzing proposals that, on their face, do not meet your parameters. Include the following factors when deciding on your criteria:

- *Return:* Most publicly traded companies have an established "hurdle rate" (the minimum required rate of return on investment) that all capital projects must meet. This rate expedites the process of allocating scarce capital resources to the most worthy projects. Work with your financial specialists to develop a hurdle rate for your unit.

- *Risk:* Determine an acceptable level of variability in the expected returns for proposed projects. What level of liquidity do you want or need?

- *Strategic fit:* Identify the essential elements of your organization's strategy. How closely must proposed projects fit within those strategies?

Review the underlying assumptions

Carefully consider the assumptions on which you base your analyses.

- Explicitly identify the key assumptions of each analysis.

- Ask which assumptions are standard within your organization and which are specific to this particular analysis.

- Consider which assumptions should be included in the sensitivity analysis (discussed below).

- Evaluate the plausibility of each assumption. Is it logically sound and internally consistent?

- Look for "errors of omission" in the assumptions and calculations. Ask your financial specialist if steps have been taken to ensure the analysis is accurate.

- Perform a post-audit on previous projects to uncover factors that may have been overlooked.

Employ appropriate analytical techniques

Cost-volume-profit analysis, also referred to as break-even analysis, may be the best analytical tool to use when all of the following conditions are met:

- Costs can be reasonably separated into fixed and variable components.

- All cost-volume-profit relationships are linear.

- Selling price will not vary with changes in volume.

Use linear break-even analysis for:

- New product decisions. Break-even analysis can be used to determine the sales volume needed to break even, given expected selling price and expected costs.

- Pricing decisions. Break-even analysis can be used to determine the increase in volume needed to justify a specific price decrease.

- Modernization or automation decisions. Break-even analysis can be used when there is an option to substitute fixed costs, such as equipment, for variable costs, usually direct labor.

Break-even analysis can also be used when the cost-volume-profit relationships are nonlinear, although this application is seldom seen in practice.

The payback period is the expected length of time it will take for the cash inflow of the investment to equal the initial cash outflow. It is best used for short-term projects of less than one year, since it does not take into account the "time value of money," (i.e., a dollar available today is more valuable than a dollar available at some future date).

Although discussions about payback periods are common in many organizations, avoid using the payback period method to the exclusion of other analytical methods. It can give others the impression that you are overly simplistic in money matters.

Net Present Value (NPV) should be used for projects that will last longer than one year, since it takes the "time value of money" into account. In general, NPV is the preferred method for making capital investment decisions.

To use the NPV, "discount" future cash flows by an appropriate interest rate to calculate their present value. Subtract the initial cash outlay to arrive at the net present value. If the NPV is a positive number, the project should be accepted according to this criterion.

Internal rate of return (IRR) is another technique that considers the time value of money. The IRR is the interest rate that will yield a net present value of zero, given the expected initial investment and the expected future cash flows.

Perform a sensitivity or "what–if" analysis

- Perform a sensitivity analysis by selecting some key data and altering it. Determine the impact that changing those factors would have. For example, what if sales volumes are ten percent lower than your best estimate? What if they are thirty percent lower? Work through some best- and worst-case scenarios.

- Ask which assumptions and estimates are "solid" and which are "soft." For each of the soft items, consider how much the actual results could differ from your estimates.

- Identify the factors that most influence the analysis. A thoughtfully designed spreadsheet will help you promptly identify the most critical variables. Identify items that are most prone to estimating errors. If necessary, identify ways to reduce the risk of estimation error. You may want to use alternative estimation methods, such as consensus estimates from experts or trend analysis.

Conduct post-audits of previous decisions

Continuously improve your decision-making process by conducting post-audits of previous decisions. Post-audits are particularly valuable for projects of a recurring nature. They should be conducted according to a predetermined schedule. The process should include the individuals involved in the original decision and answer the following questions:

- How much did actual results differ from expected results?

- Which factors most influenced the outcome?

- Were the most important factors considered in the financial analysis?

- Which factors, initially thought to be significant, had little impact on the outcome?

Document key findings to facilitate continuous improvement. Share best practices with other divisions or functions.

5. Recognize profitability and revenue potential in business opportunities.

Successful executives focus their organizations on the initiatives that will have the greatest impact. To determine which initiatives have the greatest potential, supplement your executive instincts with facts, data, and logical reasoning.

Develop a consistent, logical approach for evaluating potential opportunities

- Involve your staff and financial support people in identifying criteria for evaluating new opportunities. The list should include strategic criteria, financial considerations, and the impact on other initiatives. Disseminate these criteria to all managers in your organization.

- Beware of a tendency to scour the data you know best (e.g., market share data) while neglecting areas that are less familiar (e.g., impact on cash flow). Also, be aware of your biases and blind spots, and consider their impact on your judgment.

- Use the results of post-audits to continually improve your decision-making process.

Use facts and data to support your decisions

- Use a variety of data sources (internal vs. external information, specific vs. general) to support your decisions. Where practical, seek increased accuracy by obtaining the same information from two or more independent sources.

- If you are faced with conflicting information, ask probing questions to evaluate the accuracy, underlying assumptions, and reliability of each source and set of information.

- Avoid the temptation to gather data only for its own sake. Also, weigh the value of waiting for additional information versus the risk of delaying your decision.

- When you are faced with substantial uncertainty, look for ways to keep your options open without sacrificing potential returns. Avoid being indecisive. Take calculated risks when necessary.

6. Manage the business' overall financial performance (income statement and balance sheet).

Executives need to focus on the overriding financial goal of maximizing shareholder value. They must consider the impact of decisions and operating results on the firm's stock price and cash flow. Decisions that may seem routine, such as a change in credit policy, can have significant consequences.

Maximize shareholder value

- Be aware of the potential impact that your statements and actions can have on your organization's stock price.

- Avoid giving unintended signals to the financial marketplace.

- Understand the role of your public relations and investor relations departments in releasing financial news. The Securities and Exchange Commission (SEC) in the United States has specific procedures for disseminating information that may "materially" affect stock prices of publicly held companies.

- Ensure that everyone in your organization understands and abides by corporate information policies.

Strive to achieve stated goals

One widely accepted standard for goals is that they should be "aggressive, yet achievable." Overly optimistic goals often lack credibility for many people in an organization. Define your standards and communicate them to everyone who is involved in the preparation of budgets and plans.

- Set and pursue appropriate growth and profitability targets. Consider historical trends and future projections when setting profitability targets.

- Take a critical look at your targets. Are any elements at odds with your company's stated mission, vision, or values?

- Link targets to company strategy. Clearly articulating the linkages between targets and strategic goals will help your organization achieve them.

- Communicate goals to all managers and translate them into individual action plans. Every manager should know how to answer the question, "What do I need to do to ensure that we reach our goals?"

- Involve managers in developing contingency plans. This will guarantee that they understand the consequences of missing the targets.

Maintain the firm's optimum capital structure

- Work closely with your corporate treasury officer or CFO to understand the impact of your decisions and operating results on capital structure, risk, and cost of capital.

- Gain a working knowledge of the Capital Asset Pricing Model (CAPM). This well-known theory explains the expected return on a particular stock as the function of:
    1. The rate of return available on "risk-free" investments, such as United States Treasury Bills.
    2. The rate of return generally available in the stock market, i.e., the "market rate of return."
    3. A risk premium based on the volatility of a particular stock relative to the market.

In corporate settings, the CAPM is frequently used to develop an estimate of the required return on equity capital.

Employ appropriate risk management strategies

- Maintain a system of internal financial and operational controls to safeguard assets.

- Understand your company's tolerance level for risk and manage to that level. The most commonly used risk management tools include systems of internal control, insurance, and diversification.

- Continually scan the horizon for potential trouble spots and plan how you will address them.

RESOURCES

The resources for this chapter begin on page 434.

4
GLOBAL PERSPECTIVE

KEEP ABREAST OF IMPORTANT TRENDS THAT
IMPACT THE BUSINESS OR ORGANIZATION
(TECHNOLOGICAL, COMPETITIVE, SOCIAL,
ECONOMIC, ETC.); UNDERSTAND THE POSITION
OF THE ORGANIZATION WITHIN A
GLOBAL CONTEXT.

KEY BEHAVIORS

---

1. *Grasp the position of the business within the global marketplace; demonstrate a thorough understanding of the organization's global market position, opportunities, capabilities, and competitive threats.*
2. *Understand the impact of global trends on the organization's plans and growth.*
3. *Understand common business processes from a global perspective; ensure that business practices are aligned with the geopolitical context, foreign policy issues, and individual country strategies.*
4. *Recognize and actively pursue opportunities for global expansion and alliances.*
5. *Stay abreast of important international trends (e.g., competitive, technological, social, economic); stay abreast of and anticipate important global activities and trends that could potentially impact the business.*
6. *Have wide-ranging curiosity and interests.*

INTRODUCTION

The global economy impacts all organizations, whether or not they realize it. Globalization of the business does not mean where you do business, it means how you do business.

In the near future, very few organizations will have an international group "responsible for business over there." People will not talk about "foreign" subsidiaries. Organizations will be seen as total global entities. Everyone will be concerned about a global perspective, because "global" will define the organization. Doing business globally will be woven into the fabric of the entire organization because there will be no other way to conduct business.

Increasing your organization's and team's global capabilities is necessary to maintain, let alone grow, your organization. A global perspective includes everything: redefining your organization as global, understanding new competitors, developing new supply channels, understanding and respecting other cultures, comprehending different business processes and working with new governmental regulations and agencies, and struggling with thorny cultural and ethical issues.

Establishing your organization in the global marketplace or competing in the global marketplace will test your intellectual capabilities, your understanding of yourself and others, your ability to see the future and create competitive advantage, your ability to work through cultural complexities and clashes of cultural values, and your persistence and creativity in solving problems and seizing opportunities.

Your focused energy, honest curiosity, respect for others, and thirst for understanding the world views of others as well as the global business world is necessary. People and organizations who thrive in the global marketplace are those who learn quickly and find ways for people of many cultures to work together cooperatively. They take the time and have the capacity and willingness to find ways to incorporate the best of all worlds.

VALUABLE TIPS

- Assess leaders for global capabilities; use an assessment process that gathers information and perceptions from people from different cultures.

- Determine the match between your own organization's global strategies and those of your primary customers.

- Identify and understand the rationale behind the organization's vision of globalization. Then determine the strengths and limitations of that vision for your current competitive capabilities and geographic environment.

- Recognize that your competitors may be more experienced in particular markets or in the global market. Figure out which competitors will be most useful to learn from and study their experiences.

- Learn as much as you can about the organization's current global vision and strategy.

- Set a personal goal to develop an understanding of the mind-set and worldview of others.

- Pay particular attention to your most demanding customers. Very good, demanding customers are valued partners in understanding the future.

- Determine which business processes need to be common across the organization.

- Involve people from different geographies at the beginning of projects, not just during the implementation phase.

- Ask people to discuss how business processes are typically done in their culture before you attempt to create new ones or revise old ones.

- Assume differences between people and cultures exist until similarities are proven.

- When you propose a solution or a change, gain agreement on the end result, then ask people to implement it in the best way possible for their culture.

- Take colleagues seriously when they say things need to be done differently for their culture.

- Discuss and come to agreement on what are considered to be ethical business practices, including how the organization will deal with business practices that are seen as unethical.

- Benchmark best practices with other global organizations. Determine when global, regional, and country-specific policies and processes are appropriate.

- Challenge people to think about your products and services in terms of the core needs they fill or could fill for global customers.

- Thoroughly analyze what is required for entering a new market and determine which assumptions you are making about potential and familiar markets.

- Learn about trade agreements that affect your organization and its customers. Develop processes to keep your team up-to-date on changes that impact your business.

STRATEGIES FOR ACTION

1. Grasp the position of the business within the global marketplace.

There are many ways to be "global." In the past (and for some companies today) being a global organization meant having sales offices in other countries or forming an international group. For others, it meant getting resources from other countries, or manufacturing in other countries, or taking an advertising campaign and translating it into other languages.

Globalization now refers to how business is done, not where it is done. Globalization reflects the mind-set of everyone in the organization, not just those in the executive suite or international group. Such organizations have moved past a "not invented here" mind-set and learned to leverage the strengths of its global team members.

In this kind of global organization, an executive is expected to identify and manage the organization's core competencies and processes across the globe and leverage the global presence and network whenever possible.

Demonstrate a thorough understanding of the organization's global market position

- Understand the degree to which your organization operates within the global marketplace. Identify:
    - the percentages of your organization's revenue and profits that are derived from markets outside the home country. How is this expected to change in the next five years?
    - whether the organization has sales offices, distribution, manufacturing sites or service delivery, design capabilities, or business unit offices in different countries. What percent of the value chain lies in countries other than the company's original country of origin?
    - the mix of competitors. Are they global companies? Regional or national companies within particular countries? How is this anticipated to change in the next five years?
    - the customers. Are they global companies? A variety of national companies? Consumers from one or many countries? How is this expected to change in the next five years?

Assess leaders for global capabilities

Use an assessment process that gathers information and perceptions from people from different cultures. In the assessment process, ensure that people from different cultures are involved.

This analysis will help you to understand the urgency of developing increased global capabilities.

- If the organization is successful globally, what are the core factors of your success? Which of those factors is likely to change?

- If the organization is threatened globally, in what areas are there limitations or challenges?

- Determine the match between your own organization's global strategies and those of your primary customers. There is a big difference between a global company responding to global customers and one that needs to respond to local or national customers.

- The customer groupings may include:
    - Global customers with global customers,
    - Global customers with local customers,
    - Regional customers, or
    - Local national customers.

- Discuss the implications of these different customers with the marketing and sales groups and your executive team.

- Identify and understand the rationale behind the organization's vision of globalization. Then determine the strengths and limitations of that vision for your current competitive capabilities and geographic environment.

Become familiar with globalization models

There are at least three models for globalization. Each model has its strengths and limitations.

Global Exporter Model

The organization focuses on selling products to global customers by concentrating on products that will appeal to multiple markets. Rather than having products to meet specific country needs, it focuses on products that will meet the needs of a broad range of customer groups.

- These organizations do a great deal of research to determine the needs of the marketplace and have less product variation for local markets.

- The competitive edge comes from economies of scale in manufacturing, business processes, and customer research.

- They use efficient and highly integrated business processes.

- They tend not to move business operations, other than sales, outside their home country.

- They tend to focus on long-term results, not managing the short term market.

The success of these companies relies on their quality, product appeal to a broad global market, and efficient business processes.

The liabilities are that the organization is often tightly controlled by the home country and its mind-set. There is a lack of intellectual flexibility to thoroughly understand the changing needs of the market. They are less responsive to local preferences. They are also less responsive to changing needs. Additionally, resentment may occur in the countries in which the organization sells products, but invests little capital.

Multinational Model

In these companies, globalization first occurs by exporting the sales offices, then service, and then manufacturing. Usually research and development is the last element to be exported. Often the multinational organization develops similar products and services that allow for some customization for different customers. When product development moves from the home country to the local businesses, it provides the competitive edge for these organizations. If product development does not make this move, the products are less competitive because typically the multinational does not invest enough in market research.

Often, more of the value chain is distributed around the world to allow the multinational to draw on more resources and break through national barriers to entry. This deployment of resources makes a multinational organization more flexible to the needs of the region or country than a global exporter.

In multinationals, power, influence, and decision making is decentralized. Considerable time is spent trying to coordinate efforts across the world. The corporate office takes a strong central coordination role to try to maximize the use of resources. In recent years, multinational corporate groups have focused on finding a common vision and values, identifying core business processes, and creating common business processes.

If this describes your organization, you probably have problems with decision making, communication, and coordination. This is important, because you are trying to coordinate particular business processes through diffused layers of leadership and responsibility. Often, multinationals are less efficient than global exporters or the more traditional global/local organizations.

Global/Local Model

The global/local model of globalization is quite different from the other two. This model emphasizes local presence and responsiveness. Rather than being concerned with the global vision, goals, strategies, and coordination of particular business processes, they emphasize responding to local market needs.

Global/local companies work hard to respect local values and business processes. Organizations using this model have different products for different countries. There is little planning or communication between countries when doing business.

- Being highly responsive gives the organization a competitive advantage in the local market, but it makes it difficult for them to respond to global customers. The challenge lies in their ability to use economies of scale. It is difficult to work across countries, as there are high cultural and business process barriers. This makes it difficult for them to operate as one global business system.

Discuss your organization's global model

- Determine the model of globalization your organization fits.
    - Understand its strengths and weaknesses.
    - Consider whether another model makes sense given the organization's customers or the competitors.

- Use these models to understand the perspectives of others. Listen to understand the globalization model others have. It will be the underlying source of many disagreements.

- Communicate openly about globalization models. This will guide your discussion and choices about which direction to go.

- Expect that people will operate from their own perspective. Many do not know there are different approaches to being global.

- Discuss these models of globalization at staff meetings or an off-site meeting. Include people who have different views. Identify the impact different models will have on how you do business or work together.

- When there is a conflict among people, check to see if the underlying causes stem from different expectations based on their view of a global organization.

- Ensure that an analysis of the organization's products, positioning, pricing, distribution, customers, competitors, and threats has been conducted for each product line or business

- Look at your customers to understand how your organization or part of the organization needs to operate globally.
  - Where is your current customer base located?
  - To what degree are these local customers?
  - To what degree can these be described as global customers? For example, do they need solutions that will work across the globe, and similar services in all locations that will be responsive to a variety of people?
  - Will these customers continue to generate enough growth for your organization?
  - Who are your future customers?
  - How will the mix between local customers and global customers change?
  - How are you managing the mix between local and global responsiveness?

- The organization's competitors may be more experienced in particular markets or in the global market. Learn from them. Figure out which competitors will be most useful to learn from and study their experiences.

- Examine your competitors' business practices in markets in which you were planning to enter, but had written off. Consider what did or did not work for them.
  - What are your competitors doing?
  - What has worked successfully for them?
  - If they have competitive advantage in a market, how did they achieve it?
  - What do you anticipate as their next strategic move?
  - What is their greatest success? How did they achieve it?
  - What was their greatest failure? If they recovered, how did they do it?
  - What can you learn from their failure? Can you avoid repeating their mistakes?
  - Have they gone into markets you did not even consider?
  - Are they doing things that your organization decided not to do? How is it working?

- Examine to what extent your high potential leadership group is consistent with the need for global capabilities and experience.
    - Determine the strengths and weaknesses of the organization's bench strength from a global perspective.
    - Develop a plan to address the bench strength issues.

- Challenge your own and other's assumptions about the nationality of key executives.

- Meet with top human resources executives to understand the succession plan and process, the bench strength in the organization, and the degree to which the organization's leadership represents the organization's presence in the marketplace.

2. Understand the impact of global trends on the organization's plans and growth.

More and more organizations are operating within a global context. Change in this global context occurs at the speed of light. Therefore, an executive has to keep continual focus on the future as well as the present.

Assess your global position

- Learn as much as you can about the organization's current global vision and strategy. Thoroughly understand the value proposition offered to the organization's customers. What success has the organization had with this strategy?

- Talk with your customers and their customers to understand the industries in which they operate.
    - What keeps your customers up at night?
    - What problem resolution would allow your customers to offer significantly more value to their customers?
    - What is happening in the associated industries? How will these changes affect your customers' needs?
    - What changes do they see?
    - How do they wish you could help them?

- Pay particular attention to your most demanding customers. Very good, demanding customers are valued partners in understanding the future. Often, the demanding customers are living the future; you can gain tremendous insight into new trends and themes from them.

- Discuss your customers' view of what they expect from you and your organization. How are their expectations influenced by their view of being global and responding to customer needs?

- Review competitive analyses to determine what your competitors are doing and their plans for the future. Figure out what assumptions they hold about the future, based on their actions.

- Focus on your strongest competitors and likely competitors from other industries. Like a good customer, a strong competitor can provide excellent information about the future.

- Study how other companies operate in a particular country or culture. Arrange benchmarking visits to study the values and practices of successful global corporations. Compare these to the values and practices of your organization. Identify lessons you can learn from their successes and failures, and apply them to new markets.

- Study developing and growing economies in the world and examine the dynamics of their growth. How could they impact your business?

- Conduct an environmental scan every year as part of your planning process. Avoid becoming locked into one way of viewing the business. Use different methods and consulting resources for your scan. Encourage the participation of cross-functional representatives.

- Make sure your team knows that you want them to challenge the status quo, identify faulty assumptions, spot trends, and recognize potential global opportunities.

Assess your global strategy

Each global approach has its strengths and limitations. Periodically assess the strengths and vulnerabilities of your globalization and your global approach.

- What are your global strategic initiatives? What progress in being made?

- To what extent are you actively managing a global culture?

- How does information technology (IT) support the globalization of the business?

- Is the IT future strategy consistent with globalization?

- Have you been able to gain competitive advantage in the expected ways with your model? If not, how can you work on maximizing the strengths of your model?

- Where are the opportunities to leverage economies of scale?

- What progress has the organization made on developing mass customization capabilities that can respond quickly to local markets?

- What are you doing to increase the competence of your executives, managers, and team leaders?

If you do not have a global vision, create one with your management team. Communicate the vision to everyone in your part of the organization. Provide information about the reasons for the particular vision, so people can buy into its importance and substance.

3. Understand common business processes from a global perspective.

Business processes differ depending upon an organization's global strategy, its customers, the geopolitical context in which the organization operates, and the cultural differences within the countries with whom the organization does business or where it is located.

Determine how culture and business are intertwined in the countries where your organization currently does business, and in those where it may expand in the future.

Develop common business processes

- Determine which business processes need to be common across the organization. Use teams from across the globe for this analysis. Ask your customers. Examine the business processes of your customers and competitors.

- When your organization reaches the stage of global development where common business processes are important, you will need to understand each process and the reasons for it. Challenge your teams to work through the business processes in your areas of responsibility and note if there are differences depending upon whether they have local or global customers. What are the reasons for the differences?

- Use cross-functional teams across the globe to develop new processes rather than developing them in the home country. It will be difficult enough to get the new processes adopted without the stigma of them being imposed from corporate headquarters.

- Determine the costs of maintaining the different business processes. Have the finance department carefully examine whether the organization is getting sufficient return from this investment.

- Involve people at the beginning of process changes or improvements, not just during the implementation phase. A common complaint in almost all global companies is that the home country does not sufficiently involve the other parts of the organization at the front end.

- When you are establishing new business processes or reengineering processes, ensure participation from a variety of cultures and clarify the process objectives. This will enable team members to benefit from their diversity, yet have the same end objectives.

- Ask people to discuss how the business process is seen and typically done in their culture before an attempt is made to create a new one or revise an old one. This will allow a more thorough understanding and create more options.

Understand key cultural differences

Different business processes may be linked to some key cultural differences. Geert Hofstede, author of *Cultures and Organizations* (McGraw-Hill, 1997), identified key differences among cultures. They are relation to authority, the relationship between the individual and society, individuals' concept of masculinity and femininity, and the ways of dealing with conflict, including aggression and expression of feelings.

- Discuss with members of the executive team the similarities and differences each may have about expectations between employees and their managers and the organization; individual relationships and responsibility to one's self and to the group or organization; the expectations of men and women; expression of agreement and disagreement; and ways in which conflict is handled.

- Identify how problem solving and decision making correspond or differ in the countries where your organization is located. For example, some cultures see problems as something to be coped with rather than something to be solved.

- Assume differences exist until similarities are proven. Even if someone's words sound like the ones you want to hear, ensure that the meaning behind their words is the same as yours. When another person is talking, listen carefully to detect his or her values and beliefs. Check your understanding in a respectful and nonconfrontational manner.

- Your ability to decipher the mind-set and worldview of others is important. When you propose a solution or a change, state it in terms of the desired state or ultimate goal. Gain agreement on the end result, then allow others to implement it in the best way possible for their culture.

- Acquire basic knowledge about the economic system and business law of other countries. Business practices that are common in your country may not work or may be illegal in other countries.

- Talk to returning expatriates (executives and others) about their experiences. What did they learn about doing business abroad? What were their frustrations and successes? What would they do differently if they accepted another international assignment?

- Take colleagues seriously when they say things need to be done differently. Do not assume this is a stall tactic or someone being uncooperative. They are trying to make an important point. Treat the issues as a concern to be resolved. Even if it is a sign of lack of agreement, treating it as a problem to be resolved often works.

- Be aware that there will be natural sensitivities about particular issues depending on your global model.
    - If the organization is attempting to make decisions by taking all global points of view into account, there may be concerns about a lack of communication and the speed of decisions. Others may complain about the number or level of people representing their point of view.
    - If there is little depth of presence within a country, there will be concerns about the commitment to the country and whether you are exporting products and services that have little appeal to the local consumer. Sales and service offices in countries throughout the world may complain about not having enough control over policies and decision making for the organization. They may also complain about the home country's product development not being sensitive to the needs of the local marketplace.
    - In companies focused on local customers, responding to global customers may be difficult, because of the strong local control and focus. It may be hard to understand that global multinationals want the same product or service around the globe.

- When you are starting an operation in a new market, carefully consider the people you send as representatives.
    - Are they curious and respectful of others?
    - Are they able to suspend judgment of political beliefs?
    - Are they able to work with employees who may have been raised to believe that people from your country are enemies?

Discuss and deal with ethical issues

- Be ready to grapple with thorny ethical issues. Develop values and a code of ethics that set the standard for behavior throughout the organization. It will help employees and customers alike know what they can expect.

- Discuss and come to agreement on ethical business practices. Discuss how the organization will deal with business practices that are seen as unethical. Remember, when the organization is global, what you do in one country will be known and judged in others.

- Know what is going on, so you are not caught unaware. For example, an organization that chooses not to know how a country produces goods so cheaply is walking on shaky ethical ground.

- Know what people are doing and be responsible for it. An old adage says that if you would not be comfortable with a description of your behavior being printed on the front page of a newspaper, you probably should not be doing it.

- Wrestle with how the organization will respect local customs and beliefs and to what degree it will behave differently. Include cross-cultural groups in your discussions.

- Focus on developing standards of global behavior that are consistent throughout the organization. Find ways to make respect for individuals and cultures the dominant theme of the organization's approach.

Deal effectively with political changes

Political boundaries can change overnight as new countries emerge and old enemies become friends. Markets may suddenly open in countries that have opposing ideologies. Openly discuss issues involving politics, such as:

- Is your organization able to operate in a country that has a very different political philosophy?

- Should you support a political philosophy with which you disagree?

- How will you deal with people whose behavior has violated your and/or your country's ethical or moral standards?

- How can you avoid being accused of "exporting ideology"?

- How can your organization protect its employees and its capital during a political crisis?

Develop a set of core organizational values

Answer the following questions to determine your organization's core values:

- What does your organization value?

- To what degree do they reflect the values of the home country?

- To what degree do they reflect the values of the total global organization?

- Are these values known, shared, communicated, and managed against?

- Are the organization's actions congruent with its stated values?

- Does your organization respect cultural and value differences?

- Have values ever been compromised so your organization could operate in a certain market?

- Has your organization done things that were legal, but could be viewed as unethical?

After completing this analysis, look for opportunities to bring the organization's values in line with the global scope of the organization. Spot opportunities to increase the knowledge of and reasons behind the values. Use your communications group to develop a plan for conveying the organization's values.

Assess human resources practices

Managing people and managing human resources policies will be one of the greatest challenges you face, because there are considerable differences across the globe on these issues.

- Talk with human resources people in countries in which your part of the organization operates. What differences do they see between the human resources practices of the organization and of the local unit? To what degree are they comfortable with both practices being consistent?

- Before you go into a new country, find out what differences you can anticipate. Plan for these differences, so you are not caught unexpectedly.

- Benchmark best practices with other global organizations. Determine when global, regional, and country-specific policies and processes are appropriate.

- Determine how the organization or you will handle the perception that groups of people are not capable or worthy of jobs at a particular level.

- Discuss how you or your organization will work with people from other backgrounds who do not have the same ideas as you do about appropriate roles for women, respect for elders, etc.

4. Recognize and actively pursue opportunities for global expansion and alliances.

Global expansion represents a strong growth opportunity if your organization has products and services that meet needs or can be configured to meet needs in other countries, cultures, and regions.

Actively pursue opportunities for global expansion

- Challenge others to think about your products and services in terms of the core needs they fill with current customers. Do you see similar needs in other countries and markets? Which countries or regions do you believe provide growth opportunity?

- Where are your competitors doing business? If they are not working in a certain location, determine why. If you decide to move into one of those areas, be certain that the plan addresses the factors that prevented other companies from entering that market or made them unsuccessful.

- Conduct a thorough analysis to determine what is required for entering a new market. It may be tempting to make analogies between potential and familiar markets. What assumptions are you making? For example, one company expected that their service business would do well in a particular country, only to learn that providing service on a product which is sold in that culture indicates it was not well made to begin with.

- Look for opportunities to broaden the vertical scope of the business.

- As you or your teams identify business opportunities, identify the underlying assumptions you are making. Test whether those assumptions are accurate.

- Talk with people from other companies who are in the countries or regions you are considering. Learn from them:
  - What was the original plan?
  - How did it change? Why?
  - What were the biggest surprises?
  - What have been the three greatest challenges?
  - What advice do they have for you?

Plan alliances carefully

- As you examine the plan to enter a new market, ensure that the team has worked the entire value chain analysis and considered life cycle costs. Many organizations just focus on one part of the chain, only to discover more service support is needed or an alliance manager is needed.

- Many alliances do not achieve their original promise, so enter these with care. There should be solid rationale for the alliance, a transition plan, and a plan for growth. Additionally there needs to be clear organizational accountability for success of the relationship from both parties involved. Do not forget to look at the cultural fit. What needs to be done for the organizations to work together?

- When you are considering an alliance, keep your organization's core competencies and processes in mind. Usually most organizations retain their core competencies and processes and arrange to have their business partners handle ancillary services and processes.

- Identify the countries in which an outside organization has to have an alliance or some form of joint ownership to do business in the country.

- Talk with people inside and outside your industry about developing alliances in different parts of the world. There are countless lessons others have learned and are willing to share. They can help you understand the cultural requirements and rules of the road.

- Contact your home country's embassy or chamber of commerce for information regarding each country in which you currently do business. Also learn about countries that you have targeted for future expansion. Be sure to ask for material on trade legislation.

- Use more than one source when you search for information about a specific country. This will help you detect biased viewpoints.

- Look at partnerships with businesses outside of your industry. Do not discount unusual possibilities or configurations—they may be a way for you to introduce your product or service through a locally established product or service. This type of "odd marriage" may make sense, particularly from the point of view of the culture you are entering.

- Leverage your company's strengths and consolidate resources with your partners to ensure that you experience a successful expansion rather than an overextension.

- Look for opportunities in the public and private sector. Countries differ in regard to which sector offers most opportunity.

5. Stay abreast of important international trends.

Effective executives develop many sources of information so that they can stay on top of important international trends. Executives in most industries find that this means that they need to know far more than their industry-specific information.

Develop a broad range of information sources

- Meet regularly with executives from other functional areas to gain up-to-date information about the trends, issues, and opportunities they see. Challenge them to find fresh information and make sure their analyses add significant value. The importance of this trend information is not the information per se, but what it means to the businesses.

- Attend meetings and educational sessions with executives outside your own organization, so you learn what people in other industries are doing. It is not enough to benchmark strategies within the context of your own industry; it is critical that you are exposed to the "best of the best."

- Pay attention to advances in technology and understand their impact on critical parts of your business. If your organization is global, it cannot merely keep up, it needs to be on the leading edge of new technology.

- Scan the technical and trade magazines of your industry for an overview of new developments. Zero in on news items that interest you and share them with colleagues. If you need additional information, contact the author(s) directly; many authors list their e-mail address at the end of the article.

- Challenge others to use new technology in your organization's products and services, production and operations, and communication processes. An awareness of new developments will allow you to incorporate new technology into your planning, rather than react to it.

- Meet with the organization's technical gurus and futurists to hear them discuss what they see in the future.

- Periodically meet with the organization's most successful customers. Find out what they are doing and the trends they see.

- Benchmark other organizations to learn how they use emerging technology.

- Ask for regular analysis of investment strategies of your competitors.

- Invest in government lessons. Ensure that the organization does not rely on only one source of government information or build relationships with only one group. This is especially true for volatile or highly politicized countries.

- Use social and demographic information to influence your strategic thinking. Track market and opinion research regarding products, services, consumer attitudes, worker aspirations, generation differences, and so on.

Use information technology to maximize your competitive advantage

- Information technology (IT) is key to achieving global strategic objectives. Identify technological barriers that currently limit the productivity of your organization and the competitiveness of its products.

- Review your organization's technology strategy.
    - Is there a strategy? (If not, there should be.)
    - Is it linked to your organization's business vision and objectives?
    - Which critical assumptions underlie the strategy?
    - What do you know about the strategic skill of your technology leaders? It is critical that you have competent IT strategists, knowledgeable about the business goals and direction of the organization.
    - How many years does the IT plan encompass?
    - Where are the vulnerabilities?

- Evaluate your organization's structure:
    - What is the best way to connect the people in your organization?
    - Are your organization's systems and data available at your international locations?
    - Would more efficient communication tools and systems alleviate problems?
    - Which tools would assist teams that work within multiple time zones and work locations?

Be alert to legal issues and international trade agreements

- Trade agreements and legal accords strongly influence how business is conducted between countries. Do your homework to understand the key opportunities and constraints that face your organization.

- Learn about the agreements that affect your organization. Develop processes to keep your team up-to-date on changes that impact your business.

- Ensure that the legal group has the resources and talent to keep abreast of changes in trade agreements and how to conduct business in the other countries.

- Attend orientations and briefings about doing business in particular countries. Such meetings are often sponsored by government agencies and professional organizations.

6. Have wide-ranging curiosity and interests.

PDI research has shown that curiosity and a wide range of interests is characteristic of successful global executives. Effective executives look for knowledge and experience that will broaden their perspective. This helps them envision the future, imagine opportunities, and create those realities.

Exercise and apply your imagination

- Envision yourself as a citizen of the world rather than a particular culture. Do you see the world and its events differently? Do you behave differently?

- Imagine that you returned to work one morning to discover that your entire staff had been replaced by newly arrived, international personnel. What would you need to know about them to work effectively? What would they need to know about you?

- How are your products and services defined? Consider how you could redefine your products and services to please your most creative customer.

- Identify the fundamental constraints within which your business or organization operates. What could your company accomplish if the constraints were lifted?

- If your current international distribution sources and channels disappeared, what would you do? Outline a number of scenarios.

Develop cross-cultural awareness

- If you are currently in a global organization, take advantage of the rich knowledge within cultures at your fingertips and next door.

- Seek to understand the worldviews of others, especially when they seem very strange or different from your own. Listen to the history and rationale for each view. Remember, cultural views make sense from the point of view of the culture.

- Within each country are multiple cultures that we often ignore. Learn about regional and cultural differences in your home country and in other countries.

- Talk with people from other cultures both within your home country and from other countries. Listen to their views on how to do business, where they see new markets, and potential opportunities for improvement.

- Ask for ideas on how you can improve your cross-cultural knowledge and understanding.

- Listen to feedback you receive about your own culture. Try to avoid defensiveness so you can learn from others' comments.

- Host international students, interns, and visitors. Encourage them to share their impressions of your country and your organization, and take note of what surprises them. Ask them to describe particular aspects of their daily personal and work life.

- Open the door to another culture by learning a new language. You may need to take a total immersion course to learn about the notions and nuances of a particular country. If you already know another language, brush up on your skills by using audio- or videotapes.

- Try out your new language as you travel. Observe the reactions of your senses—how does the country look, sound, smell, taste, and feel? Keep a diary, noting what confuses, amazes, infuriates, and inspires you. Ask questions—local people are often more than willing to enlighten you.

- Contact organizations that promote international understanding. Ask for their assistance in bringing speakers and other resources in-house. Sponsor cross-cultural training.

- Each region's media present the world's events through a cultural filter. Read newspapers and watch broadcasts from other countries. What do the stories reveal about the preoccupations of people in that country? How is your home country represented in their media?

- Read or watch coverage of the same topic from two different countries and identify any differences in emphasis or interpretation. Which information is covered? Which items made the headlines? How is the story structured? Which values come through?

Develop interests outside your area of expertise

- Most people do all their learning through their work or hobbies. Make a regular practice of exposing yourself to new ideas that may not be directly relevant to your work.

- Bring in speakers or host a lecture series on new ideas or other topics that will stimulate thinking.

- Attend futurist conferences in which you learn about trends and discoveries that could impact our lives in the future.

- Host brown-bag sessions in which people from other functions discuss what they are working on and things they have learned recently.

- Join a forum on the Internet in an area of interest to you.

- Look at your university's Continuing Education offerings for executives. Consider taking a course on a subject that interests you.

- Ask your child to talk with you about what they are learning in school. You may discover they are learning things about which you know little.

RESOURCES

The resources for this chapter begin on page 436.

5
SHAPING STRATEGY

DEVELOP DISTINCTIVE STRATEGIES TO ACHIEVE
COMPETITIVE ADVANTAGE; TRANSLATE BROAD
STRATEGIES INTO SPECIFIC OBJECTIVES AND ACTION
PLANS; ALIGN THE ORGANIZATION TO SUPPORT
STRATEGIC PRIORITIES.

KEY BEHAVIORS

---

1. *Identify critical goals and success factors in different business situations.*
2. *Develop distinctive strategies to achieve and sustain competitive advantage.*
3. *Anticipate risks and devise contingency plans to manage them.*
4. *Translate broad strategies into clear objectives and practical action plans.*
5. *Focus the organization on efforts that add significant value.*
6. *Align the organization and allocate resources according to strategic priorities.*

INTRODUCTION

Shaping strategy is often seen as the ultimate responsibility of executives. The word strategy is used over and over in everyday conversations, at yearly strategic planning retreats, by consulting experts, at executive development programs and in management literature. We act as if everyone understands strategy and is talking about the same thing. That is not true.

Depending upon your viewpoint about strategy, it may be a plan, or a description of what is important, or it may be the position of the organization in the marketplace.

Strategy can be seen as a plan, an intent, or an emerging direction. There may be a real difference between your organization's intended or planned strategy and the strategy it actually executes.

The purpose of strategy is to provide direction, focus efforts, understand the organization, and provide consistency.

Key to all the approaches to strategy is the agreement that executives need to have a deep awareness of their organization's and its people's core capabilities and vulnerabilities; understand their industry, its linking industries, and the competition; and have specific strategies to gain competitive advantage.

Approaches to strategy differ in respect to the role of analysis in establishing strategy, the degree to which strategy is planned or emerges, and the role of the executive in the strategy process.

Your responsibility as an executive is to lead and participate in shaping strategy to outthink and outmaneuver your competitors and to manage the interface between strategy and the organization. Aligning strategy with the core competencies of the organization and its people and aligning the organization's resources with the strategy are essential parts of the executive's role. Gaining and maintaining competitive advantage in this day and age is a daunting task. Nevertheless, it is essential for the survival of your organization.

VALUABLE TIPS

- Identify and examine the constraints to the organization's or your business unit's greater success.

- Determine whether your current strategies and activities address the real constraints to success.

- Spend time with the executive team talking about strategy.

- Ask each business unit and function to identify their competitive differentiators or core competencies, then work together to identify the synergism between these competencies.

- Use an action learning team or cross-business unit team to map the competitive space.

- Test your organization's vision and strategies in terms of current and future personnel requirements.

- Assess each leadership team to understand the strengths and development needs of their strategic skills.

- View your company from the outside—where are you the most vulnerable?

- Meet with the organization's strategic planners and gain an understanding of the strategic analysis model they use and the reasons they recommend this approach.

- Ask each business head to identify their competitive strategy—product leadership, operational excellence (cost and efficiency) or customer intimacy—and why they chose that strategy. Then examine their plan against the strategy to see if it is consistent.

- Know which value chain activities and processes give you a competitive advantage. Also identify which activities and processes give your competitors an advantage.

- Communicate your strategic action plan as widely as possible within the organization.

- Learn about your competitors from a business standpoint, and who they are as individuals.

- Hold regular employee meetings in which you can hear specific comments and criticisms about the organization's vision and strategies.

STRATEGIES FOR ACTION

1. Identify critical goals and success factors in different business situations.

Critical success factors vary for different industries, different businesses, different stages of a business, different countries, etc. Capital may be critical to a new start up, while having enough general managers may be critical to a stable organization planning to grow by acquisition.

Determine your critical success factors

- Identify and examine the constraints to the organization's or your business unit's greater success. It is easiest to do this by looking at the value chain. What are the inputs, processes, and outputs that start as raw materials or ideas and result in products or services valued by your customers?

- Anticipate there will be internal constraints and external constraints. For example, an internal constraint may be not being able to develop people quickly enough for the roles needed; a parallel external factor may be the lack of external candidates for the same roles. Another constraint may be a lack of distribution channels in one part of the world, or a lack of technology infrastructure to support global development.

- Understand the different requirements for businesses in different stages of development. For example, start-ups need a vision, capital, and the right people, and a fast-growing company needs to add some structure and systematic processes to its growth engine.

- Study the history of the organization or business unit. How have the critical success factors changed over time?

- Notice that the critical success factors will differ by country or degree of economic development. In one country a critical success factor may be access to water, while in another it may be partial ownership by a local company.

- Learn to think like your competitors. If you were to compete against you, what would you do? Where are you most vulnerable?

- Talk with people in other functions to gain their understanding for their function's critical success factors.

- Ask your customers why they buy from you. What makes you, your services, or your products different from your competitors?

- Conduct regular market research to determine the variables that influence your customers' buying decisions.

- Consider the following when your team is discussing strategy. Use staff meetings or an off-site meeting to review this information, share learning, and challenge thinking.
  - What are the key drivers of customers' decisions today?
  - What do you anticipate will be the key drivers in the future?
  - What role will technology play in changing the industry?
  - In what ways are your customers' customers changing?
  - Where will future competition come from?
  - Which barriers to entry will no longer exist in five years?
  - What have the industry's chief limitations been in the past?
  - What influence will legislation and public policy have on your industry?

Understand and identify core competencies

One kind of critical success factor is the organization's core competencies. The organization's core competencies should provide one of the foundation blocks upon which the competitive strategy is built.

A core competence is a bundle of skills and technologies that:

- Adds to the perception of value from the customers' point of view.

- Creates competitive differentiation.

- Provides a gateway to the next product or business.

They may include such competencies as managing distribution channels, styling, and research and development. Core competencies are not things like integrity, trust, or competitive spirit. Rather, they are a bundle of concrete skills which, when combined and leveraged, supply distinct value and differentiation.

For example, automobile companies compete with one another for leadership in power trains, vehicle electronics, and styling excellence, rather than car by car. Airlines compete to develop more advanced fleet management or reservation systems, not airplanes.

Understanding and identifying core competencies enables your organization to have more competitive options, because core competencies add to the range of products and services with which the organization can compete. Core competencies last longer than one product or one business.

- What does your organization do better than any other organization?

- Ask each business unit and function to identify their competitive differentiators. Then in an off-site, lead the executive team through a process to identify the synergism between these competencies.

- Identify the basis of competition in your industry. How is this the same or different than 10 years ago? How do you anticipate it will change?

- On what basis are you trying to gain competitive advantage? If you do not have an answer, it is time for you and other executives in the organization to focus on increasing your opportunity and advantage, rather than just keeping up with the competition.

- How can the core competencies of the different business units be leveraged to create new core competencies?

- Engage an external resource expert in your industry to help identify core capabilities. Do your homework on the consultant and the firm so that you know their strengths and limitations. Take time to understand their approach to strategy, in order to match the approach with your needs.

Understand the competitive playing field

Organizations within industries become accustomed to competing with each other. If you follow the moves of your competitors over time, you can relatively easily decipher their competitive strategy and their next moves.

Organizations that follow the planning or positioning schools of strategy, which are popular approaches today, are quite easy to figure out. This is one of the vulnerabilities of both of these schools of strategy. Both of these schools argue that you cannot be all things to all people; you have to make choices. They further argue that the organization's direction needs to remain stable in order to develop competitive differentiation. Therefore, organizations that use this approach are easy to anticipate.

Some organizations follow a strategic approach that says strategy is emergent—it occurs as a result of learning and is an evolving, ever-changing process. These organizations are a challenge, because they are unpredictable. Some of them are deliberately chaotic and unpredictable. Competing with these organizations requires flexibility and fluidity.

Even more challenging is when a potential competitor appears who has not been a player in the industry. Danger lurks from the unexpected. For example, e-commerce is having a dramatic impact in many markets.

- Identify the following:
    - Who are your primary competitors in each business and region?
    - How have these competitors changed in the last three years?
    - Who will be your competitors in the future?
        - As you follow your strategy?
        - As you get larger?
        - As you move geographically?
    - Where may new competition come from?
        - What companies?
        - What industries?

- Use an action learning team or cross-business unit team to map the competitive space. Having new perspectives on this analysis can be very valuable.

- Ask your planning group to identify the strategic approach each of your primary competitors uses. With this information, you can anticipate their moves more accurately.

- Carefully read business publications to gain an understanding of why organizations make the moves they do. Challenge yourself to find competitive reasons for mergers and alliances that initially do not make sense to you. Chances are, an organization is moving to gain control over a competency platform.

Review your own capabilities and those of your team

Consider your own capabilities when it comes to developing strategy:

- How do your capabilities stack up against your competitors? How do those of your colleagues?

- How much time do you spend on strategy?

- Is strategy a priority for the team?

- Is your team better at fixing existing strategies or creating new ones?

- What is your track record of creating new opportunity?

- To what extent are your customers the most demanding in the industry?

- What amount of time do you spend catching up to your competitors rather than moving ahead of them?

- Do you spend your time as an architect for the future or simply a builder of today?

- How confident are you that the management team has the necessary capabilities to compete?

If you find that strategy is a need for your organization, invest in improving your skills. Provide opportunities for you and your team to learn about strategy.

2. Develop distinctive strategies to achieve and sustain competitive advantage.

An organization's strategy operates at many different levels. The organization itself has corporate strategy, while business units have business unit and product line strategies. When you are developing distinctive strategies, you need to understand the scope of the work you are undertaking.

Examine your corporate strategy

Corporate strategy involves three core issues: what businesses you are in and want to be in; what customers you want to serve; and what core competencies the organization brings to serve its markets.

- Identify the corporate strategy in regard to each of these issues. Check out your understanding with others.

- Ensure that you and the executive team have developed corporate strategy for the short and long term. Corporate strategy provides the framework for leveraging the organization's synergism among business units.

- Identify the factors that influence the potential threat to the corporate strategy including:
  - Possible entries into the industry.
  - Arch rivalries within the industry.
  - Possibilities of customers finding some other ways to meet their needs.
  - The consolidation of buying power, so that the financial dynamics of the industry are drastically changed.
  - A dramatic change in the power of the suppliers in the industry, so that the dynamics of the industry are changed.

- Examine how corporate strategy has taken into account or can take into account location-based determinants of competitive advantage. Local based elements of competition may be:
  - A core of highly demanding customers whose needs anticipate the rest of the market.
  - A critical mass of local suppliers whose products and services are critical to the future or competitive local companies in industries related by technology, skills, or customers.
  - Pools of skills, technology, infrastructure, or capital specialized to a particular business.
  - A context that fosters innovation, local goals, and incentives resulting in investments needed by the company, or rivalry between local competitors.

- Determine how geography and different environments can be leveraged for competitive advantage.
  - How do other industries use their geographies?
  - How do your competitors use their geographies?

- Analyze how the corporate strategy leverages diverse groups of employees.
  - How can these differences among people and their approaches, skills, and world views increase competitive advantage?

Use strategic models to help formulate strategy

- Meet with the organization's strategic planners. Ask questions to gain an understanding of the strategic analysis model they use and the reasons they recommend this approach.

- Ensure that the organization and its businesses regularly review their plans against a model of strategic analysis. Models will help you avoid errors of omission, especially if you lack experience in understanding competitive factors.

- Provide opportunities to challenge the analyses and plans of specific businesses to ensure that groupthink has not occurred.

- Make sure that the organization and its businesses have strategic direction and goals. Also, if it is your role, review them for consistency or compatibility.

- Recognize that strategic analysis has to stem from an analysis of external and internal factors.

Identify requirements for strategic advantage

According to Gary Hamel and C.K. Prahalad, competing for the future requires a change in your view of strategy. Strategy is no longer about competing against your competitors to gain market share or to develop distinctive advantage. Instead, competing for the future requires that organizations create opportunity. This demands that you outthink your current and potential competitors to gain the intellectual leadership of the industry.

- Assess your organization's ability to:
    - Understand how competition in the future will be different from today.
    - Develop processes for finding and gaining insight into tomorrow's opportunities.

- Consider your organization's view of strategy. Has your organization made the shift to viewing competitive advantage as creating opportunity?
    - Determine how to shape the industry structure rather than compete within an existing industry.
    - Determine how to compete for core competence leadership rather than product leadership.
    - Determine how to compete as a coalition rather than a single entity.

Identify the stage of competition you are in and execute against those requirements

If you believe that creating opportunity is important, then trace the phase of competition that you are in. There are three phases.

1. The first phase, *intellectual leadership*, focuses on gaining thought leadership on the core competencies of the industry, customer interface, and functionality. In this phase of competition, the focus is on identifying and creating strategic architecture.
    - The following questions will help you assess your progress in intellectual leadership:
        - Have you identified new benefits that your organization can deliver to its customers?
        - What new core competencies will be needed to deliver these benefits?
        - What interfaces will be needed for the customer to receive these benefits?

If your answers do not require making substantial changes, you have not gone far enough. The idea is to go beyond your past horizon of opportunity.

2. The second phase, *management of migration*, involves pulling together the necessary core competencies, exploring alternative product concepts, and reconfiguring the customer interface faster than the competition. This will force your competitors into longer and more expensive migration paths.
    - The next series of questions will help you assess your progress in controlling the migration path.
        - Are your resources limited to providing the necessary core competencies?
        - Have you identified the industry partner(s) you need?
        - Have you developed these alliances? Do they work well?

Again, if you are able to muster all the competencies you need within the existing businesses you have, you are not thinking far enough ahead.

3. The third phase is *competing for market share.* This involves crafting an appropriate marketing position, building a worldwide supply network, preempting competitors in critical markets, and maximizing efficiency and productivity.

- The following questions will help you assess whether or not you have reached this phase.
  - Do you have new market positioning?
  - To what extent have you developed global suppliers?
  - Have you identified the markets you need to gain global dominance?
  - Have you moved into maximizing efficiency and productivity?

Spot opportunities in the value chain

If your focus is on gaining competitive advantage rather than creating new opportunities by dramatically changing the industry, concentrate on a plan of action that will develop a business's competitive advantage, expand it, and sustain it over time.

- Review your own and your competitors' value chains. What activities and processes give you a competitive advantage? What activities and processes give your competitors an advantage? What are the major differences among your competitors?

- Learn from your competitors. For example, your competitors may have entered a market before you. What worked for them? What failed?

- Spot areas in which you are vulnerable. For example, if you know that your competitors are investing heavily in technology and you are not, you may soon be in trouble.

- Identify the barriers to entry and the competitive differentiators. How long lasting are these?

- Ensure the team realistically appraises its position, rather than gets caught in its own public relations or wishful thinking.

- Remember that denial of reality is frequently an important liability.

Consolidate your strategy

Some organizations try to be all things to all people and fail to excel at anything. According to Michael Treacy, market leaders must have the discipline to select one value proposition and manage against it.

- Look at your opportunities. Will you be more successful if you focus on total cost, best product, or a total solution strategy? Each strategy has a different focus for competitive advantage.
    - *Total cost strategy* emphasizes operating excellence. A typical area of operating excellence involves end-to-end product supply and service that is optimized and streamlined to minimize costs and hassles. In this strategy, operations are standardized, simplified, tightly controlled, and centrally controlled. Management systems are focused on integrated, reliable, high-speed transactions and compliance to norms.
    - A *best-product strategy* focuses on core processes of innovation, product development, and market expansion. Its business structure is flexible, so it can respond to entrepreneurial efforts. Its management systems are results driven and measure product success, and its culture encourages creativity, innovation, and outside-the-box thinking.
    - A *total solution* firm concentrates on customer intimacy. It focuses on the core processes of solution development, results management, and relationship management. Its structure moves decision making down in the organization to be close to the customer, and its management systems are geared toward developing specific customers. This culture focuses on specific customer solutions rather than general solutions, and thrives on lasting relationships.

- Once you select the direction of your organization, create the specific strategies for that direction.

- Recognize that the organization needs to focus on one direction, not all three simultaneously. Typically, it is not possible to achieve dominance in all three directions because of the necessary resource investment.

- Ask the leaders of each business unit to identify his or her value propositions. Each person should be able to do this. If they cannot, it may be a signal that the strategy is not clear.

- Examine business plans and strategies in relation to the business' value proposition. Inquire when you see inconsistency.

Test your strategy against organizational, industry, and customer realities

- Most organizations can come up with attractive product ideas. Use the following questions to test the potential of your product.
  - Have you identified a real product need or is the need already being filled by someone else?
  - Must the customer have this need met? How important is the need?
  - Can you build a sustained competitive advantage?
  - Will the customer see the advantage as desirable?
  - Will your approach be low cost, high quality, or a combination of the two?
  - Will it disrupt one or more competitors and give your organization a new advantage?
  - Will that advantage be short term, followed by greatly enhanced competitive inroads?
  - Is your technology sufficiently leading edge to compete?
  - Could competing technologies shoot down your idea quickly?
  - In the end, can you make a profit with this product?

- This type of reality check works best in an organization that has an open management style from the top down. Judge whether you can adequately test these ideas within your organization and if the resulting data will prove to be reliable. Also test each idea with current and future customers. Your key objective is to win their acceptance in the marketplace.

3. Anticipate risks and devise contingency plans to manage them.

"It just gets curiouser and curiouser," said Alice during her journey through Wonderland. Some would agree that business today is not only "curiouser" than before, it gets more imponderable all the time. As many traditional rules of competitive strategy become suspended or obsolete, the planning process becomes more ad hoc than orchestrated. As a result, foresight and innovation within an industry are now fundamental requirements for shaping strategy.

Anticipate the need for change

- Together with your management team, analyze the core issues of what business you are in, what your value proposition is to your customer, and what your market is. How could you change any of them?

- Examine the upstream end of your value chain. How long have you worked with the same suppliers? Could a supplier become a competitor? Suppose a key supplier went out of business. Do you have a contingency plan? Could alternative suppliers produce cost advantages due to increased competition?

- If you have a new or relatively new product that is performing well, consider how soon and in what way your competitors will enter the market against you. Will they try to emulate, substitute, or innovate a next-generation product? Do you have pricing plans that could delay competitive usurpation of your market share?

- Understand the profit engine and look for opportunities for change.
  - Identify the elements of your current profit engine. If you are in an organization in which all the competitors made a profit in the same way in the past, your industry is ripe for dramatic change.
  - The profit engine includes the market served, the value proposition put forward to the customers, the margin and value-added structure, the particular configuration of assets and skills that yields those margins, and the supporting administrative systems.
  - The profit engine affects the business you are in, the beliefs about how you make money, the products you deliver to customers, and who your competitors are.
  - How can you redefine the market served, take costs out of a particular system, or deliver the product to the customer in a different way? For example, mail order, television, and e-commerce are all changing the retail profit engine today.
  - Create a process chart and look for opportunities for change.
  - How could you improve the profit engine? How could a competitor damage your profit engine? How would you defend your profit engine in those circumstances? In each case, timing is a key consideration.

Outthink your competitors

- As you look for opportunities for thought leadership, taking control of the migration path, or competing for market share, remember that your competitors are trying to outthink you.

- Find out specifically who you are up against. Learn about your competitors from a business standpoint, and as individuals. Get to know their educational background, their track record, where they have worked, their typical mode of operation, and how they achieved competitive advantage in the past.

- Always anticipate what your competitors will do if you make a move. Staying ahead is a never-ending race. The leadership position can shift in a short amount of time. A tremendous investment can result in little advantage.

- Consider being somewhat unpredictable.

- Compete by redefining or reconfiguring the business. This will give you a competitive advantage for a longer period of time.

Anticipate competition for leadership

- Carefully assess the strength of your team's leadership in the critical parts of the value chain. Spot vulnerabilities, identify their sources, and develop strategies to minimize them.

- Watch your people. Make sure you know where the thought leadership lies in the group. Often it will not come from the people who make the most noise.

- Form a "cabinet" of colleagues to analyze risk, anticipate competitive thrusts, and predict competitive disruptions. Have this group meet regularly to make risk management an ongoing activity.

- Look within your organization for people who have great versatility and flexibility in coping with the evolving marketplace. Charge them with the mission of improvising on current strategic plans to meet unexpected or preemptive competitive strikes.

- Assess each member of your leadership team to understand the strengths and development needs of their strategic skills.

4. Translate broad strategies into clear objectives and practical action plans.

Broad strategy must drill down to each business and work unit, team, and person. Strategy must be the underpinning of what people in the organization do and how they are measured.

Identify linkage between broad organizational strategy and work unit strategy

Unless you are at the top of the organization, the vision and direction of the organization is set by others. Your responsibility is to take that vision and bring it down to the next level.

- Understanding your organization's approach to strategy will make it easier to identify objectives and action plans. They will flow directly from the strategy. For example, if you use Michael Porter's value chain, the process for implementing your strategy will include:
    - Charting the value chain.
    - Evaluating each part of the value chain for strengths and weaknesses.
    - Benchmarking competitors' values chains.
    - Identifying potential points of differentiation and excellence.

- Talk with senior executives to learn the theory behind their strategy.

- Discuss strategy with the organization's strategic planning person.

- Identify what the vision means for your part of the organization. Develop specific goals and strategies that will meet the organization's objectives. For example, if the overall strategy is to redefine your business from a book publishing company to an intellectual knowledge distribution company, meet with your team to determine how that will impact your group.

Align a balanced scorecard with strategic direction

The strategic vision and direction need to provide the anchor for any balanced scorecard approach. Linking the financial measurement system with the strategic direction makes the probability of achieving the goals more possible. Research indicates that 70% of companies fail to implement their strategy. Only 25% of managers have incentives linked to strategy, and 60% of organizations do not link their budgets to strategy.

- Determine the appropriate customer measures for your strategy. For example, if the organization targets the Global 50 the measures should focus on the Global 50, not all customers.

- Determine the internal processes and systems measures you need to capture progress. For example, a company whose strategy is product leadership will be interested in measures of time to market and percentage of revenue from new products, rather than cost per unit.

- Determine the measures of the infrastructure needed to support the strategy. A global expansion strategy will be more focused on the number of global managers ready, rather than retention.

- Make the measures and the progress visible to everyone. Ensure that executing strategy is the business of everyone in the organization.

Use the appropriate individuals or teams for action planning

Strategic initiatives require new roles and actions. Once the direction is established, create permanent and temporary structures and teams to plan and execute the strategy.

The following questions will help you evaluate your use of teams in this process:

- Are the teams composed of the right people?

- Do the teams clearly know their charter?

- Does each team have an active sponsor who knows what is required?

- Is each team responsible for developing goals against which their progress can be measured?

- Do the teams make the necessary decisions in a timely manner?

- Are the teams adding value?

When you move into new areas, use cross-functional or cross-business teams for both planning and implementation. Also use a team multi-rater feedback instrument to improve the effectiveness of the teams.

Communicate both vision and action to all important audiences

You and your team may have a vision, goals, and strategy, but that does not mean the organization does. Communication is key to strategy, alignment, and achieving specific goals. Research shows only 5% of front line employees know and understand the business strategy.

- Decide on a communication plan to provide key information to internal and external audiences. Determine the information you want each audience to receive and remember. What will they want to know?

- Communicate your strategic action plan as widely as possible within the organization. Specify the means you will use and the ends you wish to achieve. Use presentations, newsletters, posters, and other media to convey your central message.

- Hold special meetings with employees to convey your organization's broad objectives. Interpret strategies and objectives in terms of products and/or processes and actions that everyone will understand. Reserve time during the meeting for employees to ask questions of you and your team.

- Use the "bumper sticker" or "elevator speech" (1–2 sentences) technique to boil your key messages down to short phrases. If a message cannot be stated in a short phrase, it may be too complex or ambiguous.

- Use repetition to reinforce your messages. Do not make the common mistake of believing that one announcement is sufficient. Ask your advertising or communications people for a plan to drive the message home.

5. Focus the organization on efforts that add significant value.

Managing against strategy, particularly when it is long-term strategy, requires patience and persistence. Use your strategic model to determine the focus of your efforts.

Focus on priorities

Analyze your strategy for developing new opportunities. Make sure you understand the priorities of the following parts of the cycle:

- If you are in the process of developing intellectual leadership in your industry, focus on:
    - identifying new benefits for the customer,
    - identifying and managing core competencies to develop new products and services, and
    - developing new interfaces with the customer.

- If you are trying to control the migration paths, focus on:
    - identifying, building, and managing alliances and coalitions,
    - continuing to build core competencies to deliver new benefits to the customer,
    - accumulating market learning, and
    - increasing your global presence and distribution capacity.

- If you are managing for market share, focus on:
    - managing the value chain and maximizing productivity and efficiency,
    - building supplier networks,
    - creating marketing positioning messages, and
    - developing strategies for preemptive global dominance.

Review the organization's product array for areas of improvement

- Consider improving existing products to increase your market share or enter a new market. Also consider how new product ideas could lead to enhanced profitability or advances in the corporation's reputation as a leader in the industry.

- Review the percentage of your organization's annual sales that are derived from newly introduced products. Does this quota fit your organization's structure and personnel base?

- If you are in manufacturing, look for process improvements that could lead to greater capacity. Consider whether that expansion could become, in essence, a new product. Use the same conceptual approach for information systems, R&D, accounting, and other functions.

Review structures and processes for hidden cost advantages

- Examine the organization's internal processes in detail to find immediate or future economies. For example, changes and new investment in the organization's information systems could lead to downstream changes and future advantage.

- Devise a continuous management review system of the organization's value chain processes. Ask employees for suggestions on changes that will enhance cost-quality relationships.

- Establish an ongoing communication effort within the organization to emphasize the importance of both cost and quality to the organization's vision. Seek suggestions for constructive changes in procurement, work processes, and so forth.

- Always be wary of change for the sake of change. Consider the effect of any change on product quality, profitability, and future competitive advantage.

- Have your management team attend seminars and subscribe to publications that deal with process improvement, industry trends, shifts in buyers' lifestyles and preferences, and other factors that may affect future competitive issues.

- Review the human resources system for hiring, assessing, and developing talent.

- Determine the level of competency the organization needs to remain competitive. Has this been communicated? What role is your management team taking to assure the development of people?

6. Align the organization and allocate resources according to strategic priorities.

Aligning the organization to strategic priorities is critical to execution. Many executives falter with the execution of strategy.

Evaluate how strategies are carried out

- Ask that each member of your team test the alignment of the goals and resource allocations for the units that report to them.

- When you walk around and talk with people, ask what they do, why, and how their role contributes to success of the organization. People should be able to answer those questions, and you should be able to hear the alignment.

- Ensure that your people execute their plans on a timely basis. Executives who find themselves in trouble because goals are not achieved recognize too late that they have allowed "creeping excuse-ism." They have allowed themselves and others to excuse their lack of goal attainment. Usually people have good, logical reasons, but this approach, unchecked, is dangerous.

- Review plans and resource allocations so that they address the strategy and constraints to success.

Conduct regular progress reviews and look for goals alignment

- Meeting the organization's strategic goals is critical to the long-term viability of the business. Regular progress reviews are essential follow-ups to strategy formulation. Ask team members to report:
  - Their progress against goals.
  - What they learned from successes and failures.
  - Any problems, issues, or concerns.
  - What type of assistance they want from you.

- Conduct progress reviews using the existing team structure. In addition, consider using cross-functional or cross-business review teams. Have line groups review whether they are getting the support they need from the staff functions and vice versa.

- Identify teams and/or individuals who are exceeding their goals. Use the wisdom of these teams or people to help those who are having difficulty.

- Many strategic planning processes forget about the important components of a successful business strategy. Ask a team to look at where you are vulnerable. Look in particular for infrastructure issues such as business processes, technology, communication systems, etc. Then develop strategies to overcome the vulnerabilities in the short and long term.

Examine the organization's critical structural components for adequacy of resources

- Examine your organization's human resources activities (recruitment, compensation, benefits, and so forth) for competitiveness within the industry. Test their understanding of your organization's vision and strategies in terms of current and future requirements. Are people ready when they need to be? Are development and learning part of the culture?

- Can your suppliers fit both current and projected requirements? Are they sufficiently price competitive?

- Review your technical capabilities with the leaders in that area and consider whether current resources are adequate to meet future needs in the competitive arena. Ask them to help you devise strategies that will meet those requirements, either through increased budgets or a more effective use of existing resources.

- Ask your marketing and sales staffs how they perceive the organization's profit and competitive goals. If they have not already done so, ask them to give you a realistic appraisal of the viability of new products in the marketplace. Discuss competitive responses, disruptions in the industry, and other matters that may affect resource allocation.

Employ internal and external communications to keep the organization informed

- If the strategy involves a major change, develop a strong internal communications plan and allocate the needed resources to carry it out.

- At a minimum, use existing internal means like employee newsletters and bulletins to convey the message and continually reinforce it.

- If your organization is geographically widespread, use e-mail or other electronic modes of communication.

- Consider using strategically placed bulletin boards to send messages to your employees.

- Plan for the incremental release of messages and ideas to build interest in your statement.

- Provide a feedback mechanism and be sure to answer all questions or comments.

Communicate the message, then test for support

- Hold regular employee meetings in which you can hear specific comments and criticisms about the organization's vision and strategies. Be open to critical comments and listen carefully. Consider holding such meetings in an unusual or informal setting rather than a conference room or auditorium.

- Plan to spend time walking through the various areas of your organization to sample employee opinions at all levels.

- Test the effect of your external communication through focus groups, interviews, surveys, and the like.

- Take every opportunity to make customer contact. You may want to work a few shifts in the customer service area or answer their faxes and e-mail. Listen for recurrent themes of customer approval or dissatisfaction. Look for unmet needs that could suggest future product offerings or improvements.

RESOURCES

The resources for this chapter begin on page 438.

6
DRIVING EXECUTION

———

ASSIGN CLEAR AUTHORITY AND ACCOUNTABILITY;
DIRECT CHANGE WHILE MAINTAINING OPERATING
EFFECTIVENESS; INTEGRATE AND ALIGN EFFORTS
ACROSS UNITS AND FUNCTIONS; MONITOR RESULTS;
TACKLE PROBLEMS DIRECTLY AND WITH DISPATCH.

KEY BEHAVIORS

———

1. *Orchestrate the pace and process of change to maintain operating effectiveness.*
2. *Integrate efforts across functions and organizations.*
3. *Assign clear accountability backed by appropriate authority; ensure accountability for achieving business goals at multiple organizational levels.*
4. *Drive continuous improvement in all organizational processes and products.*
5. *Use benchmarks and performance measures to track progress.*
6. *Take preventive measures to avoid crisis management.*
7. *Tackle problems head-on and work to resolve them without delay; intervene to address barriers to achieving results and sources of lagging performance.*
8. *Confront problem performers directly, replacing them when appropriate.*
9. *Take decisive action in a crisis.*

INTRODUCTION

Driving execution has become increasingly complex in today's flatter and more fluid organizations. Understanding and learning to leverage complex systems of people and processes has become a mandate for today's executives. Creating connections between people and processes and aligning them with vision and strategy are key elements of success.

The best strategy in the world becomes meaningless when execution fails. Successful execution that achieves results in the near term and positions the organization for long-term stability enables executives and their organizations to reap the benefits of a fulfilled vision and strategy.

VALUABLE TIPS

- Read about change and change management in order to gain a basic understanding of the personal and organizational process.

- Determine whether you need to be the visionary, the initiator and driver of change, or its sponsor or supporter.

- Incorporate championing and managing change as normal expectations of your executive team.

- Set the expectation for integration or collaboration across units by asking for it, ensuring that it is occurring, and sponsoring opportunities for it.

- Analyze the barriers to collaboration. Ask people for feedback about what brings groups and people together, and what stimulates unproductive competition.

- Create reward and recognition systems that reinforce interdependent and joint goals.

- Encourage team members to work out problems and issues among their group, rather than coming to you for a resolution.

- When others come to you with their goals, strategies, plans, etc., listen and ask questions to understand, not to challenge or compete.

- Support success on a project by outlining the critical relationships the project manager needs to cultivate.

- Arrange for people at lower levels of the organization to work on projects from start to finish so they can see the creation of a whole product or the unfolding of an entire process.

- Treat knowledge management as an essential part of your organization's strategy; establish ways in which organizational learning and experience can be transmitted to others.

- Identify teams who can help other teams to be effective.

- Ensure that improvement goals are set for the improvement effort. In this way the effort and investment can be measured against results.

- Celebrate improvements in systems and processes.

- Help people learn to accept that continual change and improvement is the norm.

- Align measurement processes with business strategy, individual and group performance plans, and reward and recognition systems.

- Ask about and investigate the assumptions that underlie any plan. Ask others to challenge their assumptions, so that they can check their accuracy or vulnerability.

- When you are taking corrective action, make people aware of the situation and involve them as much as possible in designing and implementing a new solution.

- Anticipate as many crises as possible and have plans in place to deal with them. Put highest priority on crises that will have the largest "people" impact and affect business survival.

- Whenever possible, consult or talk to people who have experience with similar crises.

- Create and manage an effective communication plan during a crisis situation.

STRATEGIES FOR ACTION

1. Orchestrate the pace and process of change to maintain operating effectiveness.

Executives are the sponsors, champions, initiators, cheerleaders, and supporters of change. Executives need to be able to envision and drive changes themselves, but more importantly they need to be able to sponsor and support the changes championed by others. For an organization to be resilient and competitive, executives need to be continually changing and adapting. An executive is responsible for knowing when change needs to occur and must be willing to sponsor and rally support.

Additionally, effective executives ensure that while the organization adapts and changes, it also meets its goals to its stakeholders. Keeping this balance between maintaining operating effectiveness, while also changing, is a continual balancing act.

Learn about change management

- Read about change and change management in order to gain a basic understanding of the personal and organizational process.

- Adopt a model of change that makes sense to you and others in the organization. Change models help to provide a conceptual framework for what goes on when changes occur and provide good roadmaps for the issues that must be addressed.

- Determine whether you need to be the visionary, the initiator and driver of change, or its sponsor or supporter. Typically the role of an executive is that of visionary or sponsor. The role of sponsor is possible as long as you have good, effective change champions among your leadership team. If not, you may find that you need to lead the change yourself.

- When you are building your team, ensure that the team has strong change champion and change management skills. Without these you can anticipate that the team and the organization will play catch-up to the competition rather than get out in front.

- Ensure that change management plans include what needs to be done across the total value chain. Change in any part of the value chain affects the other parts.

- Communicate, communicate, and communicate about change! Remember, it is almost impossible to overcommunicate about change.

- Consider resistance to change as normal. Discover the concerns people have about proposed change. Solve the problems or potential problems they have identified, rather than simply label people as resisters.

- Incorporate championing and managing change as normal expectations of your executive team. Communicate clearly to your staff that you expect change management to be something they are doing all of the time, rather than something that occasionally needs to be done.

- Ensure that the impact of proposed change on normal operations has been taken into account during the implementation planning.

- Regularly assess the change efforts in the organization to determine whether people achieve their objectives within the planned timeframes.

Understand elements of a successful change process

In his article "Leading Change: Why Transformation Efforts Fail" (*Harvard Business Review*, March-April 1995), John Kotter discusses why transformational efforts succeed and fail. Kotter identifies eight components of a successful transformation effort. Review each component and identify opportunities for fine-tuning your skills.

- *Establish a sense of urgency:* Change efforts and projects that remain on the back burner do not get done. How can you direct the right amount of "heat" or energy toward the effort?

- *Form a powerful guiding coalition:* Influential people can be found at all levels of the organization, not only at the top. To build a board of directors for your project or change effort, meet with people informally, presell the idea, use your contacts as sounding boards, and ask others to identify individuals in the organization who are good at supporting change.

- *Create a compelling vision:* People have to understand and relate to what you are trying to do. If you cannot explain your vision in five minutes and get people to react with energy, you still have work to do.

- *Communicate the vision:* Your initiative, regardless of its size and scope, will live or die by the effectiveness of your communication. Use multiple means of communicating your vision. Use budget meetings, quarterly reviews, board meetings, and staff meetings to reinforce your vision and sustain momentum. Make a conscientious effort to "walk your talk."

- *Remove obstacles and empower others to act on the vision:* Like it or not, perception is reality to many individuals. If people perceive an obstacle, avoid arguing over it and help them figure out how it should be addressed. Act swiftly and purposefully toward individuals, systems, and processes that undermine your efforts.

- *Plan for and create short-term wins:* Individuals need to see that their efforts are yielding positive results. Work with your team to identify feasible short-term results and successes. As these wins occur, recognize and reward the individuals and teams involved.

- *Consolidate improvements and produce more change:* Efforts to improve an initiative should never have an endpoint. To sustain and increase improvement efforts, hire, reward, and promote people who represent the new, not the old. Remember that there is always someone looking for a better, faster, and different way of doing what you do.

- *Institutionalize new approaches:* Make sure people see how changes and initiatives contribute to business success. Encourage and develop a second generation of leaders to shape new initiatives and build on your successes. Encourage risk taking and nontraditional approaches and actions.

2. Integrate efforts across functions and organizations.

Effective organizations operate better when there is integration across parts of the organization. Functions, businesses, or geographies that act like individual silos are often not as effective. If work and business processes cut across functions, then organizations need to be able to focus simultaneously on the parts, the whole, and the interconnections between the two. Often competitive advantage lies in the white space.

Therefore, it is important for executives to set clear expectations for permeable boundaries between different parts of the organization and between the organization and the environment. Additionally, they need to set up and support systems that encourage this cooperation and integration.

Make collaboration an expectation

- Establish an executive team, which includes the heads of the different organizational units, as a real team with a meaningful relationship and accountability to one another.

- Set the expectation for integration or collaboration across units by asking for it, ensuring that it is occurring, and sponsoring opportunities for it.

- When an executive is sharing a plan, ask how the plan affects his or her counterpart in another business, or what conversations the person has had with the functional manager most impacted. These questions will reinforce your interest and expectation.

- Include cooperative behavior or teamwork as part of the competencies for which you hire and develop people. During performance reviews, ask others with whom the person works for feedback on these areas.

- Design an organizational structure that encourages collaboration among its work units. Use an organizational structure that strengthens what needs to be strengthened. For example, if Information Services, Global Marketing, and Distribution need to be developed as functions, then a functional organization may make sense. On the other hand, if the strategy is regional, then organizing with regional businesses is called for.

- Be aware that whatever structure is established, "silos" of some kind will result. A functional organization has difficulty with planning across the functions and across the businesses. A business unit organization has difficulty planning within the function and across businesses.

- Create reward and recognition systems that reinforce interdependent and joint goals.

- Encourage integration and cross-functional problem solving to break down department walls. Establish decision-making processes that push decisions down the organization as far as possible.

- Reach beyond the organization's boundaries to external sources, such as clients and vendors, to find ways to shorten cycle times, reduce bottlenecks, and improve responsiveness to customers.

Share information across the organization

- Sponsor or support activities in which teams from different parts of the organization learn from one another.

- Be a conduit of information. Tell people about the successes and learnings of others.

- Leverage technology to create communication vehicles that keep people updated and informed.

- Ask the human resources department to provide charts, phone directories, and other information that will help people access their peers in other areas.

- Ensure that key stakeholders of new initiatives are identified and included in the planning process.

- Create an environment that fosters dialogue. Encourage team members to work out problems and issues among their group, rather than coming to you for a resolution.

Set up cross-functional teams

- Ensure that the units work together on joint efforts. Reengineering work processes are a common opportunity for cross-unit work.

- Analyze the barriers to collaboration. Ask people for feedback about what brings groups and people together, and what stimulates unproductive competition.

- Set up cross-functional and/or cross-business teams to work on key issues and processes.
    - Identify the skills and perspectives that need to be represented on the team.
    - Keep the team size manageable, as too many people can prevent a consensus from being reached. Five to nine people is an optimal team size.
    - Set a time frame for the team's project.
    - Provide the team with the internal and external resources they need to perform successfully.
    - Give the team sufficient authority to act on appropriate matters.

3. Assign clear accountability backed by appropriate authority.

Executives who continue to function as individual contributors stifle the growth of their organizations. Effective executives drive responsibility and decision making down in the organization. This allows for others to become passionately and personally invested in the organization and its success. It allows for executives to take pleasure in watching people create and fulfill their own dreams, not just the dreams of a small number of top executives.

Delegate effectively

- Delegate results to others, not tasks.

- Let others come to you with their goals, strategies, plans, etc. Listen attentively and ask questions to understand, not to challenge or compete.

- When or if the person's plan does not meet your expectations, discuss the differences openly. Share the goals or problems; do not just dictate that the person's plan has to be different.

- Ask others how you can help or what they want from you. In this way, you are providing the help the person wants, rather than what you think they need.
    - During updates, ask what, if anything, the person wants you to do differently.
    - When you do something you thought was helpful, ask how the other person saw it.

- Check that you have surrounded yourself with many people who are more capable than you in their particular areas. Then, let them do their work.
    - Ask others for feedback about your staff.
    - Ask whether others believe you hire in your own image only.
    - Ask if others think you hire high-quality people.

- Ensure that the roles in the organization are determined by the direction and strategy of the organization.

- When you make an assignment, ask the other person to summarize so you can ensure they understand your expectations.

- Consider which people in the organization need to know who owns responsibility for the assignment. Communicate responsibilities clearly, so others know the person has the responsibility, the person can be acknowledged for their role, and the person can receive the organization's "blessing."

- If others come to you with concerns about the work, refer them (whenever possible) to the person responsible. This will keep the responsibility on the right person. In this way you will not unintentionally undermine the person. Additionally, this will allow the person to accept the impact of his or her decisions or behavior directly. This is important for learning.

- Individuals who are responsible for implementing and supporting the plan need to know what is expected of them. Ensure role clarity by communicating clear responsibilities to all parties involved in the project. Then allow people to exercise their authority to act and decide. Yield to the owner of the decision. Intervene when necessary, but do it in a way that does not undermine the credibility of the individual.

- Ensure people's success on a project by outlining the critical relationships they need to cultivate. Help them identify all the people the project will impact.

Build in accountability measures

- Initiate a culture change project that centers around employee involvement, total quality, or participative management.

- Give people responsibility for critiquing their own work or the work of their peers. Encourage employees to form peer review groups that meet regularly to discuss how processes and productivity can be improved.

- Arrange for people at lower levels of the organization to work on projects from start to finish so they can see the creation of a whole product or the unfolding of an entire process.

- Set up processes that allow employees to interact with customers, including initial calls, delivery, and follow-up. This will give them a greater sense of how their work addresses and meets customer needs.

- Initiate cross-training so people will have a broader understanding of the business and invest themselves in more than one area.

4. Drive continuous improvement in all organizational processes and products.

Quality and service are moving targets—what is considered exceptional service or quality today will be standard tomorrow. Because expectations constantly change, continuous improvement is a must.

Organizations need to go far beyond the event-driven quality programs, cost-cutting slash-and-burn efforts, and amorphous organization learning initiatives.

Executive focus on continuous learning should be a way of life. Dramatic improvements in business processes, products, and services should be included as part of normal expectations.

Focus on continuous improvement

- Review your recent speeches, interviews, position papers, and staff meeting notes or updates. What messages are you sending about continuous improvement? Is this consistent with what the organization needs?

- Continuous improvement driven only from the top will leave the organization very vulnerable. Make sure you have continuous improvement moving up and down the organization.

- Discuss continuous improvement directions and successes your peers have seen in their organizations. Ask about the role they played in these improvement processes—were they the visionary, the initiator or driver, the champion, or the sponsor? Notice how these roles differ.

- Investigate how organizations are different when the continuous improvement championing comes from the executive offices, and when it comes from throughout the organization.

- Determine whether the organization simply needs to achieve benchmark level, or whether it needs to set the standard. In areas that define the organization, competitive difference, or potential competitive differential, the organization will need to be better than others.
    - Consider what you may be able to learn from other industries. Do not just benchmark in your own industry.
    - Pay attention to articles, reports, and information about organizations that made revolutionary changes. What can you learn from these examples? How do you and your organization limit the view of what is possible?

- Require regular benchmarking on processes that are important to the organization. After the study is done, ask what will be different and what has been learned.

- Ensure that goals are set for the improvement effort. In this way the effort and investment can be measured against results. Involve the stakeholders and financial decision makers in setting the measures, so that there will be more agreement on the meaning of the outcomes.

- Celebrate improvements.

- Help people learn to accept that continual change and improvement is the norm in business.

- Deliberately shake things up by challenging the reasonableness of comfort.

Encourage organizational learning

- Establish ways in which organizational learning and experience can be transmitted to others. View knowledge management as an essential part of your organization's strategy.

- Determine whether it is most important to give people access to information and knowledge, or if it is most important to give people access to people who have had particular experience. Depending upon your answer to this, your knowledge management strategy should focus on capturing information and knowledge and getting it to people, or in identifying people with experience and connecting people to one another. This is an important distinction.

- Ensure that all primary business processes are documented and reviewed regularly. It is difficult to improve something without knowing what it is.

- As a leader, you must provide your people with the tools and knowledge they need to effectively implement continuous improvement initiatives. Make sure you have the necessary internal or external people to advise you and guide the process.

- When using external consultants, ask that knowledge transfer occurs. Consider very carefully whether you want to use consultants who are unwilling to teach your people.

- Continuous improvement depends heavily on people who hunger for ways to do it better. People must exploit their childhood curiosity, be willing to try new things, tell it like they see it, and be lifelong learners.

- Create an environment where people communicate and share information without fear—one where risk taking is the norm.

- Encourage people to push the boundaries of the status quo and current work processes. Set up structures that allow people to learn from one another through discussions, job rotation, cross-functional projects, and the like.

5. Use benchmarks and performance measures to track progress.

Performance measures are critical to organizational success. People pay attention to where the organization pays attention. Therefore, one of the primary roles of an executive is to ensure that the appropriate performance measures are in place to measure what is important.

Define performance measures

- Ensure that the organization's goals accurately reflect the goals that need to be achieved for both short- and long-term success. Most organizations use some form of balanced scorecard, in which the organizational goals focus on a number of key goals which, taken together, are seen as success. Typically these goals include financial, customer, people, and process goals.

- Anchor the balanced scorecard with the business strategy. Effective execution of strategy will not occur unless the measurement system, incentives, and resources are allocated consistently with the strategy.

- Evaluate the current measurement system. What is it measuring? Is it measuring the key variables of success? Who sees the results? What difference do they make? Is it measuring what is most important short term? long term? What should be measured that is not being measured?

- Use a team approach when you design your measurement system. Involve others early in the process to gain their buy-in. Consider partnering with a consultant to guide the process.

- Implementing any measurement system or changing which measures are used will drive changes in behavior, as "what you measure is what you get." Given the truth and power of this statement, it is essential that you exercise great care in designing or changing your measurement system so you do not unintentionally promote behaviors that are detrimental to your organization's performance in either the short or long run.

- When you are considering a measurement system, remember the following:
    - Individuals have a tendency to focus on measures that are easiest to improve in the short term, rather than on those that will drive long-term results.
    - The terms *productivity* and *performance* should not be used interchangeably. Performance refers to output or, in the case of performance appraisal, an evaluation of behavior. Productivity indicates how well a system uses its resources to achieve its goals.
    - To drive execution, a sound measurement system must be combined with effective feedback and planning systems.

- Provide feedback on the measures to everyone in the organization. Ask that teams spend time determining how to do better.

- Ask about other measurement systems. Have those functionally responsible for the measurement systems explain the rationale of different systems.

- Ensure that incentives are linked to executing the strategy.

- Make the measures and progress updates visible and easily accessible. After key measures have been defined and effective feedback and planning processes developed, communicate them completely and repeatedly.

- Post the measures, graphs, and charts on walls in conference rooms and hallways. Use technology to make the information accessible and keep it current.

- Align the measurement process with individual and group performance plans, and with reward and recognition systems. Maintain momentum by keeping individuals and teams focused on the most important measures.

Use benchmarking

Benchmarking allows a company to identify opportunities for improvement. It is part of a continuous improvement effort. Benchmarking directs efforts to be the best of the best; it also helps redirect efforts to areas in which more change is needed. Executives use benchmarking to prevent themselves and their organization from being lulled into comfort and self-satisfaction.

Effective benchmarking is purposeful, externally focused, measurement based, information intensive, objective, and action oriented. It is not simply visiting other organizations and talking to people.

- Ensure that benchmarking efforts have plans, the appropriate leadership, funding, and clear goals.

- Regularly review benchmarking efforts in the organization. Learn about the findings, recommendations, and follow-up. Often benchmarking is done but priorities for change are not identified, or if they are identified, they are not executed. Help ensure that the total benchmarking cycle occurs, so change results.

- Understand that your involvement and visibility around benchmarking send the signals that you are interested in continuous improvement, are focused on competitive advantage, are promoting cross-functional and cross-business teamwork, and want quantum leaps of improvement.

- Benchmark against companies who are leaders in your industry and other industries. Look at firms who are leading in areas in which you are trying to improve. Change your targets as your business needs evolve.

- Benchmark against organizations noted for their successes in a particular area. These organizations do not have to be in the same industry, but they must be world-class in a particular function, operation, or process.

- Benchmark internally by observing the output of various departments, divisions, and subsidiaries. Identify successful structures and duplicate them throughout the organization.

- When you read or listen to benchmark reports, make sure you understand the investigation, how the learning applies to your organization, and the recommendations. Avoid getting caught up in the detail.

6. Take preventive measures to avoid crisis management.

Adaptability and flexibility are always necessary, because things change. As much as possible, ask others to anticipate risks and build risk management into the original planning. Then people will not have to be scrambling at the last moment.

- When you are developing a plan, think ahead and consider all aspects. Outline clear action steps, timelines, and responsibilities. Also identify potential resources.

- Anticipate problems, challenges, or whether things will go as planned. Establish plans to minimize risk and prepare for contingencies.

- Ask and investigate the assumptions that underlie any plan. Ask others to challenge their assumptions, so they can check their accuracy or vulnerability.

- Solicit input from team members who will be responsible for implementation to ensure that the plan will be carried out smoothly and effectively. Work with them to identify potential obstacles and develop appropriate contingency plans.

- Sometimes new initiatives, processes, or policies run into unanticipated obstacles. Recognize the early warning signs and take appropriate action instead of blindly moving forward. Proceed more aggressively once greater organizational readiness is established.

- Take a temporary time-out to review progress and problems. Ask people who represent the affected groups and constituencies to review the plan. Make adjustments where necessary.

- Get buy-in up front and along the way. If you push the implementation too hard before gaining sufficient support, you will likely run into difficulty. You may receive public compliance but face private defiance; in other words, people may find ways to undermine your implementation efforts.

7. Tackle problems head-on and work to resolve them without delay.

When you learn of an issue that could affect your group, look into it as quickly as possible. Use this principle for problems with people, the organization, and the business. Inaction is action. Determine what needs to happen.

- Assess the seriousness of the situation. Rationalization, attempts to downplay the situation, and selective viewing of the circumstances will slow your response time.

- If appropriate, begin a formal investigation of the problem or, at a minimum, set up an informal meeting with others affected by the issue.

- Set goals for solving the problem. Create deadlines for investigating the problem and implementing the solution.

- Determine the necessary communication strategy for the situation.

- If you are reluctant to move ahead quickly on an issue, identify the reasons. People procrastinate for a number of reasons, including lack of information, an unclear course of action, lack of time to consider the issue, or fear of negative consequences. Once you have identified the obstacles, brainstorm ways to overcome them.

- The key to successful corrective action is making people aware of the situation and involving them as much as possible in designing and implementing a new solution.

- Provide information and guidance on overarching strategic issues, then ask questions to get critical data on problems and their causes.

- Encourage people to see issues from multiple perspectives and help them reach agreement on a solution.

8. Confront problem performers directly, replacing them when appropriate.

A performance problem occurs when there is a difference between what is expected and what a person does. Performance issues have many faces, including lack of results, interpersonal problems, self-management issues, and strategic mistakes.

Diagnose problems effectively

When there is a performance problem, follow this sequence to determine your actions:

1. Identify the difference between what is and what should be.
2. Determine the importance of the discrepancy.
3. Determine whether the person knew and understood the expectations.
4. Decide whether the problem is due to a skill deficiency, disagreement about goals, or disagreement about methods.
5. Decide whether coaching is adequate or if formal training is needed.
6. If necessary, determine how to align goals.

- If the problem is a function of poor communication, make sure the person is aware of specific goals and objectives. Clarify your expectations and be clear about instances in which they have not been met.

- If poor performance is due to misaligned goals, listen to the person's ideas and perspectives. Determine if there is a way to align his or her goals.

- If poor performance is due to the person's lack of skill, knowledge, or experience, provide coaching and developmental opportunities. Give more direction to people when they are working in areas in which their experience is limited.

- If organizational rewards or goal-setting policies are contributing to poor performance, identify areas where competing objectives encourage good performance in one area and poor performance in another.

Agree on a performance plan and monitor results

When you work with direct reports to resolve performance problems, try the following:

1. Reach agreement that a problem exists.

2. Determine whether the person agrees that a change in behavior will have positive outcomes.

3. If so, ask the individual to generate alternative solutions for addressing the problem.

4. Put the improvement plan in writing to solidify your agreement.

5. Offer to give effective feedback and encouragement. Also suggest that the person seek support and feedback from trusted colleagues.

6. Monitor performance. Recognize and reinforce any improvements, especially at the beginning.

9. Take decisive action in a crisis.

Executives face very different kinds of crises such as tampering with a product, losing the key executive in their largest business or function, making their largest customer dissatisfied, losing investors' confidence in the strategy, and thorny interpersonal issues. Whatever the crises, executives are called on to rapidly assess the situation and determine a course of action.

Plan for crises

- Anticipate as many crises as possible and have plans in place to deal with them. Prioritize the possible crises that will have the largest "people" impact and affect business survival as the greatest concern.

- When appropriate, do a trial run of the crisis management plan to identify areas for improvement.

- Identify the kinds of crises or problems with which you have the most difficulty making decisions. Gain insight into what causes the difficulty for you.

- Seek input from others whenever possible. Look at the problem from several points of view.

- Resist being a crisis or problem reactor; instead, be a problem solver. In a mild crisis, consider taking time to emphasize a long-term resolution. A moderately critical situation may require a balance between a short- and long-term solution. In an extremely critical situation, you may need to focus solely on a short-term answer.

- Whenever possible, gather people with whom you can consult or talk. Preferably select people who have experience with similar crises.

- Always remember that a well-managed communication plan is a necessary part of any crisis situation.

- Clearly identify the roles needed in the situation and assign responsibility and boundaries of authority.

Deal honestly and thoroughly with the issues

- Deal with underlying problems. Bring the organization's shortcomings and failures to the forefront so that corrective measures can be taken. If a crisis is related to a failing of a particular individual or work unit, deal with it in a respectful, straightforward way.

- Avoid making quick fixes. A response that only addresses the immediate, most-visible damage will not be sufficient to handle long-term repercussions.

- Look beyond the immediate circumstances and consider the impact on customers, stockholders, the industry, the community, and the environment.

- Consider ethical issues when you deal with crises. Organizations often face potentially severe penalties in the marketplace if safety and values are shoved aside to save a few dollars in a crisis situation.

RESOURCES

The resources for this chapter begin on page 440.

7
ATTRACTING AND DEVELOPING TALENT

———

ATTRACT HIGH CALIBER PEOPLE;

DEVELOP TEAMS AND TALENT WITH

DIVERSE CAPABILITIES; ACCURATELY APPRAISE

THE STRENGTHS AND WEAKNESSES OF OTHERS;

PROVIDE CONSTRUCTIVE FEEDBACK;

DEVELOP SUCCESSORS AND TALENT POOLS.

KEY BEHAVIORS

———

1. *Create an environment that provides direction and promotes continuous learning and development.*
2. *Attract and select the best high-caliber talent by recognizing organizational as well as individual needs.*
3. *Build a strong team whose members have complementary strengths.*
4. *Encourage and value diversity in the organization's talent base.*
5. *Accurately appraise the strengths and weaknesses of direct reports.*
6. *Provide accurate, motivating feedback and constructive criticism.*
7. *Recognize and unleash the full potential of others by providing the needed resources, coaching, experiences, and other support.*
8. *Develop successors and talent pools for key positions.*

INTRODUCTION

Managing the talent portfolio in your organization is critical to have the needed capabilities for short- and long-term organizational performance. Just as the investment in the organization's R&D, (research and development) is critical to success of the organization, so is the investment in C&D, or coaching and development.

It is people who think of products, create the products, serve customers, and manage the organizational systems. You can create elegant business strategies or reengineer all you want, but without the right people in the right place at the right time, your organization will not succeed.

As an executive, you have a responsibility to lead your organization in such a way that it attracts the finest people. You need top talent to develop and execute business strategies. But attracting talent alone will not supply you with all the expertise and creativity your organization needs. It is impossible for you to recruit all the talent you need from outside the organization. You need to grow it from within.

This does not happen by itself. Decreeing that development is the responsibility of individuals will not make it happen. It is the responsibility of the individual, but savvy executives also know it is the responsibility of the organization. It requires an investment in coaching and developing people. Development results from a partnership between individuals and the organization in which each takes responsibility for making development happen. You need to lead that effort, serve as a role model, and continually champion its necessity.

The people in your organization need to be world–class learners. They need to have the ability to figure out what needs to be done better and quicker than your competitors. They need to be flexible, adaptable, and resilient. They need to be able to "turn on a dime," yet also persevere when necessary.

You need to set the expectation that the organization and its people need to be constantly learning. The organization needs to have values and processes in place that make learning occur as frequently and normally as breathing. Learning needs to become the way of working in the organization.

VALUABLE TIPS

- Use a strategic performance modeling process to determine the most important competencies for the organization or for a particular position or level.

- Analyze the kind of talent you need on your team and define the qualifications necessary to fill each role.

- Identify the personnel constraints to achieving strategic business goals.

- Keep track of people who are considered strong performers in your industry.

- Develop relationships with people whom you may want to join the team in the future.

- Deliberately develop a strong network inside and outside the industry, so you know the best resources and talent.

- Learn which factors attract and retain people you want to attract to the organization.

- Develop a selection process that will give you accurate information about the candidate's skills and potential in each required competency area.

- Remember that "the best predictor of future behavior is past behavior."

- Construct an interview guide to tap into the person's experience, skills, and track record.

- Demonstrate that you are personally engaged in development by sharing your development plan, discussing your development activities, giving progress reports, taking appropriate risks in the pursuit of learning, and asking for feedback and help.

- Determine two or three behaviors which, if adopted, would result in greater focus on development and learning.

- Regularly share learning and updates at your staff meetings.

- Hold your direct reports responsible for supporting the development of their people.

- Work with each member of your team to complete a GAPS analysis.

- Make the recruiting and development of people from different backgrounds a performance criterion for you and your managers.

- When you conduct an assessment, evaluate behaviors whenever possible, rather than personality traits.

- Set objectives with each individual and the team at least once a year. Cascade these goals down from the organization's plan and objectives.

- Give frequent feedback that is directly related to people's identified development priorities.

- Develop the habit of looking for and commending positive contributions.

- Establish trusting relationships with your direct reports. Learn about their goals, values, and priorities.

- View on-the-job experiences as powerful learning devices.

- Use a team-based 360-degree survey instrument to gather perspectives regarding your team's current strengths and needs.

- Ask people about their progress, including what they are learning and their successes and failures.

- Help people figure out alternatives when they think they are stuck. When people run out of ideas, provide another way of looking at the situation.

- Establish clear expectations for your team that you and they will take an active role in developing and working the succession planning process.

- Begin your succession planning process by considering the organization's vision and future strategic business needs.

- Benchmark against organizations that have used successful succession processes and use their expertise and knowledge to help you design your system.

STRATEGIES FOR ACTION

1. Create an environment that provides direction and promotes continuous learning and development.

Individuals are responsible for their own development, but if the organization does not do its share, development becomes even harder for people. You have a choice—you can either have slow or nonexistent development, or you can invest your time in creating an environment that supports and encourages development.

Shape the environment

Use the following statements to assess the current environment:

- Open discussions with people about performance and development needs are common here.   Yes   No

- People feel like they get honest feedback.   Yes   No

- People feel responsible to focus and meet their objectives.   Yes   No

- Leaders encourage others to take appropriate risks in pursuit of learning.   Yes   No

- People here are willing to try new things.   Yes   No

- New ideas and fresh perspectives are welcomed.   Yes   No

- People can challenge the status quo here.   Yes   No

- Our culture encourages people to do new things.   Yes   No

- People here are held accountable for meeting objectives and delivering on commitments.   Yes   No

- People here trust their leaders to walk their talk.   Yes   No

If you answered "yes" to many of these statements you are on your way to a culture that supports and encourages development. If you answered no, it is likely that less development of people occurs. Development may be seen as an HR responsibility or this year's slogan. Many organizations say fine things about the importance of people and development, but they struggle to make this a reality.

- If you want to create an environment of continuous learning and development, you have to invest your own time and energy. The primary methods you can use include:
    - Set clear expectations about investments in attracting and developing people.
    - Become a visible role model.
    - Strengthen the learning climate within your own group.
    - Leverage the organizational culture, systems, and processes to promote learning.

Clarify the importance of development

Given the rapidly accelerating pace of change and shortages of people with particular skills, attracting and developing people has become a prerequisite of business success and is a clear competitive differentiator. To accomplish this objective, you can:

- Identify the constraints to achieving the strategic business goals. For most organizations, especially those in knowledge-based businesses, the primary constraint to achieving business goals is not having the right people in the right place when needed.

- Demonstrate through the strategic planning process that you cannot achieve organizational priorities without people who have the right mix of skills.

- Establish this understanding of the criticality of development to provide the rationale and motivation for the management team and employees to invest time and energy in development. Unfortunately, without this understanding, many people see development as what is done after work objectives have been completed. The new necessary understanding is that development is one of the primary business objectives of the organization.

- Create a vision with your team that supports investment in attracting, coaching, and developing employees and building a learning organization. Build a thorough understanding of the business reasons for doing this. Discuss the importance of both attracting and developing talent within the organization.

- Determine two or three behaviors which, if adopted, would result in greater focus on development and learning. For example, identify development as one of the core organizational competencies and ask that:
    - all employees regularly ask for feedback to help develop themselves.
    - your company incorporates development planning into business planning and individual goal setting.
    - all employees encourage others to learn and develop.

- Meet with your staff and your human resources support to identify the key roles in the organization. Establish a reliable method for determining the needed competencies for these roles. Then establish processes for assessing the talent and talent potential in the organization, so that you know possible successors and can begin the development process.

Establish expectations

- Establish clear expectations of the role you expect executives, managers, and employees in the organization to play with respect to development and learning.

- Develop and communicate a clear picture of the role of managers, employees, and human resources in the development of people.
    - Employees are responsible for their own development. As such they need to become aware of their strengths and development areas, their own goals and values, the perceptions of others, and the expectations of the organization.
    - Managers are responsible for helping employees develop themselves. Therefore, they need to provide access to information and opportunities for learning and practicing the new skills.
    - Human resources people have both a strategic role in helping to manage the organization's talent portfolio, and a consultant role with individual managers and employees.

- Common expectations are:
    - Managers are expected to coach and develop employees.
    - Each person is expected to work on his or her development on a regular basis.
    - Managers are expected to give employees access to information that helps them understand how they are seen by others and what is expected of them.
    - People are expected to share their knowledge and learn from one another.

- Executives and managers are expected to work with their teams to establish core practices that support development.
- Executives and managers are expected to support human resources systems and practices that attract and develop people.

Model your commitment to learning

- Demonstrate that you are personally engaged in development by sharing your development plan, discussing your development activities, giving progress reports, taking appropriate risks in the pursuit of learning, and asking for feedback and help. This public commitment to development will send a strong message to the organization and set the expectation for learning for others.

- Share your development goals.

- Tell people what you have learned.

- Talk about your learning experiences—both the successful as well as the challenging ones. Your willingness to model struggling with learning will be an important lesson for others.

- Ask others for their feedback and help.

- Tell people about your failures as well as your successes. Discuss what you did to recover from the failure or lack of success.

Establish trusting relationships with your team members

- Demonstrate a genuine interest in your team members and a desire to help them succeed.

- Build trust with others by taking time to understand them. Begin by focusing on the person and what is important to him or her, instead of what you think should be important. Act according to their best interests and the organization's.

- Find out what matters to people so you can tap into their natural motivation for development. For all practical purposes, it's impossible to motivate people to work on development unless there is a clear personal payoff for them.

- Provide information that will help them with development.

- Help each person develop and implement a plan for achieving his or her objectives.

- Make sure that your position/level in the organization doesn't intimidate people. Be clear about your motives in wanting to talk with people about their development. One real value is that people with better capabilities contribute more to the organization's success.

- Ask team members to share their expectations of you. Specifically ask how you can help them succeed in their work.

Strengthen the learning climate

- Establish processes that make learning fluid, normal, and compelling. Set up processes that allow learning to be built in to the normal course of the work you do. Don't make it an add-on to an already busy workload. For development to occur and for the workforce to be agile and adaptable, the organizational climate needs to encourage and support learning. You can play a significant role in this effort.

- Encourage learning within and across groups. Tell people about the successes of others and recommend that they ask one another for details.

- Encourage open dialogue and explore different points of view. Be open to opposing views. Never treat dissension, differences of opinion, or disagreement as obstacles. Showing frustration, even in subtle ways, will inhibit people from offering contrasting points of view in the future.

- When you disagree with someone, avoid labeling their opinions as right or wrong. Instead, use words such as "concerns," "doubts," and "questions."

- Encourage a free flow of information and ideas. Frequently ask what others have learned. Use good communication skills to examine ideas, explore questions, find out what people are learning, share best practices, etc.

- Encourage risk taking and the sharing of experiences. Regularly share learning and updates at your staff meetings.

- Support people's desire to study, learn, and investigate. Encourage people to learn things they do not have to use immediately. Learning outside of one's field of expertise is valuable because it stimulates thinking.

- Reinforce the belief that everyone needs to learn and is capable of learning. Focus on the process of learning rather than the traits of being smart.

- "Reinforce movement," rather than just rewarding performance—you need to reward progress and improvement as important things in themselves.

- Learn more about establishing a learning climate by reading the chapter on "Shaping the Environment" in *Leader As Coach* (Personnel Decisions, 1996).

- Ask for feedback about how you may unintentionally inhibit learning and the sharing of information. Do you:
    - Unintentionally "shoot the messenger" by reacting strongly to information?
    - Test people to see if they will stand up for their point of view?
    - Argue or disagree each time someone has a different opinion than yours?
    - Second-guess decisions?
    - Point out when you are right?

  Or do you:
    - Make yourself available for people to talk with you?
    - Ask what others have learned?
    - Provide information and analyses rather than asking others for their views?

Leverage the organizational culture, processes, and systems to promote learning

- You can use your position and role in the organization to leverage the policies, systems, and processes to support development and learning. Find out about the systems and programs that are supposed to result in learning and development and determine whether they accomplish the intended results. Work closely with your team and HR to create and support development processes that work.

- Request a *PDI Pipeline For Development™ Review*[1] on the organization's systems, processes, and programs that support development. This review will identify the strengths and needs for the organization's development processes. Areas to investigate include:
    - Alignment between current and future strategic business needs.
    - The clarity of the vision and purpose of each development program.
    - The alignment between programs.
    - Whether systems, processes, and programs are based on solid principles of development and learning.
    - The organizational value in these programs, especially in regard to performance, risk, and liquidity or flexibility of the workforce.

- Understand the outcomes of the current development programs and processes. Review the investment in different kinds of programs to ensure investment is made where it is needed.
    - Determine expected business outcomes for programs and initiatives.
    - Ask for evaluation of these outcomes.

GAPS GRID: CRITICAL INFORMATION FOR DEVELOPMENT

	WHERE THE PERSON IS	WHERE THE PERSON IS GOING
THE PERSON'S VIEW	**ABILITIES** How they see themselves. The person's view of their capabilities, style, and performance, especially in relation to important Goals and Standards.	**GOALS AND VALUES** What matters to the person. The motivators that energize and drive the person's behavior, including their interests, values, desires, work objectives, and career aspirations.
OTHERS' VIEWS	**PERCEPTIONS** How others see the person. How others perceive the person's capabilities, performance, style, motives, priorities, and values.	**STANDARDS** What matters to others. The success factors for the person, as defined by their roles and responsibilities, cultural norms, and other people's expectations.

- Ask that employees be responsible for performance management discussions. Have them set goals, review progress, and ask for what they need to be successful.

- Practice regular performance management, rather than wait for performance appraisal. Regularly meet to review plans, performance, and barriers to success.

- Adopt the use of PDI's GAPS grid to provide a roadmap for the information employees need to develop.

- For your own development, use the GAPS grid to seek feedback and other GAPS information for yourself. Use it to look at your goals, abilities, perceptions of others, and standards in relation to current or future roles.

SOURCES OF GAPS INFORMATION

	WHERE THE PERSON IS	WHERE THE PERSON WANTS TO GO
THE PERSON'S VIEW	**ABILITIES** • Self-assessment • Track record • Professional assessment	**GOALS AND VALUES** • Development planning • Career development discussions • Personal goal-setting • Values clarification
OTHERS' VIEWS	**PERCEPTIONS** • Direct feedback from others • 360-degree feedback • Customer feedback • Performance reviews	**STANDARDS** • Roles and responsibilities • Role models and people that others look up to • Function/role descriptions • Competency models • Organizational vision and values • Organizational strategies and priorities • Core competencies • Competitive challenges and market demands

- To help others with their development, communicate your perceptions and standards regularly.

- When coaching others, use the GAPS grid to frame discussions about the gaps between self and others' perceptions, perceptions and goals, and goals and standards or expectations.

Also, provide opportunities for employees to get the information they need to complete the grid.

- Teach people how to gather the feedback information they need for themselves. Encourage them to have current information in all GAPS areas.

- Make employee development a personal priority. Involve yourself and your team in determining the development processes you need. Use the human resources function as expert consultants to help you in the process, but do not give away the responsibility or accountability for development.

- Ask HR what you could do to be more supportive of development.

- Hold your direct reports responsible for supporting the development of their people. Ask each person to read *Leader As Coach* by David Peterson and Mary Dee Hicks, and discuss the principles at a staff meeting.

- Allow time for personal and team reflection. Tell people what you have learned from examining your own experience. Ask that the teams in the organization periodically review what they can do to encourage learning, reflection, and improvement. Ask people to identify what they learned and what they plan to do differently the next time they face a similar circumstance.

- Create a climate where high performance is the norm by establishing high standards and expectations. Establish formal and informal systems and processes that encourage, support, and facilitate individual and team development.

- Encourage risk taking and innovation. Openly and enthusiastically recognize team members who attempt to "stretch" and try new approaches. Allow people to make mistakes and learn from them. Create a safety net by intervening as needed to prevent people from being ridiculed or punished for their mistakes.

- Recognize and reward your team members when they achieve developmental objectives. Make the ties between individual accomplishments and rewards clear.

2. Attract and select the best high-caliber talent by recognizing organizational as well as individual needs.

As the organization responds to changing market needs and endeavors to create opportunities for growth, the competencies needed in the organization as a whole will change. *Organizational competencies* are competencies that everyone in the organization needs to demonstrate for the organization to achieve its goals. These include customer focus and leadership.

Each level or functional group also requires different general and technical competencies. To staff the organization and to develop people to achieve organizational performance, competencies need to be identified and managed.

Identify present and future competencies needed in the workforce

To determine the most important competencies for the organization or for a particular position or level, use a strategic performance modeling process. *Strategic performance modeling* identifies how the role(s) and expectations in the organization are changing and identifies the specific knowledge areas, skills, abilities, performance standards, and characteristics that are needed.

- Strategic performance modeling goes beyond competency modeling by providing a more thorough picture of the changing roles and actual standards of performance required. An effective strategic modeling process includes:
  - A thorough and systematic strategic analysis that identifies the organization's business goals and strategies.
  - The involvement of line management in determining the new or changing roles needed by the organization.
  - The involvement of line management in articulating the behavioral expectations of these new roles.
  - A mixture of focus groups, questionnaire processes, benchmarking, and discussions to identify critical competencies and behaviors.
  - A clear translation of strategic goals and business needs into performance requirements.
  - A comparison of important differences in performance requirements across jobs and roles.
  - The creation of a foundation for integrating multiple HR applications.
  - The use of internal and external strategic performance modeling experts to provide objective expertise.
  - A rigorous review and challenge of the identified model.

- Use the strategic performance model as a framework for assessing your current bench strength and identifying where you need additional talent. Also use it as criteria for your recruitment and selection process.

- The performance model also provides the blueprint for developing specific groups of people and provides the "S" part of the GAPS grid.

Focus attention on identifying talent and resources

- Keep track of people who are considered strong performers in your industry. Develop relationships with people whom you may want to join the team in the future.

- Deliberately develop a strong network inside and outside the industry, so you know the best resources and talent.

- Learn the factors that attract and retain people you want to attract to the organization.

Use identified needs to focus your efforts to attract talent

- Once you have identified organizational and team needs and determined that you do not have internal candidates, focus your efforts on attracting talent.

- Communicate with people inside and outside your organization about the specific kind of talent you need on your team.

- Build strong partnerships with search firms, recruiters, external advertising operations, and human resources representatives so they will understand you and your organizational environment. Enlist their help in identifying and attracting talent.
    - If you use external firms to assist in your searches, make sure you give them very focused information about the strengths you are looking for in a person. Thoroughly describe your organization's culture, values, direction, and your leadership style. The candidates they provide will only be as good as the quality of information you provide.

Critically evaluate prospective talent

- Develop a selection process that will give you accurate information about the candidate's skills and potential in each required competency area. Remember that "the best predictor of future behavior is past behavior." Construct an interview guide to tap into the person's experience, skills, and track record. Your human resources group or an external expert in this area can help you construct the interview format.

- Use tools such as behavioral interviews and guides, background history forms, and multiple interviewers. Selection improves when you involve more than one person in the evaluation of candidates. Have people who will work with the prospective candidate interview him or her. Use the performance model and interview guides to collect data for your decision.

- Read the classic, *Behavior Description Interviewing* (Allyn & Bacon, 1986), in which Lowell Hellervik and others describe a process for systematically examining an applicant's past behavior. Their method will give you concrete data for making objective hiring decisions.

- Do not make the mistake of selecting a candidate based on his or her past reputation for generally good performance. Critically assess a candidate's current strengths and weaknesses. There are some weaknesses that you simply cannot afford to have on your team, especially in executive-level positions.

- Consider using psychological testing and work simulations for critical positions. Both methods are helpful at providing distinct information about the person.
    - If you have organizational psychologists on staff, use them as a resource. Otherwise, contact an external consulting firm of organizational psychologists to provide these tests. Meet with the firm to discuss the context of the job, the requirements, and what you want to know about the candidate. It is best if the consulting firm receives this information from the hiring manager. Take time to give them good information, so their assessment will be most useful.

Use your knowledge of individual preferences, goals, and values to attract key talent

- If you want talented individuals to join your team, you need to make the position tempting. Use what you know about the individual's aspirations, motivations, and goals to attract him or her to your team. Offer to work with the candidate to design a position that addresses what is important to him or her.

- Learn about the prospective candidate during meetings or interviews. What made this individual successful in the past? What is truly important to this person? What are the person's career goals? What could prevent this person from achieving his or her goals?

- Stay in touch with people who have high potential and be willing to invest time in them. Invite them to visit you at your workplace and introduce them to key people.

- Look for individuals who share the critical values of the organization and who will contribute to attaining your vision. Find people who will bring value-added perspectives, knowledge, skills, abilities, and personal characteristics to your team.

3. **Build a strong team whose members have complementary strengths.**

The strength of each team and the organization's talent portfolio is dependent upon the current and future needs of the organization. Therefore, it is critical to identify the talent needs of the present and anticipated business priorities. With this information, you can then assess individuals and the team against these needs.

Consider the mixture and levels of talent that currently exist on your team. Determine where important gaps exist between current and future needs and implement plans to reduce those gaps. Always consider how to develop your current staff before bringing in people from outside your area.

Assess individual members of your current team

Work with each member of your team to complete a GAPS analysis. The GAPS grid provides the necessary information for identifying development directions and tapping into what motivates each person.

The left side of the grid shows an individual's current state; the right side of the grid shows where the individual wants to go.

ABILITIES: what you *can* do	GOALS AND VALUES: what you *want* to do.
PERCEPTIONS: how *others* see you	STANDARDS: what others *expect* of you

Goals and values: Ask the individual to identify personal values and goals.

Abilities: Ask the individual to identify his or her abilities and skills.

Perceptions: Give the individual information about the perceptions of others. This can be accomplished through a multi-rater feedback process, performance appraisals, informal feedback, or observations. It is important that the person have a thorough understanding of how he or she is seen by others.

Standards: Discuss your expectations for the individual. If the person is moving to another position, share any expectations you have for that job as well. Finally, share any knowledge you have about the future expectations of the organization.

One of your roles as a coach is to continually provide opportunities for the individual to discuss and update his or her GAPS. GAPS can serve as the foundation for much of your coaching with the person. Useful discussions can be based on the interactions between the different categories in the GAPS grid. For example, the difference between self-perception and others' perceptions; the difference between personal and career goals; or the difference between what matters to the person (Goals and values) and what matters to the organization (Standards and expectations).

The GAPS grid and the resulting development plan provide a solid foundation for individual development for your team members.

- Typically, the order for explaining the categories is in GAPS order. But when people have GAPS conversations, they should start with G and S: talk about what matters. Then talk about the person's capabilities (A and P) for accomplishing that. What can they do to get more of what matters to them and the organization? Where can development provide the greatest leverage in accomplishing more?

- This approach helps people avoid the "feedback trap," that is, arguing over who is right. Often, once the Standards and expectations are clear, people can self-identify their biggest development needs.

Assess your current team against the ideal team

If you want to build a strong team with complementary strengths, you need to focus on the team as a unit. Use the process listed above to identify and implement systems that will help team members understand their combined strengths and needs. Encourage team members to support one another's individual development.

After individual team members have identified their the Goals and values, Abilities, Perceptions, and Standards (GAPS), you can work with the team as a whole to identify the team's strengths and opportunities.

- Use the GAPS grid to chart the entire team, so you can assess the team's current composition, including any inconsistencies or weaknesses.

- Identify the strengths and needs that the team recognizes, identify strengths and needs that others perceive, and identify their personal goals and values. To accomplish this, you can either ask individuals to share information or you can use a group multi-rater process.

- Ask your team to help you envision ideal current and future states for the group.
    - Focus on the team as a whole rather than individual team members.
    - Take the team's vision and any strategic initiatives into account.
    - Compare your analyses of the current and ideal states of your team.
    - Determine changes and improvements needed to achieve the ideal state.
    - Identify critical deficiencies, including those that will likely occur in the future, and determine priority improvement areas.

- Ask people to share their development plans. Recommend that the team determine if the development plans address the critical issues for the team.

- Remember that your role as a coach is not to do all the coaching, but to orchestrate coaching. A tremendous amount of coaching and development can be done within the team through individuals helping one another.

- Create a list of mentors for each team that identifies the people who excel at particular competencies. Distribute the lists so people can learn from one another.

- Be aware that in some cultures there may be discomfort at being set apart as an expert. In those environments, it is better for the team to learn together.

- Consider using a team-based 360-degree survey instrument to gather perspectives regarding the team's current strengths and needs. Help your team understand its profile and ask people to identify areas where they would like to improve.

- Identify development objectives and action steps with the team. Also discuss how team members can assist each other in building the group's bench strength.

- Recognize that your team's skill mix will continue to change as individuals develop and grow and the organization changes. Reexamine your team's vision and capabilities every year. Do this more often if you are in a rapidly changing environment.

- Identify new development needs for your team and implement plans for addressing them. Periodically meet with the team to discuss their progress toward team objectives. Give the team direct and constructive feedback, and solicit feedback regarding your role. Adjust plans and action steps accordingly.

Define a strategy to fill talent gaps and round out the team

Find opportunities to develop needed skills and capabilities within your team. This will allow you to build upon the team's existing strengths without unnecessarily disrupting team dynamics. This will also give your team valuable developmental opportunities, such as new assignments, broader responsibilities, mentoring, training, special projects, or coordinating work with other units in the organization.

Sometimes it may be necessary to round out your team with people who have specific talents. In this case:

- Hire people with complementary strengths and backgrounds that will balance existing team skills.

- Always think about the developmental needs of the team as a whole in addition to the specific skills that are needed.

- Hire for the team as well as the job.

4. Encourage and value diversity in the organization's talent base.

In this day and age it seems redundant to emphasize the importance and value of diversity and variety in an organization's employee base. Your organization is becoming more and more global. You face increased sharing of resources and opportunities to work with people from other cultures.

However, it is still common in many companies to find discomfort and resistance to working with people who are different. Some organizations believe diversity is not an issue for them; this is highly unlikely. Diversity is not a U.S. racial issue—appreciating and valuing diversity applies to all cultures, regions, religions, ages, etc.

Executives need to set clear expectations that people will work together cooperatively, find ways to value one another's contributions and ways of looking at the world, and strive to understand one another's point of view and way of working.

Communicate the value of workplace diversity

- Value and encourage the organization's diversity, whether in gender, culture, race, age, religion, educational background, culture, geography, learning styles, values, organizational functions, or personality.

- Communicate the importance and benefits of a diverse workforce.

- Identify ways in which teams, composed of a variety of people, can stimulate general creativity and innovation, and generate more competitive products and practices.

- Communicate clear expectations about valuing diversity.

- Publicize the advantages that come from supporting internal diversity.
    - Your organization will gain insight into product development and market strategy for a wider range of customers.
    - Your products and services will appeal to a transcultural audience.
    - Your workforce will reflect a broader customer base due to its combination of backgrounds, experiences, and expertise.
    - Your organization will convey a positive public image.

Attract, nurture, and retain diverse employees

- Develop standards that identify your organization as "a good place to work." For example, make valuing and respecting people a core organizational value. Also, challenge and change organizational policies or practices that may be exclusionary. For example, some companies still require the managing director to be from the organization's home country.

- Hold your management team responsible for expanding your organization's talent base. Make the recruiting and development of people from different backgrounds a performance criterion for yourself and your managers. Regularly check to see if this is occurring.

- Support the unique needs of nontraditional employees. Identify policies and practices that need to be changed to reflect cultural differences. Develop relationships with people from different cultures and backgrounds, and learn from their experiences in your organization, both positive and negative.

- Identify organizations that have been publicly recognized and rewarded for their initiatives and results in diversifying and expanding their global workforces. Research their methods and determine how they achieved success. Ask representatives from these organizations to share their experiences, including the benefits that stemmed from their efforts. Use their ideas when developing your diversity strategies.

5. Accurately appraise the strengths and weaknesses of direct reports.

Regularly assess the strengths and development needs of employees in relation to current and future needs. Remember that strengths and weaknesses are dictated by business needs; they are not absolutes. Employees who matched the needs of a regionally based organization may not meet the needs of a global organization.

Before you can identify strengths and needs of direct reports, you need to understand the business objectives and strategies for the future, and the knowledge, skills, and abilities necessary to accomplish them. You need to identify strengths and development needs within this context, because the context outlines the specific needs and defines the standards at which people need to perform.

- As you think of employee needs, identify current and future organizational competencies, including:
  - *Organizational competencies.* Everyone in the organization needs these competencies, regardless of their position. They are usually derived directly from the values and mission of the organization. They include things like respect for people and customer focus.
  - *Particular level or job family competencies.* These competencies are specific to a role within the organization. For example, competencies for executives are typically different from those for managers.
  - *Job-specific competencies.* These competencies are specific to a job. For example, a software development person and a help line support person may share certain knowledge, but they also require specialized skills.

The job family or level-specific competency definitions are usually necessary for identifying the strengths and needs of your employees. When business objectives and strategies require that people take on new roles or perform in substantially different ways, it is especially critical to operate at the level of job family, level, or even a specific job.

- Strategic performance modeling identifies changes in roles, new roles the organization will need, the knowledge and abilities people need, and behavioral standards for the level at which people need to perform. This process, which is more thorough, will give you all the information you need to establish integrated human resources processes.

- If you have never used this process, ask your human resources group or an external consultant for help. Look for someone with experience in strategic performance modeling, familiarity with your industry, and (preferably) training in organizational psychology. Beware of people who know the interpersonal aspects of management and do not understand your business, your competitive context, or your mission, agenda, purpose, or objectives.

Identify direct reports' strengths and needs

- Use business needs and/or the strategic performance model as the foundation for evaluating strengths and needs. A number of methods can help you define strengths and developments needs. They include:
    - Assessment by the manager or executive.
    - Self-assessment by the individual.
    - Collaborative assessment between the individual and the manager.
    - Multi-rater feedback process in which the individual receives feedback from those who work with him or her.
    - Assessment by an organizational psychologist who is thoroughly familiar with your organization and your competency or performance model.

- The assessment process you choose will depend upon the use of the data, the importance of objectivity, and the degree to which individuals are able to evaluate particular attributes, competencies, knowledge, or culture fit. Use the following guidelines:
    - *Manager appraisal* is useful when you want a quick assessment, you believe you have the most accurate view of the person's strengths and needs, and you have very clear understanding of the current and future requirements.
    - *Self-assessment* is important for identifying the person's preset view of him or herself. People are usually willing to work on needs that they have personally identified.

      However, self-perceptions are inaccurate. Self-assessment also does not work well when the future needs are substantially different from current requirements.

    - *Multi-rater feedback* is most useful when the perceptions of others are needed. Other people can be invaluable sources of information because they may be more familiar with the person than the manager.

Also, perceptual feedback is valuable because individuals are likely to implement changes based on the perceptions of others. If the individual wants to work more effectively with others, it will be important for him or her to understand how she or he is seen. Multi-rater feedback is not as useful when the people completing the questionnaires do not understand the competencies and behaviors being rated. This most often occurs when the competencies and behaviors are new.

- *Collaborative assessment* is an effective way to combine the judgments of the manager and the individual. It is less effective if either party does not have an accurate understanding of the competencies needed.

- *Objective assessment* from an external source is valuable when the competencies are new or they are not easily measured by observation alone. For example, PDI research has shown that objective assessment provides a better measure of intellectual capabilities, strategic thinking, and certain psychological attributes than organizational observation alone. In addition, objective assessment is just that—it is objective.

• When you conduct an assessment, evaluate behaviors whenever possible, rather than personality traits. Rating behaviors allows for more accurate ratings and provides feedback that is easier to act on. For example, it is not useful to tell someone that he or she is a poor communicator. It is more useful to say, "You made comments that show that you did not listen to what the person said."

• Keep a record of the assessment you have done for each person. This assessment can be updated every six to twelve months. Ask the person to target one or two development objectives at a time. They may have a list of three to five issues they would like to develop, but keep current efforts focused on one area at a time. During the year, keep track of what you and the individual learn about strengths and needs and add it to his or her assessment folder.

• Understand each team member's personal objectives regarding career progression and development. Work with each person to identify short- and long-term career goals. Identify the skills, qualifications, and strengths he or she will need to be successful in future positions.

Design and implement systems that evaluate team member performance

- Use performance management to clarify expectations and review progress. Performance management needs to be a collaborative process, rather than a top-down process in which you dictate objectives and priorities for people.

- At least once a year, set objectives with each individual and the team. Cascade these goals down from the organization's plan and objectives. Include developmental objectives as part of the performance plan. Then set up processes to regularly review progress against objectives.

- Let your direct reports take the lead in this review. Your role is to add to their observations, if necessary.

- Conduct team reviews with teams as well as individual reviews. This reinforces the importance of the teams.

- Consider the use of multi-rater performance appraisal when it has the support of the people who are seeking feedback. You can ask others for feedback yourself or you can use a multi-rater instrument or process.

  If you use a questionnaire process, ensure it was designed specifically for use in performance appraisal.

  Multi-raters for development identify strengths and development needs; they are not good measures of which people are stronger than others.

- Don't judge the person solely on the data; meet with the person and discuss the results. Come to an agreement about what the feedback means.

- Using a multi-rater process is not a shortcut to performance appraisal. It takes time to understand and incorporate different viewpoints. Also, remember that multi-rater feedback for performance appraisal cannot take the place of good developmental multi-rater information.

6. Provide accurate, motivating feedback and constructive criticism.

Encourage team members to ask for your feedback. Invite people to help shape the process by asking, "What kind of feedback would you like?" and "How can I make this most useful to you?"

Feedback is one key to development. But much of the conventional wisdom about feedback is wrong. It is not a four-step formula or an airtight case. Feedback is information; it is a dialogue, not a delivery.

Practice the principles of feedback

- *Discovery, not delivery.* Feedback is most effective when it is exploratory; when different perspectives are discussed and examined rather than simply declared.

   The goal of feedback is joint discovery of what people are doing and how well it is working, so that people gain relevant information to sustain them in their development. Feedback discussions conducted with an attitude of exploration result in more information and deeper levels of insight.

- *Mutual understanding, not persuasion.* Feedback is most effective when both parties try to understand each other better. It's rarely productive to try to build an airtight argument convincing someone that they need to change or that their view is wrong. If both views are accepted as legitimate, people are less inclined to ignore, reject, or rebut the feedback. When both parties try to find the linkages between their perspectives, feedback becomes more relevant to things people care about and are willing to act on.

- *Adaptive, not a formula.* Feedback is most effective when it is sensitive to the person and the situation, rather than following a standard recipe. Feedback that is immediate, behavioral, and 80% positive, as some formulas suggest, might be precisely what is not called for in certain circumstances. The format and content must fit the person's view of the situation, the broader context of their work, their relationship with the feedback giver, and what will be most helpful for their development. Feedback givers need to individualize their approach and adapt it as circumstances change.

- *Process, not event.* Feedback is most effective when it is part of a regular process of inquiry rather than a single conversation. People come to understand where they stand, how they are performing, and how they might need to change through regular conversations about their performance and others' expectations. Feedback can't be limited to formal, annual performance reviews, observations on a single episode of performance, or one-time use of a feedback tool. Insight evolves across time through a series of information exchanges.

Make feedback a two-way process

Before giving feedback, think about the fact that you are beginning a dialogue, not just giving feedback. Phrase your comments so the person can hear your feedback instead of shutting it off. Put your feedback in the context of what is important to the individual and the standard or expectations.

- Make feedback normal. Communicate that feedback is important and will be discussed frequently. Give it often, in small pieces, and directly related to people's identified development priorities. If it is relevant to them and already on the table, feedback can be quick, easy, and helpful.

- Feedback can be destructive or demotivating when it serves only your needs without considering the needs of the receiver. Ease feelings of being threatened or intimidated by asking permission to share feedback rather than imposing it. Give people a safety valve; let them tell you when they have had enough or are starting to feel uncomfortable.

- Discuss the other person's view of the situation and his or her intentions. What had the person intended or planned? How did it work? What would the person do the same? differently?

- Allocate enough time to discuss feedback. Do not make the mistake of offering one of your team members critical feedback as you are hurrying down the hall to your next meeting.

- Give feedback throughout larger projects. Do not wait until the end of the project.

- Give critical feedback in private and positive recognition in public.

- Direct feedback toward behavior that the recipients can control. If you describe shortcomings based on circumstances that are beyond their control, they will become frustrated at their inability to implement your suggestions.

- Be descriptive rather than evaluative. Present your comments in an objective manner and avoid labeling the person or the behavior. Be specific rather than general. Describe observed behaviors and situations, and provide specific suggestions for improvement.

Make feedback timely and relevant

- Discuss feedback when people can best understand and use it.
    - Sometimes it's better to wait. For example, if someone knows they haven't succeeded at something, you might allow the initial sting to pass and to give the person time to sort it through alone. And if they thought they did a great job, they might want some time to enjoy their sense of accomplishment.
    - Make sure that the timing and situation are conducive to listening, mutual exploration, and discovery.
    - Keep in mind that most feedback has a relatively short half-life, so you want to have your discussion while you both still care about what happened and while pertinent details are still fresh in your memories.

- Feedback should be relevant to people's goals and values. For example,
    - Some of the best feedback heard after a presentation was, "I was bored during that second part." This wasn't behavioral, but it sure was relevant and important.
    - Since you didn't want to bore people, ask a few questions to understand where and when they were bored. But even without more detail, you know enough to take that comment and immediately do some things to liven up your presentation.
    - A specific and behavioral description might have been, "You had five overheads in a row that each contained six points. The language that you used was factual and accurate, but didn't contain lively and compelling imagery. Your commentary simply repeated what was on each slide. Your intonation was relatively flat and you didn't project much enthusiasm for your topic. You did not include any personal stories or examples of how the audience might use this...."

- Feedback should be genuine and focus on what is most important in the situation.
    - What could possibly be wrong with asking people to say more good things to others? When you follow this approach people you work with learn to count: "OK, that's one, that's two, that's three, and that's four good things. Now here comes the real message." People learn to wait for the other shoe to drop.

- Or else you deliver a feedback sandwich: Two layers of fluff with the real stuff sandwiched in between. "That was just great; you're really a great presenter. I'd like to see you do more to connect to your audience and use more examples to bring it to life and allow more time for questions and answers at the end. But you were just wonderful. Keep it up." This kind of message is contrived and people know it.
- The kind of feedback that is most important actually depends on both you and the person you are talking to. From their perspective, any of the following might be most important:
  ○ Getting accurate feedback in general
  ○ Feeling supported, valued, and accepted
  ○ Getting more information on a specific aspect of their performance that they are trying to improve
- From your perspective, these might be most important:
  ○ Improving performance in a particular area
  ○ Providing encouragement
  ○ Reinforcing what people are doing well
  ○ Building trust and rapport

Give positive feedback and recognition

- Develop the habit of looking for and commending positive contributions. People can learn as much from success as they do from failure, so help people identify what they have done well. Help them examine their performance, so they can learn about their strengths.

- Recognize that rewards should be commensurate with performance. Many leaders try to treat all team members alike, which can encourage mediocrity. When all team members receive equal rewards, superior performers feel unappreciated and poor performers recognize that they will not be penalized for their minimal efforts. Find ways to appropriately reward both individual and team accomplishments.

- Positive feedback is wonderful stuff and people are often too stingy with it. There is nothing wrong with well-earned affirmations, compliments, and praise. By all means let people know specifically and often what they are doing right. But if you have something negative to say, say it. People don't like to be coddled.

Give difficult feedback directly

- Give negative feedback when it is necessary. People will not change unless they have information that tells them it is necessary. For some people, the necessary information will be the fact that they are not getting the results they want. Or they will notice that their comments are not influential and determine that they need to develop their skills in that area. Other people will need direct feedback from you.

- Encourage people to debrief their own performance. Ask them how they did, what kind of progress they are making, and where they'd like to improve. To keep this quick and simple, just ask for the one key improvement they made and the one thing they'd most like to handle better.

- Ask them what information they'd like from you. If they ask for one of your main points, offer it directly.

- If they don't ask for some of the things that you feel are most important, offer it. "Another area for you to think about is X. Given that you are trying to be more influential as a leader, you could focus on doing more of this."

- As noted above, link your feedback to what matters to them and what matters to the organization.

- State your message clearly, directly, and precisely. Focus on the behavior, its potential impact, and its likely consequences. Concentrate on one specific behavior or incident to avoid overwhelming the receiver. For example, "You asked questions, but you didn't wait for people to answer (behavior). They may conclude you aren't really interested in their opinions (impact). As a result, they may be less likely to share their ideas and you could be cut off from valuable information (consequences)."

- Suggest specific alternatives for inappropriate behavior. People often do not know what else to do.

Use feedback as a learning experience

- Think of feedback as a change intervention and seek out ways to turn each exchange into a useful developmental experience.

- Find out what people learned from feedback experiences. Ask questions such as "What did you learn from this? What had an impact on you? What was the most valuable insight?" and "What do you think you will remember from this session when you reflect on it in a few weeks?"

- Define the next steps that will translate their insights into action. Ask questions to help people think about action steps, such as "What will you do differently as a result of this discussion?" or "In what situations can you apply this?" Encourage people to select one or two things to act on immediately.

- Recommend some best practices for learning. Suggest that they build reminders into their daily routine, seek regular feedback, and incorporate new learning objectives into their development plans.

7. Recognize and unleash the full potential of others.

Coaching and developing employees is important for executives. You have a dual role of managing a team and encouraging the development of their part of the organization through their direct reports.

Leaders can receive personal payback from coaching and development efforts, such as building stronger teams, becoming magnets for talent, and sustaining a support network.

Create development partnerships

Development occurs within partnerships between employees, their managers, and the organization. Each has to do its part for development to work.

The key to effective development is understanding what makes a difference. Organizations need to know where they are going and which knowledge, skills, abilities, and traits are necessary to get there. Individuals need to understand their personal goals and determine the linkage between their goals and the organization's.

- One of the primary roles of a coach is to provide information so people will know what is important. They orchestrate coaching and development and set the stage; it is up to the individual to develop.

- Focus five percent of your energy on coaching others. Hold conversations with people, help them learn from their experiences, offer advice or feedback, or link them with the resources they need.

Create development plans with team members

- Ensure that the performance review system you use includes a development planning process. Establish criteria regarding successful performance on the job and the accomplishment of business or organizational objectives.

- Write a development plan based on the way you write business plans; use the same principles and format.

- Be clear and specific about the changes that will happen and where they will occur. What exactly will the person be doing and in what situations?

- Follow recognized guidelines for preparing effective development plans.
    - State specific goals and activities for overcoming performance problems, building on strengths, preparing for future responsibilities, and acquiring new skills.
    - Describe the skills, knowledge, or experience that should result from the development activity.
    - Determine small steps that will lead to the ultimate goal.
    - Use job responsibilities as development opportunities.
    - Establish time frames, target dates, and checkpoints to review progress.

- Do not write development plans for other people. Expect people to be accountable for their own development.

- Ask people to focus their development plans on high-priority areas of development. A concentrated effort on twenty percent of the goals will result in eighty percent of the growth.

Create and support a development culture

- Forge a partnership; establish trusting relationships with your direct reports. Learn about them and their goals, values, and priorities. Make sure they know you will behave in ways that are respectful and helpful.

- Believe in and trust your direct reports. Assume that with the proper information they will take responsibility for their development.

- Be accessible so people will feel comfortable approaching you as a coach.

- Set the boundaries for the coaching partnership by defining what you hope to achieve through the coaching process. Set guidelines for how you will achieve the objectives.

- Recognize individual differences among your team members in the types and levels of coaching they require. The Golden Rule of Coaching is "Coach others as you would like to be coached." The Platinum Rule of coaching is "Coach others as they need to be coached."

Inspire commitment to development

Coaches inspire commitment from others by providing information and building on motivation that is already there. People change when they want to; either they already see that the change is necessary or they are able to see a personal payoff to making a recommended change.

- Make career planning or development programs available that help people look at their values and goals. Knowing their values and goals will help them identify what motivates them. Talk about your own values and goals and how they relate to your work.

- Provide people with relevant information so they can make informed choices about what to develop.

- Focus development on mutually beneficial areas by aligning their personal goals with organizational needs.

Grow skills; make needed developmental experiences available

- Identify the best way for people to learn by matching the method, the need, and the person. For example, it may be best if engineering, accounting, and other fact-based topics are learned through books, classes, and on-the-job instruction from experts. Personal values and vision might benefit more from introspection, case study, simulations, and dialogue.

- Help others identify their preferred way to learn. Know your own preferred method.

- Consider using PDI's resources, *eAdvisor*™ or DevelopMentor®, to provide learning experiences for people.

- View on-the-job experiences as powerful learning devices. People need to apply their skills in real-life situations. Consider assignments such as leading a cross-functional task force, performing a turnaround function, leading a complex project from start to finish, or managing a highly talented employee.

- To ensure that experience is a good teacher, find the right circumstances for people to use their new skills. Help people learn the right lessons from their experiences and make sure they learn these lessons quickly.

- Develop or implement training programs that address broad-based needs among your team members. After using a multi-rater feedback instrument, run group reports to identify the needs of the team. Use these group reports to identify organizational development issues.

- Support team member development through training, educational opportunities, and resources. Identify books and articles that staff members should read for skill or knowledge development. Obtain and provide financial support, and intervene to remove obstacles to team member development.

Offer useful coaching suggestions to develop team members

- Take advantage of coachable moments. If you spend five percent of your time coaching and developing people, you will recognize when they are ready to learn. Watch for the following coachable moments: successes, failures and disappointments, and requests for opinions or advice.

- Recognize that you cannot do all of the coaching yourself. Brainstorm alternative coaching strategies with your team. Consider ongoing feedback systems or try using more experienced team members to coach less experienced individuals.

- Follow up with your direct reports on the type of development they are doing with their people. You will unintentionally send a powerful message if you carefully follow up about revenue goal attainment, progress toward receiving ISO-9000 certification, or the status of a particular customer, but do not follow up on how others are developing their people.

Promote persistence

Development is not as hard as people think. If you just use brute force and effort, it is hard. If you know where to find the leverage, it still takes some effort, but it's much easier.

- Help people remain focused on their development in spite of setbacks. It is expected that people will not make constant progress toward their development objectives/priorities. There will be backsliding. Unless people have figured out how to work on their development as part of their job, they will be waylaid by everyday business activities.

- Ask people about their progress. Ask them to tell you what they are learning. Ask about their successes and failures. Help people figure out alternatives when they think they are stuck. It is amazing to discover how much people know about what they should do. When people run out of ideas, provide alternatives or another way of looking at the situation.

- Teach people how to learn for themselves.

- Make your development philosophy consistent with the old proverb: "Give a man a fish and you feed him for a day. Teach a man to fish and you feed him for a lifetime."

- Give everyone in the organization basic training in development. Teach the FIRST principles laid out in *Development FIRST: Strategies for Self-Development* (Personnel Decisions International, 1995): Focus, Implement, Reflect, Seek feedback, and Transfer learning. *Development FIRST* outlines myths and common practices that unintentionally inhibit, derail, or make development more difficult.

- Help people learn more from their experiences. This happens when they reflect on their experiences. One of the best ways to learn is to reflect on all significant experiences: What have I learned here? What exactly contributed to the outcome? What parts of this do I want to keep doing and what parts do I want to change? For example, if people do not reflect on their behavior, they will not develop.

- People usually think they can learn more from failure than success. That is because people tend to replay and examine failure. Failure often stops you in your tracks and forces you to figure out how to avoid the same thing in the future. Counteract that tendency by encouraging your people to examine their successes. Since most people have more successes than failures, examining their successes will speed up development time.

- Help your direct reports become aware of their own learning process by asking questions such as:
    - How did you know you needed to learn or develop that skill?
    - How did you decide which action to take first?
    - When you first started to work on development, what was most difficult for you?
    - How did you stick to your plan when you got discouraged?
    - How did you know when you were successful?
    - What help did you get?
    - Why did you use that particular help?

8. Develop successors and talent pools for key positions.

Executives play a critical role in managing the organization's talent portfolio. Without careful attention to developing successors and key talent pools, an organization's business options will be more limited.

Implement succession management processes in your organization

- Establish clear expectations for your team that you and they will take an active role in developing and working the succession planning process.

- Talk with executives in other organizations to learn what they do in their process.

- Include all key roles in the succession plan, not just executives.

- Begin your succession planning process by considering the organization's vision and future strategic business needs. Enlist the help of internal or external experts in designing your process and identifying the future competencies required for key positions.

- Determine the key jobs in the organization, your current bench strength, and the amount of time it will take to develop your people. Assess whether you have a pending crisis with lack of bench strength, whether it will take too long to develop people, or whether you need to change key jobs.

- Carefully evaluate potential candidates against your strategic performance model. Supplement internal judgments with external, objective assessments for key jobs. This combination of internal and external expertise will help ensure that you have a thorough and accurate assessment.

- Benchmark against organizations that have used successful succession processes and use their expertise and knowledge to help you design your system.

- Create bench strength reviews for key positions. Identify primary and secondary candidates for each key position and determine their readiness for the role.

- Prepare high-potential candidates by providing appropriate experiences and helping them develop the necessary skills. Continue to develop and update your internal talent pool as an ongoing priority.

Understand and work to satisfy other's career goals

- Help the organization clearly distinguish between succession planning and career planning. In a nutshell, succession planning is a corporate responsibility and career planning is not. Organizations plan succession, individuals plan careers. Recognize the importance of each and use them as complementary tools to ensure your organization's success.

- Use your knowledge of your team members' short- and long-term goals to suggest roles that individuals might enjoy in the future. Share your thoughts regarding their current or anticipated ability to be effective in various roles.

- Help team members fully understand which roles are available in your organization. Bring in people who know more about specific jobs to talk with team members. Help your team members fully and thoughtfully consider their range of options.

RESOURCES

The resources for this chapter begin on page 442.

[1] *PDI Pipeline For Development™ Review is a process conducted by PDI to assess the strengths and weaknesses of organizational systems, processes, and programs designed to aid the development of people. It focuses on the necessary conditions for learning and how well your programs are addressing them. It helps you find critical gaps where you have the greatest leverage.*

8
EMPOWERING OTHERS

CREATE A CLIMATE THAT FOSTERS PERSONAL
INVESTMENT AND EXCELLENCE; NURTURE
COMMITMENT TO A COMMON VISION AND
SHARED VALUES; GIVE PEOPLE OPPORTUNITY
AND LATITUDE TO GROW AND ACHIEVE;
PROMOTE COLLABORATION AND TEAMWORK.

KEY BEHAVIORS

---

1. *Create a climate where everyone stretches beyond what they thought they could do.*
2. *Create a feeling of energy, excitement, and personal investment.*
3. *Nurture commitment to a common vision and shared values.*
4. *Give people the opportunity and latitude to run their area(s) of the organization.*
5. *Promote collaboration and remove obstacles to teamwork across the organization.*
6. *Convey confidence in others' ability and desire to do their best.*
7. *Celebrate and reward significant organizational achievements.*

INTRODUCTION

Effective empowerment is a necessity in today's business environment, where people need to respond to new challenges in record time, and do more with fewer people. Executives and other leaders simply cannot accomplish their goals if they do not engage their people.

Empowered individuals and teams believe they can make a difference within their organizations. They use their talents and ideas, and see direct results from their efforts. They are not bound by layers of red tape and approvals, but have the prerogative to test ideas, make decisions, exercise discretion, and creatively handle the consequences. They also know where to get support, and can depend on their leaders to back them up.

Empowerment, done well, can infuse your organization with the energy, commitment, and brain power of your employees. Done poorly, it can be just another attempt to put a new name on old practices. Empowerment has suffered in organizations that have tried to move too fast without the necessary preparation and support. New strategies and programs have often been implemented before companies calculated the energy needed to sustain a change. In some organizations, the so-called "empowerment" of employees has really meant abandonment.

Empowerment is not a one-size-fits-all concept. It is also not a one-time gift that you bestow on your team. It is an environment and operating system from which you launch every activity. Recognizing what makes your people feel empowered is the first step to creating your system.

VALUABLE TIPS

- Develop a personal definition of meaningful empowerment.

- Find out what makes people on your team feel empowered.

- Staff your team with people who can handle challenging assignments with greater insight and skill than you.

- Give capable team members more latitude instead of retaining sole control.

- Guard against micromanaging work that you have given to your direct reports.

- Encourage and support your employees as they take responsibility and exercise authority.

- Look for challenging team projects or assignments that will stretch people beyond their current capabilities.

- Find opportunities for people to improve upon your accomplishments.

- Reward people's contributions to the success of the team.

- Provide development challenges that redefine and broaden roles.

- Create opportunities to give your team more autonomy.

- Have your team create strategic objectives and design the means to achieve them.

- Openly discuss high-level issues with your team.

- Seek substantive input from your team on critical decisions.

- Look for opportunities to collaborate with your direct reports.

- Share credit with others, particularly with your peers and direct reports.

- Encourage people on your team to teach one another.

- Ask your team if they have the latitude they need to get their work done most effectively.

STRATEGIES FOR ACTION

1. Create a climate where everyone stretches beyond what they thought they could do.

Leaders can create an environment of enthusiasm and excellence by communicating high expectations and fostering optimistic, positive attitudes about people and their work in the organization. To create a climate where everyone stretches beyond what they thought they could do, try the following suggestions.

Communicate high expectations and challenging goals

- Inspire people to excel by demonstrating excellence in your own work.

- Clearly communicate your vision of the optimal state of your organization, along with the message that you expect people to excel.

- Set high standards for routine, day-to-day tasks as well as major new assignments.

- Encourage people to think beyond current customer and organizational needs. What will your customers need tomorrow, next year, and in five years? What kind of performance goals will meet and exceed those business needs?

- Invite your team to challenge established boundaries. Help them identify "stretch" objectives to achieve organizational goals.

- Work to eliminate statements like "we've never done it this way" or "that won't work" from your team's vocabulary. Empathize with your team's perspective that change may be difficult, then begin exploring methods for overcoming the problem.

- Create an active performance review process to reinforce high performance standards. Link feedback and coaching to specific business goals.

Create an environment that reinforces risk taking and innovation

- Openly and enthusiastically recognize people who attempt to go beyond what is expected. Encourage people to look for ideas in unlikely places.

- Acknowledge and encourage all ideas, not just those that will be immediately profitable. The most obvious or popular suggestions are not always the best, so make an effort to consider innovative suggestions.

- Identify and challenge the perceived negative consequences of risk. They may include fears of losing hard-won ground, being singled out in cases of failure, relinquishing a fallback position, or lacking an adequate contingency plan.

- Help people reduce their fear of risk and failure. Make it clear that there are no failures, only mistakes that provide feedback, knowledge, and indicate next steps.

- Advocate the view that mistakes are opportunities for further learning rather than instances of humiliation and lost credibility. Give people a soft landing when they make mistakes.

- Work with your team to establish a safety net of advisors, mentors, problem-solving methods, and contingency plans. Identify both internal and external resources.

- Encourage people to believe they can do new things. Reinforce the relationship between past successes and new challenges as you coach your team. Review how and why things are moving in the right direction.

- Explore divergent thinking and discussion techniques, such as the use of metaphor and brainstorming, to help your team escape groupthink and stagnation.

Create a climate of trust in which people keep their promises

- Establish a climate where people feel comfortable and confident about making and keeping promises.

- Discuss why promises are not kept and how unfulfilled promises affect collaboration between work groups. Work with your group or the affected department to identify and rectify problems, and overcome any obstacles.

- Resist overpromising and discourage others from doing so as well. Underpromising and overdelivering is a good pattern to establish.

- Assign all action items identified at meetings, task forces, or strategic planning sessions to an accountable person or group. Ask your people to help create an appropriate follow-up system to measure their progress, and determine target dates.

- Recognize and reward people and groups for completing their action items. Link their achievements to business objectives and encourage your team to build on their successes.

Challenge others to take on tough assignments

- Model risk taking. Tell your team about a tough decision that you made and describe the issues and risks you faced.

- Remind people that a smooth path does not always lead to success; indeed, tough choices require that people take risks and push themselves beyond guaranteed outcomes.

- Encourage others to take calculated risks and schedule time with them to discuss actual or anticipated problems.

- Give people challenging assignments that will strengthen their weak areas and offer opportunities to build relationships while working on complex issues. For instance, ask a direct report to lead a cross-functional task force, carry out a new initiative, or assume oversight responsibility.

- Let people know that you are paying attention to their efforts by giving them timely, specific feedback. Positive words will encourage people, and constructive comments will enable them to make midcourse corrections to meet their goals.

- Resist taking responsibility for your employees' decisions. Avoid second-guessing, taking over, suggesting alternative strategies, or defusing confidence and enthusiasm. Instead, provide coaching and feedback to help people evaluate their decisions.

- Confront negative feelings and attitudes when they come to your attention. Such responses are common during tough assignments. Meet with people who seem to be experiencing low morale and discuss the situation. Express your confidence that things will improve.

- Ask people to call you into a discussion or activity when they think you can be of assistance. Let them take the initiative.

2. Create a feeling of energy, excitement, and personal investment.

Optimum performance occurs when an individual's professional and personal needs are met within a particular environment. Providing information and encouragement are important elements for maximizing performance. According to Dr. Warren Bennis,

> "Where there are leaders, work is stimulating, challenging, fascinating, and fun. An essential ingredient… is pulling rather than pushing people toward a goal. A 'pull' style of influence attracts and energizes people to enroll in an exciting vision of the future. It motivates through identification, rather than through rewards and punishments. Leaders articulate and embody the ideals toward which the organization strives."
>
> —*Why Leaders Can't Lead* (Jossey-Bass, 1989)

Inspire others with a sense of purpose and direction

- Enthusiasm is contagious. Convey your enthusiasm—your passion and excitement will inspire and motivate others. Enthusiasm, support, and optimism can steer others in a positive direction and renew or redirect energy when spirits are flagging.

- When you share your vision for the organization's future, make sure you leave room for your team to build on that vision.

- Build relationships with your team by demonstrating respect for each person's character and capabilities. Showing belief and confidence in your people will increase their belief and confidence in you and your leadership.

- Seek suggestions on how you can be a stronger role model. Consult persons you trust the most and ask if your actions speak as loudly as your words. Observe others whom you consider particularly strong role models and learn from their example.

Eliminate barriers to accountability

- Scan your work environment and identify factors that prevent your team from taking ownership for their work.

- Listen closely to individual team members and learn why they do or do not feel accountable. Ask your team to explore ways to encourage accountability.

- Make sure your team has the necessary tools to take initiative and handle the increased latitude. Identify and remedy any knowledge or skill deficits that may inhibit their ability to handle more responsibility.

- Support people when they make tough choices that are consistent with your organization's objectives. Respect the judgment of your group and let people know that you will stand behind them on difficult initiatives and issues.

Create an environment that makes work enjoyable

- Convey a sense of humor and encourage it in others. A sense of humor, fun, and enjoyment helps people cope more effectively with work stress and fosters creativity.

- Find humor in events and even personal errors. Show your team that it is acceptable to laugh at yourself. Take your work seriously, but do not take yourself too seriously.

- Look for opportunities to make work fun. Sponsor activities where people can get to know each other, such as team-building sessions, parties, sports activities, and volunteer work in the community.

- Recognize people's efforts to make work enjoyable.

Convey the attitude that everyone's work is important

- Reinforce the concept that each person's work is important. Regularly give your team members positive feedback that is personalized and specific.

- Highlight team members' positive contributions at staff meetings. Describe how their skills, talents, and efforts brought sound results.

- Champion effective performance by emphasizing how people's work affects you and the rest of the organization. Link specific actions to business goals and encourage people to build on their successes.

- Recognize people in low visibility jobs and encourage others to do so as well. When you describe a successful project, explain how the accuracy and timeliness of all support people, including the administrative staff, contributed to the quality of the work.

- Include support staff in your project planning meetings to gain their input and show them how their work fits into the overall project.

Expand roles and responsibilities

- Shift some of your decision-making responsibility to your team to increase their authority and accountability. For example:
  - Eliminate the need for a higher level of approval or authorization.
  - Ask employees to submit reports under their signature instead of yours.
  - Give people more control over necessary resources.
  - Arrange opportunities for your employees to attend conferences or meetings as company representatives.

- Increase your team's versatility by expanding people's current job descriptions or job profiles.

- Encourage people to take on special projects or assignments, particularly if it involves working with other areas or using previously untapped or underdeveloped skills.

- Have your direct reports prepare development plans in which they work on capabilities or skills they will need in the future, but do not necessarily need now.

3. Nurture commitment to a common vision and shared values.

Working from a shared set of values and a common vision gives leaders a sense of security. They know that people may have different ways of achieving a goal, but they will adhere to the same ground rules.

Collaborate to define your mission and shared values

- Work with your team to develop a mission statement that defines your collective purpose and goals. Encourage people to use this statement to guide their actions and interactions with others. Include the following sections:
  - A clear statement about your core business
  - Your preferred approach to customers/clients
  - How departments and individuals will work together
  - What needs to be accomplished
  - How you will measure success

- Ask your team to help you develop a set of values for your area and organization.

- Identify values that the team should share as well as values that are more personal in nature.

- Invite each member to prepare for these sessions by listing what he or she believes are the shared values.

- As a group, examine the statements, identify any differences, and reach a consensus.

- Explore what impact different values can have on the group's work and discuss options for managing the situation.

Make the vision real

- Visions have to be turned into concrete action plans for them to be meaningful and realistic for your group. Make sure your team knows how to make it a reality.

- Balance your big-picture thinking with practical action steps. Your team will lose momentum if they get stuck in seemingly endless discussions about "why."

- Discuss the vision with individual team members and answer any questions they have. Does the person have a clear understanding of the vision? Where are the gaps? Work with the person to fill in those gaps.

- Formulate and agree on the key messages your team should convey to their direct reports.

- Watch for cynicism about your area's vision. People may have seen visions come and go without having an impact on the organization. As a result, they may be cynical about a vision's ability to move people. Determine how you can make it different this time, perhaps by becoming more directly involved in making the vision real to your team.

- Invite your direct reports to describe the impact the vision has had on their actions. Are people having a hard time making the vision real? Brainstorm ways to make the vision live and breathe.

4. Give people the opportunity and latitude to run their area(s) of the organization.

Getting the best out of others requires that you effectively challenge individuals and teams with opportunities and responsibility—and that you back them up with the necessary resources. Successful executives articulate business priorities, goals, and expected outcomes, then invest people with the freedom to "run their own show."

Give your team responsibility for the whole operation

- Analyze the current level of employee involvement in the following areas: organizational strategy, operational planning, resource allocation and budgeting, and problem-solving task forces. Determine how employee roles can be expanded in each area.

- Assign an entire operation to your team. Let them set goals, determine strategies, and generate an implementation plan. Monitor their results, but let them make the decisions wherever possible. Avoid withholding parts of the process or giving people partial tasks. Let them know you are available as a resource and intervene only if you detect a serious problem.

- Give your team front-end direction to help them understand the purpose and importance of their objectives. Show them how their objectives fit into the big picture.

- Work with the team to determine how to measure and track the team's progress. Ask for and incorporate their suggestions.

- Ask your team to find ways to improve their quality, productivity, and customer service. Hold regular meetings where they can discuss how to improve processes and implement ideas for increased productivity.

- Provide appropriate "take charge" assignments. Give employees the responsibility for critiquing their own work and the work of their peers.

Back up your team

- Let employees know that you will stand with them on challenging initiatives and issues.

- Run interference for your team when they get stuck. Be an advocate if they are not getting the resources or the cooperation they need from other areas. Assist in breaking down any barriers they encounter.

- Support your team's decisions and avoid second-guessing or criticizing. This will benefit both your team and the entire organization.

- Provide helpful feedback and coaching as a way to support your team. Try to be as specific as possible. Look for opportunities to provide immediate feedback in significant situations.

5. Promote collaboration and remove obstacles to teamwork across the organization.

Creating and using teams will help you reduce silos in your organization. As you develop working relationships with people in other areas, you will learn about their goals and key challenges. This will broaden your perspective on the overall business and help you facilitate decision making between departments.

Serve as a role model of teamwork

- Demonstrate how to be an effective team member. Show others how to work with complex and troublesome issues by soliciting and using help from others. Try the following methods:
    - Facilitate discussions rather than control them.
    - Admit your limitations and deficiencies when appropriate, and accept feedback without defensiveness.
    - Advise rather than dictate.
    - Nurture creativity instead of compliance.

- Be willing to make personal changes and adjust your behavior when others give you feedback. Your instincts and habits to take over and take charge can inhibit some of the very teamwork you want. Resist those impulses.

- Illustrate that you support teamwork. Give credit where credit is due. Give your team full recognition for their accomplishments. Avoid taking personal credit for a team accomplishment.

- Curb any tendency to be uninterested in ideas that are not completely yours. Assess your reasons for pulling back from other people's ideas and look for patterns. Find a way to give attention and recognition to as many ideas as you can.

- Avoid using hidden agendas or asking for input on decisions that have already been made. These behaviors will stifle new ideas and future input.

Create an environment conducive to teamwork; discourage "we versus they" thinking

- Create a positive environment that fosters acceptance and tolerance. Establish a comfortable atmosphere in which all employees contribute ideas and ask each other for help.

- Evaluate your employees' willingness and ability to work as part of an organizational team. Encourage them to develop relationships throughout their functional area and the organization. Let them know that developing an orientation toward teamwork is part of your performance expectation.

- Foster a sense of mutual appreciation among team members. Ask two or more of your direct reports to work on a joint assignment and explain the strengths and capabilities you think they will bring to the project. Emphasize the importance of collaboration in completing the task.

- Eliminate barriers that prevent people from working together. Build teamwork among different groups through committee and task force assignments. Include representatives from various work groups, including nonmanagerial employees. Keep the teams focused on organizational goals.

- Use shared terminology within your team and educate outside groups so they understand your jargon. Language that is unclear can block communication and cause confusion.

- Show respect for other functions and professions. Avoid labels, stereotypes, and disparaging remarks about other groups or units.

- Challenge people to think of the big picture when they negotiate for resources. Encourage them to discuss how they can optimize the success of the organization by working together, instead of merely trying to increase the resource allocation for their own areas.

Use a team approach when appropriate

- Sometimes it is useful to use a team to accomplish a task, make a decision, or solve a problem. A team approach is most appropriate when:
    - An innovative approach or solution is needed.
    - Information from more than one person is required to complete a task.
    - Multiple perspectives are needed for a comprehensive understanding of the issues.
    - Enough time is available to develop a team.
    - The project, task, or activity requires considerable interdependence and coordination.
    - Full acceptance of the decisions and solutions is necessary for effective implementation.

- A team approach may not be appropriate when:
    - An activity or decision is routine or fairly simple.
    - Independent action and accountability are the most important factors for successful performance.
    - Action needs to be taken quickly.
    - Individual creativity is important for success.
    - Participants would consider the decision, task, or activity trivial.
    - Consensus or buy-in is not important for successful implementation.

- Recall specific instances when you effectively used a team approach to solve problems and when you missed opportunities to do so. Look for patterns and consider whether you often avoid team involvement on certain kinds of problems or decisions.

- Analyze decisions made in the past month to determine whether they could have benefited from some kind of team approach.

- Solicit input from a variety of groups, departments, or teams before you make decisions. Encourage representatives from each group to contribute their ideas.

- Invite your team to share success stories about collaborating with other areas. Also ask them to exchange their ideas and best practices with other groups. Guarding against the "not invented here" trap will help your group continually improve its effectiveness.

Promote an atmosphere that values diversity

- Examine your mind-set toward particular groups. Are you more likely to make jokes or treat a certain group differently? Perhaps you have never met someone from a certain group and believe you won't be able to work effectively with them. Such thoughts and attitudes will hinder your ability to work with people from those groups.

- Make an effort to get to know people from other groups so you can hear about their concerns firsthand. Knowledge and understanding will make it easier for you to challenge statements that denigrate others.

- Attend training sessions designed to raise awareness of what types of comments or behaviors are unacceptable. Even if something seems like a small issue to you, it could make others very uncomfortable.

- Ask your peers how they handle diversity issues. What advice do they have? What techniques have been effective for them?

Deal with inappropriate comments and behavior

- Discuss how you could and should handle situations when someone makes a disrespectful remark or acts inappropriately. You may want to use role plays or hypothetical scenarios to raise the awareness level within your group and bring uncomfortable issues out in the open.

- Demonstrate your leadership by clearly refusing to tolerate labeling and other prejudicial behavior. Speak out on these issues. Treat persistently unacceptable behavior as a performance issue that affects the morale of the group.

- Let people know when they said something offensive. Don't attack the person, but point out how the statement is offensive. They might not have considered a "harmless" joke as potentially damaging.

- Confront intolerant behavior, including subtle comments. Use the following approaches:
  - Ask the person for a rationale of his or her belief.
  - Discuss the impact of this belief or comment on others.
  - If the remark is an obvious put-down, offer comments like, "That's not appropriate," then change the topic to indicate you do not want to discuss your statement further.
  - If people attempt to defend their actions, reassert that intolerant comments are inappropriate.
  - Hold people responsible for changing unacceptable behavior.

- When necessary, discuss prejudicial actions or verbal patterns with someone one-on-one. If you confront them in private, there will be less ego involved and, therefore, less defensiveness.

6. Convey confidence in others' ability and desire to do their best.

Few things are as demotivating as micromanagement and second-guessing. On the other hand, communicating your confidence in someone's ability can inspire that person to take risks, try new approaches, and generally exceed his or her expectations. Leaders who successfully convey their confidence can unleash the potential of their teams.

Examine your attitudes toward people

- If you have low expectations for people, it may result in low productivity. Your expectations are communicated nonverbally as well as verbally. Imagine people at their best and help them visualize their potential.

- Solicit feedback on the kind of messages you are sending, verbally and nonverbally. If your messages are misleading or inhibiting, be prepared to change.

- Imagine people at their best and help them visualize their potential. Assume that others are acting with the highest motives.

Delegate effectively

- Identify the standards of performance for the assignment. Consider which outcomes are acceptable or unacceptable, and which outcomes would be outstanding. Explicitly convey what is necessary to accomplish the assignment. Research has shown that the more explicitly goals and criteria are presented, the more likely they are to be met.

- Ask for the person's perspective and ideas on how to accomplish the job. Express your confidence in his or her ability to successfully complete the job.

- Resist taking over when things go wrong; instead, coach him or her on how to correct the mistake.

- Show your confidence by giving your direct reports more decision-making authority.

- Accept and support your team's method of accomplishing a task and focus on the achievement of the goal. Let people know that you are available as a resource. Avoid hovering—let them find you. Set up appropriate ways for them to update you on their progress.

Recognize and praise the talents of others

- Look for opportunities to praise and highlight others' achievements. Draw attention to individual contributions, and find ways to reward and recognize specific talents.

- Value everyone's work rather than showing bias for one function over another.

- Eliminate symbols that make one group or type of employee appear to be more important than others.

- Provide verbal recognition for everyone's contributions. Use phrases that reflect the importance of collaborative efforts; for example, "This was a great example of everyone pulling together to meet a tight deadline."

- Look for opportunities to praise and highlight others' achievements. Draw attention to individual contributions and find ways to reward and recognize specific talents.

7. Celebrate and reward significant organizational achievements.

People at all organizational levels want and need recognition for their efforts and accomplishments. It motivates people by letting them know that others are genuinely pleased with their work, and that they are valuable to the organization. It is important that people at the top notice.

Reward people at the right time in the right way

- Examine the timing of your recognition and reinforcement efforts. When people perform an exemplary task, acknowledge and reward it immediately. Research shows that the sooner the reward is delivered, the more impact it will have.

- Find ways to provide encouragement throughout the duration of projects.

- When you give positive feedback or reinforcement, focus your discussion on the behavior. Giving specific feedback on good performance will encourage that behavior.

- Make the relationship between performance and its reward very clear. For example, give a person more responsibility when he or she meets his or her goals, if that is something that motivates the person.

- Expand the ways in which you recognize performance. Use a variety of nonmonetary rewards that are consistent with employees' aspirations.

- Make your employees' successes visible. Communicate their achievements to the organization in a visible and positive way, showing pride in and support for your people.

- Consider instituting a formal awards program that recognizes the achievements of successful teams.

- Do not lose sight of individual members when you reward a team. Recognize individual contributors, but avoid rewards that create unhealthy competition within the group.

- Find out what forms of recognition or rewards are most meaningful to each team. You may find it useful to schedule one-on-one meetings to discuss individual preferences.

Identify opportunities to celebrate

- Identify opportunities to celebrate team accomplishments. Anticipate milestones or project completions that you want to celebrate, put them on your calendar, and follow through.

- Openly recognize attempts by individuals and teams to go beyond what is expected.

- Reward people who overcome difficult obstacles and achieve exceptional results.

- Publicly acknowledge excellent team performance at meetings and in other communication vehicles.

- Schedule informal quarterly get-togethers.

- Celebrate when specific targets, such as sales quotas, are reached.

- Organize special team events upon the successful completion of projects.

- Organize a fun, informal contest with small prizes that everyone can win.

Align rewards to performance

- Reward high achievement through monetary rewards and compensation systems. Tie rewards to individual and team performance as they relate to organizational objectives.

- Ask your team if they think elements of the compensation or reward system are unfair. Do they feel their performance is accurately monitored and measured against primary organizational goals? Brainstorm with your team to determine what compensation and benefit systems would look like if they were more aligned to organizational goals, and more accommodating of individual needs.

- Review the performance of your team against its goals. Look for goals that are receiving either too much or too little emphasis because of the way that performance is compensated. Take action to ensure that compensation strategies support the team and organizational outcomes you seek.

Resources

The resources for this chapter begin on page 444.

9
INFLUENCING
AND NEGOTIATING

———

PROMOTE IDEAS AND PROPOSALS PERSUASIVELY;

SHAPE STAKEHOLDER OPINIONS;

PROJECT A POSITIVE IMAGE;

WORK THROUGH CONFLICTS;

NEGOTIATE WIN/WIN SOLUTIONS.

KEY BEHAVIORS

———

1. *Promote and sell ideas persuasively.*
2. *Shape the opinions of key "stakeholders"*
   (customers, shareholders, employees, etc.).
3. *Earn the respect of senior executives in the organization.*
4. *Promote and project a positive image of the organization.*
5. *Win acceptance for proposed changes and new initiatives.*
6. *Work through conflicts to create win/win results.*
7. *Negotiate skillfully to create the best outcome possible.*

INTRODUCTION

Few people make the executive ranks without knowing how to influence and negotiate with others effectively. However, this is an area in which there is always room for improvement.

The stakes are often higher at the executive level. Problems are seldom so simple that everyone agrees on one solution. Executives must do more than make decisions and give directives—they must gain willing cooperation and support from others. The success of their organizations may depend on it.

David Bradford and Allan Cohen (*Influence Without Authority*, John Wiley & Sons, 1991) note that,

> "Everyone wants to be more influential at work. There aren't many situations left where issuing orders gets desired results."

Their observation is apropos for even the most senior levels of leadership at most organizations.

Effective influence is determined by a combination of key elements. Credibility is the first element; it is built on the trust of others, acting with integrity, and an effective track record. The second element is the ability to demonstrate the value of a position. People are convinced by rational persuasion and inspiration to varying degrees. The third element stems from consultation with others and building partnerships. Nearly everyone is willing to support some initiative or plan in which they have a meaningful say.

There are often valid but competing and conflicting views on organizational issues, direction, and priorities. Participating effectively in those discussions requires both influencing and negotiating skills. Therefore, executives must be experts at the complementary skills of influencing and negotiating, and pursue negotiations in an open and sincere manner. They must engage all participants, identify and align expectations, integrate varying points of view, and negotiate terms and implementation plans.

VALUABLE TIPS

- View yourself as an influencer and negotiator.

- Identify, build, or create areas of common ground with others.

- Choose an influencing style that fits the situation.

- Use a variety of influencing techniques. This will allow you to match your technique to the individual.

- Brainstorm as many ways as possible to influence people.

- Determine what you have (resources, people, budget, authority, etc.) that other people need.

- Know the strengths and weaknesses of your negotiating style; ask experienced negotiators for their feedback.

- Always prepare for a negotiating session.

- Learn about the other party's negotiating style before you meet.

- Ask about the other party's situation instead of making assumptions about their situation.

- Determine the least you can accept before you negotiate.

- Don't sacrifice the relationship just to win.

- Remember that listening is a vital component of negotiation and influencing.

- Become aware of gender and cultural aspects of negotiation and role play situations in which you need to apply them appropriately.

- Identify role models for influencing and negotiating, and list the qualities that make them effective.

- Determine when cooperation will be more effective than competition.

STRATEGIES FOR ACTION

1. Promote and sell ideas persuasively.

Executives work with and through others, therefore they frequently use their influencing and negotiating skills. They often find that their skills are either inadequate or need to be fine-tuned for the range of situations and constituencies that confront them.

Selling ideas often comes across the best when it includes consultation, rational persuasion, inspiration, and genuine personal enthusiasm.

Know your preferred influencing style

- Identify your customary influencing approach. What are the benefits and pitfalls of your style?

- Determine what type of leader you are. Traditional leaders exercise hierarchical, bureaucratic power and authority. Transactional leaders appeal to the self-interest of others. Transformational leaders involve others as agents of positive change. Use the following questions to determine your style:
    - Do you depend primarily upon your position, power, and authority to influence others?
    - Do you freely share information with people at all levels as a means of engaging them?
    - Do you try to persuade others by drawing them into the negotiation process at an early stage?
    - Are you comfortable with a give-and-take approach to influencing?
    - Do you tell people how they have influenced you? Why or why not?
    - How much of your strategy is based on empowering employees to become change agents?

- Go to your influence strengths when they fit the situation, but use other approaches when they do not.

Identify and address needs and concerns

- Recognize that persuasive techniques do not work instantaneously—nothing can perform magic within a single meeting or conversation. Instead, use progressive, conscious steps to move people toward the acceptance of an idea.

- Try to identify shared interests, such as goals, methods, or values, and emphasize them.

- Consider the following questions:
    - How will people benefit from your idea?
    - Whose efforts might be hindered by your idea? How?
    - Can you address issues and concerns from each side?
    - Can your idea be broadened or altered to appeal to a greater number of people?
    - What type of interaction will help your case with each individual?
    - How can you promote your ideas?
    - What is the most opportune time for events and interactions?

Positively assert your ideas and proposals

- Create and use opportunities to share your position with individuals and groups. Be persistent when necessary. Focus on the positive aspects of the idea.

- Genuine enthusiasm and conviction are contagious. Express your passion and commitment when you are trying to influence others. (In part, people will be convinced if you appear convinced.)

- Watch how you convey your attitudes nonverbally. If you are excited and enthused, remember to display it through your vocal expression, facial animation, and gestures.

- Increase your emotional impact. According to Bert Decker (*You've Got to Be Believed to Be Heard*, St. Martin's Press, 1993), "to influence, persuade, or motivate people, you have to make emotional contact with them."

Use a range of influencing styles

- *Networking:* Identify people who can support you on future efforts, especially opinion leaders, and build relationships with them. Include people from inside and outside your organization.

- *Pie making:* Increase the scope and value of solutions so all parties will benefit. Find overall solutions that exceed the expectations of all parties.

- *Brokering:* Facilitate the exchange of goods and services in a win/win manner between participants.

- *Banking:* Keep track of your "assets" and the "holdings" of people around you as you influence and negotiate.

- *Leveraging power and resources:* Use status, information, services, and scarce goods to gain greater influence.

- *Inspiring:* Appeal to people's values, interests, and concerns.

2. Shape the opinions of key "stakeholders" (customers, shareholders, employees, etc.).

An important part of the executive role is shaping stakeholder opinion. Proactively meeting with people and explaining your ideas and initiatives can help you bring people on board at the beginning, instead of trying to turn around a "freight train" of opinion once it's moving.

Learn what your stakeholders need

- List all the stakeholders involved in the particular situation. Identify one or two influential representatives from each group whom you know or should know.

- Talk to your stakeholders on a regular basis. This will help you stay on top of their situations—what they need and want, their plans, current activities, how your actions affect them, etc.

- When you face a particular issue, discuss it with each stakeholder group. Find out who would be your best contact within each group. It may be your regular contact, or your contact may pave the way for you to visit with someone else who is more informed or has more stake in the issue.

- Listen to your stakeholders. What is important to them? What are their main concerns? How do they hope to benefit from your ideas?

- Realize that every situation is unique and every group has a different dynamic. Study the culture of the group you are seeking to influence.

Show how your proposals address key organizational needs and priorities

- Tie what you are proposing to real problems and opportunities. When possible, use already acknowledged problems or opportunities so you will only need to sell the solution.

- Prepare your position and rationale beforehand. Jot down the three most important points you want to make. Be ready to address the concerns you uncovered during the investigation process.

- Give a brief synopsis of the information you will be discussing before you actually present your ideas. For example, "I've asked everyone to meet today to talk about next year's marketing strategy. I have three points I wish to make, and then I would be interested in getting your input."

- When you outline your ideas, pay attention to the reaction of your stakeholders. Do they appear engaged? Are they asking questions? Look for signs that they are interested in what you are saying and want to know more.

- As you state your ideas, clearly indicate the impact they will have upon the stakeholders, focusing specifically on the issues that are of most value to them.

- Show how your proposal will produce something of acknowledged value to the organization, such as money, reduced cycle time, retentions, support for a high-priority organizational initiative, etc.

Practice reciprocation

- In their book *Influence Without Authority* Cohen and Bradford explore "currencies." Currencies refer to what people value and use for trading. They include control, innovation, excitement, stability, change, freedom, and recognition. Know the resources you have to trade and analyze the currencies of others. Once you know who holds specific currencies, you can create exchanges that will lead to satisfying alliances.

- Seek to assist others whenever you can. Look for ways to genuinely serve people, such as picking up the phone to give someone specific feedback on a good presentation, or offering to assist another executive or group on a project.

- Help other people. Notice when a colleague is overloaded and provide help or support.

- Return favors. When others assist you, find ways to assist them.

3. Earn the respect of senior executives in the organization.

Senior executives have high expectations for the leaders within their organizations. They value people who get results, are team players, and add value through their knowledge and ideas. Earning the respect of the senior executives in your organization will pave the way for your initiatives, and positively affect your career.

Know the key initiatives your organization is pursuing

- Know what the executive leadership of your organization is concerned about and the direction they are taking. Knowing the high-leverage issues in your organization and the strategic intent behind them will put you in a better position to move your agenda forward.

- Learn about the agendas of key people and their positions on important issues. A practical way to accomplish this is to participate in planning and problem-solving discussions at various levels of the organization.

- Compare your business or functional objectives with overall organizational priorities and eliminate items that are not aligned.

Demonstrate commitment to the organization

- Consciously make a commitment to your organization and its people. Decide what that means for your role—what behaviors will demonstrate your commitment?

- Be willing to sacrifice or trade off personal interests or preferences, when appropriate, to support an organizational initiative.

- When you help others, do not broadcast your magnanimity. Sometimes you may need to work behind the scenes. Willingly share credit for accomplishments.

- Be known as a leader who is not above doing any type of work that needs to be done. When the pressure is on, work side by side with your people until the crisis is over.

- Use your network to find valuable resource people who can help you solve organizational problems.

- Become "the person who knows how to get things done."

Raise your visibility within the organization

- Identify five to ten key people who are necessary for your success and invest time building rapport with each person. Influence is often as much a function of "who knows you" as it is "who you know."

- Look for opportunities to lead group initiatives. Volunteer to head a task force or project group and use a variety of techniques to increase your impact.

- Build your external "recognition factor" by serving on various boards, contributing to the community, presenting papers at professional meetings, or being interviewed as an expert or leader for business publications. This takes time but it builds visibility, and often, goodwill.

Keep your leadership informed

- Your influence will not mean much unless it is backed by the senior leadership of your organization. Watch carefully to see what is important to senior management.

- Periodically meet with your boss to let him or her know what you are doing and jointly strategize on key initiatives. Minimize surprises for those above as well as below you.

- When you realize that a decision from another area or outside the organization will have a negative impact on your part of the organization, let your boss know. Outline the anticipated impact of the decision and cite tangible consequences. If you are not able to answer a challenge or question, focus on the areas that you are able to address.

- If you avoid talking to senior management about a problem in your area, sit down and list the reasons why you hold back. Draft a list of who needs to know about the problem and specify what they need to know. Create a strategy for communicating the issue. Set a deadline and act on it.

Capitalize on your first 100 days

- The first 100 days in a new position are more than symbolic. Use this valuable window of time to set and communicate your agenda, and to produce results that people can see and appreciate. There is only one time period in which you can make a first impression.

- Initiate new programs. A job promotion is a prime time to enact change, as people are already expecting it. Listen and learn, but do not hesitate to initiate some positive changes.

- Be careful not to overpromise. People will be watching to see if your promises are credible. It is almost always better to underpromise and overdeliver.

4. Promote and project a positive image of the organization.

As an executive, you have many opportunities to promote and project a positive image of your organization. You need to be prepared to promote it at all times—client meetings, conferences, professional gatherings, community meetings, and even on your personal time. People will form an opinion of your organization based on your behavior.

Represent your organization

- Invest your time and energy in representing your organization at community and industry events.

- Consider the messages you and the organization want to send, and choose your involvements wisely so they will provide recognition and impact. Monitor your involvement so you make a real contribution, not just a show of support for publicity.

- Serve on standards-setting boards to increase your visibility and influence in the industry. Your involvement will show that you and your organizations are leaders in your industry.

- Network with your peers in other organizations and professional groups; these connections may serve you later.

- Attend supplier meetings and become familiar with the issues handled by your vendors.

Be aware of the positive and negative power of the media

- Confer with your communications or public relations staff or agency whenever you deal with a media inquiry. They will help you balance an effective use of the media with the dangers of bad press.

- Respond as quickly as possible to media requests in your area of expertise. If you do not respond, others may respond for you and about you, perhaps in a disparaging manner.

- Ask clients to supply current, value-adding accounts of how your products or services helped them. Use their stories, along with research data and new findings to shape how your organization is seen in the media.

- Enlist the help of savvy media strategists. Planned events are an excellent way to receive media coverage and shape your organization's public image.

- Identify situations that could draw your organization into the public eye. Create and rehearse a crisis management plan to avoid bad press.

- Remember, the press is always looking for crisis news, so be prepared to defend yourself from attack. Present yourselves as a caring organization, if that can be done in a sincere manner.

- If a crisis does occur, follow these principles:
    - Allow only the CEO or other specified senior executives to communicate with the public.
    - Highlight your organization's concern for the welfare of people affected by the crisis.
    - Identify key stakeholders and give them accurate, ongoing status reports.

- Use the media to your advantage. A media announcement can be an excellent place to spell out new initiatives and tell the public about the health and vigor of your organization.

5. Win acceptance for proposed changes and new initiatives.

Successful influence is a form of selling. Whether you are selling products, ideas, programs, or attitudes, your goal is to gain support and commitment. Executives need to know what is important to each person whose support they need.

Provide compelling rationales for arguments

- Create a clear, compelling picture of your idea, project, or initiative. Explain how your ideas will meet the needs and interests of others. For example, describe how your idea will solve a problem, save money, avert trouble, increase the return on investment, or improve job satisfaction. Do not expect people to draw these conclusions on their own.

- Use clear reasoning, make compelling points, and have relevant supporting information, such as examples, statistics, analogies, and quotations from experts.

- People recall images for a longer period than words. Help people connect with your ideas by linking them with graphics, illustrations, symbols, and metaphors.

- Identify reasons why people might resist your ideas. Generate key points that address their interests and concerns. Adjust your message to fit within their parameters, expand your idea to encompass what they care about, and identify how your idea can benefit them.

- No amount of influence will cover up sloppy thinking. Therefore, do your homework, run your ideas by others, incorporate their suggestions when possible, and refine your message.

Accurately anticipate the reactions of others

- Determine what style will persuade your audience. If people will be persuaded by a display of your commitment to the project, show your excitement and enthusiasm. If people are simply looking for the facts, explain your logic and reasoning.

- Before you present a new idea, make a list of the people to whom you will be submitting your plan. Determine where each person is likely to stand in relation to your proposal. Anticipate who will raise objections and come up with a rationale they can support.

- If you are presenting your ideas during a meeting, decide if there are some people you should meet with one-on-one before the meeting. This will give you a chance to learn of opposing views, which will cut down on the number of surprises that could catch you off guard during the meeting.

- Identify colleagues who seem knowledgeable about other people's positions and ask them for pointers on how to anticipate possible reactions.

- Make a point of regularly discussing your colleagues' opinions on work-related topics. Do this in a low-key manner over lunch, coffee, etc. Keep track of what you learn; remember their needs, goals, agendas, and positions on specific issues.

Find points of agreement

- When you are searching for common ground, start with basic human desires such as belonging, recognition, the desire for significance in work, and the opportunity to contribute to society.

- Clarify the interests of both parties. Concentrating on each position will prevent the negotiating process from becoming a battle of wills. Creative problem solving and searching for common ground should be the central activities.

- Figure out where the trade-offs are by asking both parties to devise creative solutions. Encourage people to think "more for you, more for me."

- When people resist your agenda, focus on understanding their issues. View their concerns as legitimate problems to be solved. Be respectful even if you have significant disagreements.

6. Work through conflicts to create win/win results.

Conflict is a whetstone that sharpens your leadership skills and character by opening your eyes to new points of view. Approach conflict with the expectation that relationships will grow if you explore opposing viewpoints.

Openly address and resolve conflict

- Do not view conflict as a breakdown in the system; instead, view it as the impetus for a new solution. Picture conflict as a fluid event.

- Allow people around you to challenge you, even to the point of conflict. Make it safe for them to freely express their views. Honest feedback will help you avoid the isolating effect of being at the top and will give you a more complete picture of each issue.

- Ask the people involved in a conflict to identify areas where they agree. Emphasize common interests and concerns before discussing areas of disagreement.

- Ask people to explain a position different from their own. It will help them understand other points of view.

Handle conflicts calmly

- Avoid taking a position too early in a discussion or debate. Maintain a relaxed attitude and keep your mind open to a number of solutions.

- Attack problems, not people.

- Stick to core issues. Complex discussions can get murky; therefore, deliberately bring the conversation back to the main points or concerns.

- Search for root causes instead of jumping to conclusions or dealing with superficial causes or symptoms.

- Paraphrase as you listen. Rephrase what the other party says to confirm that you understand his or her point of view.

- Use humor to lighten up tense or delicate negotiations. Humor can lower people's defenses and make them more receptive to your point of view. It can also help you get over tough spots.

Determine your BATNA

- In *Getting to Yes* (Penguin, 1991), Roger Fisher and William Ury outline the Harvard Negotiating Project's BATNA concept. BATNA stands for "Best Alternative To a Negotiated Agreement." A BATNA is a safeguard against failing to recognize poor options, losing sight of your original interests, or sliding into an "I have to beat you" mentality.

- Chart your satisfaction level regarding possible outcomes:
    - What is your ideal outcome?
    - What is your bottom line?
    - What is an adequate result?
    - If your negotiation process were to break down, what would your recourse be?

Pick your battles

- You will never have enough time or resources to resolve every issue that needs your attention. Focus on high-leverage opportunities and learn which obstacles offer the greatest resistance.

- No task can be done perfectly, so determine which efforts will have the greatest impact.

- Mend fences whenever possible. However, recognize that sometimes it is necessary to make enemies, if the issue is important enough. The key is to avoid making the wrong enemies and to do what you can to reduce their opposition or resistance.

7. Negotiate skillfully to create the best outcome possible.

Executives often face conflicting opinions, ideas, agendas, and methodologies as they try to accomplish their goals. Because they need to work cross-functionally, negotiation is a vital tool for getting results. Time spent developing this skill will repay executives many times over.

Prepare for negotiation

- Examine your mind-set regarding negotiation. Do you look at negotiation as an adversarial encounter or a collaborative effort? Do you begin with a defensive or an offensive posture? Do you view the process as an option-finding session?

- Study the other party's negotiating style. Then you won't be surprised at their strategies and tactics.

- If necessary, hold a preparatory meeting to lay the groundwork for the actual negotiating session.

- Separate your interests from your position by identifying the "why" behind your views. Prioritize your interests so that you do not inadvertently sacrifice a critical goal by going after a less important one.

- Identify areas of agreement and common concern.

Generate a myriad of options

- Before negotiating, collaborate with a colleague to generate some options. The more alternatives you bring to the table, the more flexibility you will have in crafting an optimal solution. Avoid searching for "one right answer."

- Include time for brainstorming during the negotiation process. Put people at ease so that they will be in a creative, problem-solving mood.

- Avoid the tendency to suggest solutions or push for closure too quickly. Occasionally step back and let ideas develop.

- Use differences as building blocks for equitable, creative outcomes.

Evaluate alternatives using objective standards and fair procedures

- Many issues are complex and include elements that no one can predict. Keep negotiations from becoming a battle of wills by focusing on objective criteria and using an equitable process.

- Agree on the criteria you will use to evaluate options.

- Keep things simple. Think of elementary ways to decide between options. Use basic processes, such as taking turns, involving a third party, drawing lots, or going "halves" on the difference.

- In his seminar on *Negotiating Rationally*, Max Bazerman encourages people to handle the unpredictable aspects of negotiation with "betting." He cites the example of an exporter who found that she could not guarantee delivery of a product because of a sudden embargo. She suggested air shipment to the customer. The customer did not want to pay the shipping fee, but needed the goods. The two parties set up a wager: They agreed that the exporter would ship the goods by air. If the boat arrived on time, the exporter would pay the air freight charge. If the boat was late, the customer would pay.

Manage unfair tactics

- *Personal attacks:* Ignore their comments and deftly steer the conversation back to the issues. Try to treat others respectfully for as long as you can—whether they deserve it or not.

- *Withholding information:* Use your knowledge of the facts to uncover missing information.

- *Mind games:* Simply say, "I don't understand." Get other people to talk; during the conversation they will reveal their real purpose.

- *Threats or increased demands:* Use your BATNA to determine your bottom line.

- *Controlling:* Call attention to the controlling behavior to reestablish the balance of power.

- *Stonewalling or stalling:* Define roles and responsibilities and set a deadline. Include a third party for accountability.

- *Irrational behavior:* Call for a time-out. Talk to the most rational member of the opposing group and identify what is prompting the behavior.

- *Lying:* Remain appropriately skeptical. Track the process to determine if the facts and assertions match.

- *Setups:* Trust your intuition. If something seems amiss, distance yourself and study the dynamics. Call for a time-out and consult with someone you trust. Bring a partner to the negotiation.

RESOURCES

The resources for this chapter begin on page 446.

IO
LEADERSHIP
VERSATILITY

PLAY A VARIETY OF LEADERSHIP ROLES
(E.G., DRIVING, DELEGATING, SUPPORTING, COACHING)
AS APPROPRIATE; ADAPT STYLE AND APPROACH
TO MATCH THE NEEDS OF DIFFERENT
INDIVIDUALS AND TEAMS.

KEY BEHAVIORS

1. *Adjust leadership style to meet the needs of different individuals and teams.*
2. *Play an evaluative, analytic leadership role when appropriate.*
3. *Play a coaching, teaching leadership role when appropriate.*
4. *Play a supportive, encouraging leadership role when appropriate.*
5. *Play a driving, demanding leadership role when appropriate.*
6. *Play a hands-off, fully delegating leadership role when appropriate.*
7. *Use a participative leadership style when appropriate.*

INTRODUCTION

The term "virtuoso" is commonly used in the arts, especially the musical arts, to refer to highly accomplished artists who demonstrate a large repertoire of skills and styles. Today's executives clearly need to be virtuoso leaders. They need to adopt their leadership style to fit the business situation, global content, and people.

Different business situations require different sets of skills and approaches. Managing resources in an emerging economy requires different skills than managing complex alliances in long established economies. Start-ups draw on clear vision, the ability to inspire others, drive and hard work, and sales skills, whereas merging two large organizations requires vision, managing complex relationships, process management skills, and team building.

Executives need to lead their part of the organization, their management team, and individuals. Sometimes they need to lead the charge, at other times they need to empower others and let go. This requires great flexibility, skill, perspective, and judgment.

As your organization confronts new and varied challenges, an agile and versatile approach is needed. What are the business challenges? Who are you leading and what do they need from you? What is the cultural content? How much experience do you and your executives and managers have with a particular situation? Should short- or long-term considerations take priority? Who knows what will work best? What risks will you face if the decision is wrong? How much time do you have? Which resources are at your disposal?

The ability to modify your style and approach to people and situations is essential for long-term success. Organizations need agile executives who can effectively utilize a number of leadership styles and options.

VALUABLE TIPS

- Determine what leadership styles and approaches your organization most needs today, and will need in the next few years.

- Identify whether your organization has a preferred method of leadership, and how that helps or hinders your work.

- Consider the individuals on your team: What type of knowledge, skill, and experience do they have? What skills do you need to lead them?

- Examine your preferred leadership style and determine when it is most appropriate and when it is not.

- Determine whether people expect you to lead in a certain way and whether that makes you more or less effective.

- Ask yourself whether you make your leadership style fit the situation or whether you expect the situation to adapt to your leadership style.

- Take time to analyze what type of leadership is required for a particular situation.

- Solicit feedback on when you should use another leadership style.

- Find a role model and study when and why he or she uses a particular leadership style.

- Guard against switching styles too frequently, it will confuse people.

- Explain why you are using a particular leadership style in a situation.

- Coach your direct reports on when they should use a particular leadership style.

STRATEGIES FOR ACTION

1. Adjust leadership style to meet the needs of different individuals and teams.

Your leadership approach needs to differ according to the person and the situation. You know that it does not make sense to lead an executive responsible for a five-year track record of increased revenue and profitability the same way you lead a functional manager new to a general management role.

A contingency approach to leadership assumes that you will consider a number of variables before choosing a leadership style that will be effective in a particular situation. Important variables to consider include:

- the nature and complexity of the assignment or issue,
- the confidence, maturity, skill, and experience of the follower,
- the time available,
- the skills and availability of the leader,
- the nature of the tasks (individual, cross-functional, or team),
- the organization's values and culture, and
- the person's culture.

Assess the people and the situation

- Assess the individuals involved. Review what you know about their strengths, experience, limitations, responsibilities, and the type of leadership and guidance they prefer.

- Assess your management team. Are you leading a cohesive and highly collaborative team or a group of mavericks? What is the team's track record? How long have they worked together? Are there conflicts within the group that could impede its effectiveness? What development needs exist in the group? Do they cooperate and readily help one another?

- Consider the situation or issue at hand. How soon does a decision need to be made? Is it a good learning opportunity?

Partner with your team

- Discuss the leadership approach you plan to use with the individual or team rather than surprising them or keeping them guessing in every situation. Let people know what to expect and give them an opportunity to share how they prefer to be led. Work out an approach that will help ensure success.

- Request that the team or individual tell you what they want from you. Talk about your leadership approach and their response so you can become partners and improve the outcome. If you choose a leadership style that is different from their preference, discuss your rationale.

- Debrief with your team and individuals. What did you do that was helpful? How could you have been more helpful? What advice do they have for you?

Adapt to cultural differences

People in different cultures see the world differently from one another. Although many global corporations create a corporate culture that is supposed to supersede the separate cultures of the countries in which the firm is located, individual people continue to be strongly influenced by powerful cultural forces.

Geert Hofstede (*Cultures and Organizations: Software of the Mind*, McGraw-Hill, 1997) has identified three dimensions of cultural differences. These three dimensions describe important differences of which executives need to be aware.

1. *Power distance* is the extent to which less powerful members of organizations accept and expect that power be distributed unequally.

   When power distance is small, employees want to be involved, consulted, and able to make decisions. They do not respond well to being told what to do. An ideal boss is participative and a resource. If you are a leader in a small power distance culture, try the following:
      - Involve direct reports in decision making.
      - Ask for the opinions of others.
      - Wait until others give their opinions before you state yours.
      - Avoid unilateral decisions.
      - Make yourself available to explain rationale.
      - Make yourself available to hear feedback.
      - Label your opinion as your point of view, rather than indicating it is "the truth."

When power distance is large, people expect to be told what to do. They are uncomfortable with the boss deferring to others. From this point of view an ideal boss is a benevolent autocrat. He or she is a leader who takes care of his or her people. In large power distance cultures:
- Be willing to make the decisions.
- Frame your request for input so that others know you are gathering data, but you will make the decision.
- Be aware that you will be unsuccessful and make other people uncomfortable if you are not willing to make decisions.

In both types of cultures:
- Discuss power distance issues, including expectations and roles. This will make the conversation less personal and more comfortable for people who want executives to be more distant.

2. In *collective societies* people are viewed as members of a group, not as individuals. Collective societies have different standards for different groups. Rules, norms, and policies apply differently, depending upon one's status. Relationships are valued over tasks.

Building relationships occurs before "doing work." Maintaining relationships is important; the relationships are not sacrificed to "get work done." The relationship between employee and employer is a moral one —each has moral responsibilities to one another. The implications for leaders include:
- Be explicit about expectations and standards.
- Expect that team rewards will be more highly valued than individual ones.
- Be aware that people will not want to stand out from their group.
- Recognize that you will be seen as an executive first, not as an individual person.
- Treat building and maintaining relationships as part of the work to be done.

Individualistic societies emphasize the person, not the group; focus on tasks, not relationships; and have more of a contractual employee/employer relationship. Work is seen as less personal. Relationships are seen as secondary. Individualistic cultures want to make decisions quickly and may be seen as abrupt or rude. Implications include:

- Be willing to "get down to business" quickly.
- Help others see the value of relationships, especially the economic value.
- Use individual incentives; they work well in these cultures.
- Understand that task orientation does not mean lack of care about people.

3. Cultures differ in the distribution of *roles between the sexes*. Research indicates that there are fewer differences among women's values in different societies than among men. Among men there is a dimension of being very assertive and competitive on one side and modest and caring on the other side. Implications for leaders include:

- Ask about the role expectations between men and women.
- Learn what is "typical" female and male executive behavior.
- Be aware that the more different you are from the expected role and the less accepting others are of cultural differences, the more challenging it will be for you and for those working with you.
- Do what you can to help others feel comfortable with you and the way you handle your role, rather than insist they "deal with it."
- Respect the point of view of others and be aware that it is truly difficult to see and understand another's cultural viewpoint, especially when a person's status is involved.
- Recognize that people fight hard to maintain their status and sense of worth. Behavior that threatens or degrades the status of others is very disruptive. The challenge is to maintain the status and sense of worth of each person.
- Watch how others handle similar situations.
- Ask for advice from others of your same culture and from different cultures. Most likely you are not the first person who has encountered these same challenges.

Stay flexible

- No single style can possibly fit all people and circumstances. Select an approach that responds to the requirements of the person, team, task, and situation.

- Keep in touch with the people around you. Talk about what they want from you and what you need from them.

- Do not fall into a rigid formula such as progressing through leadership styles. You may assume you can go from orienting to coaching to supporting to delegating, but new situations will require a tailored approach. For example:
    - Highly competent and experienced team members may encounter challenges that do not respond to a hands-off leadership style, requiring that you actively collaborate with them on some projects.
    - A new employee may enjoy and be ready for a tough assignment with little guidance. For this person, receiving instruction may be a major demotivator or downright insulting.

Cautions

- Although it is important to be versatile, if you adjust your style too much or too often, you may be seen as unpredictable or moody. Do not make changes that seem arbitrary. Explain your rationale for approaching people and situations in a flexible manner.

- If you rarely adjust your style, you may not optimize the performance of your group or unleash their full potential. Your team may not feel that you value them and they may not be as motivated and productive as they could be.

2. Play an evaluative, analytic leadership role when appropriate.

Some situations require that you supply "thought leadership" rather than direction. In this role you contribute ideas, ask questions to get at underlying assumptions, draw links to larger organizational initiatives, provide a system-wide perspective, share your expertise, and encourage others to thoroughly consider alternatives.

Challenge others

- Confirm that your team has a sound rationale for their recommendations and proposed actions. You may want to use the "five whys" or the "what will happen" techniques listed in chapter 1, "Seasoned Judgment." Careful questions will help your team examine their assumptions and further define the relevant issues.

- Challenge people to think outside of their usual paradigms. If they see a problem in a particular way, ask how else it can be seen. Ask to see their root cause analysis. Ask why they chose specific alternatives and why they rejected others.

- At times, play the devil's advocate during discussions. This will cause people to consider their position on an issue more carefully and thoroughly. When you do so, tell people why you are playing this role. Ask for their permission; otherwise, this behavior will be seen as manipulative and demeaning.

Contribute your expertise

- Add your expertise and experience by offering other approaches or ways of looking at the situation. Watch the timing of your contributions so they encourage, not discourage, thinking.

- Resist the temptation to provide answers. Instead, provide "maps" or "road signs" so people can discover the "route."

- Because you may know more about what is happening in other parts of the organization, provide linkage when others do not see it. Tell your direct reports about the connections you see, encourage them to recognize linkages, and illustrate how they can use other organizational resources.

- Make a list of possible sources of useful information and give others direction on how to access and utilize it.

Encourage learning

- Look for opportunities for team members to work together on projects so they can learn from one another.

- Deliberately set up learning pairs and teams.

- Continually ask, "What are you learning?"

- Consistently evaluate projects with your direct reports and team. Consider what went well, what did not work, and what was learned.

- Debrief successes as well as failures—it's just as important to learn from successes as failures.

- Regularly ask about the debrief sessions your direct reports are having with their teams. This will help you confirm that debriefs are happening and that people are learning from them.

Cautions

- Realize that some issues do not lend themselves to a logical, analytical approach, especially interpersonal issues. People often need to express their emotions before they are able to evaluate and analyze issues.

- Focusing on analysis may be counterproductive when you need an innovative solution. Guard against analyzing creative ideas too quickly.

3. Play a coaching, teaching leadership role when appropriate.

As a coach, your role is to help people focus on gaining competence in skills needed now and in the future, help them align their development with the needs of the organization, help them become self-directed and personally responsible for their development, and help them continually learn. The coaching style of leadership is characterized by helping others accomplish their objectives, solve their own problems, and develop the ability to continually learn and grow.

Determine what is needed

- Focus on helping people find their own answers or help. In a coaching role, you are not providing solutions.

- Before giving advice, ask for the suggestions, recommendations, or ideas from the other person.

- Before giving feedback, ask how the other person sees the situation. This teaches the other person to analyze processes and their own behavior. These skills are very important to develop.

- When someone asks for help, ask what he or she has tried, inquire about why it didn't work, and ask what he or she believes will make the difference. This method will require the person to summarize and become reacquainted with what she or he knows, and will give you important information. This process often shows that the person knows what to do, but needs reassurance or needs someone else to play a role in the solution.

- Help people identify resources that may be helpful to them.

- When it is obvious that the person has tried everything he or she could think of, you can offer suggestions.

- Present a new way of looking at the problem or issue. View the problem from the perspective of the other side. This may help the person get unstuck.

- When a person is having difficulty with a goal, walk through the vision, strategy, and steps. Periodically inquire why and what else is possible.

Recognize the value of coaching

- Sometimes people make the assumption that the skill, experience, and confidence levels of their direct reports is very high and they would not benefit from coaching. Other times people believe in the "sink or swim" approach to development. Learning only from experience is limiting and time-consuming.

- Coaching is important to the succession planning process. You need to develop bench strength. It is your responsibility to foster succession planning in your business unit and prepare your successor. Your own movement may be limited if you do not have a successor.

- For more in-depth information on coaching others, see chapter 7, "Attracting and Developing Talent."

Cautions

- When you coach, give the person what he or she needs, not what you want to provide. Otherwise the coaching approach may be intrusive and overly helpful, or too distant and aloof.

- If you rarely play a coaching role, people may flounder because they have not developed the skills they need for the future. People will not be available for opportunities when you need them.

- If you switch from being a coach to a "player" mid-project, you will frustrate your team. Your overinvolvement in a project will prevent you from coaching your team to do it on their own.

4. Play a supportive, encouraging leadership role when appropriate.

Encouraging leaders ensure that people and teams have the confidence and ability to perform independently and effectively. An encouraging, supportive leadership style usually focuses on overall individual and team development rather than specific tasks and objectives.

This style should be used when your team has the skills to succeed, but they need more confidence and initiative. Instill confidence by focusing on the strengths and accomplishments of your team and organization. Provide broad objectives, establish some checkpoints, and make yourself available at people's request.

Show support

- Listen to your team and find out what type of support they want from you. Be sure you have good rapport with each member of your team.

- Periodically check in with your team and ask for an update. This will give you an opportunity to review the status of their projects. Link your comments to your team's goals; it will show your attention and interest in what they are doing.

- Regularly declare your confidence in your team and acknowledge the difficulty of what they are doing. Express support and appreciation for their efforts.

- Ask for people's help and counsel.

- Do not forget what a powerful role model you are. Everything you do is amplified; your actions show what is truly important.

- Move beyond merely giving public support. For example, shift work to another group and free your team's time to work on a new initiative. Offer to provide resources that would otherwise be inaccessible. Identify organizational barriers and help remove them.

Help others learn

- Provide developmental opportunities by giving people challenging assignments and allowing them to deal with difficult issues.

- Utilize your management team during challenging situations, when their expertise and experience can serve as a valuable resource to the organization. Such opportunities will improve your team's effectiveness at handling difficult situations and draw out capabilities that were not previously demonstrated.

Caution

- Watch how you use this style, so you will not be perceived negatively as a cheerleader. Give positive feedback and express confidence, but also provide practical help when requested.

5. Play a driving, demanding leadership role when appropriate.

The primary purpose of a driving, demanding leadership style is to set the expectation that individuals and teams should achieve critical organizational goals in an efficient, effective, and timely manner. Use this style when the organization needs clarity and direction, and when an individual or team will not achieve goals on their own.

This style is particularly appropriate when a radical shift is required and you need to create a sense of urgency about the change. It lends itself well to situations that require one clear voice, such as turnarounds and crises.

Communicate, communicate, communicate

- Communicate the rationale behind your decisions and actions. People will be more comfortable following directions when they know the purpose for the action and sense that they are going in the right direction.

- Develop clear, simple, focused messages.

- Give people access to the information you have, so your direction makes sense.

- Differentiate the setting of direction from discussing direction.

- Repeat yourself. In times of crisis or change, some people will hear your message immediately while others will hear nothing at all. As people accept the situation and become accustomed to it, they need to hear your original message again. Give others a sense of security by repeating why the change is occurring, and restating the direction your organization is headed.

- Decide whether teams or individuals can take broad direction and run with it or whether you need to stay involved in the specific goal setting, strategy, and plan creation. You may be able to just review a plan, or you may need to provide direction for the implementation.

Monitor performance

- Closely monitor your team's performance. Monitoring their progress during critical periods will allow you to provide positive comments when they make satisfactory progress and give you time to intervene if something goes awry.

- When you are pursuing an important organizational goal, identify critical junctures during which you can give your team feedback. Then you can decide if they need guidance or if they can continue to operate independently.

- Celebrate successes. During stressful times, people need to see that progress is being made. Celebrate small successes along the way instead of waiting until the end goal is reached. A positive experience will raise the mood of your team, especially if progress has been slow or circumstances difficult.

- Let people know you are all working together. The circumstances that call for demanding leadership are often punishing for people. Encouragement and a sense of togetherness will help. During a stressful time, actively work to praise and recognize the effort your people put forward.

Cautions

- A driving and demanding leadership style must be used by both you and your direct reports, or they will be disempowered. Work to develop their abilities in this area by setting a clear expectation regarding the use of this style and modeling it appropriately.

- If you do not use this style when it is needed, your team may get sidetracked, fragmented, and lose productivity during a critical time. They may not understand the link between their actions, organizational goals, and strategy.

6. Play a hands-off, fully delegating leadership role when appropriate.

Full delegation allows your team to set goals, supervise all planning and decision making, and proceed independently. It is their responsibility to ask for help when they need it. Your role is to stay informed, monitor their progress, provide necessary resources, and handle interruptions that are beyond your team's control. Effective delegation can produce empowerment.

Assess your team

- People who demonstrate a high degree of expertise and reliability can be counted on to perform their roles well. Full delegation is appropriate when your direct reports:
    - Have the requisite knowledge, skills, or experience to do an outstanding job.
    - Want to excel at a specific assignment.
    - Are confident in their ability to do the work.
    - Are motivated to initiate action.
    - Accept responsibility for performing tasks on their own.

Delegate whenever possible

- Convey confidence in your team. Make it clear that they have your support and trust. Let your people know you want and need to delegate as much as possible.

- Consider how your people can be involved in both major and minor assignments, and delegate appropriately.

- Avoid micromanagement. Trust your people to handle the details.

- Delegate more complicated and interesting tasks in addition to routine tasks.

- Choose the right person or team for specific assignments. Determine who has the ability, experience, and confidence to complete the work, then make the assignment. Determine who will benefit by learning from the experience.

Set the context and let go

- Be sure your people understand the larger picture of business priorities and objectives.

- Be clear about your expectations. Discuss outcomes and time frames with the designated person or team, and build checkpoints and status updates into the plan where necessary.

- Keep your door open. Your direct reports need to know that you are accessible for quick updates and discussions of unexpected obstacles. A delegating style leaves the initiative primarily to the delegatee.

- Avoid the temptation to assume control from behind the scenes. If you do not, your people will quickly realize that the responsibility given to them was illusory. Reclaiming responsibility from a direct report or team will negatively affect their confidence and motivation. It should be done only in emergency situations that are critical to the organization's success, and only after you fully disclose your rationale for taking over.

- Avoid being pulled in by details. As stated above, give advice and set clear expectations about outcomes and time frames. Do not unwittingly roll up your sleeves and do the work yourself.

Caution

- If you use this style inappropriately, you may be seen as an absentee boss who overloads people with work and does nothing. It's important to watch and listen for this perception. You may need to communicate more fully about what you are doing.

7. Use a participative leadership style when appropriate.

Much of the time leaders choose a participative approach because they need their executive teams with them as they lead their organizations. Therefore, it's critical that executives develop a management team that creates a vision, sets business goals, and leads teams toward those goals.

Create the environment

- To use a participative leadership style effectively, develop the readiness of your team.

- Provide access to the information people need to understand the issues.

- Discuss and align personal and organizational goals.

- Develop processes for working through issues and making decisions.

- Develop ways to learn from your experience as a team.

- Encourage your direct reports to use participative and empowering leadership with their teams, direct reports, and each other. You should use this style whenever and wherever possible.

- Constantly clarify which decisions should be tackled participatively and which should not. Participation should lead to increased productivity, not added work and meetings.

- Ask your team to evaluate the outcomes of group decisions and efforts. Was it worth the effort? How could the group process be improved?

Cautions

- If the team or individuals are not ready for this style, you may find that everything has become a group decision. This can lead to missed deadlines and a lack of progress on issues and initiatives.

- If this style is underused, you may not have all the information you need, and make poor decisions. It is becoming increasingly rare that one person has all the needed information or perspectives.

RESOURCES

The resources for this chapter begin on page 448.

11
BUILDING ORGANIZATIONAL RELATIONSHIPS

———

CULTIVATE AN ACTIVE NETWORK OF RELATIONSHIPS

INSIDE AND OUTSIDE THE ORGANIZATION;

RELATE WELL TO KEY COLLEAGUES

(I.E., BOSSES, PEERS, COLLEAGUES, DIRECT REPORTS);

STAY IN TOUCH WITH EMPLOYEES AT ALL LEVELS.

KEY BEHAVIORS

———

1. *Cultivate a broad network to exchange ideas and rally support.*
2. *Stay in touch with people at all levels of the organization.*
3. *Relate well to bosses and higher management.*
4. *Relate well to direct reports.*
5. *Relate well to peers and colleagues.*
6. *Respect and appreciate individual differences in perspective and background.*
7. *Recognize and respond to the needs and concerns of others.*
8. *Adapt interpersonal style to meet the style of others.*
9. *Act to preserve relationships, even under difficult or heated circumstances.*
10. *Promote collaboration and remove obstacles to teamwork across the organization.*
11. *Seek to improve how the management team works together.*

INTRODUCTION

It is not unusual for CEOs of large U.S. corporations to make sure they are no more than two phone calls away from the White House. They want to be able to call the President or someone who has direct access to the Oval Office when issues and legislation come up that are of interest to their industry. They also want to learn about matters that are under consideration before they become public record or public policy.

This chapter deals with two important aspects of building organizational relationships. The first, commonly called "networking," consists of building a professional community. Through this community you can develop and maintain relationships with people inside and outside the organization who serve as advisors, information sources, sounding boards, opinion leaders, or collaborators on business initiatives.

The second aspect involves developing and maintaining a personal rapport with people in your organization. Leaders need to develop strong relationships with people on their team (above, across, and below), and with other people whose support and cooperation is vital to them and their team's success. More leaders derail because they have not developed relationships than because they are technically weak.

If you strive to identify, understand, and act upon people's needs and expectations, they will repay your efforts with high morale and increased productivity. On the other hand, if you create negative relationships in your organization, you will compromise your effectiveness. As the saying goes, "Friends come and go, but enemies accumulate." The choice is yours.

VALUABLE TIPS

- Analyze how your relationships with colleagues and direct reports in the organization impact your success and the organization's success.

- Ask for feedback on what blocks or hinders your effectiveness at building relationships.

- Make a point of meeting informally with colleagues on a regular basis.

- Encourage your colleagues to contact you for advice or support.

- Volunteer to help your colleagues when they are overwhelmed.

- Ask for assistance or counsel from colleagues when you need advice or support.

- Establish a good working relationship with at least one key member of each function or area with which you work.

- Identify "outside-the-box" relationships to help you achieve your goals.

- Guard against focusing too much on tasks and details, and not enough on people.

- Check if your work pace unintentionally puts people off.

- Name someone who is particularly effective at networking and identify specific behaviors make that person effective.

- Determine which people can give you useful information, perspectives, resources, support, or critiques.

- Attend company social events.

- Develop relationships in the external community that can help you and your organization.

- Attend professional conferences and make contacts with key people in your industry and other industries.

- Engage in community activities to connect with other business leaders.

- Use your relationship skills to help your organization build alliances.

STRATEGIES FOR ACTION

1. Cultivate a broad network to exchange ideas and rally support.

Networks are webs of people, bound to one another through trust, mutual need, and compatible goals. They are based on criteria such as professional credentials, skills, experience, position, and access. Networks provide information, support, advice, and practical assistance. They work because they benefit their members in some way.

Some networks seem to grow organically without a lot of thought and deliberate behavior. Often this occurs when people work together closely, have mutual or compatible goals, and recognize that they need one another to be most successful. Other networks need to be deliberate. They need to be grown and cultivated. They need to be recognized as strategic resources.

Identify your networks

- Look at the people with whom you work. Study organizational charts, process maps, flow charts, etc., to determine who is important to your work and the work in your part of the organization.

- Find out who is connected to you in the value chain. Also, examine the cross-functional teams in which you and your people are involved. Both are potential sources for existing or prospective networks.

- Determine who gives you advice and counsel. Who looks to you for the same? With whom does your team work most frequently? Include them in your network.

- Draw a map of your networks. This will help you understand who is included and identify opportunities to develop stronger or new relationships.

Build your internal network

- If you know little about building networks, find a strong role model. Look for people who have influence or are considered "connected." Ask people in your organization for suggestions.

- As you search for role models, remember that you may see some ways of building or maintaining relationships that are not compatible with your style. Learn what you can from people without feeling that you have to copy what someone else is doing.

- Identify people or functions that impact you and your work with whom you do not have relationships. Begin to meet with people from these areas and discuss mutual issues. Also get to know one another on an informal basis.

- Identify people who hold similar positions to yours. Choose one or two who share common job concerns and problems and meet with them informally.

- Look at your current relationships with your direct reports and the people who report to them. In what ways should you improve these relationships?

- Identify key managers and professionals at levels below yours who have knowledge or experience that will complement your skills. Find formal and informal ways to become acquainted.

- As an executive, you may discover that it is important for you to take a more significant role than you currently do with people two levels below you. Some people at that level may greatly admire you and see you as a company or industry guru. They may view having time with you as one of the advantages of working for the organization.

- Attend company social events to meet people from other areas and speak with people at a variety of organizational levels.

Establish networks outside your organization

- Consider who is in your supply chain. Are you considering changes that necessitate new or altered relationships? For example, you may decide to change the number of your suppliers. This will have an impact on the new vendors, any vendors you are dropping, and the vendors that remain.

- Consider what you can learn from people in your profession or industry and from other industries. Target the people in those organizations whom you want to add to your network.

- Benchmark an organization that is best-in-class at a particular business process. Consider developing an informal relationship with an executive from that organization to stay informed about their activities. Think about what you can offer in return, so the relationship will be beneficial to both parties.

- Establish an "environmental scanning network" that includes customers, suppliers, regulatory agencies, and related industries. Use your network to obtain information before events occur, rather than after the fact.

- Read professional newsletters and trade journals. Contact the experts mentioned who have pertinent experience or insights.

- Develop a group of government and regulatory contacts. They can alert you to upcoming legislative and regulatory agendas that may affect your organization.

Maintain your network

- Networking involves giving and sharing in addition to seeking and receiving help. Be sure you do both with the members of your network.

- Periodically stop by or telephone your contacts to stay in touch. Casual encounters and frequent contact without "wanting something" will demonstrate your interest in the other person. The frequency and tone of these meetings should be geared toward the other person's preferences rather than your own.

- The benefits of maintaining regular contact are well worth the investment. If colleagues have not heard from you in several months or years, they may not be responsive to your requests for support, as your contact will merely seem self-serving.

- Let your colleagues know they can count on you. Establish trust by maintaining confidentiality regarding sensitive information. Also, speak highly of your colleagues to others.

- Reciprocation cannot always be planned. Be open to helping when you know that a colleague is swamped or facing unexpected difficulties.

2. Stay in touch with people at all levels of the organization. A constant challenge for executives is being aware of what is happening at all levels in the company. Not only do they need to share important information, they also need to know which projects are going well and which issues need to be addressed. Staying in touch with people at all levels helps them accomplish those goals.

Stay in touch through face-to-face communication

- Decide when you should convey information in person. Some information is best communicated face-to-face, as people may have questions about the information or need to discuss their concerns and reactions.

- Be sociable and accessible. Make yourself available to others by walking around, seeking people out, having coffee, and so on. Transition times in the day (first thing in the morning, just before or after lunch, and the end of the day) are usually good times to make casual contact without being disruptive. Management by walking around (MBWA) has value.

- Let people know that you welcome questions and feedback. Find out what is going well and what their concerns are.

- Hold business- or division-wide informational meetings. Invite the entire staff, including administrative and support personnel.
    - Inform people of the organization's plans and goals and give them progress updates.
    - Ask others to comment on the organization and offer suggestions for improvement.
    - Allow time for people to ask questions.
    - Celebrate successes and contributions.

- Give each direct report some one-on-one time. Experience shows that regular, even brief, appointments with direct reports helps maintain clear direction, rapport, motivation, and productivity. In some cases, a weekly appointment will work. For others, a monthly appointment or phone conversation will be more practical and appropriate to the business.

Stay in touch through written communication

- When you receive a memo or e-mail, consider whether the information will be useful to others. If so, send them a copy and communicate your purpose for sending it.

- When you route policy memos generated by others in the organization, attach a note that explains the thrust of the policy. Highlight the parts of the policy that are most relevant and explain why the policy was made.

- As you read technical, professional, or community literature, think of who might be interested in the information. Consider sending the articles along with a personal note stating why you are sending the article. Encourage your direct reports to share information as well.

- Consider establishing an area on your intranet where people at all levels of the organization can share best practices. Also set up a place where they can send feedback on organizational policies to senior management.

- Exchange monthly activity reports with colleagues you do not see regularly.

Stay in touch through the telephone

- Consider contacting the top fifteen to fifty people on your network at least once a month. In many cases, telephone calls will be your only way to maintain such frequent contact.

- Use phone calls to alert others to actions, decisions, or developments that may interest them. Offer to send them any documentation or additional information they need.

- When you want to get input quickly from a number of people, make a series of phone calls. The response rate for phone inquiries is considerably higher than for written requests.

- If you hear a good word about someone you know, call them up and pass along the compliment.

- Use voice mail to stay in touch, but do not let it take the place of actual conversations.

3. Relate well to bosses and higher management.

Relationships with your boss and colleagues in higher management are vital to your success. As you work on initiatives, you will learn a great deal from their wisdom and experience, and gain a greater insight into how the organization truly works.

Develop a positive working relationship with your boss

- Develop an effective relationship with your boss by following a simple process: Concentrate more on what your boss needs from you than on what you want from your boss. Deliver on the results you are asked to achieve!

- Take the time to get to know your boss. What are his or her business goals? Personal goals? What is important to him or her? What irritates him or her? Find out what your boss respects and appreciates. Talk with your boss and people who have worked with him or her to get this information.

- Figure out how you can complement your boss's strengths, development needs, and personal priorities. For example, your boss may be excellent at giving feedback but not receiving it, which is causing him or her to miss important information. Make it your job to listen to people throughout the organization and capsulize their views for your boss.

- When you receive negative feedback or treatment from your boss, give him or her the benefit of the doubt regarding his or her intentions. Very few bosses truly set out to make the lives of others miserable. Check to be certain you understand what the message was, rather than focusing on how the message was delivered.

- Keep your boss informed so there are no surprises. Be open, direct, and respectful, as well as timely, in your communication.

- Say "please" and "thank you" and give compliments. Your boss is human and likes to receive sincere appreciation. Make a point of sharing when his or her help has been useful.

- Let your boss know what will help your team. Help your boss find a constructive way in which to relate to you and the team.

- Ask your boss for feedback and coaching, and thank him or her for providing constructive comments. Implement what you agree on during coaching sessions at the earliest opportunity.

- Develop an informal relationship with your boss, which will increase familiarity and rapport. Express appreciation for opportunities and shared confidences.

Give feedback to your boss

- Communicate your intention to share helpful feedback with your boss, and let him or her determine when he or she would like to receive it. When your boss is ready, give clear, specific feedback. Include both genuine compliments and constructive suggestions, if appropriate.

- Be aware of possible style issues, and adjust to them. For example, does your boss prefer to hear ideas and news in writing or face-to-face? What time of day is your boss available for informal feedback?

- Remember that most people want to be effective leaders. If you can figure out a way to deliver the message, many people will appreciate the advice. However, also remember that what you want may not be the best for you or the organization. There are times when your ideas are not necessarily right.

- Tell your boss when his or her positively intended decision or action was negatively perceived by others. It may be the only way he or she will hear about people's reaction.

Develop relationships with others in higher management

- Establish some level of familiarity and rapport with executives in higher management within your business unit, related units and functions, and corporate offices.

- Select two or three senior executives in your organization whom you respect a great deal. Meet with them to convey your respect and ask for their advice on one or more business matters. Ask about their area of expertise, what their experiences have taught them, and what advice or cautions they would give new executives.

- If you think developing relationships with specific executives will concern your boss, discuss your plans and rationale with him or her.

- Attend executive socials and meetings where you will have the opportunity to converse with colleagues that you do not normally see.

4. Relate well to direct reports.

Your direct reports are your ticket to getting results within the organization. You will find it extremely difficult to achieve your goals without their cooperation. If you relate well to them, you will understand what motivates and drives them, and will be able to channel their energies in a positive direction.

Be approachable

- Make it easy for your direct reports to keep in contact with you. Establish an open-door policy and set aside regular blocks of time during the week when you will be available.

- Spend more time "managing by walking around" or consider moving closer to your employees' work area. Being nearby will give you opportunities to ask questions and show your interest in day-to-day operations.

- If your direct reports view you as unapproachable, determine why you give this impression. Are you unavailable? Do you appear uninterested in their problems? Do you become angry when people inform you of problems? Do you look too busy? Ask for feedback from an assistant or a direct report who knows you well.

- Tell your direct reports how you plan to be more accessible and approachable, then follow through. Stating your plans in public will make you more accountable, and show that you are making a sincere effort to change your behavior.

Practice effective interpersonal communication

- Show sincere interest in your direct reports and know what is important to each individual.

- Practice simple courtesies like saying "please" and "thank you."

- Be sure to listen to your direct reports. Draw out their thoughts, ideas, and feelings in addition to sharing yours.

- Demonstrate respect for all people, even those with whom you disagree or lack understanding.

- Utilize your direct reports' ideas and experience by asking for their advice and involvement.

- Recognize and praise their contributions.

- If you invite direct reports to discuss problems, be prepared to respond nondefensively if they disagree with you. A "shoot the messenger" reaction will prevent you from receiving honest feedback in the future.

Be an active listener

- When a direct report has an important issue to discuss, give him or her your full attention. Meet in a place where you can reduce or eliminate distractions and interruptions.

- If you cannot give the person your undivided attention and the issue is important, reschedule the conversation.

- Give nonverbal attention to the speaker. Maintain regular eye contact, sit up or lean forward, turn toward the person talking, nod your head to indicate you are following the person's explanation, smile when appropriate (to show humor, irony, empathy), and the like.

- Resist interrupting a person in the middle of an explanation.

- Ask questions. Asking questions for information and elaboration may be the most underused interpersonal communication skill. Ask open-ended questions to encourage the speaker to elaborate on the topic. This will prevent you from jumping to conclusions before you hear the full story or issue.

5. Relate well to peers and colleagues.

Many executives know how to work the "streets" or formal avenues by which work is accomplished. These structures and systems handle the routine demands of an organization with reasonable effectiveness and efficiency, but they are not always adequate for tough issues. Executives who rely solely on the streets will not be totally effective. They must also work the "alleys," or informal pathways of communication and influence, to gather ideas, build support, and guide action. Many times those informal pathways are built on relationships with peers and colleagues.

Plan your network

- Draw a map of your potential network of peers and colleagues. Include lateral individuals (your peers, including those in other units or functions) and vertical individuals (upper- or lower-level coworkers in your area). List their names, their functional responsibilities, and the ways in which they can support you.

- Determine what you have to offer your network. For example:
    - you have special knowledge or expertise.
    - you can get an idea accepted by key people in the organization.
    - you can access other resources, including temporarily lending personnel from your department.

- Select at least one goal that you want to achieve. Then identify the people or groups whose support could make or break your effort. What is your current relationship with each group? What obstacles do you face? How will your proposal benefit them?

Develop your network

- Start small. Make it easy for peers and colleagues to help you. If you ask for too much, people may not be able to respond favorably and may even consider the request presumptuous. Remember, advice and information are easier to give than resources or public support.

- Let others know that you will reciprocate. If they help you, reassure them that you will help them in some way.

- When you need assistance, such as advice or input on a proposal, directly state your needs to the individual whose help you need.

- Always ask for another person's help rather than demand it. Show appreciation for what they can provide instead of pushing too hard for what you want.

- If you need support or backing from several people, show how your proposal will benefit them. This is especially important when you are trying to influence people outside of your domain.

- Involve your direct reports in a team approach to networking. Make each person responsible for developing and maintaining a good rapport and working relationship with several colleagues in other parts of the organization. This will keep you and others on your team from becoming overloaded.

6. Respect and appreciate individual differences in perspective and background.

Organizations vary in their appreciation of and accommodation to differences in people's perspectives and background. At one end of the range are organizations in which many people, if not all, come from the same background. They are from the same country or part of the country, have similar socioeconomic backgrounds, attend the same schools, and so on. People in this type of organization are sometimes suspicious of people with different backgrounds. These organizations are often filled with divisions and factions. People think the group in power is not respectful of the points of view of those with less power.

At the other end of the range are organizations in which people come from many different backgrounds and have diverse views. They are often unified by a common set of values or the pursuit of a worthy mission. Differences in expertise, status, gender, or ethnicity are secondary to the dedication they feel and the contributions they make to the whole organization.

Executives can have a direct influence over which type their organization is going to be.

Check your own prejudgments

- Examine your mind-set toward particular groups. Are you more likely to make jokes or treat a certain group differently? Perhaps you have never met someone from a certain group and believe you won't be able to work effectively with them. Such thoughts and attitudes will hinder your ability to challenge comments made about those groups.

- Reflect on your experiences in working with people from other backgrounds, and answer the following questions:
    - Do you seek out or tend to avoid people who are different from you?
    - Do you expect more from people like yourself?
    - Do you give less feedback to people from other groups for fear of being accused of racism or discrimination?
    - Do you avoid working with people if English is not their first language?

- Use your answers to determine your personal barriers to developing strong partnerships with people from diverse backgrounds.

- Challenge your assumptions about others. For example, you may assume that someone in a wheelchair cannot do a particular job. Instead of acting on that assumption, ask the person how he or she would perform the essential functions of the job. Consider reasonable accommodations.

Be a role model

- Identify people from different cultures and backgrounds within your department and begin to develop rapport with them. For example, ask about their experiences in your organization, both positive and negative.

- As you develop relationships, remember that you must be genuine. If you are getting to know people in an insincere way, they will pick up on your attitude and question your motives.

- Look for opportunities to mentor employees from diverse backgrounds. Help them learn the ropes in your area, including informal bits of knowledge that they might otherwise not learn.

- Hire people with a variety of experiences, approaches, backgrounds, and ethnicities.

- Actively seek information from people with different backgrounds and include them in decision making and problem solving.

- When you have an opportunity to form a project team, look for people who have diverse experiences and opinions. Deliberately select people who can bring different points of view.

- Hold casual conversations with a wide range of people and invite them to be part of informal work-related activities, such as lunches and social events.

Create an environment of acceptance

- Describe your organization's environment. Do your people respond favorably to diversity and cultural differences or do they tend to be aloof and suspicious of people who are different from themselves?

- Make sure people with different perspectives and experiences are actively welcomed, not merely tolerated.

- Develop an atmosphere in which it is safe for all employees to express ideas or views that differ from the norm or conventional thinking.

- Ensure that your physical surroundings represent different cultures. For example, put artwork and magazines in your reception area that reflect a number of styles and cultures.

- Implement training programs designed to develop a greater awareness of and sensitivity to differences. Pace the delivery of new information during workshops and other training, and allow time for discussion and debriefing.

Confront prejudging behavior

- Confront intolerant behavior. It is your responsibility to take the lead in defining behaviors that are unacceptable in the workplace. Discouraging and refusing to accept ethnic, racist, sexist, or other disparaging comments and behaviors will strongly influence the conduct of your group.

- Let people know when they have said something offensive. Don't attack the person, but point out how the statement is offensive. They might not have considered a "harmless" joke as potentially damaging.

- Recognize and confront aspects of your organizational culture that keep capable employees from being fully included and successful within your organization. Form an official task force to address issues of diversity and encourage team members who represent diverse backgrounds to join.

- Ask people from other countries, cultures, and market groups for ideas about how the organization can be more effective.

Champion diversity efforts

- Analyze your workgroup or department and other areas. Which groups have a diverse composition? What difference has it made to their productivity and creativity?

- Keep track of what you have learned from being on diverse teams. Refer to your experiences as you advocate for more diversity in your group.

- Identify policies and practices that need to be changed to reflect cultural differences and take the lead in changing them.

- Encourage your peers and others to frame diverse views and opinions as valuable instead of detrimental. Why do they seem different? What can you learn from them?

- Remember that changing attitudes in yourself and others will take time. Be persistent and keep striving to increase your understanding.

- Look for organizations that have been publicly recognized and rewarded for expanding their diverse and global workforces. What lessons can you learn from them?

Hold managers accountable

- Set clear, behavioral expectations in your area regarding the acceptance, appreciation, and the use of diversity.

- Hold managers accountable for making the necessary changes in their departments. Use formal channels, such as performance reviews and departmental goals.

- Establish baseline measurements from which you can evaluate your efforts to promote, manage, and value diversity. Once you have established these measures, monitor your progress on a regular basis.

7. Recognize and respond to the needs and concerns of others.

There is therapeutic value in knowing the boss is willing to listen to one's concerns—even if nothing can be done. Just taking the time to listen will convey interest in and respect for the other person.

Focus on understanding others

- "Seek first to understand, then to be understood," is one of the basic principles of Stephen Covey's book, *The Seven Habits Of Highly Effective People* (Simon & Schuster, 1989). As he indicates, it takes courage and consideration to not be understood first.

- Learn about people's needs and preferences. Some people value prestige and recognition, others value achievement, challenging assignments, or promotions. Once you know what is important to an individual, you can develop appropriate opportunities and rewards.

- Do not allow yourself to become so busy, preoccupied, or self-centered that you fail to notice the needs and concerns of others. Strengthen your relationships with others by showing sincere interest in them and what is important to them.

- Work on the attitude and skills of empathy. Draw other people out. Learn about what excites and motivates them. Listen to people's concerns.

- Collaborate with your direct reports on planning, setting goals, and evaluating their work. This will help you align personal preferences with organizational needs and heighten their sense of personal accountability. Assigning jobs that people want to take on will increase their motivation and productivity levels.

8. Adapt interpersonal style to meet the style of others.

People respond more favorably to those with whom they feel comfortable. Adjusting to another person's style is one way to help them feel more comfortable. However, executives should guard against adapting to others in an insincere way or their behavior will be perceived as manipulative and unethical.

Understand and accept individual styles

- Be a role model for understanding and accepting individual styles.

- Don't expect people to adapt to your style simply because you hold a particular position within the organization.

- Build genuine rapport by adjusting your style, energy, emotion level, and approach to better match the person you are working with.

- Make a sincere effort to understand and empathize with others. People can tell when you are pretending.

- Consider taking a personality test to gain insight into your personal style.

- Guard against relying on an informal system for categorizing people. Instead, use tools, such as the Myers–Briggs Type Indicator,® for understanding differing interpersonal styles. Remember, category systems should be used to give insight, not to create labels or excuses.

- Resist the tendency to be critical of people who operate with different interpersonal styles. People behave as they do for reasons based on personality, experience, or culture. Make an effort to understand why they act as they do.

- Don't confuse style with unacceptable behavior. If an employee is acting inappropriately, you need to deal with the situation directly, not excuse it as a style issue.

9. Act to preserve relationships, even under difficult or heated circumstances.

Relationships that do not remain at a constant level are common. Even the closest relationships become strained at times. The key is recognizing the importance of the relationship.

Recognize the importance of the relationship

- Focus on why the relationship is important. Think about your history with the person and what you would lose if you were no longer in contact.

- Recognize that pride can cause a great deal of damage. Determine whether your pride is more important than the long-term relationship.

- Acknowledge up front that certain situations may get heated or overly stressful. Agree beforehand that you will take a break when the circumstances require it.

- Resist the tendency to personalize disagreement. When a person does not like your idea, it does not necessarily mean he or she doesn't like you.

- Avoid personal attacks or put-downs when you challenge someone's idea or analysis. This will help you both focus on substantive issues and avoid damaging your relationship.

- When you have a heated exchange with someone close to you, take time when the situation has cooled down to affirm each other and reinforce the importance of the relationship.

- Avoid sarcasm. Humor can defuse tension in many situations, but sarcasm can hurt and alienate people.

10. Promote collaboration and remove obstacles to teamwork across the organization.

Many initiatives require the cooperation and combined effort of teams across the organization. Obstacles can become serious impediments if they are not addressed and are left to calcify. Executives need to identify and directly address those obstacles, so the organization can work efficiently.

Define teamwork and discuss roles

- Meet with the team and define what you mean by "teamwork." What does it mean in your area, or in the context of specific projects? Define your term so everyone has a similar understanding.

- Openly discuss the obstacles that people face as they work with teams across the organization. Are they systemic, interpersonal, or situational?

- Develop a vision and charter to help your team focus on relevant issues.

- Clarify the role of each team in larger initiatives.

- Assign people to teams, projects, and task forces because of what they offer as participants, not because of their position or power.

- Move toward team-based appraisals and rewards rather than focus on individual performance. Evaluate people on their willingness and ability to work as teams in the organization.

Promote teamwork across the organization

- Emphasize common goals whenever you work with your team or confer with others on organizational matters.

- Determine which structures and processes are conducive to teamwork and collaboration, and build them into projects.

- Constantly solicit ideas on how you can improve teamwork across the organization.

- Encourage people across the organization to share best practices and innovative ideas for improving teamwork.

- Point out how teams can benefit from collaboration. Outline solid business reasons, using concrete examples and statistics.

- Watch for "we versus they" thinking and discussions. Check yourself and caution others when they talk in those terms.

- Set up shared assignments (where a person's time is split between two departments) for some people in your group and ask colleagues in other functions and units to do the same.

- Require project teams or task forces to include one or more people from outside the immediate and most logical group of people.

11. Seek to improve how the management team works together.

As an executive you belong to at least two teams. You are part of a team led by your boss and you lead a team of your direct reports. You can most directly affect these two teams.

Strengthen the teamwork of your direct reports

- Meet with your direct reports on a regular basis so they feel like a team. Develop shared goals and discuss your progress.

- Help team members better understand one another. Ask each one to share information about the work they are doing.

- Have a retreat or team-building session with your direct reports at least once or twice a year. Use this time for planning, creating and/or recommitting to a vision, proposing joint projects, and making necessary decisions together.

Strengthen your role as a team member

- Encourage your boss to view you and your colleagues as a team, rather than simply viewing you as a collection of individual executives with differing responsibilities.

- Bring issues that require discussion and collaboration with other team members to your boss's staff meetings. Tell your colleagues that you want to use them as sounding boards and advisors.

- Offer to partner with one or more colleagues on projects, problems, or organizational initiatives.

- Ask for and offer suggestions on how you and your colleagues can cooperate and collaborate more frequently and effectively. Work to champion and implement some of those suggestions.

RESOURCES

The resources for this chapter begin on page 450.

12
INSPIRING
TRUST

———

ESTABLISH OPEN, CANDID, TRUSTING RELATIONSHIPS;
TREAT ALL INDIVIDUALS FAIRLY AND WITH RESPECT;
BEHAVE IN ACCORDANCE WITH EXPRESSED BELIEFS
AND COMMITMENTS; MAINTAIN HIGH STANDARDS
OF INTEGRITY.

KEY BEHAVIORS

———

1. *Establish open, candid, and trusting relationships.*
2. *Maintain high standards of personal integrity.*
3. *Behave in accordance with expressed beliefs and commitments.*
4. *Collaborate as a team player; never undermine others for own gain.*
5. *Treat others fairly and consistently.*

INTRODUCTION

Imagine that you are playing a game of Ping-Pong in a room where curtains hang behind you and your opponent. As you play the game, bowling balls roll out from under the curtains and across the floor. Sometimes you get hit, at other times you are able to step aside. While you dodge bowling balls, someone randomly interjects rule changes for the game, which often result in a loss of points for you. Would it be difficult for you to maintain your concentration and motivation under these circumstances? This scenario illustrates the effect of low trust in a business environment. People find it very difficult to maintain the necessary emotional equilibrium to be motivated and productive in such surroundings.

Nowhere is the task of defining executive leadership more challenging and less tangible than in the domain of trust. Also, no responsibility is more important. By its very definition, trust is not something executives do. It is something they earn through their behavior, principles, character, personal qualities, and relationships. Trust may not be necessary for asserting power and control, but it is essential for winning commitment and loyal support from others.

Trust operates on multiple levels. To some degree trust is both a character and a competence issue. People want to know if you are honest and open about your agenda and actions, and if they can trust your intentions. They also want to know if you have the skills, resources, time, and wherewithal to deliver on your commitments.

Executives not only have to earn personal trust, they also need to set the stage for trust in their organizations. To maximize their organization's value, they must earn the trust of important stakeholders such as employees, customers, and stockholders.

Acting in ways that are consistent with your expressed values and beliefs, living up to your commitments, and treating people fairly will help earn the trust of others. A persistent, good faith effort on your part will send an important message to the people in your organization and make many of the things you are trying to accomplish easier. Your team will willingly follow your lead, even in ambiguous circumstances, if they know you are honest, competent, and trustworthy.

Your behavior sets the expectation for your part of the organization. By watching the behavior of others, you will be able to discern the type of example you set.

Inspiring trust is a very subtle and multifaceted phenomenon. This chapter will help you develop trusting relationships with those you lead, and help you understand why trust breaks down.

VALUABLE TIPS

- Remember the law of the harvest; in a relationship area such as trust, you will reap what you sow.

- Trust is difficult and takes time to build—but it is easy to destroy.

- Building trust often begins by building a personal relationship with others through listening to what is on their minds and hearts.

- Maintain sufficient consistency or predictability so people know what to count on from you.

- Be accessible to your people—executives who are inaccessible cannot possibly expect to be trusted just because they have a title.

- Go out and talk to your people and other constituents to find out what they value.

- Deliver on your commitments and encourage others to do the same.

- Avoid careless communication; if you are clear about what you mean, there is less likelihood that others will find your statements misleading.

- Never knowingly mislead or lie.

- Be open with others when discussing conduct that might look to others as inconsistent or incompatible with a prior promise.

- Consciously display your leadership values, principles, and ethics in the actions you take and decisions you make.

- Find a common ground on issues and build support and consensus around a core of shared principles and values.

- Admit your mistakes or your part in them and resist putting a self-serving spin on the truth.

- Protect the interests of those who are not present and those who have less power than you.

- Convey the same thinking and position in a public discussion or meeting that you share in a private conversation.

- Apply your company's code of business ethics judiciously.

- Work actively to rebuild trust after the organization goes through a difficult period.

STRATEGIES FOR ACTION

1. Establish open, candid, and trusting relationships.

Trust is a quality of the reciprocal relationship between you and the people you are leading. Trust can expand or contract; therefore, you must regularly monitor its level.

As Kouzes and Posner (*Credibility: How Leaders Gain and Lose It, Why People Demand It*, Jossey-Bass 1995) note,

> "Leadership is a relationship, and strong relationships are built on mutual understanding. Leadership is a dialogue, not a monologue. Constituents come to believe in their leaders—to see them as worthy of their trust—when they believe that the leaders have their best interests at heart."

Build trusting relationships

- Trusting relationships are established and sustained by each party's willingness to appreciate the other's needs. People will grant you greater trust if four conditions are met:
    - You are clear about your expectations, intentions, and agenda.
    - They believe what you say.
    - They believe that you understand their interests.
    - They believe that you will protect their interests.

- Honesty and the appreciation of mutual interests are the baselines of any enduring relationship. They are indispensable for leading people through a period of crisis or change. People will allow you to lead them into uncharted territory if they believe you are competent, that you care about them and their concerns, and that you will tell them the truth.

- Consider your experience with gaining the trust of others.
    - Who are your models of trusted leaders? What did you learn from them?
    - How have you earned the trust of people who initially mistrusted you?
    - What is your experience in helping others establish trust?
    - How have you regained trust that was lost?
    - What is your experience in gaining the trust of people from other cultures?

Demonstrate competence

- An impeccable character is not sufficient to inspire trust; ethical leaders also need to convince people they know what they are doing. People will not rally behind your initiative unless they believe you have the knowledge, judgment, and ability to make critical decisions and get the job done. This does not imply that you must know everything. Those who claim to know everything are often suspect.

- You are in your position because you have expertise of genuine value. Build credibility with others by tactfully demonstrating confidence in your ability. Share information about your background and expertise. Provide others with information on your experience as it relates to the current challenges in your position, but avoid overstating your accomplishments or expertise.

- Establish your credibility each time you assume a new role, begin an assignment with new people, or undergo a significant shift in responsibility. You cannot assume that the extent of your expertise is known.

- Demonstrate competence without resorting to self-aggrandizement. Identify what you lack without losing your ability to guide and influence those who have the expertise you need. Be willing to listen and learn from a predecessor or others who may be familiar with your new responsibilities.

- Maintain credibility across the organization. The perception of your expertise needs to be fostered, so others will continue to count on you. Consider volunteering for new assignments where your expertise will be of value to others.

Demonstrate trust in others

- Remember that trust is reciprocal. If you do not trust people, they will have a difficult time trusting you.

- Eliminate policies, checkpoints, reviews, and sign-offs that provide no value other than to verify that people did what they said they would do. Organizational policies and procedures are often scar tissue from former organizational mistakes or injuries. Consider whether the procedures are still relevant and necessary, or whether they merely convey a lack of trust.

- Give your direct reports greater latitude, authority, and choice. Openly negotiate the degree of latitude people have and how they can earn more. Work with others to establish clear boundaries on authority and autonomy. Stick to your part of the arrangement and expect them to do the same.

- Assume that people want to do a good job. Provide training, coaching, and support to help them improve. Remove roadblocks that may be interfering with their effectiveness. Do not punish or criticize errors until you understand all sides of the story. Presume that people have done things for a good reason and they will try to avoid similar problems in the future.

Show real understanding of others

- People will not trust you to act in their best interests until you demonstrate that you genuinely understand their needs and priorities. Practice good listening skills. Until you listen well, you cannot fully understand others, and they will not feel completely understood.

- Understanding other people's viewpoints is not the same as agreeing with them. When you disagree with others' opinions, challenge yourself to see issues from their point of view. Your goal is to make them feel that you understand and respect their views, even if you continue to disagree.

- Ask people about their needs, goals, and priorities. Find out what they enjoy about their work and what frustrates them. Show that you have taken their interests into account and allocate opportunities in accordance with their expressed interests.

- Look for opportunities to protect and obtain the things that are important to people, and ask for opinions from those who have placed a priority on a particular issue.

- When priorities clash and you cannot give people what they want, let them know that you considered their interests and that you did what you could to promote and protect their views.

Demonstrate candor

- Open yourself up to others in a genuine way. Let people see multiple dimensions of your life and personality. Share your history, interests, hopes, and needs, and allow people to discover the real person behind your title.

- Failing to share what is on your mind can be counterproductive. People are cautious about leaders they do not understand; therefore, more will be lost than gained by cultivating a mystique.

- Tell your direct reports about your expectations, priorities, and intentions. If you neglect this step, they will spend time trying to read your mind instead of directing their energy toward achieving organizational goals. Leaders who are trusted make themselves known and make their positions clear.

- Complexity and ambiguity, present in most organizations, leave a great deal of latitude for misunderstandings. Never assume that people know implicitly what you are trying to accomplish. Many executives find that their good intentions backfire due to misinterpretations. As you act, communicate the purpose behind your actions.

- Hold formal and informal discussions with your direct reports. Share your thoughts and the reasons behind your decisions. Connect your expectations, priorities, and goals to the activities of your direct reports.

Be accessible

- It is hard to sustain trust if you are out of touch. Create opportunities for people to find you and talk about their concerns. Hearing both good and bad news will improve your decisions, minimize the number of surprises you face, and prevent crises.

- Open, trusting relationships cannot flourish in settings that are based on hierarchy and privilege. A posture of special privilege will prevent candid exchanges and insulate you from people and information. Minimize real and perceived barriers that create distance and convey the message that you are superior or off-limits.

- Review your organization's practices regarding office space, perks, and resources. Eliminate special treatment that suggests organizational rules do not apply to everyone.

- Seek feedback on the type of first impression you make on others and find out how others generally view you. People may be hesitant to open up and speak candidly with you if you come across as an extremely serious or intense person. If you are seen as unapproachable, investigate the reasons why you give that impression. Are you unavailable? Do you appear uninterested in the concerns of others? Do you become angry when you are informed about problems? Do you seem aloof? Adjust your leadership style and actions to display the kind of image you prefer.

- If your people often have trouble reaching you, consider holding at least one transition time each day during which you don't schedule appointments or meetings. The most obvious transition times are first thing in the morning as people are coming in, just before lunch, just after lunch, and toward the end of the day.

Actively avoid behaviors and actions that undermine trust

- You and other organizational leaders undermine trust when you:
    - Breach the faith of others through unethical behavior.
    - Operate from a posture of privilege rather than partnership.
    - Assume, for the most part, that people are fundamentally untrustworthy.
    - Fail to readily and clearly communicate direction, purpose, priorities, and information.

- Trust can also be undermined when:
    - The organization does not consistently deliver on its promises.
    - Members of your organization do not trust each other because of obvious internal contradictions and inconsistencies.
    - People do not maintain necessary confidentiality.
    - People are open and honest about successes, but not problems and mistakes.

Support organizational alignment

- It takes more than one person to build trust; trust requires a relationship. Executives can act in ways that will foster and help inspire trust. For example, evaluate the following issues:
    - How do your organization's policies and practices show trust and commitment to employees?
    - How can you make business policies and practices consistently respectful of employees throughout the world?
    - Do you consciously integrate high ethical standards and fairness into your organizational policies and practices? Does the organization have a code of ethics?
    - How do your organization's business practices and policies reflect its view of people? Are people competent and valued or are they expendable resources?
    - How do you advocate high standards of ethics and fairness across the organization? How is that conveyed to people?

- Emphasize integrity, concern for people, ethics, and orientation to company values and policies in documents such as handbooks, policy statements, business practices, and the like.

2. Maintain high standards of personal integrity.

The trust that others bestow on you must be anchored in your personal integrity. Therefore, an important step in building trust is being clear with yourself and others about what you stand for and what guides your behavior.

Personal integrity, built on a clear sense of your guiding beliefs and values, is the foundation of trust. Your actions must flow naturally from who you are. Develop a strong core of guiding principles and make a consistent and good faith effort to demonstrate them in your daily conduct. No one can be a perfect role model, but others will notice and respect a sincere effort.

Develop a leadership credo

- Be clear about what assumptions, values, and beliefs guide your decisions, actions, and relationships.

- Articulate the underlying values and principles that guide your leadership, decision making, and treatment of others.
    - What constitutes your spiritual core? What assumptions, values, and beliefs guide you in your daily life?
    - What values do you refer to when you make tough decisions?
    - What values and principles do you promote and fight for in your organization?

- Draft a credo that articulates how your beliefs, values, and principles guide your leadership. Begin with the following sentence: "This is what I believe and stand for as a leader: _____." Resist listing platitudes that do not sincerely express what you believe. When it is complete, set it aside for a few weeks. When you return to the document, consider whether or not it inspires you, and how it affects your current role.

- Interview leaders whom you admire and ask them to describe their leadership credo. What are their guiding values and principles? How do they apply values to their leadership? Evaluate whether or not their values inspire you and consider incorporating them into your credo.

- Share your credo with several people who know you well. Encourage them to describe instances in which you acted in accordance with your values and principles, and situations where your behavior was inconsistent. Ask for suggestions on how to convey your credo in a manner that is clear, practical, and compelling.

- Read Max DePree's books, *Leadership is an Art* (Dell Publishing, 1989) and *Leadership Jazz* (Dell Publishing, 1993). They will give you an example of a well-developed leadership credo by a CEO who led a successful and highly regarded company for a number of years.

Make ethical choices

- Consider the following questions when you are faced with problems and decisions that pose ethical issues:
  - What consequences will my decision have in the short-term? In the long-term?
  - Is the situation harmful or dangerous to others?
  - If someone else came to me with this problem, what advice would I offer?
  - How does this decision measure up against my personal standards and the organization's values?
  - Are my needs, the needs of those I report to, or the needs of those I advise, preventing me from seeing the full problem?
  - What would I think and feel if I were on the "receiving" end of the decision?

- Once you have decided on a course of action, consider the following questions:
  - Will I be proud of my decision a year from now?
  - If the situation and my actions were taken to a higher level in the organization, would the people I admire in senior management approve?
  - Am I willing to face the inherent risks of this action, including the consequences for my career? Am I willing to take the heat for a controversial decision that I believe is ethically right?
  - Am I able to look at myself in the mirror and say that I am comfortable with this action? Would my family be comfortable with my actions if they were told about the situation or if it were reported in the media?

- Executive leadership can be lonely. Develop a trusted resource to serve as a sounding board for the ethical issues you face.
  - Choose someone who can tell it to you straight.
  - Seek guidance from ethical and spiritual mentors.
  - Consult with people in your organization who are known for making principled decisions during difficult times.
  - Identify people from other organizations who have faced similar situations and ask them how they handled the problem.

3. Behave in accordance with expressed beliefs and commitments.

Executives lead and influence others through personal relationships and encounters. You and other executives set and maintain standards and norms, and exhibit and promote preferred ways of acting. People view you as role model to some degree; therefore, you need to be an advocate for ethics and high standards in organizational relationships.

Serve as a role model

- Your position and personal power give you a great deal of potential influence over the standards that will be followed in your organization. Be conscientious about "walking your talk." Resist saying too much until, or unless, your conduct demonstrates your stated beliefs.

- Trust is earned, in part, by consistently displaying trustworthy patterns of behavior. Do other people view you as reliable and consistent?
    - Is your behavior predictable and consistent with your stated positions?
    - Do you follow through on promises and avoid excuses?
    - How do you respond to constructive criticism?
    - How do you treat confidences?
    - How do you convey negative information?
    - Do you take responsibility for your mistakes and omissions?
    - Do you put the interests of others on a par with your own?

- Promote fairness through your actions and consider whether or not your decisions treat people equally. Regardless of their role or position, people should be afforded respect.

- Be vigilant in protecting the interests of those who are not present or those who do not have a formal voice in decisions that affect them.

- When you feel the need to question others' motives, guard against jumping to conclusions or accusations. Resist blaming others. Try to be as objective as possible.

Maintain your standards under pressure

- When you weigh decisions against your guiding principles, you may find that the right choice is not always in your best interest, particularly in the short-term. Business challenges and poor results may tempt you to cut corners and justify exceptions to your standards. Stay the course and expect the same of others, even when temptation seems irresistible.

- Your standards and principles will be particularly tested in circumstances where the tide of opinion is against them. At such critical moments, challenge your colleagues. Openly compare their opinions and decisions against the organization's values and ethics criteria. Encourage others to do the same.

- Every day you have opportunities to promote your values and determine acceptable boundaries for decision making. Demonstrate your values when you discuss problems, make decisions, talk about personnel issues, explore new strategies, and respond to crises.

- When trust is shaken, make a good faith effort to rebuild it. Often your reactions to events show more about what you stand for than how you act when you are on your best behavior.

Maintain a strong focus on ethics in your organization

- Challenge others to take ethical considerations into account before they make decisions.

- Encourage others to question practices they cannot support. When ethical concerns are brought to your attention, respond to them in a serious manner.

- Create a safety zone where people can raise sensitive ethical questions, and protect employees who are willing to raise concerns. Encourage open-door policies whereby people can talk with their bosses without revealing names or confidential information. Permit employees to go to higher levels in the organization with their problems when it is necessary to get constructive action.

- Establish forums for discussing ethical concerns that are relevant to your industry. Inform and involve your colleagues (or boss if appropriate) when you find yourself in situations that create ethical dilemmas. Share your problems and ask for their input and advice.

- Write, revise, or expand your organizational code of ethics. Refer to the code regularly and distribute it widely. Emphasize organizational values in handbooks, policy statements, and job descriptions. Provide training in business ethics during employee orientation and offer seminars for existing personnel.

- Encourage, support, and reward behavior that upholds high ethical standards. Deal swiftly and consistently with people who violate organizational ethics, regardless of their position or status.

Establish consistent, fair organizational practices

- Audit business practices for consistency and honesty. Does your organization conduct informal business according to organizational policies and professional standards? Do supervisors and managers consistently uphold standards of fairness or do they tacitly compromise ethics by looking the other way?

- Review your practices regarding hiring, promotions, and dismissals. Do you retain and promote people who embody organizational values and advocate their use? Do you reject, dismiss, and discipline people who do not?

- Minimize arbitrary inequities in compensation and rewards. Ask your direct reports if employment practices, such as compensation, promotions, bonuses, assignments, and perks, are perceived as fair and equitable. People usually accept a situation in which rewards are granted on the basis of contribution, tenure, and merit, but they often resent rewards based on favoritism.

4. Collaborate as a team player; never undermine others for own gain.

Trust cannot be established when people doubt someone's motives or feel that they will be undermined. In such cases, people focus on their own agendas instead of working toward a common goal. Executives need to take the lead in establishing a collaborative environment for their teams.

Be a role model for collaboration

- Actively break down barriers and vested interests that prevent cooperation between teams. Watch for excessive territoriality in others and bring it to their attention. Catch yourself when you are more concerned about your team's success than that of the organization.

- Watch for actions and attitudes that reflect the interests of individuals or subgroups. Propose alternative actions that will serve broader organizational interests.

- Seek to find a common ground for agreement on which everyone can stand. Show how individual values, concerns, and interests can be served by coming to consensus on a set of common values.

- Serve as a coach and facilitator in meetings, particularly when there is friction within your own staff. Model appropriate listening and cooperative behaviors when dealing with opposing parties. Facilitate a discussion of mutual goals and try to find areas of agreement.

Do not view circumstances as a zero-sum game

- The basic premise of the "zero-sum game" metaphor states that when a person or group gains something, others must lose a similar amount. When competition is fierce, the temptation to go for the win can be overwhelming.

- To counterbalance this lure, step back from the situation, take a long-term view, and look for win/win solutions. Weigh the implications of pressing for personal gain (or the gain of some group) versus a negotiated outcome where all parties' interests are protected. Consider the following questions:
    - What do I stand to gain or lose in the ongoing relationship?
    - What will it take for me to trust the motives of the other party?
    - Am I willing to invest the time and effort required to devise a collaborative solution?
    - What are the short- and long-term implications of each option?

Demonstrate reliability and protect confidential information

- Resist the urge to make empty promises to buy yourself time or prevent others from pressuring you. Also avoid making statements that others will misconstrue as promises. Clear, unambiguous statements will help you prevent confusion.

- Do not make commitments you cannot keep. Tackle only what you have a reasonable chance of accomplishing. Develop the habit of asking for more time to consider a decision rather than making unwise commitments. Make realistic time and resource estimates, and consult others before promising their time.

- Set organizational guidelines for handling confidential information, such as personnel and salary data. Abide by these guidelines and convey the expectation that others should follow suit.

- Publicly support positions that you privately pledged to endorse. If you promised someone that you would support them on a project, do not remain silent when it is presented in a meeting.

5. Treat others fairly and consistently.

People are very cognizant of how they are treated compared to others inside or outside their group. If you tend to treat one group more or less favorably, even if it is unintentional, it can harm your reputation and your ability to work with them. It is important that you monitor how you treat various groups, and make a conscious effort to be consistent in your behavior.

Audit your personal consistency

- The following statements describe someone who is unduly inconsistent and unpredictable. If they apply to you, people probably have trouble trusting you, predicting your actions, and counting on you to protect their interests.
    - Do you frequently change your mind?
    - Are you known for the "initiative of the month"?
    - Do you routinely shortcut procedures and policies in the name of expediency?
    - Are you seen as someone whose decisions can be swayed by the last person who talked to you?
    - Do you placate people by giving in to their demands or complaints?
    - Do you say "yes" when you know you cannot deliver?

- Make every effort to behave and act in a consistent manner. Resist overcommitting or committing too quickly to a particular position. Weigh your decision in light of the principles and priorities that relate to the issue.

- Do not make snap decisions. Take time to think through the implications of a particular action. You may want to list the pros and cons of the issue and wait a day before making your decision. This will prompt you to consider more factors and lessen the perception that you are easily swayed by others.

- When you change direction, explain your reasons. Allow yourself to hear that others think the change is unnecessary or that it makes no sense to them.

Admit mistakes and limitations

- People often believe that executives do not admit their mistakes. Public relations and spin control have taught them that people in power have the capacity to cover up the full truth and protect themselves.

- When you make a mistake, surprise people with your candor, your willingness to admit fault, and your desire to make amends. Remember, most people will forgive mistakes of judgment, but they will not easily forgive cover-ups or mistakes caused by ill intentions. Avoid exacerbating mistakes with excuses.

- When trust has been breached, make amends by following the RESTORE model.
    - *Return* to your core values. Reflect on your priorities and guiding principles, and determine how they affected your actions.
    - *Evaluate* what went wrong. Be honest with yourself. Identify your role in the situation and determine what you could have done differently. Gather information on any problems your conduct may have caused and take responsibility for your actions.
    - *Structure* what you need to do to make amends. Strategically plan how you will approach the problem and confront the people whose trust has been damaged.
    - *Talk* with people. Admit your mistakes and apologize for any problems they may have caused. Be willing to say "I'm sorry."
    - *Offer* resolution and restitution. Ask what you can do to make things right.
    - *Reaffirm* your desire for a trusting relationship. Discuss terms for continuing your relationship and consider ways to regain trust in the future.
    - *Eliminate* the chance of repeating your mistake. Identify traps you walked into and avoid them in the future. Enlist the help of others to prevent the problem from recurring.

RESOURCES

The resources for this chapter begin on page 452.

13
FOSTERING
OPEN DIALOGUE

PROMOTE A FREE FLOW OF INFORMATION
AND COMMUNICATION THROUGHOUT THE
ORGANIZATION (UPWARD, DOWNWARD,
AND ACROSS); LISTEN ACTIVELY; ENCOURAGE
OPEN EXPRESSION OF IDEAS AND OPINIONS.

KEY BEHAVIORS

1. *Create open channels of communication.*
2. *Keep others well informed.*
3. *Express ideas clearly and concisely.*
4. *Promote frank discussion of tough issues.*
5. *Express opinions without intimidating others.*
6. *Listen carefully to input and feedback.*
7. *Ask questions to clarify ambiguous messages.*
8. *Encourage others to express contrary views.*
9. *Exhibit nonverbal behaviors that show receptivity to others' ideas.*

INTRODUCTION

The changing environment of today's organizations presents executives with unusual communication challenges and opportunities. Technology has made it easier and faster to get the word out; unfortunately, the word itself has become more problematic. Open dialogue and executive forthrightness are valuable concepts—when they work. However, they do not always get the expected results.

Dynamic workplaces demand open communication so people can hear and talk about business and organizational changes, concerns, events, policies, problems, and opportunities. Multidirectional and multichannel communication help people keep their bearings in a turbulent environment. Managing those directions and channels is an executive imperative.

Executives directly affect the degree of openness allowed in organizational interactions by demonstrating the ground rules for one-on-one and group communication. As role models, they must use communication styles that convey clear messages, facilitate dialogue across functions and areas, and determine and clarify boundaries for larger discussions.

Executive behavior does more to foster open dialogue in an organization than any other factor. Executives can directly affect the degree of openness allowed in their organizations by establishing and demonstrating communication styles, structures, and systems that facilitate open discussion of more routine as well as difficult issues. They can also support solid, trustworthy relationships between people at all levels in an organization by sharing information and going beyond communicating only what is necessary.

VALUABLE TIPS

- View sharing information as an opportunity rather than a burden.

- Encourage your leadership team to regularly keep one another informed and share information.

- Find out what your direct reports and others in the organization want to know.

- Hold periodic meetings, even multiple level ones, to share information about recent developments in the organization.

- Regularly solicit information from your direct reports and people across the organization, especially on the most important issues.

- Use the "streets and alleys" in your communication efforts (that is, informal as well as structured communication opportunities).

- Actively encourage and welcome discussion of difficult or controversial issues.

- Consider cultural differences when you communicate with others.

- Regularly check with people to see if they understood the intent of your message.

- Ask others for clarification if you are not sure of a message's meaning.

- Ask your direct reports and others to contact people across the organization to get the information they need.

- Use a variety of communication tools and opportunities.

- Express disagreement with others without intimidating, belittling, or silencing them.

- Seek to understand others before making sure that you are understood.

- Express appreciation and respect for others when they share contrary opinions or sensitive feelings.

- Ask for suggestions from people in your part of the organization how you can more effectively foster open dialogue.

- Do not "shoot the messenger" of bad news when they have accurate information.

- Resist the tendency to let crisis management methods abandon communication strategies in favor of expediency.

- Update the people in your organization on important issues even when nothing new has developed.

- Recognize and use effective communicators in your organization.

- Use electronic information channels to pass along and clarify information that does not require a face-to-face exchange.

STRATEGIES FOR ACTION

1. Create open channels of communication.

Effective executive communicators promote sharing of information throughout the organization, which includes using active upward, downward, and lateral communication. They let people know that they value open channels of communication, and make sure their practices support their platitudes about communication.

Define your role

- Explore what fostering open channels of communication means to you. What part does it play in your success as an executive, in your team's success, and in your organization's success?

- Meet with your boss to discuss his or her view of the role communication should play in your current position. Ask for details regarding your communication priorities, specific activities whose frequency you should increase or decrease, and how you can prepare yourself for future roles.

- Ask for input and feedback from your direct reports and others on your current ability to foster open communication. Where do they see room for improvement? Again, ask for specific suggestions.

Approach communication in a systematic way

- Find motivated people on your leadership team and across the organization who have excellent communication skills. Form alliances with them to discuss strategies, approaches, and action steps for fostering open dialogue.

- Take advantage of the diverse styles and approaches to communication that already exist in your organization.

- Use, support, and expand existing systems that encourage an open exchange of ideas and information.

- Maximize the conditions that foster open communication in your organization and minimize any factors that inhibit dialogue.

- Create a personal communication strategy for reaching all of your important constituencies inside and outside the organization.

Promote sharing of information throughout the organization

- Set aside some time during meetings to discuss communication issues within the team. If it is practical, schedule weekly meetings. Weekly meetings of short duration are more effective than infrequent meetings that go on for hours.

- Provide mechanisms that give employees an opportunity to bring their questions, concerns, complaints, and suggestions to senior management. This may take many forms: regularly scheduled feedback sessions between employees and top executives; organization-wide employee attitude or opinion surveys; hotlines where employees can voice their concerns, ideas, and opinions; and anonymous suggestion boxes using both paper and e-mail options.

- Provide avenues for information to flow from the top down in your organization. Employees who are informed about what is happening in their organization will be more active and involved. In addition to newsletters and memos, try using more immediate and engaging vehicles such as face-to-face meetings, e-mail, and internal broadcasts.

- Encourage time- and talent-sharing across functions. Set an example by sharing members of your team with areas that are under pressure. Create cross-functional teams or temporary task forces to work on organizational projects or issues. Make sure that a variety of functions, levels, and experience is represented on the team. Such teams will increase communication across functions, and provide more holistic solutions to problems and issues.

Define an ideal communication environment

The following example shows one executive team's ideal communication environment. They defined seven characteristics:

- *Open and accessible:* Create a nonthreatening atmosphere that identifies issues and solutions and focuses on issue-based problem solving. Encourage people to give information and suggestions upward, downward, and laterally.

- *Results oriented:* Clearly communicate the organization's direction and departmental responsibilities. Use daily communication to build rapport, share information, increase understanding, and solve problems. Encourage constructive, problem-solving feedback.

- *Supportive:* Praise people for doing good work. Stress a sense of teamwork on the group level and evaluate success in terms of what is best for the organization as a whole. Support cooperation and coordination of efforts between groups.

- *Dynamic:* Make organizational processes fluid, flexible, and growth oriented within a basic structure. Keep bureaucracy at a minimum.

- *Risk taking:* Create a work environment where taking risks is encouraged. Communicate all ideas, even if they are inappropriate or impractical.

- *Thorough:* Assimilate new employees quickly. Provide basic policies and policy interpretations as needed. Clearly communicate and manage accountability for results.

- *Anticipatory:* Plan ahead to prevent "fire fighting" and crisis management. Conduct anticipatory problem solving to aid resource planning and coordination.

Increase your cross-cultural communication skills

- Learn more about your communication style. In *Workforce America!* (Irwin Professional Publishing, 1990) Marilyn Loden and Judith Rosener specify eleven basic elements of communication. The opposite ends of a spectrum are shown for each element. Based on your day-to-day interactions, determine where you fit on each spectrum and pay special attention to any elements where you are close to one end.
    1. Mode of interaction: initiating vs. listening
    2. Reference point: individual vs. group
    3. Authority base: facts vs. intuition
    4. Degree of self-disclosure: impersonal vs. personal
    5. Mode of expression: rational vs. emotional
    6. Method of support: challenge vs. agreement
    7. Method of disagreement: confrontation vs. compliance
    8. Vocal characteristics: low vs. high
    9. Method of assertion: direct vs. indirect
    10. Physical proximity: distant vs. close
    11. Reliance on protocol: high vs. low

- Identify where organizational traditions, practices, and culture restrict communication to one style, limiting diverse expressions and opinions.

- Examine your personal preferences regarding communication styles. Do you feel some styles are better than others? Becoming aware of your personal preferences and assumptions will help you recognize how different styles can interfere with the open exchange of ideas and information.

- Use cross-cultural communication skills in all of your interactions, not only those where obvious differences are involved. Differences in background and experience can have a profound effect on the way messages are sent and received. Openness and awareness will help you engage others in productive cross-cultural dialogue.

- In general, remember that different is merely different, not better or worse. This will help you avoid the judgmental attitude that people may have about differences in communication and other areas.

2. Keep others well informed.

The communication demands at the senior levels of any organization are relentless. Most actions and decisions require some form and often multiple forms of communication. Executives must proactively drive this process, and encourage it throughout their area, unit, or function.

Share information strategically

- When appropriate, share the context for your decisions and talk about their implications. Link them to the goals of your department, the work of other groups, and the organization's broader vision and strategic priorities.

- Share the responsibility for keeping others well informed by delegating certain communication tasks. Increasing the connection points will broaden your capabilities and empower others on your team.

- Use a "cascade" approach to communication whenever appropriate. That is, let your direct reports know what they should actively communicate further down the organization. Your communication with them is just the first step in the communication effort.

- Include a feedback or upward communication mechanism with any major downward communication effort. Let your direct reports know you want to hear what people in the organization are saying and feeling.

Communicate proactively during change

- When significant organizational changes are coming, convey information at the following stages:
    1. in advance, to prepare people for the upcoming changes,
    2. when the change is officially announced,
    3. during the implementation process, and
    4. following the change process to determine its effect on people's understanding, attitudes, and productivity.

- Thoroughly inform all people who will be affected by a change. Answer questions during the process, but resist being drawn into speculation. Be a role model for sharing information by being clear about what you can and cannot say.

- Multidirectional communication (up, down, and across) produces employees who are better informed and more involved. It creates an "early warning system" that allows you to identify potential problems and take action before an issue becomes a crisis, especially during times of change. Be sure to create vertical and horizontal communication flows in your area.

Use the media to your advantage

- Learning how to interact with the media is not something that comes naturally to all executives, but it can mean the difference between success and failure. Consult your public relations department or agency for coaching and training.

- Build credibility with the media. Maintain open and active communication channels and address negative issues head-on. Silence or stonewalling the media can turn a routine story into an investigation.

- Participate in the interview process instead of letting outside sources speak for or about your organization. This will help your organization receive balanced and accurate coverage by the media during a public relations crisis.

Use a wide variety of communication channels and media

- Set up systems for communicating with your boss, your direct reports, the organization, and outside constituencies.

- When deciding on the vehicle for your message, consider your overall goals. Are you primarily informing, soliciting ideas, or gathering information? Is this a onetime event or part of an overall organizational initiative?

- People may not pay attention to the same communication vehicle every time. Therefore, important messages should be sent through at least two channels. For example, follow an announcement or presentation with a written memo or e-mail.

- Keep up-to-date on emerging communication media. Expand your options beyond organizational newsletters and the lunch room bulletin board. Voice mail, e-mail, video conferencing, and televised organizational newscasts can increase the speed and effectiveness of your message.

3. Express ideas clearly and concisely.

Many people believe that being verbose indicates knowledge or power. However, it can bar effective communication by obscuring your main points and distracting the listener. Expressing yourself clearly and concisely includes both content and delivery (or nonverbal) features of communication.

Speak with precision

- Ask a trusted colleague to signal you when you stray off the topic or become redundant. Follow the cue to be concise.

- Pay attention to the behavior of your listeners. If they appear restless, you are losing their interest. Get back on track.

- Determine whether your key points are getting through by asking people to summarize what you said. Their feedback will alert you to any lack of precision on your part.

Speak with enthusiasm and expressiveness

- Your communication style, whether in conversations or presentations, can directly impact your ability to convince and influence others. Ask a trusted colleague with whom you regularly interact to evaluate your style and its impact in a variety of situations. Determine whether you need to speak more slowly, use less jargon, or change your style in some other way.

- Watch how you communicate your attitudes nonverbally. Others will make decisions about your attitudes toward yourself, toward issues, and toward themselves based on what you convey nonverbally. Energy and expressiveness show interest, enthusiasm, and conviction.

- Videotape a meeting or presentation during which you are trying to persuade others. View the tape and assess whether your tone of voice and inflection accurately reflected the importance of the topic and showed an appropriate level of enthusiasm toward the audience and the setting. Identify areas that need improvement and create a development plan.

Sharpen your presentation skills

- Formal and informal presentations are opportunities for high-impact communication, so be well prepared. Formulate a clear purpose statement and identify key messages that support your theme. Before you begin speaking, use the following questions to analyze the needs of your audience:
    1. Who is the audience?
    2. What are their attitudes? Do they have experience with the topic?
    3. How diverse is the audience?
    4. How can I discuss the topic and issues in a way that relates to everyone?
    5. What kind of response or outcome do I want?

- Use nonverbal cues to increase your impact. Expressing yourself in nonverbal ways can make the difference between an apathetic reception and an enthusiastic response. Increase the use of these cues to supplement your message and clarify your content.

- Use stories, examples, and anecdotes to communicate with others. According to David Armstrong in *Managing by Storying Around* (Doubleday & Company, 1992) storytelling is a powerful tool that adds an element of fun to interactions, communicates corporate culture, recognizes heroic deeds, and empowers people by letting them know what is expected of them.

- Coach others on their presentation skills. Observing and giving feedback to others will sensitize you to your own communication issues.

- Note additional suggestions in chapter 14, "High-Impact Delivery."

Make sure your message is understood

- If your work requires that you speak in technical terms, make a conscious effort to translate, explain, or give examples for language that may be unfamiliar to some of your listeners.

- Encourage people to ask questions. Sometimes, to protect their egos, people choose to remain confused rather than ask questions. Make it easy and safe for people to seek clarification. Avoid sarcasm or disparaging remarks. Express appreciation for questions that lead to a better understanding of the issue.

- When speaking with people whose native language is different than yours, follow these tips given by Sondra Thiederman in *Profiting in America's Multicultural Marketplace* (The Free Press, 1992):
    - Do not shout.
    - Speak slowly and distinctly.
    - Emphasize key words.
    - Use visual aids.
    - Cover small amounts of information at one time.
    - Be aware of your tone of voice.
    - Recap and repeat frequently.
    - Take care not to patronize.
    - Check for understanding.
    - Say as precisely as you can what you mean.
    - Avoid idioms and slang.
    - Choose interpreters carefully.
    - Learn a few words of the other person's language.

4. Promote frank discussion of tough issues.

Taking a stand and resolving important issues require persistence, clear communication, a strong emphasis on paying attention to and working with others, and the courage to stand behind your convictions. Let people know where you stand on important issues, even if your position is unpopular with some people. Also, let people know you value honest, vigorous discussion and debate on issues.

Demonstrate leadership courage

• Show respect and concern for people by confronting tough issues head-on. In the long run, no one will benefit if the issues that need to be addressed and resolved are ignored or the differences are trivialized.

• It is crucial that you respond quickly when important individual or team issues surface. Addressing problems promptly will show your team that you are not intimidated by having to deal with difficult issues.

• When you face a tough decision, listen carefully to the input of others and make sure you understand their positions. Carefully analyze the alternatives before you settle on a course of action and clearly state your views.

Challenge others to make tough choices

• Model risk taking. When appropriate, tell your direct reports about the risks and issues that you consider before making a tough decision.

• Help others develop confidence in their decision-making ability. Lend your expertise, but stop short of making the decision for them.

• Fully support your people when they make tough choices. If a decision backfires, provide assistance through damage control and repair.

Encourage others to engage in appropriate discussion and debate on issues

• Take an active role in establishing a climate that encourages a respectful exchange of ideas, debate on issues, and constructive criticism.

• Regularly discuss difficult, controversial issues at staff meetings. Ask two or three persons with different positions to prepare their initial thinking and statements for the discussion.

• Don't forget the "people" side of these debates. Be prepared to deal with others' reactions and feelings during and after the process. Acknowledge reactions and work to rebuild the cohesiveness of the group, if necessary.

5. Express opinions without intimidating others.

Even executives with an open style and a flat organization receive some degree of deferential treatment. Formal authority and power over people's careers and livelihoods inhibit people's willingness to openly disagree with executives. Therefore, they need to be aware of indirect messages that are sent by their direct reports and to have the skills to draw out those messages.

Develop sensitivity to power and status differences

- Executives often intimidate others when they express their opinions. Ask your colleagues to let you know if you are coming on too strong. When they say you do, find out which behaviors gave that impression.

- When you suspect that you have imposed your viewpoint, explain that you were trying to encourage an open discussion.

- Arrange your office to encourage open communication. Create an uncluttered space that allows for work discussions and provides comfortable, accessible seating for casual drop-ins. Avoid having a desk between you and the person with whom you are meeting. Even if your layout options are limited, move out from behind your desk when you greet people.

Focus on understanding others

- Whenever possible, focus on understanding others before you confirm that they understand you. People will believe that you are more open-minded if you try to understand their perspective first.

- Increase your use of open-ended questions; they will encourage others to speak at length and show that you are interested in hearing their views. Form open-ended questions from almost any action verb, including "elaborate," "compare," "illustrate," "give," "tell," "share," and "paint." Such questions will encourage in-depth exchanges of information and make your conversations livelier, more engaging for others, and more interesting for you.

- Be patient with others. They may be less confident or articulate than you are and may feel somewhat intimidated. Create opportunities for interaction when you have the time to be patient.

Make your communication style less intimidating

- Consciously make an effort to connect with people on a personal level. Ask about their interests, experiences, aspirations, and frustrations. People will find you more approachable if they get to know you outside of meetings.

- When you are angry or disappointed, be very cautious about expressing your opinions. Despite your best intentions, your dissatisfaction with a situation can be perceived as criticism by some individuals. Gather your thoughts before you speak and focus on events, circumstances, and situations, rather than individuals.

- Use "I" statements and "whole messages" when you express your opinions. "I am not sure we have fully explored the alternatives on this issue" sounds less accusatory or blaming than "You have not investigated this issue fully." Whole messages, which include observations, thoughts, feelings, and goals, provide the context for an "I" message.
  - For example, "As I listen to the discussion, I hear many risks but few alternative suggestions. I believe we need to broaden our focus and look at opportunities as well as threats. Otherwise, I'm concerned that we'll get stuck here and not make any progress. I ask that we balance our discussion as we go forward."

- Establish an open-door policy. This does not mean that you must be available at all times, but rather that you set aside regular blocks of time for talking with your direct reports about their concerns. Remember, an open door works only if there is an open mind behind it.

6. Listen carefully to input and feedback.

When you listen to others, work to understand what they are trying to communicate. According to Stephen Covey in *The Seven Habits of Highly Effective People* (Simon & Schuster, 1989) "Most people do not listen with the intent to understand; they listen with the intent to reply."

Review basic listening skills

- Listen to people without interrupting. Pause or ask questions instead of jumping in with your response. This will allow the other person to be fully heard and feel fully heard.

- Monitor your conversations to see how often you interrupt others or cut off the end of their sentences. Do you tend to interrupt more with direct reports than with peers? Do you interrupt more on topics you are familiar with?

- Confirm that you understand what the other person said by paraphrasing what you heard in your own words. It shows that you are listening, checks your interpretation of the message, and encourages the speaker to explore the issue more fully. When you paraphrase, use simple, declarative statements. Lengthy sentences will dominate the conversation and prevent the other person from expanding on his or her views.

- Use reflective statements, especially during tense or upsetting situations. When you use them, focus on the speaker's emotions or feelings. This will create a basis for rapport, make the speaker feel understood, and encourage the speaker to express his or her emotions.

- Use summary statements to restate the speaker's core themes and feelings. This will not imply evaluation or agreement, but it will help you review areas of agreement or disagreement and summarize action items or positions on issues.

- Learn to tolerate silence as a listener. This will convey your interest in what another person has to say and prevent you from making a premature response.

Listen for the total message

- Effective listening goes beyond hearing words and facts. You must process the information to understand the total message. Listen for the purpose or intent behind the message.

- Identify the speaker's main thoughts and ideas, and determine the frame of reference for the message. Try to view ideas from the speaker's perspective and comprehend the feelings behind his or her words. If you are in doubt, ask the person.

- The speaker's nonverbal behavior is part of the message. Watch for clenched fists, crossed arms, facial expressions, and so forth. If you are not sufficiently clear about the meaning of a behavior, ask the speaker what he or she is thinking and feeling.

Sharpen your feedback-seeking skills

- Feedback is a two-way exchange. Consider forming a feedback partnership with a trusted colleague in which you both give and receive feedback.

- Use discernment when choosing someone to give you feedback. Make sure they have the time, skills, and experience to give you helpful information.

- Look for someone who gives an honest opinion, provides constructive comments, and excels in the area in which you are seeking feedback. Let your feedback sources know which skills and behaviors you are working on. Being specific and clear about feedback topics will help them give you pertinent information.

- Ask for feedback only when you are ready to receive it openly and nondefensively. Soliciting feedback when you are not ready to hear it will set the stage for an unsuccessful interaction. Know yourself: Are you someone who wants to hear feedback immediately after an event or do you prefer to form your own assessment first?

- Learn to filter feedback. Information from another person can give you valuable insights into your behavior and skills, but remember that it is only one perspective.

Use a variety of methods to gather information

- Practice "management by walking around" and ask employees for ideas and comments, both positive and negative. Write down what you hear and tell people about any action you take as a result of their ideas or information.

- Set aside time during meetings to ask for and listen to feedback on your ideas, decisions, and plans before you finalize and implement them.

- Conduct employee opinion surveys to gather information in a nonthreatening way. After the responses are compiled, publish the results. Schedule meetings with direct reports to address specific questions and concerns, and solicit ideas on how to utilize suggestions.

7. Ask questions to clarify ambiguous messages.

In a perfect world, every issue would be crystal clear, and every person would understand exactly what was meant during conversations. Because that is not the case, executives must become masters at clarifying ambiguous information.

- Sometimes people would rather be confused than appear confused. Seek clarification whenever it will be helpful to your understanding of an issue or situation. It is likely that if you were confused, someone else probably was as well.

- Show respect for others by clarifying any questions you have, rather than making assumptions.

- If you suspect that there has been a misunderstanding, try to clarify the situation by asking questions. Asking questions may be the most underused interpersonal skill—use this skill for getting the whole story.

- Even though you are trying to clarify information, avoid relying on closed questions that yield a "yes" or "no" answer. Give people a chance to expand on their remarks.

8. Encourage others to express contrary views.

Executives who develop a reputation for "shoot the messenger" behavior will significantly limit the type of information people will share with them. Good information, even if the news is bad, is always worth hearing.

Be open to the expression of opposing views

- When you disagree with someone, avoid labeling his or her opinions as right or wrong. If people feel that their opinions will be judged, they will be hesitant to speak up. Instead, use words such as "concerns," "doubts," and "questions."

- Never treat dissension, differences of opinion, or disagreement as obstacles. Showing frustration with people expressing contrary views, even in subtle ways, will inhibit them from offering contrasting points of view in the future.

- Guard against groupthink, a phenomenon in which a group fosters a feeling of infallibility by suppressing dissension and opposing views. It stems from pressure to reach agreement under tight deadlines and results in pseudo-consensus, or the appearance of group agreement, even though individuals still have deeply felt reservations and concerns.

Listen carefully when others express contrary views

- Make a point of listening attentively when others express differing points of view on an issue.

- When people express a point of view with which you strongly disagree, wait until they have finished speaking. Restate the main points of the argument and ask them to verify your accuracy. Indicate points of agreement if you can do so honestly and sincerely. Then, and only then, specifically state which points you disagree with and why.

- Respond nondefensively when contrary viewpoints are expressed.

- Request additional contextual or historical information that will help you understand the issue from another point of view.

- Ask how the other party would resolve the difference of opinion.

Be aware of cultural differences

- Consider the cultural perspective. The expression of contrary views is affected by a culture's values and its view of power. For example, individuals from cultures that value balance and harmony may avoid direct or negative confrontations. Also, cultures in which a hierarchical relationship is expected and welcomed may not tolerate contrary views as easily as cultures in which people are accustomed to having more egalitarian relationships.

- Show respect for differences and take cultural differences into account as you develop channels for the expression of contrary views.

- Monitor your reactions to situations in which people from different levels, functions, or cultures express contrary views. Are you accustomed to hearing differences of opinions from certain groups of people, but not from others?

9. Exhibit nonverbal behaviors that show receptivity to others' ideas.

You communicate your attitudes nonverbally. Others interpret the attitudes you have toward your self (confidence, arrogance, uncertainty), toward your issue (interest, enthusiasm, conviction, apathy), and toward the listeners or audience (arrogant, aloof, condescending or warm, open, approachable, respectful) based on what you are doing nonverbally.

Leverage your nonverbal impact

- Recognize that over 90% of the information people pick up about attitudes is from nonverbal cues. If your nonverbal message is inconsistent with your verbal message, most people will believe that your nonverbal message is more accurate.

- Increase your awareness of nonverbal cues. Study how others use eye contact, posture, facial expressions, head nods and hand motions to convey messages. Compare what gestures and nonverbal messages mean across countries and cultures.

- Use regular eye contact when someone is talking. However, avoid relentless eye contact or staring.

- Show openness by using positive hand movements (e.g., hands open, palms up). Resist fidgety hand movements. They convey nervousness or impatience.

- Occasionally nod your head or make a brief utterance (e.g., "I see," "really," or "go on") to convey interest.

- Guard against revealing body cues of boredom or indifference when another person is presenting ideas.

- Use genuine smiles when appropriate. Keep in mind a smile can be a show of warmth, humor, empathy, irony, or the like.

Choose the right setting for conversations

- Talk with others in a physical setting that is conducive to open conversation. Because your office is your territory, a neutral location may be more conducive for others.

- Ask others what time, place, or arrangement would make them more comfortable when they are discussing and debating issues.

- Initiate a more relaxed posture or sitting position. Sit on the same level as others do. Avoid more prominent positions, such as the head of a table.

- Use space effectively. Establish a close-enough proximity to someone that it shows interest in them and what they have to say. However, be aware of gender, culture, and power issues.

RESOURCES

The resources for this chapter begin on page 454.

14
HIGH–IMPACT DELIVERY

DELIVER CLEAR, CONVINCING,

AND WELL–ORGANIZED PRESENTATIONS;

PROJECT CREDIBILITY AND POISE

EVEN IN HIGHLY VISIBLE,

ADVERSARIAL SITUATIONS.

KEY BEHAVIORS

---

1. *Approach communication as a strategic issue.*
2. *Deliver clear, well-organized presentations.*
3. *Build confidence and inspire support through a convincing presentation style.*
4. *Use vivid language, examples, and illustrations to convey key ideas.*
5. *Project a credible executive image with polish and poise.*
6. *Handle questions well in highly visible, adversarial situations.*
7. *Communicate clearly through the news media.*
8. *Lead effective meetings.*

INTRODUCTION

Communication, or the "currency of leadership," is the central process and tool for transacting the responsibilities of leadership. Nearly every important executive task involves some form of communication.

Changes that surround you and your organization present new obstacles and opportunities almost every day. Each issue and situation entails a communication role for you. Your people want to know, and indeed, need to know, what is going on. It is your job to tell them both the good news and the bad. What communication demands accompany your executive responsibilities? More demanding and challenging communication assignments than earlier career assignments are likely required.

Executives have a wide range of communication and information delivery systems available. Effective executive communication requires thoughtful, systematic planning, use of a variety of communication tools and media, and high impact, skillful delivery. Therefore, you are encouraged to start with a strategic perspective before moving on to discrete communication transactions and skills.

VALUABLE TIPS

- Use communication strategies and activities as essential disciplines and tools for achieving business objectives.

- Find an internal communication coach and meet regularly to exchange ideas and gain assistance.

- Seek feedback on your communication effectiveness from a trusted colleague.

- Reduce or eliminate speech patterns that may annoy others and reduce your effectiveness.

- Outline your introduction, core content, and conclusion and stick to it.

- Use nonverbal, verbal, and visual features to enhance your message and impact.

- Project confidence and conviction when you communicate.

- If you are overly nervous or anxious, focus on the positive reasons for conveying a message.

- Be animated—use appropriate gestures and body language to emphasize your statements.

- Vary your voice volume, pitch, and pace to sustain interest and convey emphasis.

- Watch for nonverbal cues of disinterest or lack of understanding in others so you can clarify your point or add emphasis.

- Use a balanced stance and erect posture; keep your weight evenly distributed on both feet to avoid swaying and slouching.

- Pause to think for a moment before answering a difficult question.

- Be a "problem solver" rather than a "blame placer" when communication breakdowns occur.

- Assist and encourage other executives and managers as they develop their communication roles.

STRATEGIES FOR ACTION

1. Approach communication as a strategic issue.

Executives are often so familiar with issues and topics that they assume others understand the importance and business relevance of those subjects. Many people in organizations do not have that understanding. Whenever possible, executives should position their remarks within a strategic context.

Communicate in terms of strategic priorities and goals

- People are looking for direction from their leaders. Regularly transmit and interpret the organization's strategic direction, priorities, and objectives.

- Whenever possible, relate your message to important business issues in the organization.

- Periodically convey the strategic priorities and goals of the organization to key audiences.

- Translate strategic priorities and goals into concrete implementations and actions that people can use.

- Regularly share success stories.

- Be as clear and specific as you can about the implications of decisions and business developments. People need to know how decisions affect them and their part of the organization. Give enough background to indicate why the subject of your message is relevant, significant, and timely.

Use communication as a learning opportunity for your team

- Give the "whys" (business purpose and rationale) in addition to the "whats" and "hows" of organizational plans, policies, and actions.

- Link your communication to other activities and events within the organization, such as business planning, continuous improvement and reengineering efforts, restructuring, and improving customer service. Information that is linked to a larger purpose or initiative will be taken more seriously.

- Educate employees on developments within your industry that may affect the way your organization does business. Competition may dictate that your organization make certain changes.

Use multiple vehicles of communication

- Remember that messages, even important ones, seldom register with people the first time they are heard. Advertisers understand that repetition is essential for reaching an audience. Moving an audience through awareness, understanding, acceptance, and action takes time and multiple exposures to a message. Relentlessly repeat your messages—especially the most important ones.

- Use a variety of communication vehicles, channels, and methods to reinforce your messages and make them accessible to the intended recipients. Some people respond better to spoken messages, others to written ones.

- Use at least two different communication media for your most important messages.

2. Deliver clear, well-organized presentations.

Audiences respond best to messages that are clear and unambiguous. They want to know what the topic is, some relevant and pertinent facts, and why it matters to them. Upfront preparation can make this possible every time you give a presentation.

Tailor your presentation to the needs of your audience

- Analyze the situation by responding to the following questions:
    - What prompted the presentation? What is the occasion and the specific purpose?
    - What will people be expecting to hear about the topic?
    - Are you an appropriate spokesperson for the topic?
    - What kind of response or outcome do you want? What do you want the audience to do as a result of your presentation?
    - Who will be in attendance? What are their attitudes and experiences with the topic?
    - How diverse is the audience? Can you discuss the topic or issue in a way that includes and relates to everyone?
    - When will the presentation take place?
    - Are you one of several presenters? Is there a possibility that your time may be cut short?
    - What are the physical arrangements of the room? Are they conducive to the type of presentation you wish to give? If not, what adjustments can be made to improve them?
    - How could you improvise if your best-laid plans fall through?

Focus attention on central themes

- Articulate your presentation goal in a clear, concise statement. Make sure the audience knows what you want them to do or understand.

- Select a structure for organizing the key points of your presentation. Popular structures include: chronological, logical, and a simple-to-complex progression.

- Develop an introduction that captures people's attention, states your purpose for the presentation, and presents an overview of the key messages.

- Provide some background information on the subject during your opening remarks so listeners will know why the topic is important.

- Develop the core content (body) with up to five key messages. State your key messages in simple, declarative sentences, using action verbs. Word them concisely, precisely, and, when possible, positively.

- Incorporate your supporting material under each point.

- Develop a conclusion that emphasizes the kind of response you want from the audience.

Develop your content

- Direct your content toward the level of knowledge of the decision makers in the audience. Also be prepared to provide background information for those who are less informed.

- Appeal to the different perspectives represented in the audience by emphasizing multiple elements of your topic. Choose supporting material that is relevant and convincing to the specific audience.

- Use a good mix and variety of supporting material, such as anecdotes, comparisons, and quotations. Many presenters rely too heavily on statistics and explanations.

- Sequence material to maximize understanding. Organize supporting ideas and observations so that they lead to your goal.

- Use engaging transitions between each key message or topic to help the audience see the connections.

- Reduce or eliminate repetitious phrases like "it seems to me" and "it is likely." They are unnecessary filler words.

- Avoid presenting verbatim from the text. Even if you prefer to write out your presentation for practice purposes, reduce your words to an outline form for the actual presentation.

3. Build confidence and inspire support through a convincing presentation style.

Effective communication is deceptively difficult, as messages contain verbal, nonverbal, and visual aspects. The degree to which they are understood is influenced by the content and context in which the message occurs, the confidence, competence, and background of participants, and the chemistry between the communicators.

Develop audience confidence in your presentation abilities

- Remember to consider the six C's of communication dynamics: context, content, confidence, competence, chemistry, and cross-cultural effects. The six C's will help you package the message and propel its delivery.

- If you are presenting to an audience that does not know you, walk around and talk to people in the audience before you speak. Ask about their interest in your topic and let them get to know you. Then focus your presentation directly to your audience's interests in the topic.

- Focus on the audience and make every effort to connect with them. Engage the listeners by asking rhetorical or actual questions, and prompt them to think about the issues. Visualize yourself talking to each person individually.

- Make your presentation a positive experience for all concerned. Have an optimistic and positive mind-set as you prepare and deliver it. Remember that communication, not performance, is the essential element in a presentation.

- Be personable and professional, which will lead people to like and respect you.

- Show that you know what you are talking about—provide quality content.

Use nonverbal cues to increase your impact

- Learn about how people communicate their attitudes nonverbally, including attitudes about themselves (confidence or anxiety), their subject matter (conviction or boredom), and their audience (arrogant, aloof, and condescending or open, approachable, and engaging). Expressiveness can make the difference between an apathetic reception and an enthusiastic response from the listeners.

- Be aware of your nonverbal messages. View a tape of your speech. Turn the sound off and look for ways that you could enhance your message with nonverbal elements, such as eye contact, stance, body movements, and arm gestures.

- Increase the use of nonverbal cues to supplement your verbal message and clarify your intent:
    - Show general liveliness through your body language and facial animation.
    - Direct regular, sustained eye contact at all parts of the audience.
    - Vary your vocal pitch, volume, tone, and pace for interest and emphasis. Pause occasionally to let your listeners grasp your message.
    - Use a variety of full-length arm and hand gestures, when appropriate, to emphasize or help describe what you are saying.
    - Maintain a relaxed, yet erect, posture and stance. For example, put one hand in your pocket or gesture naturally with both hands to convey greater conviction or emphasize a point.

- Find opportunities to smile. Smiles indicate humor, warmth, irony, or empathy. A smile will convey your personable side. The best presenters come across as both personable and professional.

- Make sure your confidence, conviction, and interest come through. Your enthusiasm will convey conviction and engage your listeners.

Manage anxiety

- Dispel the notion that you need to eliminate anxiety before you can give a successful presentation. Most people do not and should not eliminate it. Channel this energy into improved expressiveness.

- Find ways to relax before presentations. Techniques such as deep breathing, positive thinking, and connecting with your audience in advance will help calm your nerves.

- Realize that anxiety decreases with experience, but it does not disappear. Anxiety is not as noticeable to your listeners as it is to you.

- Consider that the physiological responses of anxiety and adrenaline are very similar: increased heart rate, sweaty palms, weak knees, light-headedness, and butterflies in the stomach. These responses are very common and indicate that the mind and body are getting ready for the presentation.

- Engage in mental scanning. Before you present, visualize the actual room, the audience, and your position in the room. Imagine what you are going to do from the moment you open your mouth.

- Come to grips with your fear of making a mistake. The belief that a good speaker does not make mistakes is both untrue and unhealthy.

Adjust to the situation and audience

- Remain flexible when you face unexpected audience reactions, questions, schedule changes, or equipment failures.

- Be prepared to change your approach if people appear distracted or you see blank stares. Pick up the pace.

- Delete supporting material if you need to shorten your remarks.

- Encourage people to ask questions.

- Use examples to keep remarks sufficiently concrete.

- Remember that audiences have more tolerance for content in the morning. Make afternoon speeches livelier.

Use feedback to improve your delivery

- Cultivate critics. Find people whose opinions you value and trust and ask them to critique your presentation content and style.

- Practice in front of a colleague and ask for comments and suggestions for improvement.

- When appropriate, get feedback from your audience through questionnaires or informal comments.

- Videotape your practice sessions and your actual presentations. You may find that you use your skills differently in rehearsal than in presentations.

- Immediately after each presentation, ask yourself and trusted others the following questions. Then apply what you learned to your next presentation.
    - What points did I miss?
    - Which points could have been omitted?
    - Did I stay focused on the key issues?
    - What worked well in my delivery as well as my content and visuals?
    - How might I have kept the audience more interested?
    - How might I deliver the presentation more concisely?

4. Use vivid language, examples, and illustrations to convey key ideas.

Most people remember a story longer than a statistic or explanation. Vivid language, examples, and illustrations will make your presentations memorable and enjoyable.

Add variety to your presentation

- Improve and vary your vocabulary to increase your impact.

- Avoid unusual, long nouns or technical terms.

- Develop your use of strong action verbs.

- Break compound and complex sentences into simpler sentences. Spoken language is simpler in structure and shorter in sentence length than written documents.

- Guard against relying only on explanations. Explanations can sound abstract and vague if they are not accompanied by concrete supporting material.

- Use a wide variety of supporting materials, including vivid examples, comparisons, analogies, and quotes from customers or industry experts.

- Use real-life examples, especially situations that are familiar to your listeners. If a real example is not available or you want to protect anonymity, use a hypothetical example that is realistic.

- Try to mix serious and humorous statements. Humor is not limited to telling jokes. Often the best presentation humor comes from a humorous story or a humor or ironic twist on a serious example.

Use visual aids effectively

- Visually reinforce important messages and information. Become familiar with different types of visual aids, including their advantages and disadvantages.

- Determine which visual aids will enhance your presentation. Keep in mind that visual aids should complement, not duplicate, your verbal presentation.

- Be sure your material is clear and the font size is large enough to be read from the back of the room.

- Double- or triple-proofread overheads, slides, and computer presentation materials for errors in spelling, numbers, sequence, etc.

- Follow this sequence for using a visual aid:
    1. Determine where it will fit in the presentation.
    2. Prepare a transition to introduce it to the audience.
    3. Show the visual aid.
    4. Describe its essential components (but do not read it verbatim).
    5. Make your point.
    6. Transition into the next segment of the presentation. Bring the attention back to you.

- Speak to your audience, not to your visual aid. Resist looking at the screen when you use an overhead. It is okay to glance at the transparency or computer screen, as you would your presentation notes, but look at your audience as much as possible.

- Avoid standing between the visual aid and your audience.

- Know which presentation software and equipment are commonly used in your organization.

- Before the presentation, make sure the visuals and equipment are in place and that the equipment works properly.

5. Project a credible executive image with polish and poise.

Expectations for executive communication are high. People expect executives to be experienced communicators, at ease with groups, and in command of their message. The extent to which you can present with polish and poise can add to or detract from your message.

Present a credible image

- In general, dress at the level of your audience or one step above. However, if an audience expects you to dress "in uniform" despite their casual attire, you may want to meet that expectation.

- Be sure to do your homework. Effective preparation and accurate information are the keys to credibility.

- Match your delivery to the message. If you are delivering an alarming message, be calm. If you are trying to energize people, show enthusiasm.

- Be prepared to objectively discuss the pros and cons of your main ideas. Be honest. Share your concerns and convictions.

- Resist using too much hyperbole (exaggeration for the sake of emphasis).

Build on your experiences

- Nearly all executives are highly experienced communicators, and their habits (including less effective ones) can become ingrained. Reflect on your communication experiences:
    - What aspects of your communication have been most successful for you?
    - How can you use those experiences and successes in your current position?
    - Which negative communication experiences taught you lessons? Have you or others tried things that did not work out well?

- Although each opportunity is not a formal presentation, try approaching all of your messages as if they were. It will teach you how to lend high impact to your communication delivery.

- Seek out assignments that require you to make presentations to groups. Volunteer for membership on committees, task forces, and other projects that involve speaking opportunities.

- Pursue speaking opportunities in your community or professional associations.

- Coach others on developing their skills; often the teacher learns as much as, or more than, the pupil.

- Identify a good role model or potential mentor and observe the person. Ask the person for recommendations on how to be highly effective and credible as an executive communicator.

- If feasible, take a class with a professional presentation coach. Also consider attending an executive communication seminar that features extensive feedback and/or videotaped sessions.

Ten commandments for clear, compelling, credible executive communication

1. *Tell it straight.* Tell the truth. People can sense double-talk. Do not talk down to an audience, talk across.

2. *Be human.* No organization is perfect. Admit mistakes once in a while. Tell people how you are handling a difficult situation.

3. *Keep it simple.* Simplify your message to clarify complex issues, but do not be simplistic.

4. *Look for the drama.* Let the excitement of your message come through. Genuine enthusiasm and conviction are contagious.

5. *Be a good listener.* Get out and talk to people. Ask them for their ideas.

6. *Recognize everyone.* Your audience includes people of diverse gender, cultures, races, and status. Let people know they are genuinely appreciated.

7. *Package your message attractively.* Use compelling stories and interesting visuals. Make your communication convey action.

8. *Keep it concise.* Get to the point and keep your focus on what is important to the audience, not to you.

9. *Avoid jargon.* Do not focus on a particular group. Speak in terms the entire audience will understand.

10. *Saying won't make it so.* Provide good information and a genuine performance. If you cannot "walk the talk" then at least "stumble the mumble" and let people know you are making a good faith effort.

6. Handle questions well in highly visible, adversarial situations.

Media interviews, board meetings, stockholder meetings, annual meetings—all are situations in which executives are "on stage." They often need to explain, persuade, defend, define or redefine, and convince. Handling questions is a vital part of this role.

Demonstrate poise in front of groups

- Try to follow the two-thirds/one-third guideline. Allocate two-thirds of your time to presenting and one-third to questions and answers. If the audience and situation require it, allow even more of your time for questions and discussion.

- Be ready. Think of potential "why" questions and prepare your responses beforehand.

- Speak to the entire audience when you answer questions and watch for their reactions.

- Pause to think before answering. It will give you a chance to take a deep breath and come up with an effective response.

- If you take questions during your presentation, answer simple ones immediately. However, do not let specific questions disrupt the flow of your presentation. If someone asks a question that relates to a later point, ask if they can wait to see if the presentation will fully answer it.

- Answer concisely. Usually fifteen to forty-five second answers are sufficient. Answers of more than a minute may seem like stonewalling.

- When you answer lengthy questions, first restate the question more concisely, then give a brief synopsis of your answer before going into detail.

- Encourage people to ask follow-up questions if they want more information.

- Inject some humor if you can. Be careful not to do so in a way that conveys sarcasm or puts someone down.

- Follow through on all promises to supply information.

- Handle mistakes smoothly. If you ignore glitches and go on, your audience will stay with you. If you become flustered or distressed, they will focus on the mistake.

Maintain control of the situation

- Convey a sense of respect for the listeners in all circumstances, even if audience members become hostile. If you do receive negative reactions, make every effort to respond respectfully.

- If you receive an aggressive or hostile question, first empathize with the emotion, then try to respond to the substantive issue raised by the question.

- Maintain control and stay on track; do not digress into tangents. Relate your answers to your key messages whenever possible.

- Be honest. If you do not know the answer, admit it. If a question can be better answered by someone else, invite that person to respond.

- Provide a "capper." After the question and answer session, take fifteen to thirty seconds to restate your key messages, give a final emphasis, and/or remind the listeners of the next steps to be taken.

7. Communicate clearly through the news media.

The media is an important communication channel. Understanding the media's needs, carefully planning your message, and preparing in advance can maximize your potential for positive results from an interview.

Follow basic media interview principles

- Be aware of your organization's public relations procedures and guidelines.

- Confer with your public relations or communications representative. This person may be internal to the organization or on the staff of the public relations agency used by your organization.

- Answer questions. Give the requested information if it is available or provide the information when it becomes available. If you are not able to reveal the information, explain why.

- Be truthful and accurate. Provide accurate information even if the story does not speak well of your organization. Never attempt to mislead a news reporter—the word will spread among the media that you cannot be trusted.

- Explain yourself. Provide background information and data that explain your organization. Be prepared to explain how and why decisions were made.

- Rarely correct errors. Seek a correction only if a major factual error or significant omission skewed the entire story's accuracy or misstated a key piece of information.

- Be consistent. Talk to the media during bad times as well as good times—it is essential for establishing your credibility. Johnson and Johnson came out of the Tylenol® tampering scare in the 1980s with a favorable company image, in part because of their forthrightness and willingness to communicate actively with the media.

Prepare for a media interview

- Whenever possible, determine your communication objective for an interview. (The interviewer has an objective and so should you.)

- Try to identify one to three priority messages and state each in a simple, declarative sentence.

- Identify possible interview topics and gather relevant background materials. Anticipate the more difficult or troublesome questions that may be asked. Prepare answers of 25 to 100 words to each question.

- Rehearse your interview if possible. There is no substitute for trying out your responses in front of someone.

- Do not attempt to memorize answers or read answers from prepared notes. However, it is acceptable to use a sheet of relevant statistics or other key facts during an interview.

Respond to the interviewer

- Establish and maintain a cooperative and pleasant atmosphere.

- Start with a comment that emphasizes common ground with your potential audience. Remember who your audience is: the interviewer is not the audience, but an intermediary between you and the audience.

- Restate your key messages when the opportunity arises.

- Avoid "off the record" answers. Assume everything you say may be reported.

- Humor is often appropriate, provided it is in good taste and not subject to misinterpretation.

- During the interview, ask yourself if your communications objectives are being met. If not, tell the interviewer that you have some important information that has not been covered.

Tips and techniques for responding to questions

- If you believe the premise of the question is wrong, begin your answer with a qualifying statement.

- Respond to a direct question with an equally direct answer. Do not mislead the interviewer with your answer.

- Begin your response with a concise summary of your answer. Include the most important point(s) and facts. Be prepared to back up your initial answer with specific support for your position, such as examples, facts or statistics.

- Do not "overanswer." You may confuse, rather than enlighten the interviewer. Or you may inadvertently disclose information that you did not intend to reveal.

- When working with reporters, don't:
    - Argue with the reporter or lose control.
    - Criticize the questions.
    - Respond sarcastically. A reporter might take you literally.
    - Exaggerate the facts, lie, or mislead. Reporters can often spot attempts to misdirect them, and they will brand you as an unreliable source.
    - Repeat an objectionable question in order to deny it.
    - Use technical jargon, acronyms or buzzwords—unless your audience clearly knows enough about the subject.
    - Make a statement if you do not want it quoted.
    - Ask to see a story before it is published or broadcast. Although a few news people permit this, most consider it an affront to their independence.

8. Lead effective meetings.

Regular communication and continual information exchanges are essential to an executive's effectiveness within the organization. For most executives, the meeting is the most common setting for that information exchange.

Prepare for your meetings

- Determine if a meeting is necessary. Is there really a need to gather people to discuss one or more issues? Consider whether you are holding meetings for a reason or out of habit.

- Be sure your meetings have a clear purpose and agenda. Is the purpose to exchange information, gain support, solve a problem, generate new ideas, arrive at a decision, check progress, or establish plans? You and others need to know the purpose and expected outcomes of each meeting.

- Distribute meeting agendas in advance whenever possible. It is a courtesy to the attendees and helps them prepare for the planned topics and discussions. At the executive level, you may want to include an addendum to the agenda that gives a brief description (two sentences to two paragraphs or more) on each topic listed.

- Invite the appropriate people to each meeting. Include those who can make a contribution and those who have a definite need for the information that will be covered.

- Consider the location and timing. What room or location will be most appropriate to the meeting's purpose? Will schedule constraints, major activities, or deadlines interfere with the meeting?

Keep your meetings moving forward

- Maintain a balance between permissiveness and progress. When appropriate, use brainstorming and other divergent discussion processes. However, make sure the discussion leads to the type of clarity, decision, or commitment that is needed.

- Set clear time parameters for the meeting to make it more productive. Meetings that are sixty to ninety minutes long tend to stay more focused. Longer meetings are more effective when they are divided into shorter segments with periodic breaks.

- Request that all presentations be well organized and concise. You or the presenter should make the purpose of the presentation clear.

- Listen attentively to others. It will help you set a positive tone, and make the meeting more efficient and effective by influencing the group's ability to achieve understanding and reach necessary decisions.

- Ask questions. They are an excellent tool for monitoring and facilitating discussions. Knowing how to ask the right questions can be more important than knowing the answers. Questions will help you draw out contributions, assure that all relevant points of view are explored, and balance participation between attendees.

- Periodically summarize the major points in a discussion. It will help people focus on the issue and stay on track with the agenda.

- Whenever possible, start and end meetings on time. You and others have busy schedules, and a casual approach to meeting times can interfere with other important meetings and activities. Starting and ending on time shows a sense of respect for others. If you will be late, designate someone else to start the meeting on time.

Follow up your meetings

- Whenever appropriate, prepare a meeting summary within 48 hours. Because you and other attendees are busy, a written summary will help everyone remember what was discussed and decided.

- Document the events, including the conclusions reached by the group and a list of action items that will require follow-up. Identify the person(s) who will be responsible for each action item and the target date for its completion. If relevant, indicate if and when a follow-up meeting is planned.

- Distribute the summary to all attendees and anyone else who needs to be informed about the decisions made and actions taken.

RESOURCES

The resources for this chapter begin on page 456.

15
DRIVE FOR STAKEHOLDER SUCCESS

SET AND PURSUE AGGRESSIVE GOALS; DRIVE FOR RESULTS; DEMONSTRATE A STRONG COMMITMENT TO ORGANIZATIONAL SUCCESS; WORK TO DO WHAT IS BEST FOR ALL STAKEHOLDERS (CUSTOMERS, SHAREHOLDERS, EMPLOYEES, ETC.).

KEY BEHAVIORS

1. *Establish aggressive goals and drive for results.*
2. *Place organizational success above individual gain.*
3. *Effectively balance the competing priorities of different constituencies.*
4. *Convey a commitment to understanding and doing what is best for shareholders.*
5. *Convey a commitment to understanding and doing what is best for employees.*
6. *Convey a commitment to understanding and doing what is best for customers.*
7. *Model a strong work ethic.*

INTRODUCTION

Executive leadership is a balancing act. Organizations need leaders who can successfully respond to the needs and expectations of multiple stakeholders, including shareholders, customers, employees, boards of directors, government regulators, and local communities.

In science one learns that a valid scientific theory specifies the conditions that are necessary and sufficient to explain a phenomenon. For example, fire requires three conditions: a source of fuel, a source of heat, and oxygen. Together, they are necessary and sufficient for producing combustion. If any condition is missing, regardless of the quantity of the others, fire will not appear.

This metaphor applies to business leadership. Attention to shareholders, employees, and customers are essential for business success. Executives who ignore any of these important stakeholders will lack the sufficient conditions necessary to achieve and sustain business success.

VALUABLE TIPS

- Focus on developing commitment and personal ownership of goals.

- When you give your people the responsibility to set goals, respect the level of goals they set.

- Do not send mixed messages regarding the authority people have.

- Be careful with the issue of urgency; some executives overdo it.

- Check for alignment between organizational goals and business unit goals.

- Talk about the success of others and tell people about the role others have played in your success.

- Clearly define the needs, wants, and expectations of the stakeholders who have your highest priority.

- Take individual and institutional investor expectations into account when you make business recommendations and decisions.

- Communicate regularly with all stakeholders using a variety of media.

- When you consider important operating decisions, ask, "If I owned this business, what would I do?"

- Make yourself available to your staff.

- Encourage cooperation rather than competition between work units.

- Include people at all levels in as much planning, decision making, and problem solving as appropriate.

- Evaluate your employees on their willingness and ability to work as part of a team in the organization.

- Encourage your direct reports to develop relationships throughout the organization, not just within their own functional area.

- Acquire knowledge in customer's industries to understand the trends that may impact them in the future.

- Provide strategic value to customers, such that you will be invited to contribute to their strategic planning processes.

- Whenever practical, integrate your business processes with those of your customers.

- Take time to meet with customers personally.

STRATEGIES FOR ACTION

1. Establish aggressive goals and drive for results.

Effective executives focus on achieving results through and with others. They provide an organization's overall direction, clearly state which results are required, and prioritize business issues and activities. They determine which goals will be pursued and, to a large degree, measure their success in terms of the results achieved. By taking the vital step of addressing stakeholder expectations, they let the organization know what they are trying to accomplish.

Begin the goal-setting process

- Involve your team thoroughly in the goal-setting process and make sure they are involving their own teams as well. Business experience as well as business literature has documented that the more involved people are in goal setting, the more committed they are to the goals.

- Review the competitive situation with your team and make sure everyone has a similar view. If there is disagreement, determine what needs to happen to bring the team into agreement.

- Set big picture goals with your team, then allow them to work with their own people to determine specific goals and strategies.

- Recognize that involvement in the goal-setting process does not eliminate an executive's responsibility for setting forth a challenge. State the challenge broadly, so your team and the teams below them can determine specific goals and strategies.

- If you have an experienced leadership team, set the challenge with them, not for them. Use their experience and knowledge in key areas.

- Have the leadership team utilize the knowledge of people who are lower in the organization. Ask them to provide feedback on the feasibility of the goals, especially when you are charting new territory. For example, a pharmaceutical team may need input on what is reasonable for the release of a new drug or treatment.

- Use a balanced scorecard approach to setting goals, as long as it is anchored by the business vision and strategy.

- Periodically examine your planning process to make sure it is working for you. Be careful about always using the same approach to examine your competitive environment. Involve enough people or gather sufficient information outside your organization to avoid a myopic view.

- Anticipate the moves that your competitors will make and consider how they will respond to your strategy and goals.

- Always anticipate what will not go as planned, so you can plan for contingencies.

Support the goal-setting process

- Honor the goal-setting process used by the group. It will demoralize people and send confusing messages if you arbitrarily change goals after they are set.

- If you have given your people the responsibility to set goals, then respect the level of goals they set. If you have concerns that their goals will not be challenging enough, build in a review process. Do not send mixed messages on the authority people have.

- Ensure that business, team, and individual goals are aligned.

- Periodically review progress toward the goals. Ask for monthly and quarterly updates.

- Use monthly and quarterly reports to identify potential problems and solve existing problems. Do not use them for punishing people.

- Provide regular feedback on the measures. Expect that teams will work to improve scores.

- Use teams to help others when they are having difficulty. An organization is only as strong as the teams and people in it. A team having difficulty should get help from other groups, not condemnation.

- Make the necessary, tough decisions when you have a leader who is not able to accomplish his or her goals. Carefully identify the problems, including systemic problems and those that are beyond anyone's control. Provide very direct, specific, behavioral feedback and give help to the person and the team. But when you have to, make the call.

Focus on achieving results

- Focus on results that impact all stakeholders: customers, employees, the community, stockholders, etc. Do not just focus on short-term business results. Set goals for results in regard to each stakeholder group.

- Emphasize the need for results, not just activities or long hours. If people are not as productive as they should be, ask them to review the following occupancy, efficiency, and effectiveness criteria.

  - *Occupancy:* Are people occupied with priority activities or do shortages, delays, and other obstacles hamper them? Focus your team's efforts on high-payoff goals and activities that others, such as senior managers, deem important or critical.

  - *Efficiency:* Are people spending the proper amount of time, effort, and other resources on tasks? For instance, are staff members meeting for four hours to resolve something that should be completed in one and one-half hours? Identify situations in which your team is seeking unnecessary permission or approval, and eliminate them.

  - *Effectiveness:* Are people giving attention to the highest priority tasks or are they spending time on less important tasks that should be delegated to someone else?

- Tell your team how their efforts contribute to the organization's bottom line and its success. Analyze goals that have been accomplished in your organization and point out how your team did or did not impact those results.

- Be sure to measure a number of variables and expect continual improvement—even beyond the aggressive goals originally set. Communicate your team's results to as wide an audience as appropriate.

- Monitor your communication and energy to ascertain whether you have a balanced focus that will give you the results you want.

- Recognize that in order to attain quality results, you need quality processes. Encourage your staff to improve work processes whenever and wherever possible to produce better results.

- Benchmark your organization against other respected organizations in your industry. Also stimulate your creative thinking by benchmarking against the "best-in-class" for productivity in other industries.

Convey a sense of urgency when appropriate

- If your team and their people understand the business context and set goals, you can expect that they will have a strong sense of urgency. If they do not have that sense, or you joined them during the middle of the year, you may need to set an expectation of urgency.

- Be careful with this issue; some executives overdo it. When executives give the impression that everything is urgent and must be addressed immediately, it sets the stage for burnout.

- Think about your team's work priorities and key projects over the last several months. Did you:
  - Convey too little urgency?
  - Convey so much urgency that your staff was unclear about which priorities and projects they should pursue?
  - Convey a sense of urgency on your projects, but not on the work of others?
  - Convey a sense of urgency only on certain kinds of tasks or issues?

- Communicate a sense of urgency about goals, tasks, and projects that are both pressing and important. Expressing great urgency over every project will create unnecessary "brushfires" for your people and undermine your executive credibility. If your team feels that you do not identify genuine priorities, they will make their own decisions about what is critical.

- If you are in an organization that is bogged down by bureaucracy and inefficiencies, create a need for change based on the competitive situation, customer needs, or morale. See chapter 16, "Entrepreneurial Risk Taking" for more details.

- Follow your team's progress on high-priority projects and continue to convey an appropriate sense of urgency. Set review checkpoints ahead of the actual deadlines.

- Identify effective role models. Look for executives who display an appropriate amount of urgency toward important projects and tasks of less significance. Ask them how they prioritize projects, how they show a sense of urgency (verbally and nonverbally), and what strategies work well for them.

- Request feedback from a colleague (another executive or someone on your staff) on how well you communicate a sense of urgency on projects and tasks. Ask him or her to list occasions when you displayed an appropriate or inappropriate amount of urgency and to note any observed patterns.

2. Place organizational success above individual gain.

The best guarantee of a long and successful career is the attainment of positive results for all stakeholders. Executives are in a position to help their organizations achieve success. Focusing on factors that contribute to organizational success should be your highest priority when making decisions.

Make sure business priorities are clear

- Extend the business planning process to your part of the organization. Even if you inherit plans from others, spend time clarifying strategic priorities and the implications for your staff, business unit, and function.

- Check for alignment between organizational goals and business unit goals. Then evaluate whether the actual work of the team matches the goals.

- Prioritize goals, projects, and tasks on a daily basis. You may find it useful to create A, B, and C categories, especially for goals. Put no more than three goals in the A category, three in the B category, and the remainder in the C category.

- Periodically review priorities with your leadership team. When you find a larger number of important priorities than can be accomplished, treat it as a problem. Work with the team to determine what can be done. For example:
    - Lower the priority.
    - Use more people.
    - Add or borrow staff.
    - Reengineer the process.
    - Redefine a successful outcome.

Act with organizational integrity

- Support decisions and actions that you believe contribute to the success of your organization—even if the decisions or actions are unpopular.

- Honestly assess whether you avoid communicating accurate, but negative, information upward. Is it because the information may reflect badly on you? Small problems that are ignored often become larger problems that hold serious implications for an organization.

- Resist the urge to make promises to prevent others from pressuring you or to buy yourself time. It may help in the short run, but ultimately it will undermine your leadership credibility. Also avoid making statements that others may misinterpret as promises.

- Report on your successes and failures with equal candor. Your willingness to admit mistakes will encourage others to do the same, thus circumventing the problems that stem from selfish attempts to hide mistakes.

Make sacrifices for the good of the organization

- Before you act, think about the impact your behavior will have on the organization.

- When you face a tough decision, analyze the data as it relates to high-priority objectives. This will help you choose a reasonable course and establish your reputation as a results-oriented decision maker.

- Successful executives always consider the important constituencies first, even if it means personal sacrifice. Resist the temptation to follow the path of least resistance if it is not in the best interests of the organization. Decisions based on personal priorities or preferences will not result in long-term gain for you or your organization. Set the example for your organization.

- Review your behavior and the feedback you have received. If you consistently look out for yourself and have no concern for your colleagues and their success, broaden your focus to include others.

- Share credit with others. Talk about the success of others and tell people about the role others have played in your success.

3. Effectively balance the competing priorities of different constituencies.

Surveys and interviews with business leaders confirm the importance of serving multiple constituencies. Because demands often seem relentless, executives must develop a systematic approach to help them respond to the needs of their most important stakeholders.

Identify your constituencies

- Decide how you will relate effectively to each constituency. Each group has legitimate needs and expectations; some need more attention than others. Most executives focus on particular areas, according to their specific responsibilities and the nature of their organization's products and services.

- The following list identifies different groups that comprise today's complex stakeholder environment.
    - Board of Directors
    - Bosses
    - Stockholders
    - Community at Large
    - Suppliers/Vendors
    - Strategic Alliances
    - Customers/Clients
    - Direct Reports
    - Internal Peers/Colleagues
    - External Peer Network
    - Others

- Examine the list and identify your important stakeholders. Double underline the highest priority stakeholders. In most cases that will include shareholders, employees, and customers. Single underline the second-highest priority groups. This category might include the board of directors and internal peers or colleagues.

- If you are the CEO, CFO, or similar senior officer of your organization or division, financial analysts may be high-priority stakeholders for you. Some experts believe that the ultimate competition is for capital. If that is true for your organization, it is imperative that you actively and effectively work with the analyst community. After all, analysts' recommendations strongly affect the decisions of investors.

- Before you work with financial analysts, you may want to identify a mentor experienced in dealing with them. Regularly consult with your mentor to shape your approach.

Define the needs of your priority stakeholders

- Clearly define the needs, wants, and expectations of your highest-priority stakeholders, such as shareholders, employees, and customers. Periodically review and update your knowledge of each group.

- Develop a set of questions to ask each stakeholder group in order to collect information and demonstrate interest in their point of view.
    - What does our organization do well?
    - Where and how do we need to improve?
    - What are my strengths?
    - What are my limitations?
    - What do you think I am missing or don't understand?
    - What advice do you have for me?
    - If you were in this role, what would you do differently?

- Identify common expectations across stakeholder groups. For example, two or more groups may expect products and services to be of the highest quality. Others may expect the enterprise to have sound management and planned growth.

Make smart, balanced decisions

- Make sure you seek information on what your constituencies "can live with," even though they may not agree with a particular decision.

- Determine the competing needs, wants, and expectations of your stakeholder groups. Identifying the alternatives that each constituency can live with should help you reduce the number of high-conflict issues.

- When you make decisions, consider what is best for each constituency. Base your decisions on principles and the practical realities of each situation. Obviously, you cannot maximize the interests of each stakeholder group on every decision.

- When you must make a tough, and perhaps controversial decision, do what you can to address the interests and perspectives of the various parties. Tell people that you wish you could achieve agreement or at least acceptance, but you cannot. Therefore, your decision must be based on your judgment about what is best for the organization. It is permissible to show that you are sincerely anguished about the decision.

4. Convey a commitment to understanding and doing what is best for shareholders.

Executive leaders always need to consider the stewardship of the organization's resources, including its financial resources. Each major decision's short- and long-term impact on financial results needs to be considered. Of course, excessive focus on short-term performance can undermine the long-term health and viability of an enterprise.

Due to the large number of individual and institutional shareholders in today's market, many companies develop their own shareholder profile. Executives need to know their company's shareholder profile. Once they know what individual and institutional investors are expecting, they can take that into account when they make business recommendations and decisions.

Provide the information shareholders need

- Give shareholders information that will enable them to realistically appraise their investment and judge the competence of management. Include the traditional financial information any investor would expect, along with information about the organization's long-range plans, marketplace opportunities, and potential.

- If your company's stock is publicly traded, follow SEC guidelines and rules.
    - The Securities and Exchange Commission was established by the federal government to protect investors by standardizing the type of information they receive.
    - Two of their most important rules deal with reporting methods and "full and timely disclosure." Corporations must immediately tell the public and the SEC about any changes that could affect the value of the securities it issues.
    - If you have questions, confer with your legal staff and the executive responsible for your company's shareholder relations.

- Become familiar with your organization's investor relations communication plan. If it contains only quarterly results, work with your internal staff or a public relations agency to build a plan that is more elaborate and strategic. Use this opportunity to learn about your industry and business.

Ensure shareholder value

- Make sure the management reward system is closely tied to performance for the owners and shareholders of the business. The performance measures should be both short- and long-term.

- Work with your finance group to determine a useful measure of value.

- If your organization's earnings are low, the contributing causes may be due to poor management decisions or they may be beyond management's control. In either case, give shareholders the reasons for the poor earnings and inform them of what is being done to improve performance.

- If there are small or nonexistent dividends, it may be a result of low earnings or investment decisions. Explain the reasons why earnings are low and assure shareholders how conditions will improve, if you are confident they will improve.

- If you decide to reinvest earnings in the business rather than pay dividends, tell shareholders the rationale behind this strategy, forecast its probable duration, and predict how it will affect future earnings, dividends, and corporate assets.

Manage the profitability of your business

- Set budget and profitability goals that will challenge you and your organization. Ensure that everyone who is responsible for meeting your organization's stated financial goals knows what the goals are and what they are expected to deliver toward those goals.

- Regularly stress the importance of improving processes that lead to profitability, as profitability is usually an outcome measure of other sound approaches to the business.

- Build and maintain an effective working relationship with your organization's information systems area. Ask them to create operating and budget-monitoring reports that give you the information you need to make sound business decisions. Generate the reports on a schedule that will be most useful for you. Do not accept the status quo; keep pressing until you are comfortable with both the processes and the resulting numbers.

- When you consider important operating decisions, ask, "If I owned this business, what would I do?" Every employee, manager, and executive should constantly think like an owner and teach others to do the same.

- Conduct quarterly or periodic reviews that track your organization's progress toward business goals. Make sure you understand what is happening in the business, and then make changes in your assumptions and forecasts if necessary. When appropriate, involve your team in the process so you can share information and find opportunities to maximize the use of resources.

5. Convey a commitment to understanding and doing what is best for employees.

Employees are critical to the success of your organization. In these days of downsizing, labor shortages, and restructuring, keeping employees and providing a motivating environment are big challenges. For many employees, a tremendous range of employment choices exists. Executives who really understand this are rare.

Many employees have taken a cautious attitude toward organizations. Organizations, like people, usually get what they give. A business enterprise must be attractive to shareholders in order to obtain the capital needed to fund the company. Customers' needs must be met in order to sell products and services.

Employees' interests must be served so that an organization can attract and maintain people who provide quality goods and services. The quality of employees is an especially critical factor for organizations that provide services.

Assess employee satisfaction

- Listen to employees one-on-one, in focus groups, and in exit interviews.

- Ask people why they stay.

- Meet with new employees after they have been on the job for three months. Learn how they see the organization. Ask:
    - What are the differences, if any, in how people are treated?
    - Would you recommend that others work here? Why? Why not?
    - What is valued in the organization?
    - How are employees treated?

- Consider using a 360-degree feedback process to measure employee satisfaction with leadership. This feedback is often more useful to managers than employee surveys because it focuses on what the individual can do differently.

- Review characteristics of companies considered the best for which to work. How does your organization compare?

Maintain active communication with internal constituencies

- Communicate regularly to let people know you care about them. As an added benefit, direct contact with employees will give you unfiltered information.

- Develop a communication and access plan that will reach internal audiences. Specify important internal audiences with whom you should communicate on a periodic basis. These may include your staff, managers inside your unit who do not report to you directly, other employees in your area, and employees outside your unit.

- Identify the communication method you wish to use with each constituency. Methods may include appointments, presentations, meetings, e-mail, voice mail, letters, memos, reports, organizational publications, video programs, and satellite broadcasts. Remember that employees nearly always prefer face-to-face communication, so consider that first wherever possible.

- Always convey important messages through two or more channels. This will reinforce the message and provide at least two opportunities for people to receive the information.

- Decide how often you will communicate with each audience: daily, weekly, monthly, or quarterly.

- Select your content. Formulate your communication objectives and key messages.

- Build in feedback mechanisms that allow you to hear the issues and concerns of your people. If possible, provide a feedback tool that is anonymous.

- Review your communication plan every quarter. Look for gaps and unnecessary duplication.

- Make yourself available. Let your staff know when you are in the office.

- Visit people. Walk around.

Foster an environment of teamwork

- Encourage cooperation rather than competition between work units. Make sure that groups set their goals in harmony with one another and that the goals are mutually supportive.

- Provide a structure conducive to teamwork. Too much hierarchy, whether formal or informal, can impede teamwork. Also provide the necessary resources for team success. Those resources may include clear direction, up-to-date information, proper staffing, and appropriate funding.

- Be an example of an effective team leader and team member.

- Acknowledge successful team accomplishments. Share stories of efforts, projects, and initiatives that demonstrate effective teamwork.

- Include people at all levels in as much planning, decision making, and problem solving as appropriate. If direct involvement is not practical, at least discuss the impact the decision will have on their work requirements.

- Evaluate your employees on their willingness and ability to work as part of a team in the organization. Encourage them to develop relationships throughout the organization, not just within their own functional area.

- Provide feedback when you see "silos," barriers, etc.

Value everyone's contribution

- People want their work to make a difference. Thank people publicly and privately for their contributions.

- Notice when your staff is working particularly hard or putting in long hours. Acknowledge the effort. Encourage them to tell you what they are working on.

- Publicly value administrative work. Create a climate where everyone's work has value.

- Minimize the overt symbols that make one group or type of employee appear to be more important than others, but do not ignore the needs of some to have special recognition. Seek help and consultation from your human resources group to create the right balance.

- Publicly acknowledge excellent individual and team performance through formal and informal methods, such as meetings and publications.

- Reinforce and recognize the attainment of goals. Praise the accomplishments of less visible employees as often you praise people who are in the spotlight. Behind-the-scenes contributors seldom get the recognition they deserve. Be specific about what has been accomplished. Specificity will greatly enhance the value and impact of recognition.

- Give your staff feedback if you see any of them devaluing the contributions of others.

6. Convey a commitment to understanding and doing what is best for customers.

Customer satisfaction needs to be a "given" if your organization is to be successful. To do this, the organization needs to work on building customer loyalty.

Customer loyalty goes beyond simply being satisfied or meeting requirements. It means that your customers value you and the organization to such a degree that they would not consider using another vendor. Loyal customers invite you to take part in their business planning process and integrate an understanding of your plans into theirs. They know that their success is paramount to you. Because of this, there are many, many relationships among the business leaders and regular employees of both organizations.

Learn about your customers

- Study your customers. This is especially critical if you have been away from direct customer contact for while. Who are the customers? How many do you have? How does the number of customers fit with your resources to manage the customer relationships? Why do customers buy from you? What is important to them?

- Personally meet with customers to learn how they use your products and services. Which ones do they use? Talk to the actual people who use them. Use this information to determine how you can increase each product's value.

- Know who the customers are as people, as well as customers.

- Collect and consume feedback from customers. Read customer survey reports. Use this feedback to improve service, products, services, and your relationships with customers.

- Conduct a service-profit chain analysis for your business. Begin the process by asking the following questions:
    - How do we define loyal customers?
    - Do measurements of customer profitability include profits from referrals?
    - What proportion of business development expenditures and incentives are directed toward the retention of existing customers?
    - Why do our customers defect?
    - How do we obtain customer feedback in our organization?
    - How is information concerning customer satisfaction used to solve customer problems?

- If your direct customers are groups within your organization, find out whether they are utilizing your products or services or going to outside vendors. If it is the latter, work with them to identify their needs and discover why they are choosing an external vendor. Then develop a proposal that meets their needs, or restructure your pricing so that it is more competitive.

- Keep on top of changes in your industry and your customers' industries. Read trade journals and industry reports, and join a professional association or one of its special interest groups.

Develop a deep understanding of customers' businesses

- Rather than simply understanding what your customers say are their requirements, challenge your staff to develop a deep understanding of your customers, their businesses, their competitors, and their customers.

- Ask your customers to explain the value proposition they present to their customers. Continue to investigate their value proposition and how they plan to deliver on it until you truly understand it. Then identify ways in which your organization can be of more value.

- Identify your customers' value chains, how they add value at each part of the value chain to their customers, and the challenges they have.

- Challenge your people to develop industry relationships, so you can provide new information to your customers about their industry, their competitors, or their customers.

Align business strategies with customers' strategies

- Recognize that the success of your organization is tied to the success of your customers. Therefore, your business strategies need to be related to theirs to ensure that you will meet their future needs.

- Understand your customer's business strategies. Map their value change, learn about their strategies to enhance the value, then develop your strategies to complement their business strategies.

- Compare your existing business strategies to those of your customers. Where are they compatible and where are they different? What does this tell you? If your strategy is not related, plan how you will develop a new customer base.

- When you are working on your unit's business strategy, assign prework consisting of readings that will help people understand your customers' strategies.

Learn how to add more value to your customers

- Use PDI's Customer Review Process to build deeper relationships with customers. This thorough and systematic information-gathering process results in:
    - a new understanding of the customer's business.
    - an idea of how you can add value.
    - a stronger relationship between you and the customer.

- Deliver on requirements absolutely and consistently.

- Once your ability to deliver on requirements is stable, focus on adding value. Determine how to add value by understanding customers' current and future needs.

- Identify unmet needs and frustrations by leveraging relationships in all parts and levels of the organization. During your planning process, determine which of these can be added to your core capabilities and plan accordingly.

Maximize customer satisfaction and loyalty

- Personally demonstrate consistent care and concern for customers. Customers are precious! Treat them as such.

- Actively build relationship equity with customers. Establish and maintain relationships so you will have an inside track when a new business opportunity arises.

- Talk to people who are not your customers and find out why.

- Thank customers for their business.

- Monitor how easy it is to work with your organization. Ask for and listen to feedback.

- Design a system that measures what you promise to customers. Customer-oriented organizations utilize measurement and related feedback systems that determine how well employees are focusing their energy and efforts on areas that are vital to customers.

- Make sure front-line employees are empowered to deal with customer needs and concerns.

- Look for ways to give people and your organizational structure more flexibility. Flexibility will enable you to tap into the creative energy of your employees more effectively.

7. Model a strong work ethic.

Organizations look for committed people who are willing to invest themselves in their work. Committed executives set high standards of performance, establish aggressive goals, and work hard to achieve them. They also take pride in their work and place work high on their priority list. In fact, those who work the most hours are typically the most successful in their organizations.

Still, a strong work ethic must be balanced with life priorities. There is a saying that, "Too many people worship their work, work at their play, and play at their worship."

Seek out new work challenges

- Talk with your boss about your desire to broaden the range of your executive responsibilities. Indicate your interests and ideas. However, make sure that you have mastered your current job before you ask for more. Performing well in all aspects of executive responsibility is the best route to interesting assignments and advancement.

- Ask your boss what additional skills or experience you need for broader responsibility.

- Identify customer, technological, and business issues that will be critical to your organization's future success and develop additional expertise in those areas. Find opportunities to share your customer knowledge and explain how trends may affect your business.

- Gain experience and add challenge to your work by taking on special projects, joining task forces, or moving laterally to a different functional area.

- Be realistic about what you can handle. Consider your strengths and interests, and set your goals accordingly. Do not set yourself up for failure by taking on too much at one time, or too soon.

Readily put in extra time and effort

- Even if you are generally a hard worker, there are times when executive jobs require even more effort to complete a project, deal with a problem, or catch up on routine responsibilities. When these situations arise, be responsible, tenacious, and creative.

- If you cannot put in extra time, clearly explain your reasons, show your concern, and find others who can help.

- If you frequently work long hours beyond the point of being productive, check to see if your situation matches that of other executives in the organization. You may discover that you need to hire more people, reprioritize responsibilities, and eliminate or delegate more work. Or you may simply need to become more comfortable with extra hours.

- Some organizational cultures discourage long hours. You are likely to know if you are in such a culture. If so, be careful not to make your hard work too visible. Some colleagues may try to discredit your enthusiasm and effort by attributing it to poor organization or merely trying to impress a boss.

- Look at the long-term consequences of working extended hours. "Going the extra mile" shows others that you are willing to do whatever it takes to get the job done. As a result, you will probably find yourself involved in many interesting and challenging assignments. On the other hand, working extended hours may keep you from important goals and priorities outside of work. You need to decide which area has higher priority at any point in time and accept the consequences of your decision.

Initiate activities on your own

- Do not wait for assignments—simply decide what needs to be done in your area of the business and do it.

- Watch for opportunities to help other departments or business units. This will give you more knowledge of other areas and add to your reputation as a team player.

- Take the initiative to propose recommendations for organizational problems or opportunities outside your area. Determine how you can provide input to those directly responsible without alienating them.

- Identify areas that need improvement and work to address specific problems. The traditional adage of "if it's not broken, don't fix it," has been replaced by "if it's not broken, improve it anyway." If you wait until your technological or organizational strategy is truly broken, it may be too late.

- Adopt the view that your responsibilities go beyond your specific executive accountabilities. Identify and seize opportunities wherever they appear in the organization.

RESOURCES

The resources for this chapter begin on page 458.

16
ENTREPRENEURIAL RISK TAKING

CHAMPION NEW IDEAS AND INITIATIVES;
IDENTIFY NEW BUSINESS OPPORTUNITIES
AND MAKE THEM A REALITY;
FOSTER INNOVATION AND RISK TAKING.

KEY BEHAVIORS

1. *Create an environment that encourages innovation and risk taking.*
2. *Champion breakthrough ideas and initiatives.*
3. *Pursue new business opportunities and make them a reality.*
4. *Put own career at risk when necessary to support entrepreneurial ventures.*

INTRODUCTION

Entrepreneurial organizations and leaders are pioneers. They follow a clear and compelling vision that is strongly connected to the marketplace.

Entrepreneurial leaders and organizations have a high degree of self-confidence. In *Built to Last,* (HarperBusiness, 1994) James Collins and Jerry Porras describe this high degree of self-confidence (and sometimes arrogance) as the "hubris factor." These organizations set "Big Hairy Audacious Goals" (BHAGs) that require a certain level of unreasonable confidence. As Collins and Porras note:

> "The BHAGs looked more audacious to outsiders than to insiders. The visionary companies didn't see their audacity as taunting the gods. It simply never occurred to them that they couldn't do what they set out to do."

These entrepreneurial leaders are highly motivated by the vision, purpose, and ideas that give birth to their venture. They communicate a vision, then spend a great deal of face-to-face time with their people to nurture that vision and execute against the goals.

VALUABLE TIPS

- Express appreciation for creative, innovative ideas.

- Regularly help champion and implement the ideas your people suggest.

- Be willing to try different things, keep those that work, and put a quick, easy end to those that do not seem promising.

- Provide incentives for experimentation and risk taking.

- Deliberately moderate your own interest in contributing; allow the team the fun of creating.

- Make it easy for people to network across functions so they can identify and work with people who have important expertise.

- Facilitate and encourage conversations, sharing, and work across business units, functions, and disciplines.

- Ask for a business rationale for experiments, projects, and tests.

- Tie rewards to achieving positive outcomes.

- Make rewards for initiative, experimentation, and innovation larger than the rewards for safe behavior.

- Work to create a meritocracy where rewards are based on results rather than activity.

- Recognize what is at stake and make sure people, especially project leaders, are protected and rewarded for taking risks.

- Make sure experimentation and "pilot testing" are part of an innovation plan.

- Let customers know when they are participating in a trial launch so you can get their feedback.

- Identify risks as early as possible and do everything you can to avoid unnecessary risks.

- Develop plans to deal with potential failures and mistakes.

- Focus your attention and energy on initiatives that are most important to you and the success of the organization.

- Focus on a small number of initiatives and do not become too fragmented. Concentrate on those in which you have interest and competence.

STRATEGIES FOR ACTION

1. Create an environment that encourages innovation and risk taking.

Innovation and risk taking are necessary to ensure long-term survival and healthy growth in today's business climate. Competitive challenges and technology require that organizations change fast and radically. Incremental process improvements often aren't enough.

A natural tension between control and latitude exists in innovative development efforts. When people are given more latitude, they have more opportunities to try new ideas. Because this degree of latitude and encouragement for risk taking increases risk for the organization, clear overall direction, clear goals, and solid risk evaluation processes are needed.

Create an empowering climate for new ideas

- In highly entrepreneurial companies, people believe they have the ability to influence and contribute to the future of their company by creating viable new products, services or processes. Let your people know they can make these contributions.

- Empowerment is key. Encourage people to openly present their ideas without fear of criticism or ridicule. Let people know that innovative thinking is a part of everyone's job, regardless of their function or level of responsibility.

- Establish a pattern and norm where people encourage, rather than criticize, new ideas. Ask people to first discuss what they like about an idea, rather than what they dislike.

- Set aside time at staff meetings and other gatherings to discuss new, creative, even wild ideas. Emphasize that ideas need not be fully developed before they are shared.

- Express appreciation for creative, innovative ideas. Regularly help champion and implement the ideas your people suggest.

- Ask your team to investigate their ideas. Let the team decide if and how an idea should be pursued. After they have developed their thoughts, have them report back to you. Listen, encourage, and ask the team how you can help them pursue the idea or innovation.

Encourage experimentation

- Be willing to try new and different things. Keep those that work and put a quick, easy end to those that do not seem promising.

- Rather than following a two- to three-year timeline, test projects by moving directly to implementation. Encourage experiments.

- Keep projects small as long as possible. This will make it easier to end the project and try something else if it does not work. If an ill-advised project grows too quickly, the momentum may be too great to stop.

- Create ways to do a lot of small experiments where you can learn from mistakes. Mistakes can be worthwhile and teach valuable lessons if they come from a genuine effort to try out ideas, concepts, or products. However, watch to see that you do not make the same mistakes over and over. Repeated mistakes are costly and unacceptable.

- Provide incentives for experimentation and risk taking. The incentives may be in the form of dedicated time on a favorite project, bonus compensation, promotional opportunities, or salary increases.

- Consider setting up an undesignated budget for internally generated ideas. Some companies have a group of internal venture capitalists who makes decisions about funding proposals and projects.

Foster a sense of ownership

- Create opportunities for individuals and teams to become involved. People do their best work when they feel highly invested in what they are doing. Exhilaration and passion come from taking a promising idea and carrying it through.

- Encourage individual ownership of ideas and creative projects. A sense of ownership often depends on the degree to which individuals associate their personal success with a project's success. Highly committed people carry ideas further, with more energy and vigor, than those who are not as highly committed.

- Encourage team ownership of projects. Teams often derive a sense of identity from projects in which they are involved in all phases, from conception through development, testing, refining, and implementation. When a team feels ownership, they put additional creativity, insight, dedication, and effort into a project.

- Give the team the fun of creating; deliberately moderate your own contributions.

Create a supportive organizational system

- Innovation is not a well-controlled process. Instead, it relies on trial and error, experimentation, freedom from constraints and defined ways of doing things, autonomy and latitude, and the ability to be playful. Keep bureaucracy at a minimum; it tends to limit action, slow down decision making, and discourage risk taking.

- Keep the organization as flat as possible. Make policy and administrative requirements clear and simple. This will enable swift and regular communication between the people working on innovations and the ultimate decision makers.

- Make it easy for people to network across functions. This will help them locate others who want to help on a project and bring important expertise to their effort.

- Let the project leader facilitate team meetings. Hold back your ideas until others have had a chance to contribute. As an executive, you may influence the team more than you expect.

- Let people across the organization know that you are interested in creativity and innovation. Be sure to inform the line management and line functions as well as the design and development functions.

- Facilitate and encourage conversations, sharing and work across business units, functions, and disciplines.

- In general, do what you can to create jobs, structures, and assignments that attract bright, energetic people. Then give those people opportunities to grow, develop, and experiment with innovative ideas.

Provide people with the business context

- Be sure people have a clear, solid understanding of how the business works. This will make it easier for them to determine how promising an idea might be.

- Make sure people have a clear vision of where your team, function/unit, and organization are going. This will help them link specific design decisions or innovations to the growth of the organization's strategic capabilities. It will also help them find the value link to customers and end users.

- Ask people to give you a business rationale for their experiments, projects, and tests. They should be able to present and defend their idea, concept, and plan with sufficient clarity, and link it to your overall business vision and strategy.

- Emphasize the real necessity for product innovation. Share stories from your organization's history or stories from other industries that show how an innovation improved an organization's competitive position.

- Remind people that the organization cannot compromise on performance. Experimentation and risk taking need to be thoughtful, thorough, and disciplined. Creative efforts cannot be sloppy or haphazard. When people make mistakes, they must own them. They must take responsibility for their actions and move on.

2. Champion breakthrough ideas and initiatives.

Honest communication of real world economic threats and needs can be used to create an atmosphere in which people take appropriate risks. Many businesses continue to be viable only because of the new products and ideas they develop. After all, "necessity is the mother of invention."

Provide incentives for innovation

- Set very challenging stretch goals. When you do so, people will more readily see that risk and innovation are needed to achieve those goals.

- Tie rewards to achieving positive outcomes. The rewards for initiative, experimentation, and innovation should be larger than the rewards for safe behavior. Work to create a meritocracy where rewards are based on results rather than activity.

- Provide a soft landing for failure. Some experiments will not work out. Do not let that be a career derailer for people. If they fear that failure on a risky project will result in serious damage to their careers, they will understandably avoid risk.

- Share the risk. You and other senior-level people should be project champions and run interference when necessary. You should also provide encouragement and guidance throughout the project.

Give initiatives attention and support

- Recognize that executive sponsorship of new initiatives is a powerful way for you to support entrepreneurial efforts.

- Listen to creative, speculative, and even wild ideas. Listening is a simple but important way to "walk your talk" about innovation. The quickest way to dampen creativity is to act negatively when someone comes to you with a new idea.

- Be involved in periodic reviews, especially on larger projects. Do what you can to keep the project going forward. Refocus projects when necessary.

- Be as supportive as you can, but make tough decisions when the situation requires it. When you redirect an effort and cause disruption, show others compassion. As the saying goes, "Be hardheaded and softhearted."

- Ask people what type of encouragement and guidance will help them be successful. Tell your people to let you know how you can be most helpful to them.

- Protect experimental efforts when necessary. Well-meaning executive colleagues and other people may challenge you on some of the activities. Be sure to let them know that the innovative efforts are taking place with your full support.

Encourage the right types of innovation

- Be careful in this area. Innovative ideas may emerge at any time during an exploratory effort, but there are times when you should discourage innovation.

- Actively support innovative ideas at the beginning of any creative effort or project. When you move into the implementation phase of a project, maximize efficiency, productivity, and results. Be available throughout the innovation effort to guide and advise your team when those questions come up.

- Champion and guide innovative efforts that stem from perceived problems, expressed customer needs, and research findings (research is often ignored). Any of these three reasons will provide a solid rationale for experimental initiatives.

3. Pursue new business opportunities and make them a reality.

Strategic alliances, mergers, and acquisitions occur daily. In the midst of all the excitement, it's important to remember that 70% of mergers and acquisitions do not achieve the intended goals. Therefore, it is incumbent upon executives to study both successful and unsuccessful cases to glean important lessons.

Create partnerships

- When you are planning a substantial project, look for groups or units within your organization where a strategic alliance makes sense. The alliance could be based on similar technologies, production processes, sales and distribution systems, or the like.

- Consider forming creative alliances to secure the necessary resources. Look to other units for funding, facilities, and people with particular expertise. If the alliance results in an innovative product or service, it will benefit both groups.

- Look up- and downstream from your area. Would other units be especially interested in what your team is doing? Will your team depend on other departments for a successful implementation?

- Identify when a partnership may be helpful for sponsorship reasons. The political support of other executives and groups may be crucial for the success of some initiatives.

Assess the risks required

- Most organizations and executives are more willing to take technical and marketing risks than managerial risks. The first two areas are usually understood to be a necessary part of doing business. Even though you may be more comfortable with them, avoid technical or marketing initiatives that take on unnecessary or excessive risk.

- Recognize what is at stake and make sure people, especially project leaders, are protected and rewarded for taking risks. Because technical and marketing risks are associated with a project, they are seldom personalized. However, managerial risk is another matter. The personal exposure, visibility, and risk for executives and project leaders are greater.

- Provide the support and protection needed for technical innovations. Technical developments always contain some unknowns. Discovery and learning are fundamental to the process. Because technical advancements involve trial and error, they hold a certain risk.

- When necessary, distribute risk across projects. For example, charter one team to come up with breakthrough ideas on product design and a second team to focus on process improvements. Have a third team focus on worker training and development to improve efficiency.

- Make sure experimentation and pilot testing are part of an innovation plan. Customer preferences and reactions are often difficult to predict; therefore, market testing for new products and services is essential. Let customers know they are participating in a trial launch so you can get their feedback.

Be decisive and move forward when necessary

- Often you must act with incomplete knowledge. If you always wait until your information is complete, you will miss some windows of opportunity. Learn to use your hunches, "gut reactions," and intuition. Make a decision and move forward.

- Visionary thinking, as discussed in chapter 2, is important for entrepreneurial risk taking and industry leadership. If you want to take the industry lead in an area, you need to do more than simply respond to customers. You must create new territory.

- Decide how far you should test the limits of your business. Are your organization's internal processes and capabilities available? Is there market readiness for what you and your team have in mind? You may need to make trade-offs to move forward on your initiative.

- When you move forward on an initiative be sure to communicate the new direction and the reasons for it. Provide a compelling business rationale. Be sure to inform all of the stakeholders and constituencies that may be affected, and hopefully, benefited by the innovation.

- Remember, there are times when you should just do it! At those times, be ready to improvise and adjust the plan as you proceed.

Do your homework

- Secure resources for your project early in the process when things begin to take shape. Be sure you have the funding, people, and infrastructure lined up to successfully launch or implement an initiative.

- Conduct a rigorous competitive analysis. Be aware of how your present competition might react to your innovation and where future competition will appear.

- Minimize risks by identifying them as early as possible. Develop plans to deal with potential failures and mistakes. Do everything you can to avoid unnecessary risks.

- Midcourse corrections are necessary for nearly every innovation. Devise a method for tracking and measuring success. Use it to gather good information and make adjustments before mistakes become too costly.

4. Put own career at risk when necessary to support entrepreneurial ventures.

Some executives are and will continue to be averse to risk. However, most executives need to become more comfortable with risk taking, as entrepreneurial efforts are essential for the sustained success of nearly every organization.

Develop a risk profile

- Become comfortable with turbulence, uncertainty, and ambiguity.

- Create enthusiasm and emotional energy. Creative ideas can empower people and stimulate positive emotional energy.

- Be bold with your ideas. Remember, an exciting, challenging, provocative idea, goal, or vision will stimulate your people. Charisma is not enough.

Choose your priorities

- Although not every battle is worth fighting, some are. If necessary, be willing to put yourself on the line to champion an innovative cause. This will send a powerful message to your people, your leadership, and the organization.

- Discernment requires wisdom and judgment. Consider both the obvious issues as well as the nuances and subtleties of any potential innovation. Decide when something is worth an all-out effort.

- Focus your attention and energy on initiatives that are most important to you and the success of the organization. Focus on a small number and do not become too fragmented. Concentrate on those in which you have interest and competence.

Put yourself on the line

- Let people know that they are allowed to make the wrong decisions at times. Try to absorb or filter criticism that comes from others in the organization.

- When an experiment does not work, readily share failure and responsibility. Your people need to know they can count on you, especially in difficult circumstances. Also, remember to freely give and share credit with your people.

- There are times when you may need to take huge risks. Industries are full of stories of a champion who put his or her career on the line to make sure a project moved forward. Some entrepreneurial initiatives do require that level of conviction and commitment. If you face this situation, make sure your initiative is consistent with the strategic vision and priorities of your organization.

RESOURCES

The resources for this chapter begin on page 460.

17
MATURE
CONFIDENCE

REALISTICALLY APPRAISE OWN STRENGTHS
AND WEAKNESSES; SHARE CREDIT AND VISIBILITY;
MAINTAIN AND PROJECT CONFIDENCE,
EVEN WHEN NOT SUPPORTED BY OTHERS.

KEY BEHAVIORS

---

1. *Project self-assurance and unshakable confidence.*
2. *Stand up to criticism and make "lonely" decisions.*
3. *Maintain a sense of humor.*
4. *Readily share credit and give opportunities for visibility to others.*
5. *Realistically appraise own strengths and weaknesses.*
6. *Seek and accept constructive criticism.*
7. *Acknowledge own mistakes and limitations.*

INTRODUCTION

When one thinks of a confident executive, what comes to mind? Someone of a certain age? Someone with a strong ego? Someone who always has the answers?

Executives with mature confidence are realistic, secure in their knowledge, capabilities, and experience, and always looking for ways to learn more. In other words, they accept where they're at, but they're not satisfied in staying there. They are secure enough to keep growing.

Executives with mature confidence are easy to be around. They are not threatened by others—even those with strong personalities and ideas. They welcome good ideas from a number of sources. They have enough confidence in their abilities that they can seek out and delight in the abilities of others. Giving others credit does not take away from their glory. In fact, they recognize that knowing their strengths and limitations is the first step in designing strong teams who can complement their abilities.

Executives with mature confidence accept the responsibility of being a leader. They understand that they must occasionally make tough, unpopular decisions, and that their ability to be open about those decisions has a great effect on the morale of their organizations.

Mature confidence comes when an executive knows what he or she has to offer and is willing to do it to the best of his or her ability.

VALUABLE TIPS

- Convey confidence and optimism in yourself, your work, and your organization.

- Surround yourself with competent people.

- Draw on the talents of people at all levels of the organization.

- Involve other people in decisions that affect them. Let them know what impact they had on your final decision.

- Don't interrupt when people are giving you feedback.

- Thank people for constructive criticism and recognize that it can be risky to give feedback to someone at your level.

- Create an environment that fosters feedback and learning from mistakes.

- Assess your strengths and limitations every quarter and adjust your development plan accordingly.

- Develop a feedback network with three peers. Meet monthly to discuss issues and share progress reports.

- Publicly and privately express your confidence and support for others.

- Take time to recognize and reward successes.

- Exhibit a sense of humor, especially during stressful situations.

- Set realistic standards of professionalism and performance for yourself and others.

- Share your honest convictions, even though they may be unpopular.

STRATEGIES FOR ACTION

1. Project self-assurance and unshakable confidence.

Executives need a great deal of confidence and a strong ego; it fact, it is unlikely they would achieve an executive position without it. The key is to act confidently without stepping over the line into egocentrism.

Display confidence and self-assurance

- Consider how you currently display confidence and self-assurance. In which situations are you more likely to show confidence? Why? Do you feel more knowledgeable in those areas?

- Ask a mentor or trusted colleagues to give you feedback on how you display confidence and self-assurance. Give them a definition of what you see as confidence vs. ego so they will know what kind of information you are looking for. Urge them to be honest; insincere flattery will not help you improve.

- Think about a colleague who is self-assured and confident. What behaviors give that impression?

- Consider how you react when a leader lacks confidence in his or her plans or abilities. What behaviors make you think they lack confidence? Are you displaying any of those behaviors?

Identify situations in which you lack confidence

- Consider situations in which you feel or have been told by others that you seem to lack confidence. Why do you lack confidence in those situations? Do you lack skill or experience? Is it triggered by the people involved? Identifying what causes your reaction will help you determine how you can change it.

- Choose a situation that makes you feel a lack of confidence. List three things that would give you more confidence the next time it occurs. Then practice those five things regularly for a month. The next time you face a similar situation, record whether your practice made you more confident.

- Examine whether you are reluctant to be a learner. One clue is that you may not want to take any chances in areas where you are not already confident that you will succeed. If so, start small. Learn something in an area where the stakes are low. Then move on to more visible opportunities.

- Resist negative self-talk. Sometimes people think, "I never handle those situations well." As an old adage suggests, whether you think you can or you think you can't, you are probably right.

Convey more confidence in your interactions with others

- Good posture and expressive gestures create a confident impression.
    - When you meet people, shake hands firmly and look directly into their eyes.
    - When you speak, use a clear, strong voice and assert your views in a direct manner. Avoid diluting your comments with phrases such as "don't you think," and "maybe I'm wrong, but." These are referred to as verbal "take aways."

- Record yourself on audio- or videotape in a variety of settings—meetings, presentations, phone discussions—and look for behaviors that convey a lack of self-confidence. You may be too soft-spoken, hesitant, or overly tentative in your suggestions. Make a note of these behaviors and consciously try to eliminate them in the future.

2. Stand up to criticism and make "lonely" decisions.

Executive decisions are where confidence in one's abilities, awareness of one's limitations, and recognition of one's responsibilities come together. You need to develop the strength to make decisions, even when you know you will be criticized. As Harry Truman said, "The buck stops here."

Prepare for tough decision making and criticism

- Recognize that you will need to make some unpopular decisions. Criticism comes with the territory.

- Do not view criticism as an enemy. If you fear it, you will lose the value of honest and valid criticism. You may also avoid taking risks and subsequently miss opportunities.

- Listen carefully to criticism and evaluate whether the comments are valid. If they are, decide how to respond to specific points.

- Clarify your overall values. Develop a leadership creed that you can follow when you make tough decisions. Share this creed with your team. (Note the discussion on leadership creeds in chapter 12, "Inspiring Trust.")

- Look in the newspaper and business magazines for examples of how other leaders respond to criticism and pay special attention to their tactics. Which actions and statements ring true, which sound defensive, which display confidence, and which ring hollow?

- Develop a relationship with a public relations advisor you can trust. Use his or her expertise and support when you face public criticism.

Use an objective, systematic approach to problems

• Every time you need to make a difficult decision, list the important factors that you need to consider. Focus on the ultimate goal and be as objective as possible.

• Once you have developed your criteria, list them in order of importance according to what is best for the organization.

• Use your list to generate alternative solutions. Analyze your options carefully and determine a course of action that will meet the most important criteria.

• Involve others whenever possible (and appropriate) in the problem-solving or decision-making process. Input from key people will enhance the quality of your analyses and build a firm base of support for your actions.

• When you deal with areas of uncertainty or risk, turn to people in your organization who have faced similar situations. They may be able to help you determine how to proceed.

• Consider difficult problems or decisions in light of your deeply held convictions and values. Before you take a stand, determine your bottom line. How long will you stand your ground, and how firmly will you push people in a particular direction?

Communicate your decisions

• Anticipate aspects of a decision on which you may be challenged or criticized. Be prepared to respond in a constructive manner.

• Openly acknowledge that your position may be unpopular.

• When you are challenged, restate your position clearly and ensure that your point of view is understood.

• Strengthen your argument by explaining the rationale behind your decision. Explain your criteria, research, and experience, and offer supporting data for people to review.

• Remember, your goal is to win wider acceptance for even the most controversial decisions, not to arrive at a conclusion that pleases everyone.

• Talk with your colleagues about how they make decisions and deal with people's reactions. Incorporate their ideas and strategies as you make and communicate your decisions.

3. Maintain a sense of humor.

Laughter is a basic physical response that releases tension and helps you put things into perspective. It is not possible to laugh and worry at the same time. When it seems as if there is no solution to a problem, take a break through humor.

- Learn to laugh at yourself, even when you are dealing with formidable executive responsibilities. Leaders who take themselves too seriously can lose their effectiveness.

- Spend time with friends and colleagues who display a good sense of humor. Note what they do and how they use humor.

- Watch how others use humor in business settings and incorporate effective methods into your work.

- Seek feedback from a trusted colleague or team member on whether you come across as overly serious. Ask for specific examples and suggestions on when you can use humor to project a more relaxed image.

- When you face an adverse situation, step back for a minute and look for a humorous angle. Humor can help you relax and allow ideas to flow.

- When appropriate, use cartoons projected on overhead slides to start meetings or presentations. This will help you establish a more relaxed tone.

- Humor is highly personal. When you do use humor, consider what effect your words will have on all members of your audience. Be especially sensitive to issues of diversity. Do not let humor turn into sarcasm or put-downs of others.

- Collect a few humorous books, tapes, and videos. When you find yourself losing your sense of humor, rely on someone else's—take the evening off and read a book, or watch a video with your family or friends.

4. Readily share credit and give opportunities for visibility to others.

As an executive, you have a tremendous opportunity to give your people credit and visibility. Sharing credit and providing opportunities can be tremendous motivators. It makes people feel like they are valued for who they are instead of treated like pawns in some game the leader is playing.

Give others credit and recognition for their accomplishments

- Readily share credit. However, don't share credit indiscriminately or it will lose its effectiveness. Make sure the recognition matches the contribution.

- Tell your team that you appreciate their contributions. Be specific about what they did well. Praise the accomplishments of less visible employees as often as you acknowledge people who are regularly in the spotlight.

- Track projects so that you are sufficiently aware of your team's accomplishments and successes.

- Celebrate completed projects (or difficult project phases) with a team breakfast or lunch, or similar events.

- Announce individual and team accomplishments through a variety of communication channels.

- Publicize strong performance in company newsletters, meetings, and other communication vehicles.

- Send team members personal memos and post congratulatory notes on the bulletin board.

- Display complimentary customer letters in a public area.

- Consider instituting a formal awards program with certificates, plaques, traveling trophies, or other items. Always describe the specific efforts of the individual or team as you present an award.

Involve others in highly visible projects

- Identify projects that offer a high degree of visibility. A high-level, cross-functional task force is an excellent example of a high-visibility opportunity.

- Develop a list of visible projects—current, pending, and proposed—and look for ways to involve others in their implementation.

- Keep track of people's particular skills so that you can fully utilize their skills during projects.

- Remember developmental goals as you search for involvement opportunities. Try to delegate projects or responsibilities that are in line with individual career objectives and interests.

- Ask your direct reports for new project ideas, then assign full responsibility for completing them. Give people the support and latitude they need to succeed in such visible projects.

5. Realistically appraise own strengths and weaknesses.

Knowledge of your strengths and weaknesses is key to your success as an executive. If you are unaware of them or unwilling to look at them, your growth as an executive and individual will be blocked.

Assess your skills

- To see yourself objectively, you need a mirror. Select confidants whom you trust and whose judgment you respect. Periodically ask them for feedback. Listen to their comments; you may not agree with them completely, but the information will help you form a more realistic view of yourself.

- Use a formal instrument (questionnaire or rating scale) to measure your performance in a number of areas. Choose an instrument that asks for input from you, your direct reports, your peers, and your boss, and that gives you a report that targets areas for improvement. The anonymity assured by this process will permit others to give you candid feedback.

- Consider participating in a comprehensive assessment of your abilities, personal traits, and interpersonal style. Select a residential leadership program that performs assessments using tests, organizational and peer feedback, and simulations. Such assessments can be conducted individually or in the context of a group. Objective, multiperspective feedback will be especially valuable if you have not been assessed in the past.

- Reflect on several recently completed projects that were successful or not as successful as you had anticipated. How did your personal strengths or weaknesses contribute to each outcome?

- Be careful about self-deception. People practice a certain amount of self-deception in order to see themselves in a positive light. Within reason, self-deception can help people feel confident, allow them to conquer their fears, and encourage them to meet difficult challenges. However, it can also prevent people from realistically appraising their strengths and weaknesses.

Recognize your strengths

- Don't shy away from recognizing your strengths because you are afraid you will step over the line into egotism. Your strengths got you where you are today; keep using them.

- Make a list of your strengths, accomplishments, and successes, and refer to it whenever you feel a lack of confidence. No one can do everything perfectly. Accentuate the things you do well.

- Take on assignments and tasks that use your best skills. Also pursue challenges that will stretch your skills.

- Coach and mentor others in areas of your strength. This will force you to think more comprehensively about your strength, how you developed it, and how you can use it further.

6. Seek and accept constructive criticism.

The odds of people voluntarily telling an executive something they may not want to hear are low. There is a high degree of perceived risk in giving an executive constructive criticism, especially from people at other levels or within other areas of the organization. It is up to you to seek and accept constructive criticism.

Solicit feedback

- Actively seek constructive criticism instead of waiting for others to give you feedback. People are often intimidated by executive power and position and are reluctant to say anything negative. You need to be proactive.

- How you ask for feedback can determine whether you receive honest, useful information. People need to know why you're asking and what you intend to do with the information.

- Ask for feedback on neutral territory. If you call people to your office, they may be intimidated, or at least inhibited, by the setting.

- Ask several individuals whom you trust and respect to answer the following questions:
  - What do you think I do particularly well as an executive? Where do I need work?
  - How would you describe my style?
  - Have you observed specific situations, such as managing meetings, delegating, handling crises, and the like, in which I could have performed more effectively?

- Consider the feedback: Which actions were effective and which were ineffective? Plan what you will do differently the next time.

- Solicit feedback when you complete projects. If someone gives you vague feedback ("nice job"), ask for specific details on what you did well and where you could improve your performance.

- Ask some coworkers to monitor your progress during future projects. Tell them specifically which behaviors you are trying to improve, so they can target their feedback.

Tips for receiving feedback

- When someone is giving you feedback, do not argue, explain, or debate. Maintain a listening and learning attitude. Offering excuses can appear defensive and make you seem uninterested in other people's concerns.

- If you find yourself interrupting during feedback, immediately stop yourself and listen.

- Guard against asking too many follow-up questions at one time, especially "why" questions. People may perceive your behavior as defensive instead of inquisitive.

- Use discretion when you share your point of view. First, summarize the other person's comments to ensure that you understood them fully. Then, share your point of view—if the other person is ready to hear it.

- Ask trusted colleagues to caution you when you appear defensive. Try to eliminate or change the behavior they have labeled as defensive, even if you do not agree with their point of view.

- When someone brings a mistake to your attention, acknowledge that they are taking a risk. Postpone your response until you have had enough time to weigh their input and investigate the issue further.

7. Acknowledge own mistakes and limitations.

Successful people make mistakes. They differ from unsuccessful people in that they learn from these experiences. If you have not weathered setbacks in your organizational life, you have probably not taken many risks or stretched yourself by taking on tough and difficult goals.

In *Learning to Lead* (Addison–Wesley, 1994), Warren Bennis and Joan Goldsmith describe executives who make mistakes. They indicate that such executives:

> "…simply don't think about failure. One of them said during an interview that 'a mistake is just another way of doing things.' Another said, 'If I have an art form of leadership, it is to make as many mistakes as quickly as I can in order to learn.'"

How you deal with mistakes and limitations can play a large role in your development and success as an executive.

Deal with mistakes

- Look at a failure or mistake as a challenge. View it as an opportunity to think creatively. Brainstorm ways to get around whatever obstacles it presents.

- Consider a failure or mistake a learning experience. Review the events that led up to it, and assess your attitude and behavior at the time. For example,
    - Did you neglect to get buy-in from others?
    - Did you take a high-handed approach with others?
    - Did you fail to do your homework?

- After you have assessed the situation, decide how you can change your attitude or behavior to achieve a more favorable outcome next time.

- Take responsibility for your mistakes. Don't blame others or make excuses.

- Focus on the process rather than the outcome. Thwarted plans may mean that you neglected to build relationships with internal or external people who are important to organizational goals. Focus on the conditions and causes of the setback rather than the outcome.

- Don't dwell on the past. No one is perfect. If you are pushing your boundaries, you are bound to make mistakes and occasionally fail. Dust yourself off and move forward.

Deal with limitations

- Compensate for your shortcomings by surrounding yourself with people who are skilled in the areas where you are less effective. Even at the highest organizational levels, executives need to work with others to get the job done.

- Improve your competence by pushing yourself to take on challenging work, even if you lack some of the necessary skills. Identify someone who has the skills you need and draw them into the project.

- Model the behavior of people who are skilled in areas where you need development. Learning can often be accelerated if you have a good example to follow.

Set realistic standards for yourself

- Compile a list of the important skills, knowledge, and abilities that are necessary to succeed in your position. Next, write a description of superior and inferior performance for each area. Strive to make your standards challenging, attainable, and pragmatic.

- Most performance measurements occur on a continuum. Be realistic about the level of performance at which you can and should perform.

- Avoid black-and-white thinking that views performance as a complete success or a total failure. Many times you can be successful by turning in an acceptable performance.

- Regularly monitor your performance and compare it to your standards. When you accomplish a goal, take time to congratulate and reward yourself. Enjoy the feeling of personal accomplishment that accompanies your achievements.

RESOURCES

The resources for this chapter begin on page 462.

18
ADAPTABILITY

—

MAINTAIN A POSITIVE OUTLOOK;
RESIST STRESS AND WORK
CONSTRUCTIVELY UNDER PRESSURE;
RESPOND RESOURCEFULLY TO
CHANGE AND AMBIGUITY.

KEY BEHAVIORS

—

1. *Respond resourcefully to new demands and challenges.*
2. *Work constructively and calmly under stress and pressure.*
3. *Work effectively in ambiguous situations.*
4. *Cope effectively with political realities.*
5. *Handle tense situations without overreacting or becoming overly emotional.*
6. *Maintain a constructive, positive outlook even when plans are thwarted.*

INTRODUCTION

In recent years the executive role has been compared to a rafting trip down the Colorado River. There have been a lot of white-water rapids to navigate and it has been nearly impossible to see around the bends in the river. Because some people have dropped out, the remaining crew is bruised and exhausted from the trip.

Successful executives must use an array of techniques to steer their organizations through a constantly changing marketplace. They must maintain a confident attitude, foster resourcefulness in their team, calmly handle tense situations, and display organizational savvy to navigate the white water.

Today's executives face a barrage of challenges, from determining their e-commerce strategy to dealing with a global economy. In order to survive (and thrive), executives need to accommodate different work styles, environments, and perspectives. They need to be able to respond quickly to changing circumstances, see things from different angles, try new methods, and always watch for what's coming next.

Adaptability is an essential weapon in the successful executive's arsenal. It helps an executive be resourceful, work under stressful conditions, and remain positive in the face of adversity. This helps them build successful coalitions and charge ahead, even when ambiguity is the only certainty.

Valuable Tips

- Seek out challenging situations in which you must be adaptable.

- Anticipate a positive outcome to stressful situations. Your mind-set can make a tremendous difference in the outcome.

- Practice different coping strategies on the job and see which ones work best for you.

- Focus on the right activity at the right time. Otherwise, you may get overwhelmed.

- Break problems down into manageable parts and take things one at a time.

- Do not view outcomes as either a total success or a total failure; things are rarely so black and white.

- Coach others on strategies that will increase their adaptability and creativity.

- Invest time in creating and supporting systems that encourage adaptability.

- Be a problem solver rather than a problem reactor.

- Develop an "early warning system" that effectively detects changes in your organizational environment and the marketplace.

- Establish an internal group to monitor events that affect your business.

- Consult with outside experts who track emerging trends in your industry. Start to prepare now for what will likely affect your organization.

- Actively participate in your organization's political influence processes. Recognize that politics can be played in a positive way.

- Become active in an industry association to broaden your network. Stay in regular contact with your network members.

STRATEGIES FOR ACTION

1. Respond resourcefully to new demands and challenges.

If the only tool you have is a hammer, you will treat every problem like a nail. Executives need more than one approach or viewpoint; they need to be willing to open their minds and creatively consider the best approach to a new demand or challenge. A resourceful response may involve a slight tweak to an existing process, a combination of previously unmatched elements, or an entirely new approach.

Create a climate of adaptability

- Identify the general attitude regarding adaptability in your organization and in your area. How do people react to new situations or new solutions?

- Assess your team's general attitude toward adaptability. Do they see it as an asset or a risk not worth taking?

- If there are obstacles to adaptability, determine whether they are systemic. Does innovation seem almost impossible due to existing procedures?

- Determine the business reason for being adaptable in your area. It is more likely that your team and other people will try to be adaptable if they can see a bottom-line benefit.

- Model an attitude of adaptability. Begin with low-risk situations, such as changing the setting or structure of your staff meetings. Let people know that you are trying something new and tell them why. Ask for their reactions and comments.

- Regularly take time in staff meetings to brainstorm innovative solutions to recurring or new problems. Reinforce why creativity is important in your area and for the organization.

Anticipate new demands, challenges, and obstacles

- Be proactive about identifying opportunities and threats. For example, as you read business publications, think about how you, your team, and your organization could be affected by specific situations.

- Look for fracture lines. According to Gareth Morgan in *Riding the Waves of Change* (Jossey-Bass, 1988), fracture lines are "forces that come together, gather momentum, and have an ability to reshape the future of entire industries or services." For example, consider how the emergence of e-commerce could or does affect how you sell or distribute your products.

- View your organization from the eyes of your competitors. What market forces are you ignoring? Where could your competitors take the lead?

- Identify an opportunity and list all the obstacles that will prevent you from taking advantage of it. How can you begin changing those obstacles today?

- Think about a situation in which your failure to anticipate changes in the work environment resulted in lost time and productivity. How did you become aware of the missed opportunity? What would you do differently now?

- Set the expectation that people throughout the organization should proactively look for ways to respond to new demands and challenges. Create performance goals in this area to show that this issue is a serious one for the long-term growth of your organization.

2. Work constructively and calmly under stress and pressure.

Executives are guaranteed stress and pressure. They deal with more issues, more people, more situations, more decisions, and more demands on their time. Their demands are relentless. Therefore, they have to create ways to accomplish their goals and work constructively.

Identify your stress points

- List situations that cause you stress and look for patterns. Do certain people or groups cause you repeated stress? Are you more stressed by internal or external issues?

- Ask trusted colleagues to share their perceptions of what causes you stress or where they see you exhibiting stress. Do you tend to overreact to certain situations or problems? Are you showing stress in situations where you thought you appeared calm?

- Determine whether your work habits contribute to your stress. Do you procrastinate? Do you neglect to communicate your intentions? Do you micromanage others?

- Identify how stress and pressure interfere with your ability to reach your goals. Choose one goal and track your progress over the next month. Record every stressful incident related to the goal. How did you react to the stress? How did it interfere?

Manage stress and pressure

- Assess your current stress management techniques by completing a coping strategies checklist; you will find an example in Leatz and Stolar's book, *Career Success—Personal Stress* (McGraw-Hill, 1992).

- Explore and implement psychological techniques, such as positive self-talk, emotional expression, and effective worrying.

- Maintain and cultivate your sense of humor. A well-developed sense of humor will help you and those around you deal more effectively with stress.

- Develop a network of people who handle stress successfully; they can provide support and serve as role models.

- When you are particularly stressed, talk to a trusted colleague. Blowing off steam with someone you trust will allow you to regain your perspective.

- Examine your eating habits and start an exercise program. List reasons for making a change in your diet or lifestyle, and write a plan. Be realistic in your expectations—expect to slip occasionally.

- Monitor your caffeine and nicotine intake. Stimulants can take a toll on your overall fitness and affect your ability to cope with stress over the long run.

- Do not underestimate the importance of sleep in managing stress. Sleep needs vary among individuals; make sure you get a sufficient amount.

- Take vacations two to four times a year; once a quarter is a good pattern. For highly pressured positions, a two-week vacation can help more than two one-week vacations.

- Spend time with family and friends, and make time to pursue hobbies and leisure activities.

Focus on your priorities

- Know the top three goals that you want to achieve each quarter and each year. When you are pulled in competing directions, determine whether those tasks will help you achieve your overall goals.

- Practice saying "no." Role play situations with a mentor or trusted advisor in which you have to deny a request and defend your answer.

- Maintain your focus. Explore various systems to keep you on track, such as software programs. For example, PDI's DevelopMentor® features "QuickTrack," a tool that gives you automatic reminders about the priorities you have set.

- Tell your colleagues about your priorities. Ask them to remind you of them during particularly stressful periods, when you may be tempted to get off track.

3. Work effectively in ambiguous situations.

Ambiguity can cause people a great deal of stress, especially people who like to plan ahead and know all the options. When you move into the executive realm, issues are often less clear-cut than at other managerial levels. Answers are not always forthcoming or clear, and your ability to work within those parameters is crucial.

According to Stephen Covey, "People can't live with change if there's not a changeless core inside them. A key to the ability to change is a changeless sense of who you are, what you are about, and what you value." (*Principle-Centered Leadership*, Summit Books, 1991.) Identifying and committing to your "changeless core" will create an internal anchor that helps you work effectively in ambiguous situations.

Clarify personal and work values

- Develop a leadership creed that captures the essence of what leadership means to you and share it with others. Regularly evaluate whether your actions are consistent with your beliefs.

- Write a personal mission statement. Where do you get your sense of worth, your direction in life, your perspective on life, and your capacity to act? How do you define success?

- Examine how your personal values influence your work values. For example, to what extent do the following items motivate you in your work: recognition, security, money, power, growth and development, self-expression, leadership, excitement, achievement, making a difference, and close working relationships.

- Think about the legacy you want to leave with your team and your organization. What accomplishments or qualities do you want to be remembered for? Evaluate what you are currently doing—is it consistent with the legacy you want to leave?

- Encourage people on your team and others across the organization to think about their values. Make an effort to illustrate the connection between clear values and working effectively in ambiguous situations.

Increase your tolerance for ambiguity

- Change your expectations about the environment in which you operate. In other words, expect ambiguity.

- You may not be able to change an ambiguous situation, but you can change your reaction to it. Assess your reactions to past ambiguous situations. Did you:
     - Try to control what was happening?
     - Enjoy the excitement of the unknown?
     - Wait for others to explain what was expected?
     - Worry about whether or not you were making the right decision?
     - Use the opportunity to try new behaviors?

- Examine your ideas about how you exercise control. Feeling a loss of control may be one of the most difficult aspects of leading in ambiguous circumstances.

- Focus on the big picture. There are always less ambiguous areas of your life. Give yourself a break once in a while—focus on areas where you feel more comfortable and circumstances are more concrete and predictable.

- Find people in your organization who deal effectively with ambiguity. Ask them to share their experiences and describe the lessons they learned, the skills they used, and the outcomes they achieved.

- Improve your intuition and observation skills. In the past, most executives were rewarded for a "take charge," "let's get this thing done" attitude. In ambiguous, constantly changing environments, executives need to know when it is appropriate to sit back, listen, and observe.

Broaden your response options and capabilities

- According to Nancy Schlossberg's book, *Overwhelmed: Coping With Life's Ups and Downs* (The Free Press, 1989), change is typically met with four resources: your situation, your self, your supports, and your coping strategies. The following questions will help you identify your response options and capabilities.

  - *Assess your situation.* Does the new situation require change in your current role, routine, assumptions, or relationships? What level of control do you have in the situation? Will other stressors and changes in your life hinder your ability to deal effectively with this situation? Have you faced similar circumstances in the past? Can you plan for this type of change in advance? Do you view the situation as primarily positive or negative?

  - *Assess yourself.* What is your general approach to challenge and change? What inner resources do you have to deal with this change? Which types of stress challenge you and which types overwhelm you?

  - *Assess your supports.* Do you have, or do you know where to find, people who can provide resources such as time, information, and expertise? Do you know someone who has been through a similar experience? Have your usual systems of support been interrupted by this change?

  - *Assess your strategies.* Can you negotiate your way out of what seems like a no-win situation? What positive actions are within your control? Who can you go to for advice? How can you assert yourself?

- Determine the outcome you want to achieve, then brainstorm with colleagues, a trusted advisor, or a mentor to generate possible responses. Weigh possible responses in terms of benefits, cost, and the likelihood of success.

- Because a new demand or challenge may consume a significant amount of time and attention, determine which tasks can be delegated or delayed. Channel your energy toward the most important project.

4. Cope effectively with political realities.

You may be personally comfortable with change and new approaches. You may also be enthusiastic about trying new strategies and brilliant at outlining why the changes will benefit the organization. However, every organization has constituencies that have vested interests in keeping things just the way they are. Your challenge is not only to adapt to outside circumstances, but to figure out how to work within internal political structures.

Understand team and organizational politics

- Think about the word "politics." What thoughts and feelings come to mind? Are they positive or negative? What do they indicate about your view of politics within the organization and beyond?

- Learn the political rules and landscape of your team and organization. Observe who makes the decisions, how the decisions are made, and how resources are allocated.

- Consider a situation in which your team was divided because of organizational politics.
    - What role did you play in resolving the issue?
    - Did it alter your assumptions about how things are done in your organization?
    - How could you promote a more positive political process in the future?

- Maintain a broad network of relationships across the organization to increase your understanding of internal politics. Your network will give you access to important information that may not be communicated through formal channels.

- Use both the "streets" as well as the "alleys," i.e., the formal and informal networks at your organization.

Assess your political temperament

- Ask a trusted colleague to describe your reputation in the political arena. Do you fight too many or too few battles? Do you fight the wrong battles? Are you viewed as stubborn and unwilling to compromise? Are you seen as someone who gives in at the first sign of resistance?

- Analyze the way in which you deal with internal politics. Does it motivate and energize you or cause you to feel stress?

- Assess whether you have a desire to win every battle. How does this affect your ability to work with people?

- Review how often you made trade-offs in the last year. Are you satisfied with the results? How did it affect your reputation as a politically savvy executive?

- Consider how you handle issues that are politically volatile. How has your approach worked? How could you make your approach more effective?

Create a positive political climate

- Determine how you can use internal politics in a positive way. For example, politics can be used to promote shared values and create an environment in which people commit to common goals.

- Discuss with your team how you can foster a positive political climate within your group and with groups across the organization.

- Communicate the benefits of teamwork and offer support and encouragement to others. Enlist their cooperation as you look for ways to work collaboratively.

- Foster a win/win attitude. If others are working from a win/lose position, resist the temptation to respond in kind.

- Deal with people directly, especially when you have a difference of opinion. Encourage others to do the same. A positive political climate requires open and honest relationships.

- When you disagree with other individuals or groups, concentrate on common goals. Remember to attack problems and not people.

- Avoid pushing others to achieve closure before the alternatives are adequately explored. This can cause polarized positions.

- Recognize the cost of pushing your agenda at all costs. Even though you may win, the cooperation of the "losers" could be lost. In other words, public compliance may be undermined by private defiance.

5. Handle tense situations without overreacting or becoming overly emotional.

Everyone becomes upset and occasionally loses it. But some people are emotional, habitually short tempered, or overreact to situations. Their behavior undermines people's trust and confidence. It also shuts them off from feedback that could prove valuable or vital. Emotions in the workplace are acceptable, tantrums are not.

Recognize your trigger points

- Identify situations or people that cause you to overreact. What triggers the emotion or reaction? Pinpointing why something or someone bothers you can help you control your reaction when it occurs.

- Ask colleagues to observe your behavior when you are involved in a stressful situation. Tell them to watch for signs such as clenched fists, impatience, or irritability. Later, as they describe your actions, try to remember the instances when you exhibited those behaviors.

- During the next month, write down each situation in which you were tempted to (or became) overly emotional or overreacted. What patterns do you see? What can you learn from those patterns?

- When you know what type of people or situations cause you to overreact, role play those situations with a trusted peer. This will give you a chance to try different coping methods in a safe environment. You will also get immediate feedback on what works or doesn't work.

Respond appropriately

- Assess your attitudes toward conflict. Do you see it as something that should be managed, resolved, or negotiated? Are you comfortable dealing with conflict? What is your conflict management style?

- Don't avoid conflict simply because you are afraid you're going to overreact or become emotional. The only way to become more comfortable with conflict is to face it and practice different coping techniques.

- Consider the consequences of overreacting or becoming highly emotional. How do people react to you after the occurrence? How does it affect your ability to work with others? How does it affect your reputation?

- Avoid responding immediately during a confrontation. Instead, take a moment to regain your equilibrium and avoid doing or saying anything you will later regret.

- If you become overly emotional during a situation that is not urgent, put the issue aside for a few days. Return to the problem when you are ready to review it more objectively.

- If you cannot set the problem aside, try to respond like an impartial third party while you work on the problem. If you grow too involved, take a short break to calm down and think objectively.

- Over the next few weeks monitor your reactions to conflict on your team or within your organization. Record the cause of the conflict, the sequence of events, your role, and how you felt about the outcome. How did you behave during each situation? Was it appropriate to the situation?

- Talk to your peers about their experiences in this area. If you are a new executive, you may be surprised by the number of situations in which there is conflict. You may also be surprised by the intensity of people's reactions to your ideas or statements, which in turn can make you overly emotional.

6. Maintain a constructive, positive outlook, even when plans are thwarted.

Leaders often deal with large-scale plans in which certain elements are accepted and others are rejected or thwarted. When this happens, they cannot let the setback stop them entirely. They have to focus on the big picture and reflect on what they have been able to do. Then they have to regroup and keep driving their initiatives. A positive, constructive outlook helps them achieve their goals.

Maintain a positive mind-set

- Think optimistically. Anticipating a positive outcome can increase your chance of success and expand your feeling of well-being. Conversely, anticipating a negative outcome can turn into a self-fulfilling prophecy.

- Frame difficult challenges as learning opportunities. Every situation can teach you something of value; view each instance as an occasion for growth.

- Adopt a can-do attitude and approach challenges from a problem-solving perspective. Divide problems into manageable parts and solve one at a time.

- Spend your energy looking for alternative solutions instead of focusing on why things cannot be done.

- Imagine yourself in a situation in which you are pessimistic. Then picture how you would respond to the same situation if you felt a high level of optimism. Compare the two scenarios. Do this exercise whenever you feel yourself automatically reverting to a pessimistic mind-set.

- Relabel your experiences to lessen your personal stress. Any event can be viewed as negative or potentially harmful; identifying an incident as such can trigger a stress reaction. Reducing the threat message you send yourself is the first step toward lowering your stress level. It will help you think of negative outcomes as disappointments rather than failures.

Focus on the right things

- Focus on the actual event, not the supposed consequences. What did people actually say and do? Is your plan completely thwarted or only one aspect of it?

- Consider whether you are reacting to the current situation or the accumulation of similar situations.

- Keep the situation in perspective. Look at how it fits into the overall picture of your career and life. Recognize that the world will not end because of the outcome of one situation.

- Adjust your expectations. If you achieve your objectives 100 percent of the time, it only proves your standards are not high enough.

- Don't dwell on disappointments. Turn your attention to current projects and increase your momentum on a different high-priority goal. After a few weeks you will be able to review the thwarted project with a more balanced perspective.

- Concentrate on the things you can control rather than the things you cannot.

- Control your attitude. Although it is natural to be frustrated or angry when things do not go your way, concentrate on general objectives to maintain your perspective. Learning from temporary setbacks will increase your chances of succeeding in the future.

- Review past situations for lessons learned; even adverse experiences are worthwhile if you learn something. Remember, this encounter may be preparing you for a more important challenge in the future.

RESOURCES

The resources for this chapter begin on page 464.

19
CAREER AND SELF-DIRECTION

CONVEY A CLEAR SENSE OF PERSONAL

GOALS AND VALUES; MANAGE TIME EFFICIENTLY;

PURSUE CONTINUOUS LEARNING

AND SELF-DEVELOPMENT.

KEY BEHAVIORS

1. *Convey a clear sense of personal goals and values.*
2. *Make personal, career, and organizational goals compatible.*
3. *Achieve an effective balance between work and personal life.*
4. *Manage time according to priorities; use time economically and efficiently.*
5. *Pursue continuous learning and self-development.*

INTRODUCTION

Few people enjoy being in an isolated area with no directions and an unspecified destination. However, each day people go to work at jobs or careers that they "fell into," and have no idea what's coming next. Plus, they have no idea how to find direction or meaning in what they do.

Organizations are influenced by who their leaders are and what they do. If the leaders are unclear about their personal goals and values, it will lead to a general sense of unease about the organization's goals and values. Leaders who can communicate values and vision in a way that resonates with people's aspirations will be more successful than those who do not. Also, leaders who know where they are going in their own careers are in a better position to lead their organizations.

Powerful and influential leaders are candid with themselves and others about who they are, what drives them, and which principles guide their thinking and actions. They effectively articulate direction for their organizations and determine which goals will be pursued. Then they shape their organization's mission by providing a map, a compass, and a specific destination.

VALUABLE TIPS

- Periodically clarify your priorities and guiding principles; they may change as you enter new phases of your career.

- Align your values, priorities, and principles with how you spend your time and energy.

- Determine the type of contribution you wish to make and legacy you wish to leave, then create a concrete plan to make them happen.

- Identify three ways to spend more time doing what you care about most.

- Become more familiar with development and development planning, and create an ongoing plan that you update frequently.

- Identify the competencies that will be necessary for success in your future. Ask experienced executives for their ideas on how you can develop those skills.

- Regularly evaluate and get feedback on your performance and skills.

- Work on your development every day for a minimum of five minutes.

- Reflect on what you learn every day. What should you do differently next time and what should you repeat?

- Cultivate interests, activities, and friendships outside of work; this will enrich your life and complement your work.

- Coach others on their career and life planning. In this capacity, act as a role model and share your development experience with them.

STRATEGIES FOR ACTION

1. Convey a clear sense of personal goals and values.

Your personal goals and values are the foundation for your decisions and actions. If you are unclear about what your goals and values are, it will hinder your ability to set a course for your personal growth and for the organization's growth.

Reflect on the beliefs and values that drive your mission as a leader

- Recognize that this process is not a one-time event. You should set aside a two-hour block to begin reflecting on your beliefs and values, then schedule regular times to continue your work.

- Use the following questions to begin identifying and clarifying your values, goals, and priorities:
    - What brings you the greatest amount of satisfaction in your life?
    - What do you want to accomplish within your lifetime?
    - How would you describe your life mission? How can you most powerfully express your life mission in your work?
    - What sparks your interest and energizes you?
    - How can you best serve others and make a meaningful contribution in their lives?
    - How often do you review your life priorities?
    - Are you comfortable with the amount of time and energy you devote to each important aspect of your life?
    - How do you maintain balance and proportion in your life?
    - Do you enjoy going to work each day? What do you enjoy?
    - Do you feel good about the type of work you are doing? What do you feel best about?
    - What truly motivates you to do your best work?

- Write down your values and beliefs. The process of writing them will help you achieve greater clarity.

- Review your values. Determine whether each of the following is something that (a) you try to avoid; (b) is nice to have; or (c) is essential to you. Which item would you be willing to give up first, which last?
  - Achievement or a sense of accomplishment
  - Financial security
  - Recognition from others (inside or outside of an organization)
  - Professional growth
  - Family
  - Spirituality
  - Adventure (challenge, exploration, risk)
  - Others (not listed here)

- Outline some principles, beliefs, or rules that guide your actions. Consider how you would like to behave and how you actually behave.

- Spend some time thinking critically about what you have discovered. Does your actual behavior reflect your principles? In what ways does your behavior contradict your principles? Which negative beliefs are holding you back? What are some of the pushes and pulls that cause these contradictions?

Update your short- and long-term goals

- Think about your professional and personal legacy and determine the important contributions you want to make.

- Contemplate your future priorities. What do you want to achieve that you have not already done? What do you feel passionate about? What important contributions can you make in your current role? In your career?

- On the left-hand side of a piece of paper, write your current age at the top, then list your age in five-year increments. Note what you would like to accomplish at each stage. Include professional, personal, family, and community aspirations, priorities, and goals. Then take each goal and answer the following questions:
  - How can you accomplish your objectives?
  - What sacrifices or trade-offs are you willing to make?
  - Whose support is needed to get where you want to go?
  - Are you satisfied with the work and life balance represented?

Articulate a personal mission statement

- Become familiar with personal mission statements. A well-crafted mission statement:
    - Includes your values, principles, and vision—who you are and what you want to be.
    - Captures the contributions that you want to make.
    - Addresses the roles in life that you feel are important: work, family, community, and so forth.
    - Expresses something of your inner spirit, aspirations, hopes, and dreams.

- Take a personal retreat to begin creating your personal mission statement. Use the work you did identifying and clarifying your values.

- Ask a close and trusted colleague or friend to review a draft of your mission statement. He or she should serve as a sounding board and not have a stake in the outcome of your mission. Presenting and explaining your statement to this person will make it clearer and more powerful.

- At some point in the process, read other mission statements. Reading personal and organizational mission statements can inspire you, give you fresh ideas, and provide new perspectives. However, make sure that your statement ultimately reflects your vision and values, not those of other people.

- Maintain your mission statement. This is a challenging, ongoing task that requires time to hone the statement and make it come to life. Test it out regularly against reality, then revise it as circumstances (and you) change. Make it a living, breathing document.

- Read Max Dupree's *Leadership is an Art* (Dell Books, 1990) and *Leadership Jazz* (Dell Books, 1993). They capture and convey a successful leader's mission statement.

- Write down what success means to you. You may want to define success in more than one area.

2. Make personal, career, and organizational goals compatible.

As an executive, it is critically important that your goals for personal and career development fit well with the goals of your organization. There should be substantial alignment between your personal goals, the direction of your career, and the short- and long-range goals of your organization.

Evaluate the alignment between your goals and organizational goals

- Take a long, hard look at your organization and your role within it. Consider the following questions:
    - Where is organizational energy directed?
    - What are the policies and practices for allocating resources (people, finances, etc.)?
    - What are the organization's strategic plans?
    - Which tactics will be used to implement the strategy?
    - What does the strategic direction require of executive leadership?

- Think about the fit between your current role and your values and goals. The best fit is when you can contribute to your organization's success and thoroughly enjoy what you are doing.
    - Is there a discrepancy between what you aspire to and what your organization is asking of you?
    - How well do your current work and nonwork roles utilize your talents?
    - To what extent does your work interest and energize you?
    - To what extent are you serving others and making a meaningful contribution to their lives?

Resolve conflicting goals

- Identify any goals in which your personal, career, and organizational priorities diverge. How do they conflict? Generate alternatives for bringing the conflicted areas into line with your life priorities, then outline what needs to change so that your goals will be met.

- Delegate work that fulfills the organization's goals, but does not help you meet your professional goals.

- Forge a new direction for the organization that allows you to pursue your priorities and helps your organization prosper.

- Fulfill goals from different areas with the same activity. For example, serve as a mentor for young people within your community.

Link goals with opportunities

- Regularly search for new opportunities that will allow you to realize your personal and professional goals. Scan your organization to find existing opportunities and determine which opportunities you can create.

- When you find an opportunity—or it finds you—evaluate its benefits in terms of your values, principles, priorities, and goals.
    - What contributions will the opportunity allow you to make?
    - Which skills will be developed by taking on the new work challenge?
    - Will you be able to accomplish things that you had not thought about or planned to pursue?

- Imagine yourself handling the new challenge.
    - What impact will the job have on your daily routine?
    - Where will you be in five years if you take advantage of this opportunity?
    - Where will you be if you do not take advantage of it?

- Weigh the benefits of the opportunity against its costs. Balance your desire to take advantage of unanticipated circumstances with the continued pursuit of your overall mission.

3. Achieve an effective balance between work and personal life.

Balance is achieved when people allocate their personal resources (such as time, energy, and money) in a way that enables some meaningful fulfillment of all their important life priorities. This does not necessarily mean that at every point in time people devote a proportionate amount of attention to each life priority. Rather, it means that they allocate time, attention, and resources to the things that matter most to them.

Review your balance between work and home

- Schedule an annual life balance audit during which you compare the amount of time and energy you devote to different life areas to your values, principles, and purpose.

- Ask your colleagues, friends, and family for their feedback on how well you balance your work and home lives. You may find that their perceptions differ from yours.

- Keep track of how you spend your time during the next month. How many times did you stay late at work? How often were you with your family or friends? How often did you cancel personal activities to handle work responsibilities?

- If you have a family, tell them why your work is important to you and explain how work and family fit into the type of contribution you wish to make.

- If you are not investing your time wisely according to your definition of success, determine where you can make adjustments.

Identify what energizes you at work and home

- Recall times when you felt enthusiastic, alert, and productive at work or home. Describe several tasks that consistently left you ready to tackle any project.

- List activities and projects you do most frequently at home and work, from paying bills to chairing meetings. Think about your responses to each activity. For example, do you feel renewed or exhausted after a morning run? Do you feel accomplishment or frustration after a board meeting?

- Analyze your transitions between work and home. Think about mornings when you found it difficult to concentrate on getting things done at work. What activities occurred during the previous evening? Consider the evenings when you were too exhausted to muster much enthusiasm to do anything around home or with family members. What happened at work?

- Track your energy level for two weeks. Choose a period that reflects a typical level of demand at work and at home. At the end of the two weeks, look for patterns. How did your activities at work influence what you did at home, and vice versa? What combination of tasks made you feel enthusiastic and alert?

Spend nonwork time on fulfilling activities

- Evaluate how you spend nonwork time in terms of your overall goals. Transition out of activities that are inconsistent with your personal mission and priorities.

- Treat family time as seriously as a business commitment. Schedule time for family activities on your calendar. Also take advantage of unexpected opportunities to spend time with your family. For example, if it is important for you to spend time with your son or daughter, set aside lower priority and less urgent tasks to free up some time.

- Schedule time for your own activities. It is easy to push aside commitments if other people are not involved, because you only disappoint yourself. However, social activities, pursuing hobbies, and regular exercise are critical ways of relaxing and reducing stress.

- Hire someone else to do the chores you dislike. Collaborate with other family members to get tasks done; perhaps someone else will enjoy doing the chores that you dislike. Tackle large jobs, such as cleaning the garage, as a team.

- When you must fulfill responsibilities that leave you feeling drained and irritable, reward yourself by scheduling activities that pick up your spirits and renew your drive.

- Schedule at least one two-week (or more) vacation a year. Be sure to include an activity during that break that you thoroughly enjoy. Also consider trying new activities.

4. Manage time according to priorities; use time economically and efficiently.

Executives constantly face the challenge of self-management. Failure to give attention to time management often leads to burnout (from overwork and lack of balance) or rust-out (a gradual erosion of motivation and productivity that accompanies a loss of personal direction, purpose, and growth).

Each new career level requires that you reconsider how you invest your time and energy. As you read this section, review your time management strategies in light of the unique and broadened expectations of executive performance.

Establish priorities based on urgent and important tasks

- Become familiar with Stephen Covey's definition of tasks (*First Things First*, Fireside, 1996). According to Covey, tasks that contribute to your overall objectives and give meaning to life are "Important." Tasks with tight deadlines and pressing problems are "Urgent."

- Base your priorities on tasks that you perceive as Important, rather than the tasks that are merely Urgent. Covey provides four categories that combine Important and Urgent tasks.
  1. Quadrant I tasks are both Urgent and Important. They include handling crises and meeting deadlines. Although you need to devote some of your time to these tasks, spending all of your time here will eventually generate intolerable levels of stress and preclude time for valuable long-range planning and preparation.
  2. Quadrant II represents tasks that are Important but not Urgent. Investing in Quadrant II tasks will increase your capacity to lead by giving you time to prepare and plan for projects. These tasks will strengthen your capabilities and those of your team.
  3. Quadrant III activities are Urgent but not Important. Many daily interruptions fall in this category. You need to carefully differentiate between Quadrant I and III activities, and decrease the time you spend on Quadrant III tasks.
  4. Quadrant IV activities are neither Urgent nor Important. They are truly a waste of time. If you find yourself spending much time here, it may be an indication that you are feeling overwhelmed or burned-out.

Manage time according to your priorities

- Know what important tasks you need to accomplish each week, month, quarter, and year. When new projects or tasks arise, see whether they will help you attain your priority goals.

- Maintain a single list of tasks that need to be done. Add any item, no matter how big or small, to the list.

- Prioritize each item as you add them to your calendar. Pay attention to when you function best; if you lack energy in the morning, do not plan to work on complex projects that require concentration when you first arrive at work.

- At the end of each workday, determine what you have accomplished and what you have left undone. Revise the next day's schedule as needed.

Streamline processes that use up your time

- Guard against being dominated by technology—cell phones, pagers, e-mail, etc. Be responsive to people who leave you messages, but maintain your focus on what needs to be done. Schedule two or three periods each day to return messages.

- Schedule a time each day to handle incoming paper—mail, memos, faxes, periodicals, etc. Make a decision about each item: throw it away, route it to someone else, file it, or place it in an action file.

- Prepare for meetings whether you are the leader or a participant. Request an agenda for each meeting you are asked to attend and consider what you will get out of each meeting. If your expertise is not essential, ask one of your staff members to attend in your place. Explain to the meeting leader why you will not be attending the meeting.

- Consider making your direct reports the point of contact with colleagues and clients who call regularly. This will help them develop their skills, free up your time, and provide prompt service to clients. Clarify what type of problems or requests should still be referred to you.

- When you need a period of uninterrupted time to complete a project, consider working at home. Create a location in your home that you use only for work. Make sure your assistant and relevant others know where you can be reached if a genuine crisis arises.

- When people drop by to see you, let them know up front how much time you can spend with them. If possible, set aside regular blocks of time when you can be interrupted. Reserve the rest of your day to work on important tasks that require concentration.

5. Pursue continuous learning and self-development.

The reward for continual learning is not a diploma, it is an expanded mind. You are fortunate because you live in a world where there is always something to discover. Instead of viewing learning as an onerous task, look at it as an adventure. Explore new areas of thought, try new approaches, take a chance by being a novice again. Be proactive, wise, enterprising, confident, and bold. You may not be able to learn everything, but you can greatly develop your mind and capabilities.

Use the Development FIRST model for your development

The FIRST model described in *Development FIRST: Strategies for Self-Development* (Personnel Decisions International, 1995) can be used as a road map for development. It outlines five essential steps:

1. **F**ocus your efforts on one or two high-priority development goals.

2. **I**mplement something every day. Constantly take on new challenges and stretch your comfort zone. Frequent efforts will lead to greater learning than sporadic efforts.

3. **R**eflect on what you are learning. Take stock of your progress on a regular basis to consolidate your learning and correct your course.

4. **S**eek information, feedback, and support. Steady, reliable information will help you form an accurate description of your progress.

5. **T**ransfer learning into next steps. Periodically step back and assess your accomplishments. If necessary, readjust your goals. Make them more realistic, more challenging, or more meaningful.

Assess where you are and where you want to go

According to David Peterson and Mary Dee Hicks in *Leader As Coach* (Personnel Decisions International, 1996) people need to assess where they are now, and where they want and need to be in the future. The GAPS model will help you determine your current state by looking at your Goals and Abilities, and the Perceptions and Standards of others.

- The left side of the grid (right) shows where you are now, the right side of the grid shows where you want to go. Finding the gaps between the two sides will help you identify development targets.

- The top of the grid shows your views and goals, the bottom of the grid shows other's views and standards. Comparing them will point out discrepancies between your perceptions and the perceptions of your coworkers, and whether your goals will help you meet the established standards for a particular skill or competency.

ABILITIES: what you *can* do.	**G**OALS AND **V**ALUES: what you *want* to do.
PERCEPTIONS: how *others* see you.	**S**TANDARDS: what others *expect* of you.

Focus on your priorities

- Determine your incentives for developing your capabilities.
  First, determine your personal reasons, such as:
  - I need to be more effective in my job.
  - I want to be up-to-date on technology.
  - I want to be more versatile in my current role.

- Second, move on to organizational reasons for development, such as:
  - This will improve our ability to deliver services effectively.
  - This knowledge will keep us on the cutting edge.
  - This will help us deepen our organizational expertise in a specific area.

- Third, consider the return on your investment for developing a particular area. Assess:
  - the difficulty of achieving the goal (easy, moderate, or difficult).
  - the cost of achieving the goal (money, time, effort, organizational support).
  - the payback (cost and effort compared to the potential payback).

- Choose one or two development goals that matter most to you and the organization, regardless of whether they are strengths or development needs.

- Remember that the amount of effort it takes to set personal goals and think through your development will repay you many times over.

Implement something every day

- Regular activity is key. Try to practice a skill, read an article, or the like, every day.

- Use your time efficiently (link your goals with on-the-job opportunities. For example:
  - Join cross-functional teams to learn about subjects beyond the scope of your present job.
  - Practice a new skill on a routine task.
  - Assume new responsibilities that will force you to think and act differently.
  - Try to meet difficult standards, such as creating a new operating unit in record time.

- Make development a job priority.

- Schedule development activities on your calendar.

- Share your development goals with others. Ask them to keep you accountable.

- Build development activities into your daily routine. Spend at least five minutes a day working on a new skill.

- Set reasonable goals. Break large goals into smaller steps so that you do not become overwhelmed.

Reflect on learning

- Establish a regular time to reflect, such as every week or month.

- Take time to check your development progress. This will help you assess what you have learned and determine how you can leverage it in the future. Consider the following questions:
  - What did you try?
  - How did it work?
  - What do you want to repeat or do differently next time?
  - How did you manage obstacles to your development?
  - How does your current skill level compare to your goal?
  - How can your new skills be used in different situations?

- Look at the context in which you work. Are certain situations or people more challenging than others? What are the common elements among those people or situations?

- Analyze the larger patterns and trends regarding your development. How does your skill compare with what it was when you first started your development? What challenges keep arising?

- Stay open and alert to learning opportunities. You may come across new situations in which you can hone your skills, or you may learn lessons that you were not expecting to learn.

- Take stock of your mistakes. Try to extract the right lessons from your mistakes. Figure out what went wrong, the part you played in the situation, and what you can do differently next time as a result of this experience.

- Confront obstacles to your development, such as procrastination, fear of failure, and feeling stuck. Plan how you will counteract your personal obstacles. Also ask your peers for suggestions on how they handle obstacles.

Seek feedback, information, and support

- Actively solicit the feedback you need to grow and develop. Many people are reluctant to give feedback, especially negative feedback. As a result, if you wait for others to offer their feedback, you may never get it.

- When you solicit feedback, ask questions that effectively uncover what you are trying to learn about yourself. Examples of these questions include:
    - What do you think I do particularly well as a leader? In what areas do I need work?
    - What one thing holds me back the most?
    - Have you observed specific situations in which I could have performed better in terms of motivating others, managing meetings or groups, coaching employees, delegating, handling crises, and so forth?
    - Where are my interpersonal skills strong, and where are they weak?

- Actively seek feedback from your boss on a continuing basis. He or she can be a valuable source of feedback. Ask for specific comments, suggestions, and feedback in areas you are attempting to improve.

- Encourage your employees and peers to provide feedback. Ask them how you can be more effective in your job. Also ask what you might change to help them be more effective in their jobs.

- Solicit feedback from others at the end of projects. Ask them what you did that was effective and what you did that was not effective.

- When someone gives you vague feedback (for example, "nice job"), either positive or negative, ask for specifics on what you did well or where your performance was lacking.

- After receiving feedback from others, ask yourself these questions:
    - Is the feedback valid and accurate?
    - Is the feedback important?
    - Do I want to change my behavior or approach? If yes, how can I change it?

- Once you have thought about the feedback and have decided how you'd like to do things differently the next time, ask people to observe you in this specific area on a future project and give you additional feedback.

Transfer your learning

- When you reach a development objective, celebrate your accomplishment! Your success can build your self-confidence, so take time to acknowledge it.

- Review the major lessons you learned while developing a skill.

- Continue to create opportunities to use your new skill.

- Consider advancing to the next level of mastery in a particular skill. Continue to push yourself in more complex situations, and benchmark yourself against the experts in the field.

- Cross-train in related areas and look for related ideas and connections.

- Teach others the new skill to deepen your expertise.

- Focus on a new development goal. Use the new knowledge and skills you have acquired as you work on the next goal.

RESOURCES

The resources for this chapter begin on page 466.

20
CROSS-FUNCTIONAL CAPACITY

———

UNDERSTAND THE ROLE AND INTERRELATIONSHIP OF EACH ORGANIZATIONAL FUNCTION (E.G., MARKETING, SALES, OPERATIONS, FINANCE, HUMAN RESOURCES); HAVE EXPERIENCE AND SKILL IN MANAGING ACROSS FUNCTIONAL AND ORGANIZATIONAL LINES.

KEY BEHAVIORS

———

1. *Know how to get things done in a complex, multilevel organization.*
2. *Understand the role and interrelationship of each management function.*
3. *Understand operations, production, and manufacturing functions.*
4. *Understand marketing, sales, and service functions.*
5. *Understand how to use staff functions effectively.*
6. *Consider all management functions when developing plans and implementing changes.*
7. *Display strong general management skills.*

INTRODUCTION

Whether your organizational metaphor is a machine or an organism, you need to know how the entire entity works. Executives constantly work with and through other people, groups, teams, functions, and departments to attain their important organizational goals. The more they know about those groups, the more they can accomplish.

Acquiring and demonstrating cross-functional skills can be challenging. It requires a concentrated effort to learn about functional areas and integrate the information into a coherent whole. Executives need to take advantage of the fact that their work requires cooperation between groups, and use those opportunities to learn as much as possible from their colleagues at all levels of the organization.

The reward for developing cross-functional capability is an expanded set of career options, a clearer understanding of the organization's strengths and weaknesses, a broader network of colleagues, and a greater capacity to achieve one's strategic goals.

VALUABLE TIPS

- Gain familiarity with the core functions, systems, and processes of your organization.

- Identify the current and future issues and challenges facing each function.

- Determine how each function and core process adds value to the organization.

- Know who to call in each function when you need information.

- Form strong relationships with people in other functions and units so you can get the help and cooperation you need.

- Determine what help or support from other functions would make your unit more successful.

- Identify how your group can help or support other functions more effectively.

- Leverage the strengths of other parts of the organization to build your area's core competencies.

- Support organizational systems and processes that facilitate cross-functional efforts.

- Learn from people who have done a particularly effective job leading cross-functional, multilevel initiatives.

- Benchmark the most effective functions within the organization.

- Take advantage of opportunities to socialize with your peers in other functions.

- Make a point of meeting executives from other organizations who serve in different functions than you.

STRATEGIES FOR ACTION

1. Know how to get things done in a complex, multilevel organization.

As executives rise in an organization, they face an increasingly complex web of people, functions, and processes through which they must work to accomplish their goals. They don't have the luxury of ignoring other groups while they work on their own problems or issues. They not only have to know all the components, they need to know how to put them together. Understanding the big picture helps them get things done.

Acquire a wide-angle view of the organization

- Analyze your organization's formal structure to get an understanding of the organization as a whole. Study how the various functions relate to each other, and look for overlaps and similarities.

- Review your organization's overall strategies, including corporate strategy (what businesses you are or should be in), functional strategy (the value chain elements and operational methods used), and the business strategy (how to position the organization's products and services in the marketplace and fight the competition).

- Analyze your organization's strategic plans, goals, and operating philosophy. Choose specific functional or departmental strategies and evaluate them to see how well they match key organizational strategies.

- Become familiar with paradigms and tools for analyzing business and organizational processes, such as value chain analysis and systems thinking. Apply them to your organization—what insights do you gain from different tools?

- Consider each major activity in the value chain. What are the drivers of customer value, cost structure, and asset investment? How is each managed? What are the potential vulnerabilities?

- Read available job descriptions for your boss, your peers in other divisions, and individuals at other levels. Identify the critical responsibilities of senior executives and try to understand the various unit and functional leadership requirements.

Integrate work across functions

- Work to reduce functional silos and an overly isolated view of work in your organization.

- Discover the links between the processes in your area and other areas, and share the information with your peers in those groups.

- Ask your team to work with other areas so activities on the value chain will be planned and coordinated more carefully.

- Establish the expectation that your direct reports will consult and involve one another when they plan their strategies. Set standards for the level of involvement you want and reinforce it through the performance review process.

2. Understand the role and interrelationship of each management function.

Knowing what each function does and who the key decision makers are is key to accomplishing cross-functional tasks. It's like knowing the alphabet before you can make words. Executives are not only responsible for making "words," they must also be able to put them into "sentences."

Learn about each functional area

- Learn who guides and what drives the organization in various units and functional areas.

- Arrange to meet individually with your peers in each functional area. Ask about their plans, visions, challenges, how they view the connection between their area and yours, and ideas they have for how your two groups could work together.

- Learn about the work styles in each function. This will help you work more effectively with each group.

- Read internal and external publications about your organization. Newsletters can be especially helpful—look for articles about special accomplishments, upcoming products, new contracts, and completed projects.

- Study reports and documents that describe best practices, procedures, and other information related to the core functions of your organization.

- If your organization is implementing an organization-wide initiative, volunteer to serve on the steering committee or task force. You will meet peers from other functional areas and broaden your perspective.

- Make use of informal opportunities to reach out to colleagues. Meet for lunch, take a few minutes to get a cup of coffee, or play a round of golf.

Openly exchange information and ideas

- Learn when key information will be discussed in each functional area and participate in their meetings if appropriate. You will acquire a working knowledge of topics that are important to each group and hear firsthand accounts of how specific issues affect their area.

- Plan across the value chain, rather than having each group work separately. When you and your team draft a plan, ask your up- and downstream colleagues to review it. Consider holding a combined meeting of your respective leadership teams to discuss and critique plans.

- Set up cross-functional teams to work on complex, recurring problems and pursue business opportunities.

- Meet regularly with staff functions integral to your team's success. Spend time educating them about your area and the business as a whole, so they can provide targeted expertise to your area.

- Volunteer to explain your area's role in the organization to other areas. Ask other executives to reciprocate by participating in your staff meetings and giving presentations about their areas of responsibility.

3. Understand operations, production, and manufacturing functions.

Many executives work in broad functional areas, such as engineering, design, assembly, distribution, planning, and plant management. Because such functions must be closely intertwined, it is important to have a strong working knowledge of manufacturing, operational, and production issues, strategies, and practicalities.

Identify core operational issues

- Develop a working knowledge of the operational issues that face your organization. For example, learn about materials acquisition, inventory management, distribution, capital equipment purchases, and facility management.

- Find out which operational issues are unique to your organization. What factors cause this? For example, the location and layout of a production plant may determine how much inventory can be stored at one time.

- Study an operations project that intersects with your area. Consciously observe how the operations leaders perceive and solve issues and problems.

- Take one operations issue and learn about it in depth. For example, study the issue of suppliers.
    - Who are the key suppliers?
    - Could a key supplier become a competitive threat?
    - Where are the strategic vulnerabilities? Do you have alternative suppliers ready to go?
    - What is the difference between a vendor, a sole supplier, and an alliance?
    - What are the dynamics of your suppliers' marketplace? Could developments in their industry impact their relationship with your organization?

Understand production issues

- Meet with your peers in production so you can learn firsthand what they do. How does the production area intersect with your area? How can you work together?

- Learn how the production area is set up. For example, is work done on a sequential, segmented assembly process or is it done by teams who create the whole product?

- Find out what changes the production area has made in the last few years. How has that affected their productivity and output?

- Analyze how agile the production area is. What feedback mechanisms and data measurements do they use? Can they respond to real-time feedback?

- Determine how well employee input is utilized. Are their improvement suggestions used? Are they given the latitude to make decisions that positively affect the output in their area?

- Learn some of the concepts of production, such as just-in-time inventory management.

- Find out if the production area outsources and their rationale for doing so.

- Study how the production area manages projects. Benchmark their best practices.

- Develop a working knowledge of complexity theory, an increasingly popular set of concepts and practices in recent years.

Learn the dynamics of the manufacturing environment

- Regularly visit the manufacturing area and walk the floor with one of your peers. Occasionally go through the plant with one of your peer's direct reports to gain a different perspective.

- Visit other plants in your organization and observe how they are run. Note any differences between products, volume, production processes, or procedures. Such visits will allow you to learn how diverse factors affect execution.

- Ask manufacturing executives and managers to tell you how they believe they are perceived in the value chain. Identify their key frustrations in working with other groups in the organization.

- Meet with manufacturing executives and discuss ways to exchange information and expertise between your groups. Identify specific knowledge and skills from the manufacturing group that can help your department improve.

- Strongly consider taking an assignment within a manufacturing unit. This will give you a more thorough understanding of the issues that affect them on a daily basis.

- Learn about current topics for manufacturing, such as the theory of constraints, cycle time, inventory management, and supply chain dynamics.

- Brush up on technology jargon used in manufacturing. Become familiar with terms such as EDI (electronic data interchange), CAD (computer-aided design), CAM (computer-aided manufacturing), and CIM (computer-integrated manufacturing).

- Learn how pollution regulations affect your manufacturing area. What do you do with byproducts of production? How does that affect your reputation in the community?

4. Understand marketing, sales, and service functions.

Pleasing customers is the cornerstone of business success. While every function of an organization is connected to customers, the marketing, sales, and service functions often have the most direct contact with customers. Therefore, knowing what they do and developing a strong partnership with them is particularly important.

Gain a better understanding of the marketing function

- Identify executive colleagues who shape your organization's marketing strategy and ask them how strategic considerations influence their decisions.

- Learn about your organization's short- and long-term strategic marketing plans.
    - How is your organization positioned?
    - How is the market segmented?
    - How is the approach tailored to different market segments?
    - What is your marketing department's approach toward your competitors?
    - How do they use market research, pricing strategies, advertising, public relations, promotions, product packaging, and other marketing components?
    - What is the current and future role in Internet marketing (e-commerce)?

- Ask experts about core marketing processes and factors, such as consumer analysis, market analysis, competitive analysis, and marketing mix.

- Read market analyses conducted by your marketing department and others. What is the focus—what are they paying attention to?

- Learn how the marketing strategy for a product line is determined. Identify which factors are considered, how strategies are developed, how objectives are formed, and how to identify vulnerable elements of a plan.

- Ask to participate in the strategic planning for a new product or a product in trouble.

- Pay attention to how your competitors establish their visibility in the marketplace. What kind of advertising do they use? Who is their target audience? How does this compare to your organization's actions?

Learn about your customers

- Ask customers about how they feel about your organization. To what degree do your products and services meet or exceed their expectations?

- Determine the percentage of new customers that come from customer referrals.

- Talk to people who are not your customers and find out why. Find out what it would take for them to become your customers.

- Check to see what your customers are saying about you on the Internet. In some cases, disgruntled customers have developed web sites dedicated to publicizing negative information about particular organizations.

- Measure how well you keep your promises to customers.

- Develop a solid customer feedback mechanism and pay attention to the information you receive. What actions have you taken in the last six months that were directly related to customer feedback?

- Identify the areas in which your customers perceive you have a competitive advantage. Explore how you can excel even more in those areas.

- Examine the issue of customer retention.
    - How do you define loyal customers?
    - How much time and money do you direct toward retaining current customers?
    - Why do your customers defect?

- Determine how well your employees are focusing their energy and efforts on areas that are vital to customers.

Gain a better understanding of the sales function

- Meet with your peers in the sales function to learn about their key sales strategies.

- Analyze the sales strategies. How do they vary for specific products and services? For different customer sets or markets?

- Learn about relationship- and transaction-focused strategies. Does your sales group use one strategy for high-end products and services and another for lower end products and services?

- Find out how sales information is generated and used in your organization.

- Learn the cost of sales for your area. Are sales costs going up or down? What is causing the shift?

- Discuss whether your organization's current sales approach will continue to be competitive and sustainable.

- Arrange to accompany salespeople in the field. Listen to how they position your products and services. Go out with both individuals and sales teams to see how the sales calls differ.

- Ask the sales group how you can help them. Talk with sales people about their concerns and issues with your functional area. End the conversation with an action plan.

Gain a better understanding of the customer service function

- Broaden your knowledge of the customer service area. Become familiar with key customer service policies and practices.

- Learn how the quality of customer service is measured in your organization.

- Encourage all employees to share customer feedback and suggest ways to make the organization more responsive to customer needs. Demonstrate that you take your employees' input seriously by acting on their comments and suggestions.

- Monitor how easy it is to work with your organization. Ask customers about their experiences, both positive and negative. What changes can you make in response to their feedback?

- Meet weekly with your staff to discuss the most frequent complaints made by customers about your area.

- Survey your customers to see how your organization stacks up against your competition in terms of customer service. Where do they have an advantage? What can you do to challenge their approach to customer service?

- Benchmark your customer service department against organizations known for excellence in this area.

5. Understand how to use staff functions effectively.

Staff functions advise, serve, and support the line functions. They include human resources, communications, finance and accounting, legal, information services, and the like. A basic knowledge of each staff function will help you assemble more effective teams and coordinate their efforts to maximum advantage.

Develop your understanding of the financial function

- Ask people in the finance function about key issues that the organization deals with on a regular basis.

- Identify which financial controls operate in your organization. How do these controls impact your department?

- Review key financial measures that are used in your organization and industry.

- Learn what role the financial function plays in formulating your organization's strategy. What impact do they have on decision making?

- Study your organization's budgeting process. Do you have a solid understanding of how it works? What key trade-offs were part of this year's budgeting process? How were they made? Who was involved?

- Find out about your organization's investment strategy. What is your risk strategy? What is your acquisition strategy?

- Analyze annual reports from the last few years to understand more about the financial health of your organization.

- If you need to acquire more financial skills, attend an executive course or seminar for nonfinancial executives at a university.

Develop your understanding of the human resources role

- Study your organization's human resources strategy. How does it support the organization's overall business goals?

- Learn about the key human resources issues that will impact the business in the next three to five years. How does HR plan to address them?

- Discuss how employees provide a competitive advantage for your organization. How does your organization show that it values its employees?

- Investigate how talent is selected and utilized within your organization. Is there a current and adequate succession management plan?

- Learn about your organization's development program for employees. What are the individual's and the manager's roles in development? What development resources are available for individuals and groups?

- Learn which core competencies are required for your organization to succeed. Do people receive training and encouragement in developing those competencies?

Develop your understanding of the legal role

- Identify the key legal issues in your area. They may include acquisitions, mergers, divestitures, employment contracts and terminations, and customer and pricing agreements.

- Build relationships with the members of the legal staff who support your department. Learn what type of help they currently provide and explore how they could help you further.

- Become familiar with the important laws and regulations that affect your department and organization.

- Develop an understanding of how intellectual property, vendor relationships, and client relationships are protected in your organization.

Develop your understanding of the information systems/information technology (IS/IT) role

- Meet with key IS/IT leaders to discuss the current state of information systems and technology in your organization. Ask for their assessment of the organization's strengths and weaknesses in the technology area.

- Learn how IS/IT currently interacts with your group. Do they play a significant role? How has that role changed in the past two years? How will it change in the next two years?

- Work with an IS/IT colleague to plan how information technology could change the way you work in your area. What would it take to make significant changes in productivity or efficiency?

- Give your IS/IT colleagues feedback on the type of information they currently provide. Is the information timely and accessible? Is the format understandable and useful to you?

- Discuss how IS/IT can help you integrate processes across functions in your organization.

- Ask technology vendors to periodically meet with you and your staff to discuss new products and developments.

- Meet with recently hired technical employees and ask them to assess your organization's technical capacities. How does it compare to other organizations?

6. Consider all management functions when developing plans and implementing changes.

Executive decisions are often made at a level that affects entire business units or the organization as a whole. Because the consequences can be far-reaching, such decisions cannot be made lightly. Sufficient preparation and analysis must precede a change, and effective communication and explanation must follow it.

Involve affected parties in planning

- Ask your direct reports to identify who should be included in the planning process. Involve the people and departments whose support will be necessary to implement the change. Remember, it is better to ask for feedback from the affected parties than to guess what their reactions will be.

- Try to involve others in each phase of the planning process: defining the problem or opportunity, generating options, selecting criteria for making the final decision, making the final call, and planning implementation.

- Involve the same people in every phase or include different people in each, depending on the input needed.

Define roles and responsibilities

- Discuss the role of each function during the change initiative. People need to be able to see the overall picture.

- If you change roles or assign new responsibilities during a project, announce it to everyone involved in the process.

- Keep track of any instances of unclear or inadequate definitions of roles and responsibilities. After you clear up the misunderstanding, communicate with each person involved in the process to make sure everyone has the same information. Note the cause of each misunderstanding so you can improve your definitions in the future.

- If you anticipate that people will disagree about how the roles and responsibilities were assigned, talk with each person first to explain your rationale. Deal respectfully with their concerns. Be clear about what you want, particularly with those you will rely upon as supporters.

Communicate during the change process

- Whenever there is a major change initiative in process, communicate, communicate, communicate! Expect that some people will not get the complete message the first, second, or even third time they hear it.

- Share the "whys" driving the change, not just the what, who, how, and when.

- Because you hold a high position in an organization, it is important that you realize your thoughts and feelings may be diluted and changed when you communicate through others. Determine when people need to hear a clear, definitive message from you, and when other people should be responsible for communicating a message.

- Organize the information you want to convey and gather the necessary supporting data. You will communicate more clearly if you are well prepared.

- Monitor your communications for mixed messages. If you believe you are sending them or receive feedback that you are, restate your message to clarify any misunderstanding.

- Ask a trusted colleague for feedback on your ability to openly communicate your ideas, intentions, and feelings. Do you seem sincere or does it seem forced? Are you able to get your point across?

- Encourage people to openly express their thoughts and feelings about the change. Listen carefully, try to understand their concerns, and take them seriously. Then discuss your rationale for implementing the change.

7. Display strong general management skills.

If your experience has been in one particular function rather than in the management of multiple functions or an entire business, you may not possess strong general management skills. Or you may have strong general management skills, but the perception is that you are only good in the last area you managed. In either case, it is up to you to develop the skills and/or change the perception to build your expertise and credibility.

Understand the general management role

- Develop a clear understanding of the expectations for your role. Discuss your role with your boss so you know which areas are critical, which are important, and which can be put on hold when necessary.

- Determine where your general management skills are strong and where you need to develop knowledge or experience.
    - Ask for specific feedback from your boss, trusted colleagues, or selected members of your external network.
    - Use a GAPS grid (discussed in chapter 19) to assess your abilities against the standards for your position.
    - Participate in a formal assessment process from a human resources consulting firm, such as Personnel Decisions International.

- Identify a role model. How does that person display strong general management skills? How does the person handle areas in which he or she is not as strong?

- Interview an experienced general manager whom you admire. Find out how he or she developed skills in this area. What advice does he or she have for people who are new in this role? What tips does he or she have for someone in your position within your organization's culture?

Build your general management skills

- Create a targeted development plan that will expand your general management skills, knowledge, and experience.

- Manage at least two departments in your current position.

- Assume responsibility for a project requiring multiple management skills, such as new product development, a new plant start-up, or a major technology introduction.

- Staff your team with individuals who are strong in areas in which you have less knowledge, skill, or experience. Learn as much as you can from their insight and judgment.

- Seek out a coach in this area. Regularly meet with him or her to discuss your experiences and growth in this area. Make sure you are both clear about the expectations for the coaching relationship.

- Talk to several executive colleagues who have successful general management track records. Read the articles, newsletters, and books they recommend.

- Consider retaining consultants or advisors who can expand your knowledge of specific functions or activities. Actively use them as your teachers.

- Attend an executive school or seminar designed for general managers and concentrate on the topics with which you have less familiarity.

RESOURCES

The resources for this chapter begin on page 468.

21
INDUSTRY
KNOWLEDGE

KNOW WHAT IT TAKES TO BE SUCCESSFUL IN
THIS INDUSTRY; HAVE THOROUGH KNOWLEDGE OF
THIS INDUSTRY'S HISTORY, CUSTOMERS,
AND COMPETITIVE ENVIRONMENT.

KEY BEHAVIORS

---

1. *Know what it takes to be successful in this industry.*
2. *Have thorough knowledge of this industry's history and growth patterns.*
3. *Apply knowledge of products and processes to understand key issues within own unit and across the organization.*
4. *Display deep insight into the competition's strengths, weaknesses, and strategies.*
5. *Have experience and know-how in a variety of industries.*

INTRODUCTION

What is industry knowledge? How do you acquire it if you are in an industry that changes every three months? Does knowing the history of an industry matter in a world where everything is changing?

Absolutely! Executives need to know their industries like the back of their hands. They need to be immersed and steeped in knowledge and insight. Paradoxically, they also need to be able to step outside of their industry and see it with the eyes of an outsider. Having both viewpoints helps them recognize and capitalize on good business opportunities.

The sheer amount of information can be staggering—where does one start? Savvy executives start by asking questions. How has the industry changed since they began their careers? More important, how is it going to change in the next few years? What part are they going to play in leading those changes? Also, what can they learn from other industries? Have competitors taken their companies into new arenas?

Joel Barker, a popular U.S. futurist, claims that anticipation and innovation are more critical to organizational success than ever. Executives are in a key role to make sure those two events happen, and industry knowledge is their starting point.

VALUABLE TIPS

- Don't just learn industry knowledge—create it.

- Create a mental map of your industry and update it frequently.

- Learn about the intangibles of your industry.

- Determine how e-commerce does and will affect your organization and industry.

- Explain the special competencies of your business to someone who has never heard of your industry.

- List your industry's key developments in the last six months.

- Study the solutions being tried by a wide range of industries.

- Look for competitive information in unexpected places.

- Maximize the rate at which people in your organization learn and apply knowledge.

- Regularly read leading articles about your industry.

- Track how well your team shares knowledge with each other and their respective areas.

- Investigate your organization's opportunity cost of not developing and sharing knowledge.

- Make sure people don't walk out the door with the knowledge you need to take your organization to the next level.

- Document and share learnings across the organization.

- Set aside time each quarter (or periodically) to explore and chart new business opportunities.

- Hire direct reports who have a wide mix of industry knowledge and experience. Look for both depth and breadth.

- Envision where you want to take the industry in the next five years.

STRATEGIES FOR ACTION

1. Know what it takes to be successful in this industry.

Every industry has success factors that organizations must meet. The key is knowing what those factors are going to be in the future. Some industries are changing so rapidly that executives must rethink their businesses every few months instead of years. Other industries are on the brink of expanding, changing their boundaries, and transforming into new configurations. Your task is to not only meet the challenges of your industry, but lead at the edge of the curve.

Understand your organization's current position

- Determine your organization's current position within the industry. What factors contributed to this position? Are you satisfied with the trajectory the organization is on?

- List the skills or capabilities that make your organization unique within your industry. In which skills and capabilities do you excel?

- Examine how you measure up against your competitors in the industry. Where are you winning? Where are they ahead?

- Understand your current competitive strategy. Are you competing on the basis of best total cost, best product, or best total solution? (These strategies are described by Michael Treacy and Fred Wiersema in their book *The Discipline of Market Leaders,* Perseus Press, 1997.)

- Know why your customers make their choices. This will help you determine if the factors in which you have chosen to excel are the most important to your customers.

- Determine who has the best customers in the industry. Why? What factors drive the best customers to select those organizations?

Keep abreast of broad industry developments

- Determine how the industry is changing. What factors impact the industry? How could the success factors change?

- Ask your colleagues and coworkers to identify important trends in your industry. Compare their answers. What themes emerge?

- Create a model of your industry and display each competitor's unique assets. Look for potential overlaps, gaps, and synergies; also look for possible mergers and alliances that your company could pursue.

- Find out who, if anyone, has business environmental scanning responsibility in your organization. Read their reports and discuss their findings with your peers.

- Study market research to identify which factors influence your customers' choice of vendor. How have those factors changed in the past few years? What will make them change in the future?

- Ask experts to help you recognize key trends. Use their knowledge and expertise to stay on top of current information.

- Build an informal network of peers in organizations comparable to yours and exchange stories about successes and failures.

- Broaden your contacts and meet leaders in your field by joining professional and industry organizations.

- Attend university- and industry-sponsored seminars on new developments in your field.

- Become familiar with the type of business and industry information you can find on the Internet. A good place to start is **www.ceo-express.com.**

- Stay up-to-date on your industry and general business reading, including:
  - Trade and professional publications
  - Abstracts of key business articles and books
  - Publications such as *Fortune, Forbes, Business Week,* the *Wall Street Journal, Fast Company,* and *The New York Times*
  - Business publications from countries outside your own

Stay up-to-date on "best in class" practices

- Read and learn what you can about organizations in your industry that are cutting edge or have a state-of-the-art process or product. What learnings can be applied to your organization?

- Interview people within your organization who have come from other organizations. They can share important expertise from their industries.

- Create a team that will develop and maintain benchmarking data. Compare your processes to those of other organizations and identify opportunities for improvement.

- Benchmark against companies that are leaders in your industry. Look at firms that are leading in areas in which you are trying to improve. Change your targets as your business needs evolve.

- Benchmark against organizations noted for their successes in a particular area. These organizations do not have to be in the same industry, but they must be world-class in a particular functional or operational area.

2. Have thorough knowledge of this industry's history and growth patterns.

Knowing how your industry began and grew is important. Before you can critique or change something, you should know how it was created, the challenges involved, the roadblocks people faced, and how they worked with available resources. This information will help you pinpoint which issues were dealt with well, and give you clues on how you can deal with current and future issues.

Learn about the industry's history

- If you are new to your industry, talk to your boss and experienced colleagues for suggestions on how you can quickly get up-to-speed. What areas should you focus on first?

- Research the history of your industry. How did it begin? What was its market impetus?

- Dig up the myths, legends, stories, and decisions that shape the industry's sense of self and its sense of purpose. What does history tell you about the industry's possible strengths or weaknesses?

- Who are the heroes, sages, and elders of your industry? What were their specific achievements? How do those achievements impact the future of your organization and the industry?

- Examine how your industry dealt with transitions in its structure, philosophy, and mission.

- Consider how your industry's history can be both a boon and a barrier to organizational success. Does it hinder innovation? Does success prevent organizations from taking risks?

- Look for patterns of entrenched thinking within your industry, and especially within your organization.

- Identify the innovators within your industry. What changes are they making? How will that affect your organization?

Understand the industry's growth patterns

- Review your industry's growth patterns. Look for points of stability, decline, and rejuvenation.

- Identify trends that sparked a change in the past. What was the pattern? Do you see anything similar today?

- Examine how technology impacted past growth, then identify three to five emerging technologies that will influence your industry in the future.

- Find out what type of industry information your marketing department is tracking and learn how to use that data to understand and predict growth patterns.

- Examine factors that may currently affect your growth, such as:
    - Global interdependence
    - Changing definitions of quality, speed, and efficiency
    - Mass customization
    - Rapid technological change
    - Newly emerging domestic and international markets
    - Being digital
    - The emergence of e-commerce
    - Government policies and political shifts
    - Changing supplier relationships
    - New relationships between workers and employers; "free agents"

Envision the future of your industry

- Forecast significant changes in your industry and anticipate their impact. Begin strategizing now how you could deal effectively with those changes.

- Gather your senior managers once a month to discuss the future and how it may impact your business. Assign a relevant future-oriented article or book to read, and discuss how the author's analysis applies to your organization or industry.

- Ask your senior management team to consider the following questions:
    - Does your organization take the lead in defining the industry and its future?
    - Are you building the strategic architecture you will need in the future?
    - Do you compete for opportunity in addition to market share?

- Invite futurists to speak at your organization. Build in time for discussions on their assumptions and the implications of their predictions for the industry and your organization.

- Create a team whose sole purpose is to envision the future. Invite people from inside and outside of your company, including futurists, technology mavens, current industry leaders, strategists, and dreamers. Take their input seriously—sometimes an unusual, unexpected, or unorthodox idea is the key to maintaining a competitive edge.

- Identify five emerging opportunities that could positively impact your company's future. Then identify five areas where current or future competition could put you out of business unless you take immediate action.

- Tackle at least one new project each year that challenges you to think seriously about the future of your industry and organization.

3. Apply knowledge of products and processes to understand key issues.

At the executive level it is not possible or necessary for you to have detailed knowledge of every process that produces your organization's products and services. However, as a decision maker with input into the direction and strategy of your organization, you need to be aware of the various work processes, how they relate to one another, and the key issues around them. You can also play a key role in promoting learning and knowledge sharing across the organization.

Understand the organization's products

- Analyze the market for your organization's current products. Which markets are you in? Which products meet the needs of those markets? What is the current basis of your competitive advantage? Where do the margins come from?

- Examine products and markets across your organization's businesses. What are the commonalties? Where are the differences?

- Learn which products are on the development path. Are these products line extensions or do they meet significantly different needs?

- Consider what spurred product development in the past. Have you been a customer-led or technology-led company? How do you think that will change in the future?

- Find out how far ahead you are in product development. It is important that product development be focused on both near- and long-term product innovation at any given time.

Understand and leverage core processes

- Develop an understanding of core processes. There are at least two views of core processes:
    1. A core process is similar across a number of product lines or businesses. It is important to identify, define, and chart each process so it can be managed across the organization, not just in each work group.

2. A core process is unique and offers a significant point of differentiation from an organization's competitors. It delivers significant value to the customer and sets the organization apart. It is a strategic advantage and needs to be managed as such.

- Articulate both types of core processes within your organization. Every leader should have a shared understanding of what they are and how they can be leveraged.

- Ask a process team to focus on your organization's core processes. Identify which processes are, or should be, common across product lines and businesses in your organization.

- Determine if these processes bring strategic advantage to the organization. If they do not, how could they become a strategic advantage?

- Regularly examine whether your core processes still differentiate your organization and bring competitive advantage, or whether they have become the norm in the industry. Do not be lulled into complacency—keep challenging people who tell you everything is all right.

Understand and leverage core competencies

- Develop a strong understanding of the core competencies in your organization. A *core competence* is a bundle of skills and technologies that delivers a fundamental benefit as perceived by the customer.

- Work with your team to determine the core competencies in your area. Use the following criteria:
    - A core competence must be unique; it must offer something that competitors do not.
    - A core competence must be extendible; that is, you must be able to imagine what else can be done with the competence.
    - A core competence must be difficult to duplicate.
    - A core competence must be current. Core competencies can become core capabilities when others in the industry catch up.

- Manage core competencies as strategic assets. Develop and acquire the skills or technologies you need for your core competencies. Also consider aligning with other organizations to achieve the necessary combinations of skills and technologies.

- Find new ways to leverage the skills and technologies embedded in your core competencies. For example, find a new market for a current product.

- Look for opportunities to establish the core platform upon which others build their products. Provide an engine that drives a number of products; for example, provide the chip in every computer.

Coordinate planning across units and the organization

- Conduct strategic planning sessions with your colleagues across the organization to share strategic information, coordinate work, talk about the future of the business, and create opportunities. This will help your organization or unit leverage core competencies by moving from parallel planning to joint planning and collaboration.

- Review large-scale plans with your colleagues in the value chain, both upstream and downstream. Listen carefully to their reactions and input.

- When you review plans with your leadership team, ask how other functions and businesses were involved in the analysis and preparation. This will reinforce the concept that you want people to work together.

- When problems or a new opportunity arises, determine who should be involved. Guard against involvement for the sake of involvement. Involve people in plans and processes in which they can add value.

Practice knowledge management

- Find out how you currently capture, track, and teach the knowledge you have in your organization. In today's knowledge economy, your intellectual capital is vital.

- Become familiar with the basic concepts of knowledge management.

- Analyze the cost of not sharing information. What would you do if a key person left the organization tomorrow? What expertise will you lose? How much time would it take to replace that expertise? Is it replaceable?

- Create an environment where learning is encouraged, supported, and valued:
    - Support people's desire to study, learn, and investigate.
    - Encourage people to learn things they do not have to use immediately.
    - Reinforce the belief that people in the organization are smart, have insight, and are creative.

- Encourage a free flow of information and ideas, and encourage people to summarize and document their learnings, readings, and the like.
- Give people the freedom to fail.
- Communicate the importance of managing knowledge to people in your area and across the organization.
- Work with your peers to determine how you can coordinate your knowledge management efforts.

4. Display deep insight into the competition's strengths, weaknesses, and strategies.

Thoroughly understanding your competitors is a fundamental business practice. Unless you know the marketplace and your competitor's capabilities, you can't respond proactively and appropriately, or plan a suitable strategy. Developing that insight takes time, effort, and a great deal of thought and reflection. But the ROI is invaluable.

Study your competitors

- Begin with the following questions to analyze the competition:
  - Do your competitors dominate a certain market segment?
  - Do your competitors have a unique product or selling angle?
  - Which activities give your competitors a key advantage?
  - What are the major differences among your competitors in terms of their strengths and weaknesses?
  - Do your competitors have ideas or practices that would work well in your organization?

- Analyze data on your competitors' strengths and weaknesses in the areas of strategy, products, pricing, and practices. Distribute written reports of your analysis to relevant people in your organization to promote general awareness and discussion.

- Pay attention to what your competitors are doing, especially when it is out of character or new. Figure out what it means.

- Study competitors who are gone. Why did they fail? What lessons can you learn?

- Consider where you're getting your competitive information. Are you using the same sources as everyone else? Are you digging deeper than your competitors?

- Network with your industry peers from other geographical areas. Because they do not view you as a direct competitor, they may be more willing to share information.

Understand your competitors' unique skills and capabilities

- Study your competitors' strategies. Are they competing for best total cost, best product, or best total solution? Meet with your team to discuss the implications for your organizational strategy.

- Use a model created by Kenichi Ohmae to determine the unique features of your competitors and define performance relative to them (see his book, *The Mind of the Strategist*, McGraw Hill, 1996, for details). Then look for gaps that your organization can profitably fill.

- Analyze your ability to provide the best deal to your customers according to a process prescribed by Michael Treacy and Fred Wiersema in *The Discipline of Market Leaders*. Compare your deal-making ability to that of your competitors.

Know where competition will come from in the future

- Stay on top of technological advances, company mergers, and new competitors. Be alert to the problems and opportunities that these shifts can present to your organization.

- Look for competitors that are poised to take advantage of competitive changes. Analyze their resources, partnerships, distribution channels, positioning, brain power, and flexibility.

- Cultivate a sense of urgency within your organization—new competitors can emerge at any time and threaten your organization. Periodically discuss how you could handle unexpected sources of competition. Plan your countermoves.

- Identify vulnerabilities in your organization's profit engine. How might a competitor take advantage of those vulnerabilities? What different assumptions might a competitor make?

5. Have experience and know-how in a variety of industries.

The more you know, the more options you have. Developing your experience and knowledge in a variety of industries will enable you to apply principles from one discipline to another and look at old problems in new ways.

Develop a knowledge base about various industries

- Create a spot on your organization's intranet where you collect information on other industries. Track how often people are using it and what type of information they need.

- Read case studies from different industries. Look for innovative solutions that you could apply in your organization.

- Hire managers who have experience in distinctly different industries. Take advantage of their industry knowledge as you plan strategy and form objectives.

- Surround yourself with people who are insatiably curious. Find ways to use their ever-increasing knowledge within your organization.

- Join formal or informal groups that exchange business-related information. Look for associations based on common bonds, such as products, target markets, location, and organizational size.

- Create, join, or offer to chair a cross-industry task force that works on common problems and tries to identify new industries. This will give you a chance to study those issues in depth.

Explore synergies between your industry and other industries

- Expand your definition of your industry. What are the current boundaries? What could make those boundaries shift?

- Ask your senior management team to envision partnership possibilities between your organization and a company in another industry. What type of products and competencies could result?

- Look for partnerships or unusual alliances that, if realized, could revolutionize your industry.

- Take advantage of opportunities to talk to industry experts. Find out how they view the industry and whom they view as potential competitors or allies.

- Ask peers in related industries about processes, systems, products, and services that they use. Look for opportunities to experiment with their procedures and practices within your organization.

RESOURCES

The resources for this chapter begin on page 470.

RESOURCES

—————

EDUCATION IS NOT THE FILLING OF A PAIL,

BUT THE LIGHTING OF A FIRE.

– WILLIAM BUTLER YEATS

—————

THE ABILITY TO LEARN FASTER THAN

YOUR COMPETITION MAY BE THE ONLY

SUSTAINABLE COMPETITIVE ADVANTAGE.

– ARIE DE GEUS

**Chapter 1
Seasoned
Judgment**

Bazerman, Max H. *Judgment in Managerial Decision Making.* New York: John Wiley & Sons, 1997. ISBN: 0471178071.
Bazerman covers many aspects of decision making, including biases, uncertainty, fairness, motivation, regret, negotiation, and group decisions.

Browne, M. Neil, and Keeley, Stuart M. *Asking the Right Questions: A Guide to Critical Thinking.* Englewood Cliffs, NJ: Prentice Hall, 1997. ISBN: 0137581866.
This text helps readers bridge the gap between blind acceptance of information and critical analysis and synthesis. It teaches them to react rationally to alternative points of view and develop a solid foundation for making personal choices about what to accept and what to reject as they read and listen.

Hammond, John S., et al. *Smart Choices: A Practical Guide to Making Better Decisions.* Boston: Harvard Business School Press, 1998. ISBN: 0875848575.
Smart Choices outlines eight elements involved in making the right decision, from identifying exactly what the decision is and specifying your objectives to considering risk tolerance and looking at how today's decisions influence future decisions.

Klein, Gary. *Sources of Power: How People Make Decisions.* MIT Press, 1998. ISBN: 0262112272.
Klein presents an overview of naturalistic decision making and explains the strengths people bring to difficult tasks. His work is based on observations of people acting under real-life constraints such as time pressure, high stakes, personal responsibility, and shifting conditions.

Mitroff, Ian I. *Smart Thinking for Crazy Times: The Art of Solving the Right Problems.* San Francisco: Berrett-Koehler, 1998. ISBN: 1576750205.
Mitroff demonstrates that the majority of serious management errors can be traced to one fundamental flaw: solving the wrong problems. He introduces a process to help readers focus on the right problems, frame them correctly, and implement appropriate solutions.

SEMINARS

Critical Thinking: Real-World, Real-Time Decisions
University of Pennsylvania, Wharton Executive Education

Participants learn a sound process for framing problems and making decisions, including identifying the key elements of the decision, defining the right problem, and identifying tradeoffs and choices.

Length: 3 days
Cost: $4,350
Location: Philadelphia, PA
Telephone: 215/898-1776
Fax. 215/898-2064
www.wharton.upenn.edu/execed

Effective Decision Making
Harvard University, John F. Kennedy School of Government.

This program is designed for senior executives in the public, private, and nonprofit sectors. It focuses on making wise choices in the face of risk and uncertainty.

Length: 2 days
Cost: $1,950
Location: Boston, MA and Washington, DC
Telephone: 781/239-1111
Fax: 781/239-1546
www.ksg.harvard.edu

Program for Executives
Carnegie Mellon University

This program covers strategic skills, analytical thinking, leadership skills, and decision making. Coursework includes readings, case studies, discussion, role plays, simulation, and videotaping.

Length: 4 weeks
Cost: $17,400
Location: Pittsburgh, PA
Telephone: 412/268-2304
Fax: 412/268-2485
www.heinz.cmu.edu/exec-ed

**Chapter 2
Visionary
Thinking**

Cochrane, Peter. *Tips for Time Travelers*. New York: McGraw-Hill, 1998. ISBN: 0070120706.
A renowned business leader and irreverent futurist offers commentary on how today's dramatic advances in technology will alter the way we live and think. The technology is inevitable; Cochrane argues that the only question is whether we will embrace it or fear it.

Kotter, John. *Leading Change*. Boston: Harvard Business School Press, 1996. ISBN: 0875847471.
One of the world's foremost experts on business leadership distills 25 years of experience and wisdom into this visionary guide. He outlines what it will take to lead the organization of the 21st century.

Martin, Chuck. *Net Future: The 7 Cybertrends That Will Drive Your Business, Create New Wealth, and Define Your Future.* New York: McGraw-Hill, 1998. ISBN: 007041131X.
Author and cyber expert Chuck Martin identifies seven revolutionary trends that will profoundly affect and change the way we do business. He offers solid advice and tips on how to benefit best in an increasingly wired world.

Schwartz, Peter. *Art of the Long View: Planning for the Future in an Uncertain World.* New York: Doubleday & Company, 1996. ISBN: 0385267320.
Schwartz offers specific techniques for personal and organizational visioning, based on scenarios of the future. He includes numerous exercises that have been used with leading companies worldwide.

Sherman, Howard, and Schultz, Ron. *Open Boundaries: Creating Business Innovation through Complexity*. Reading, MA: Perseus Press, 1998. ISBN: 0738200050.
Open Boundaries helps readers understand, analyze, and nurture the creative process. The authors discuss a decision-making approach that thrives on ambiguity and unpredictability, rather than a linear cause-and-effect method.

SEMINARS

Advanced Management Program
Duke University, The Fuqua School of Business
This program outlines the forces that are changing business, discusses strategies for future success, and covers how to align strategic direction, organizational systems, and business relationships.
Length: 2 weeks
Cost: $19,000, including room and meals
Location: Durham, NC
Telephone: 919/660-8011
Fax: 919/681-7761
www.fuqua.duke/edu/

Creating the Future: The Challenge of Transformational Leadership
University of Virginia, Darden Executive Education
This program covers leadership strategies to help organizations compete effectively in a complex, changing world.
Length: 1 week
Cost: $4,950
Location: Charlottesville, VA
Telephone: 804/924-3000
Fax: 804/982-2833
www.darden.virginia.edu/execed/

Winning in the Next Millennium: Strategies for Driving Change
University of Pennsylvania, Wharton Executive Education
This conference addresses the challenges associated with creating and leading a world-class organization. Participants receive the latest insights in electronic commerce, biotechnology, globalization, competitive realities, and changing customer demographics.
Length: 4 days
Cost: $3,750
Location: Philadelphia, PA
Telephone: 215/898-1776
Fax: 215/898-2064
www.wharton.upenn.edu/execed

Chapter 3
Financial Acumen

Droms, William G. *Finance and Accounting for Nonfinancial Managers: All the Basics You Need to Know*. Reading, MA: Perseus Press, 1998. ISBN: 0201311399.

This book is specifically designed for people who are relatively untrained in the areas of accounting and finance, but need to learn more for continued professional growth. The reader will gain an understanding of the basic concepts used in financial analyses.

Fraser, Lyn M. *Understanding Financial Statements*. Englewood Cliffs, NJ: Prentice-Hall, 1997. ISBN: 0136191150.

Fraser's thorough discussion of concepts, theories, and analytical techniques is illustrated with practical case histories. This is a good resource for executives who want to increase their facility for understanding and interpreting the information in published financial statements.

Hickel, James. *The Cost-Effective Organization: How to Create It, How to Maintain It*. Lakewood, CO: Glenbridge Publishers, 1993. ISBN: 094443522X.

Hickel addresses two related subjects: how to conduct a thorough analysis of an organization to identify and eliminate unnecessary expenses, and how to ensure that those expenses don't creep back into the organization's budget. He discusses the need for vigilant management and the cooperation of all employees during all phases of the business cycle.

Higgins, Robert. *Analysis for Financial Management*. Chicago: Irwin Professional Publishing, 1995. ISBN: 0256135681.

Higgins, a professor at the University of Washington, presents financial information in a clear, concise manner. Used at top business schools across the country, this book will give both beginners and experienced financial professionals a wealth of information.

SEMINARS

Finance and Accounting for the Nonfinancial Executive
Columbia University
This program covers income statements, balance sheets, cash flow statements, modern costing analysis, and accounting issues in a global environment. It also teaches participants how to manage for financial excellence.
Length: 1 week
Cost: $5,950
Location: Harriman, NY
Telephone: 212/854-0013
Fax: 212/316-1473
www.gsb.columbia.edu/execed

Finance for the Nonfinancial Manager
University of Michigan
This program helps participants improve communication with people in financial areas, develop financial policy, and better understand the impact of financial decisions on their organization's profitability.
Length: 5 days
Cost: $5,200
Location: Ann Arbor, MI
Telephone: 734/763-3154
Fax: 734/763-9467
www.umich.edu/execed

Financial Issues in Global Competition
Thunderbird Executive Education
The program gives participants a deeper understanding of the global financial environment, including cross-border financial issues that affect competitiveness and performance.
Length: 1 week
Cost: $4,500
Location: Phoenix, AZ
Telephone: 602/978-7635
Fax: 602/978-0362
www.t-bird.edu/execed

**Chapter 4
Global
Perspective**

Bryan, Lowell L, et al. *Race for the World: Strategies to Build a Great Global Firm.* Boston: Harvard Business School Press, 1999. ISBN: 087584846X.

The authors explain how firms can drive their transition from national to global markets by pursuing and capturing entire portfolios of global opportunities. They describe companies who use intangible assets to think and act differently from past multinational models.

Hofstede, Geert H. *Cultures and Organizations: Software of the Mind.* New York: McGraw-Hill, 1997. ISBN: 0070293074.

Hofstede's theory of intercultural cooperation is based on his study of worldwide sites where dissimilar cultures coexist. He believes cooperation is not only possible, but mandatory for solving global survival issues.

Mazarr, Michael. *Global Trends 2005: An Owner's Manual for the Next Decade.* New York: St Martins Press, 1999. ISBN: 0312218990.

The transformation from an industrial to a knowledge economy and society is generating profound new challenges and opening up unprecedented possibilities. Mazarr provides a vision of the future and a handbook for understanding daily events.

Mulgan, Geoff. *Connexity: How to Live in a Connected World.* Boston: Harvard Business School Press, 1998. ISBN: 0875848508.

Mulgan's central issue is the fundamental conflict between the freedom to behave without considering the consequences (as many in the West are able to do) and interdependence between societies and cultures. The author argues that reciprocity, or the golden rule, "is the most important idea for a developed democratic society."

SEMINARS

**International Executive Program
INSEAD**

This program prepares participants for broader organizational responsibilities within a global marketplace. Basic organizational functions, financial analysis, and negotiation techniques are highlighted.

Length: 6 weeks
Cost: Fr 135,000
Location: Call vendor
Telephone: (33) 60 72 42 90
Fax: (33) 60 74 55 13
www.insead.fr

The International Forum
University of Pennsylvania, The Wharton School
This program gives participants an opportunity to explore global strategic issues. Senior business leaders test their thinking, their priorities, and their concerns against peers with similar responsibilities but different perspectives.
Length: 3 series of 4-day sessions
Cost: $40,000 for all three sessions, $28,500 for any two sessions, $15,900 for any one session
Locations: Call vendor
Telephone: 215/772-0266
Fax: 215/772-0357
www.wharton.upenn.edu/execed

The Oxford Advanced Management Programme
University of Oxford, Templeton College
This program is design for senior managers who have fifteen to twenty years experience. Participants examine business from a strategic, global perspective.
Length: 4 weeks
Cost: £14,000
Location: Oxford, United Kingdom
Telephone: (44) 1865 422500
Fax: (44) 1865 422501
www.templeton.ox.ac.uk/

Program for Global Leadership
Harvard University
This program is designed to address regional and global issues and how they affect the role of upper-level general managers.
Length: 4 weeks
Cost: $29,500
Location: Asia, South America, or Massachusetts
Telephone: 617/495-6555
Fax: 617/496-4345
www.exed.hbs.edu/

**Chapter 5
Shaping Strategy**

Day, George (ed.). *Wharton on Dynamic Competitive Strategy.* New York: John Wiley & Sons, 1997. ISBN: 0471172073.
Executives can use this advanced tool box of innovative methods, techniques, and approaches when they face competitive challenges. The topics are handled by experts in the field and are linked by common themes.

Downes, Larry. *Unleashing the Killer App: Digital Strategies for Market Dominance.* Boston: Harvard Business School Press, 1999.
ISBN: 087584801X.
When technologies, products, and services converge in radical, creative new ways, a "killer app" can emerge—a new application so powerful that it transforms industries, redefines markets, and annihilates the competition. Downes provides the tools and techniques you need to create the killer app within your organization.

Fahey, Liam. *Competitors: Outwitting, Outmaneuvering, and Outperforming.* New York: John Wiley & Sons, 1998. ISBN: 0471295620.
Fahey's approach, called "competitive learning," provides an integrated approach for successfully winning over the competition. Knowing the competition's broader competitive environment and its organizational culture can help companies make better decisions and become more efficient and productive.

Keller, Kevin Lane. *Strategic Brand Management: Building, Measuring, and Managing Brand Equity.* Englewood Cliffs, NJ: Prentice Hall.
ISBN: 0131201158.
Finely focused on "how-to" and "why," this book contains specific tactical guidelines for building, measuring, and managing brand equity.

Labovitz, George, and Rosansky, Victor. *The Power of Alignment.* New York: John Wiley & Sons, 1997. ISBN: 0471177903.
The authors identify five key elements that exist in every company and provide a specific framework for refining and linking those elements for organizational growth and sustained success.

Slywotzky, Adrian. *Profit Patterns: 30 Ways to Anticipate and Profit from Strategic Forces Reshaping Your Business.* New York: Random House, 1999.
ISBN: 0812931181.
Slywotzky provides a method to see order beneath the surface chaos. Pattern thinking helps people anticipate the likely direction of changes, reveals the economic meaning of these changes, and provides the tools to capitalize on them.

SEMINARS

The MIT Executive Short Course in Corporate Strategy
Massachusetts Institute of Technology

This program focuses on modern corporate strategy and strategic management, and promotes an exchange of ideas among top scholars and corporate executives.
Length: 5 days
Cost: $5,600
Location: Cambridge, MA
Telephone: 617/258-8984
Fax: 617/252-1200
www.mit.edu/sloan-exec-ed

Strategy Formulation and Implementation
Columbia University

This program covers formulating, communicating, and implementing business strategies. The first week covers competitive dynamics, industry analysis, financial analysis, and strategy formulation; the second week focuses on issues and processes that are related to strategy implementation.
Length: 2 weeks
Cost: $13,500
Location: Harriman, NY
Telephone: 212/854-0013
Fax: 212/316-1473
www.gsb.columbia.edu/execed/

Strategy: Formulation and Implementation
University of Michigan

This program explores a broad set of strategic management issues and provides executives with concepts and practical applications for long-range organizational planning, strategy formulation, and implementation.
Length: 6 days
Cost: $5,520
Location: Ann Arbor, MI and Hong Kong
Telephone: 734/763-4229
Fax: 734/764-4267
www.bus.umich.edu/

**Chapter 6
Driving
Execution**

Galloway, Dianne. *Mapping Work Processes*. Milwaukee, WI: ASQC Quality Press, 1994. ISBN: 0873892666.
Galloway's book focuses on action, not theory. Topics include process mapping, flowcharts, quality tools, process management, process improvement, and TQM.

Harrington, H. James, et al. *Business Process Improvement Workbook: Documentation, Analysis, Design, and Management of Business Process Improvement*. New York: McGraw-Hill, 1997. ISBN: 0070267790.
This hands-on implementation guide tells how to document a company's processes, analyze current effectiveness, design new processes, use system enablers, and much more. Lists, charts, and appendices are included.

Keen, Peter G.W., and Knapp, Ellen M. *Every Manager's Guide to Business Processes: A Glossary of Key Terms & Concepts for Today's Business Leader*. Boston: Harvard Business School Press, 1995. ISBN: 0875845754.
This guide gives a simple, but not simplistic, review of key terms and concepts, focusing on exactly what they mean in today's business environment.
It provides a comprehensive, cross-disciplinary summary of business process fundamentals and business process innovation.

Smith, Douglas K. *Taking Charge of Change: 10 Principles for Managing People and Performance*. Reading, MA: Perseus Press, 1997. ISBN: 0201916045.
Thinking of great ideas is easy compared to making changes, especially in large, complex organizations. This book provides the diagnostic tools managers need to assess their particular needs for change and the tool kit required to implement those changes.

Ulrich, Dave, Zenger, Jack, and Smallwood, Norm. *Results-Based Leadership*. Boston: Harvard Business School Press, 1999. ISBN: 0875848710.
The authors reveal how to produce results that can be measured and integrated into any business strategy or corporate culture. They argue that it is not enough to gauge leaders by personal traits such as character, style, and values, but they also need to achieve results.

SEMINARS

Leading Organizational Change
Cornell University, Johnson Graduate School of Management
The current business environment requires that individuals, teams, and organizations be equipped to lead and manage all types of change, including strategic, structural, cultural, and technological. This program is designed to provide a full range of necessary strategies, frameworks, and skills.
Length: 5 days
Price: $5,100
Location: Ithaca, NY
Telephone: 607/255-4251
Fax: 607/255-0018
www.gsm.cornell.edu

Leading Organizational Change
University of Pennsylvania, The Wharton School
This program views change as a natural process that can be continuously nurtured within organizations. Participants develop and practice the skills needed to recognize and facilitate change through simulations, case studies, and group presentations.
Length: 5 days
Cost: $6,950
Location: Philadelphia, PA
Telephone: 215/898-1776
Fax: 215/898-2064
www.wharton.upenn.edu/execed

Management of Change in Complex Organizations
Massachusetts Institute of Technology, Sloan School of Management
This program provides a research-based perspective on a number of emerging managerial problems and considers the various ways these problems can and should be addressed.
Length: 1 week
Cost: $5,600
Location: Dedham, MA
Telephone: 617/253-7345
Fax: 617/252-1200
mitsloan.mit.edu

**Chapter 7
Attracting and
Developing Talent**

Buckingham, Marcus, and Coffman, Curt. *First, Break All the Rules: What the World's Greatest Managers Do Differently*. New York: Simon & Schuster; 1999. ISBN: 0684852861.
Buckingham and Coffman explain how the best managers select an employee for talent rather than skills or experience, set expectations for them, build on their unique strengths rather than trying to fix their weaknesses, and develop them.

Cross, Elsie and White, Margaret (eds.) *The Diversity Factor: Capturing the Competitive Advantage of a Changing Workforce*. Chicago: Irwin Professional Publishing, 1996. ISBN: 0786308583.
This collection of the most-requested articles from the quarterly journal *The Diversity Factor*, provides both theoretical and practical information that will help organizations learn to manage diversity successfully.

Davis, Brian L., et al. *Successful Manager's Handbook: Development Suggestions for Today's Managers*. Minneapolis: Personnel Decisions International, 1996. ISBN: 0972577017.
This handbook is filled with on-the-job development suggestions and recommended resources for developing fundamental management skills. Based on Personnel Decisions' extensive research and practice in the area of management assessment and development, it is organized around nine core factors that are critical to managerial success.

McCall, Morgan W. *High Flyers: Developing the Next Generation of Leaders*. Boston: Harvard Business School Press, 1997. ISBN: 0875843360.
McCall presents a strategic framework for identifying and developing future executives. He believes leaders remain open to continuous learning and are able to learn from their experiences. The key is getting them the right experiences.

Peterson, David B., and Hicks, Mary Dee. *Leader As Coach: Strategies for Coaching and Developing Others*. Minneapolis: Personnel Decisions International, 1996. ISBN: 0938529145.
Leaders must equip employees with the tools, knowledge, and opportunities they need to develop themselves and become more effective. This book shows how purposeful coaching can direct energy and fuel systematic growth in the competencies your organization needs.

SEMINARS

Advanced Program in Human Resource Management
University of California, Los Angeles, The Anderson School

Participants will explore the relationship between human resources and business performance, and learn how to measure the impact of their human resources initiatives. They learn how to best build and utilize employee teams for positive organizational results, identify innovative approaches to effective employee training and feedback, and apply the latest assessment tools to measure job performance.

Length: 5 days
Cost: $4,875
Location: Los Angeles, CA
Telephone: 310/825-2001
Fax: 310/206-7539
www.anderson.ucla.edu/

Managing Managers and Professionals
Berkeley Center for Executive Development, Haas School of Business

Each participant's motives, competencies, managerial style, and organizational climate are assessed and analyzed to identify key areas on which to focus and improve.

Length: 5 days
Cost: $4,750
Location: Berkeley, CA
Telephone: 510/642-4735
Fax: 510/642-2388
E-Mail: bced@haas.berkeley.edu

Program for Manager Development
Duke University, The Fuqua School of Business

This seminar is designed to improve the managerial performance of high-potential executives and prepare them for future leadership in their organizations.

Length: 2 weeks
Cost: $9,500
Location: Durham, NC
Telephone: 919/660-8011
Fax: 919/681-7761
www.fuqua.duke.edu/

**Chapter 8
Empowering
Others**

Bradford, David L., and Cohen, Allan R. *Managing for Excellence: The Guide to Developing High Performance in Contemporary Organizations.* New York: John Wiley & Sons, 1997. ISBN: 0471127248.
The authors focus on the manager as coach and discuss how to develop overarching goals that tie employees' interests to the needs of the department. Other topics include building shared-responsibility teams and motivating employees to do even routine jobs creatively.

Petzinger, Thomas. *The New Pioneers: The Men and Women Who Are Transforming the Workplace and Marketplace.* New York: Simon & Schuster, 1999. ISBN: 0684846365.
Tom Petzinger, one of America's most-read business columnists, reveals how a dynamic generation of innovators and entrepreneurs is creating a collaborative new workplace, a value-added marketplace, and an economy overflowing with opportunity.

Pfeffer, Jeffrey. *The Human Equation: Building Profits by Putting People First.* Boston: Harvard Business School Press, 1998. ISBN: 0875848419.
Pfeffer uses evidence, analysis, and real-life examples to prove a direct correlation between effective people management and profits. He builds a strong business case that the culture and capabilities of an organization, derived from the way it manages its people, are the real and enduring sources of competitive advantage.

Pinchot, Gifford, and Pinchot, Elizabeth. *The Intelligent Organization: Engaging the Talent & Initiative of Everyone in the Workplace.* San Francisco: Berrett-Koehler, 1996. ISBN: 1881052982.
The Pinchots show how an organization can respond more effectively to customers, partners, and competitors by developing and engaging the intelligence, business judgment, and wide-system responsibility of all its members. They include examples of how these changes are already being implemented in diverse organizations.

SEMINARS

Leadership for Extraordinary Performance
University of Virginia, Darden Executive Education
This program examines how to develop vision and leadership that inspire others to extraordinary performance. Participants will learn how to gain support from key people and manage the fulfillment of individual and group commitments.
Length: 1 week
Cost: $5,300
Location: Call vendor
Telephone: 804/924-3000
Fax: 804/982-2833
www.darden.virginia.edu/execed/

Managing Teams for Innovation and Success
Stanford University, Graduate School of Business
This program is designed for teams or individuals who want a new approach for enhancing organizational effectiveness.
Length: 1 week
Cost: $6,300
Location: Stanford, CA
Telephone: 650/725-2608
Fax: 650/723-3950
www.gsb.stanford.edu/eep

Mobilizing People
IMD – International Institute for Management Development
This program will help managers improve their ability to influence others, particularly their ability to mobilize people to meet corporate, divisional, team, or project objectives.
Length: 2 weeks
Cost: Fr16,000
Location: Lausanne, Switzerland
Telephone: (41) 21 618 0342
Fax: (41) 21 618 0715
www.imd.ch

**Chapter 9
Influencing and
Negotiating**

Kozicki, Stephen. *Creative Negotiating: Proven Techniques for Getting What You Want from Any Negotiation.* Holbrook, MA: Adams Media Corporation, 1998. ISBN: 1558507973.
This book is written in a friendly, approachable style, with anecdotes, illustrations, and diagrams. The author focuses on flexibility, careful planning, and four basic rules: there are no rules, everything is negotiable, always ask for a better deal, and learn to say no.

Levine, Stewart. *Getting to Resolution: Turning Conflict into Collaboration.* San Francisco: Berrett-Koehler, 1998. ISBN: 1576750051.
According to Levine, people's inability to reach true resolution of conflict undermines their ability to forge successful business and personal relationships. He provides a new set of tools for resolving personal and business conflicts.

Rusk, Tom, and Miller, D. Patrick. *The Power of Ethical Persuasion: Winning Through Understanding at Work and at Home.* New York: Penguin Books, 1994. ISBN: 0140172149.
People can break through the barriers that stand in the way of communication by applying the ethical principles of respect, understanding, caring, and fairness. The authors show how to reach satisfying resolutions, even in high-stakes negotiations that are filled with strong emotions and defensive reactions.

Shell, G. Richard. *Bargaining for Advantage: Negotiation Strategies for Reasonable People.* New York: Viking Press, 1999. ISBN: 0670881333.
Bargaining for Advantage focuses on six key emotional leverage points that researchers have shown help the best negotiators succeed. It answers questions such as: how can you achieve your goals even when you are short on bargaining power?

Ury, William L. *Getting Past No: Negotiating Your Way from Confrontation to Cooperation.* New York: Bantam Doubleday Dell Publishing, 1993. ISBN: 0553371312.
Ury shows readers how to stay cool under pressure, stand up for themselves without provoking opposition, deal with underhanded tactics, find mutually agreeable options, and more.

SEMINARS

Negotiation Dynamics
INSEAD

This program provides strategies for handling a variety of negotiation situations, including negotiating within and between organizations, negotiating in complex multiparty situations, and negotiating in long-term relationships.
Length: 1 week
Cost: Fr28,000
Location: Call vendor
Telephone: (33) 60 72 42 90
Fax: (33) 60 74 55 13
www.insead.fr

Negotiation and Influence Strategies
Stanford University

This highly interactive program teaches participants how to implement negotiation strategies more effectively and emphasizes coalitions, networks, relationships, and ethics.
Length: 5 days
Cost: $6,300
Location: Stanford, CA
Telephone: 650/725-2608
Fax: 650/723-3950
www.gsb.stanford.edu/eep

Negotiate for Success
Rice University

Participants will learn how to master cooperative and competitive negotiation techniques, maximize power positions, and create opportunities for both parties to win.
Length: 3 days
Cost: $1,475
Location: Houston, TX
Telephone: 713/527-6060
Fax: 713/285-5131
www.rice.edu/execdev

**Chapter 10
Leadership
Versatility**

Conger, Jay A. *Winning 'Em Over: A New Model for Managing in the Age of Persuasion*. New York: Simon & Schuster, 1998. ISBN: 0684807726. Conger outlines four crucial components of effective managing by persuasion: building one's credibility, finding common ground so that others have a stake in one's ideas, finding compelling positions and evidence, and emotionally connecting with coworkers so that solutions resonate with them on a personal level.

Farson, Richard. *Management of the Absurd: Paradoxes in Leadership*. New York: Simon & Schuster, 1996. ISBN: 0684800802.
Farson challenges leaders to look past trendy quick fixes and facile formulas and deal with the real dilemmas and complexities of managing people and organizations.

Hughes, Richard L.; Ginnett, Robert C.; and Curphy, Gordon J. *Leadership: Enhancing the Lessons of Experience*. 2nd ed. Burr Ridge, IL: Richard D. Irwin, 1995. ISBN: 0256162123.
This textbook is based on the premise that leadership is a process, not a position. The authors look at how leadership develops and how it is measured. They examine leadership as an art and a science, and compare it to other concepts, such as power and influence.

Kouzes, James M., and Posner, Barry Z. *The Leadership Challenge: How to Keep Getting Extraordinary Things Done in Organizations*. San Francisco: Jossey-Bass, 1996. ISBN: 0787902691
This revised and updated book is an essential tool for leaders in business, government, education, communities, and all across society as they prepare themselves for the demands of 21st century leadership.

Vecchio, Robert, ed. *Leadership: Understanding the Dynamics of Power and Influence in Organization*. Notre Dame, Ind: University of Notre Dame Press, 1997. ISBN: 0268013160.
This anthology delivers the very best in the areas of general management and leadership. Six facets of leadership are explored: the myths and facts of what leaders do, power and influence, dysfunctional aspects of leadership, models of leadership, alternative views of leadership, and emerging issues.

SEMINARS

Advanced Leadership Program
University of Minnesota, Carlson School of Management
Participants will develop knowledge and skills to extend their leadership influence, develop a personal leadership strategy, and understand the sources and practice of courage and credibility.
Length: 4 days
Cost: $2,200
Location: Minneapolis, MN
Telephone: 612/624-2545
Fax: 612/626-9264
www.csom.umn.edu/edc

Impact Leadership
Personnel Decisions International
Participants in this workshop will learn more about their assets as a leader, learn how to enlist others in their vision, and establish their own leadership agenda. Working alone and in small groups, participants will identify leadership opportunities, set priorities, plan action steps, mark milestones, and set goals to continue developing their personal and interpersonal leadership.
Length: 3-5½ days
In-house delivery only; program tailored to meet your needs.
Location: Call vendor
Telephone: 800/633-4410
Fax: 612/904-7120
www.personneldecisions.com

Leadership at the Peak
Center for Creative Leadership
Participants evaluate themselves as leaders, identify specific development goals, strengthen their understanding of the reasons for executive success and failure, and acquire new ways to develop and learn as senior executives.
Length: 1 week
Cost: $8,900
Location: Colorado Springs, CO
Telephone: 336/545-2810
Fax: 336/282-3284
www.ccl.org

**Chapter 11
Building
Organizational
Relationships**

Ashkenas, Ron, et al. *The Boundaryless Organization: Breaking the Chains of Organizational Structure.* San Francisco: Jossey-Bass, 1995. ISBN: 078790113X.
Four top management strategists show how leading companies are breaking boundaries in all directions—vertical, horizontal, external, and geographic—and achieving stellar results.

Bolton, Robert, and Bolton, Dorothy. *People Styles at Work: Making Bad Relationships Good and Good Relationships Better.* New York: AMACOM, 1996. ISBN: 0814477232.
According to the authors, it is possible to overcome personality conflicts by understanding other people's differences instead of merely reacting to them emotionally. They present a comprehensive behavioral science model for understanding four different "people styles"—driver, analytical, amiable, and expressive.

Maurer, Rick. *Feedback Toolkit: 16 Tools for Better Communication in the Workplace.* Portland, OR: Productivity Press, 1994. ISBN: 1563270560.
This short, easy-to-read book is filled with practical how-to's (and how not-to's). Maurer's six-step framework and creative approaches to giving and receiving feedback will help both individuals and groups improve their skills.

Oshry, Barry. *Seeing Systems: Unlocking the Mysteries of Organizational Life.* San Francisco: Berrett-Koehler, 1996. ISBN: 1881052990.
Oshry explains why so many efforts to create more satisfying and productive human systems end in disappointment, lost opportunities, broken relationships, and failed partnerships. He provides a new view of these systemic relationships and patterns, enabling people to recognize and stop destructive patterns of behavior.

SEMINARS

Strategies for Enhancing Executive Influence
Harvard University, John F. Kennedy School of Government
This program gives senior executives research-based influence strategies, techniques for analyzing influence situations, and guidelines for planning influence strategies inside and outside the organization.
Length: 2 days
Cost: $1,450–$1,950
Location: Cambridge, MA
Telephone: 781/239-1111
Fax: 781/239-1546
www.ksg.harvard.edu

Positive People Skills
Ashridge
This program will raise participants' awareness of their interpersonal skills and help them manage relationships more effectively.
Length: 1 week
Cost: £2,990 + VAT
Location: Berkhamsted, United Kingdom
Telephone: 44 (0) 1442 843491
Fax: 44 (0) 1442 841209
www.ashridge.org.uk

**Chapter 12
Inspiring Trust**

Barrett, Richard. *Liberating the Corporate Soul: Building a Visionary Organization*. Boston: Butterworth-Heinemann, 1998. ISBN: 0750670711. Barret provides leaders with the tools they need to develop, implement, and monitor a values-driven corporate culture.

Dalla Costa, John. *The Ethical Imperative: Why Moral Leadership is Good Business*. Reading, MA: Addison-Wesley, 1998. ISBN: 0201339838. The author believes corporate ethics must be a fundamental component of any business. He provides a practical model that people can use to establish their own "ethical orientation" and outlines a global ethic for the global economy.

Hagberg, Janet O. *Real Power: Stages of Personal Power in Organizations*. Salem, WI: Sheffield Publishing Company, 1994. ISBN: 1879215179. Hagberg focuses on a number of power paradigms, including leadership, how women and men view and use power, and six stages of power.

Hesselbein, Frances (ed) and Cohen, Paul (ed). *Leader to Leader: Enduring Insights on Leadership from the Drucker Foundation's Award-Winning Journal*. San Francisco: Jossey-Bass Publishers, 1999. ISBN: 0787947261. A "who's who" of world-class business leaders, best-selling authors, and leading management gurus share their most important lessons on leadership.

Kouzes, James M., and Posner, Barry Z. *Credibility: How Leaders Gain and Lose It, Why People Demand It*. San Francisco: Jossey-Bass, 1995. ISBN: 0787900567. Kouzes and Posner assert that credibility is the foundation of leadership. They believe leaders can encourage greater initiative, risk taking, and productivity by demonstrating trust in employees and resolving conflicts on the basis of principles instead of positions.

SEMINARS

Executive Seminar
The Aspen Institute
This values-based seminar gathers leaders from public, private, and other sectors to discuss the forces at work in society and the global community. Classic readings from Plato to Jefferson are used to stimulate thinking on vision and integrity.
Length: 1 week
Cost: $5,500
Location: Aspen, CO
Telephone: 970/544-7915
Fax: 970/544-7983
www.aspeninstitute.org

The Executive Leadership Program
Vanderbilt University, Owen Graduate School of Management
This program focuses on the qualities of leadership and new ways to lead and motivate others.
Length: 3 days
Cost: $1,750
Location: Nashville, TN
Telephone: 615/322-2513
Fax: 615/343-2293
www.vanderbilt.edu

**Chapter 13
Fostering Open
Dialogue**

Ellinor, Linda, and Gerard, Glenna. *Dialogue: Rediscover the Transforming Power of Conversation*. New York: John Wiley & Sons, 1998. ISBN: 0471174661.
Dialogue breaks down barriers, creates partnerships, and helps team members achieve optimal results. In this book, readers learn how to use the full range of Dialogue methods, including its four fundamental techniques: suspension of judgment, listening, identification of assumptions, and inquiring/reflection.

Krisco, Kim. *Leadership and the Art of Conversation: Conversation as a Management Tool*. Prima, 1997. ISBN: 0761510303.
Conversation is the most powerful—and underutilized—management tool. If you can change the way you talk to people, you can become a more effective executive virtually overnight. With this book, you'll learn how to use the "ordinary" conversations you have with people at work every day to boost productivity, inspire peak performance, and achieve success.

McCallister, Linda. *I Wish I'd Said That*. New York: John Wiley & Sons, 1997. ISBN: 0471176877.
Six major styles of communication are described in detail: noble, magistrate, candidate, senator, Socratic, and reflective. Recognizing these communication styles will help people control interactions without building resentment. The author includes a communication style profile test, so readers can identify their particular style.

Stone, Douglas; Patton, Bruce; and Heen, Sheila. *Difficult Conversations: How to Discuss What Matters Most*. New York: Viking Press, 1999. ISBN: 0670883395.
Everyone dreads certain types of conversations, and often handles them poorly. The authors teach readers how to handle these dialogues with more success and less anxiety.

SEMINARS

**Communications Strategy: Managing Communications
for the Changing Marketplace
Northwestern University, Kellogg Graduate School of Management**
The program emphasizes how best to coordinate and manage various modes
of commercial communication in order to sustain a competitive advantage.
Length: 4 days
Cost: $3,200
Location: Evanston, IL
Telephone: 847/467-7000
Fax: 847/491-4323
www.kellogg.nwu.edu/

**Persuasion and Influencing Skills
Vanderbilt University, Owen Graduate School of Management**
The program helps participants communicate more effectively, listen
effectively, negotiate successfully, and conduct productive meetings.
Length: 3 days
Cost: $1,550
Location: Nashville, TN
Telephone: 615/322-2513
Fax: 615/343-2293
www.vanderbilt.edu

Chapter 14
High-Impact
Delivery

Mosvick, Roger K., and Nelson, Robert B. *We've Got to Start Meeting Like This: A Guide to Successful Meeting Management.* Indianapolis, IN: Park Avenue, 1996. ISBN: 1571120696.
A tremendous amount of time is lost in business every day because of ineffective meetings. This book demonstrates how to have fewer meetings and get better results.

Ringle, William. *Techedge: Using Computers to Present and Persuade.* Englewood Cliffs, NJ: Prentice Hall, 1998. ISBN: 020527305X.
Ringle's book is meant for both novices and experts. He covers topics such as choosing a laptop computer for presentations, using the Internet to research topics, creating interesting slide presentations by adding multimedia enhancements, and using microphones and projectors.

Urech, Elizabeth. *Speaking Globally: Effective Presentations Across International and Cultural Boundaries.* London: Kogan Page Ltd., 1998. ISBN: 0749422211.
Because executives are faced with multicultural and multilingual workforces in a global economy, they need to communicate effectively with all types of audiences. Urech outlines tools and techniques, highlights pitfalls and perils, and provides country-by-country guidelines.

Wilder, Lilyan. *7 Steps to Fearless Speaking.* New York: John Wiley & Sons, 1999. ISBN: 0471321591
This seven-step program for improving oral communications skills tells how to improve one's voice, structure a presentation, use props, and demonstrate conviction.

Woodall, Marian K. *Thinking on Your Feet: How to Communicate Under Pressure.* Professional Business Communications, 1996. ISBN: 0941159965.
This concise book outlines techniques for improving the quality of responses to difficult questions. The author provides guidance on how to quickly and clearly formulate answers and improve the delivery of the message.

SEMINARS

Effective Executive Speaking
American Management Association
This seminar is designed for every executive with some speaking experience who must speak in front of a group, make a presentation, sell ideas to others, or face cameras and microphones.
Length: 3 days
Cost: $1,445
Location: Call vendor
Phone: 800-262-9699
www.amanet.org/seminars

Speaking With Impact
Personnel Decisions International
This seminar gives participants feedback on their current skill level and teaches them how to develop a unique speaking style. Participants will learn how to motivate their audiences and gain confidence in all aspects of public speaking.
Length: 2 days
In-house delivery only.
Locations: Call vendor
Telephone: 800/633-4410
Fax: 612/904-7120
www.personneldecisions.com

**Chapter 15
Drive for
Stakeholder
Success**

Kaplan, Robert S., and Norton, David P. *The Balanced Scorecard: Translating Strategy Into Action*. Boston: Harvard Business School Press, 1996. ISBN: 0875846513.
The authors provide a framework for translating a company's vision and strategy into a coherent set of performance measures. In addition, they discuss how one can channel employees' energies, abilities, and specific knowledge toward long-term goals.

Knight, James A. *Value-Based Management: Developing a Systematic Approach to Creating Shareholder Value*. New York: McGraw-Hill, 1997. ISBN: 0786311339
Knight clearly defines the nature of corporate value, and explains how enhancing it can create positive reverberations throughout an organization. He describes companies that have successfully managed for value, and explains how value-added management creates the optimal balance between short- and long-term decisions.

Reichheld, Frederick F. *The Loyalty Effect: The Hidden Force Behind Growth, Profits, and Lasting Value*. Boston: Harvard Business School Press, 1996. ISBN: 0875844480.
Reichheld outlines how loyalty-based management can create highly profitable organizations. He links value creation, growth, and profits to loyal customers, employees, and owners. His conclusions show how even a small improvement in customer retention can double profits for a company.

Seybold, Patricia B., and Marshak, Ronni. *Customers.Com: How to Create a Profitable Business Strategy for the Internet and Beyond*. New York: Times Books, 1998. ISBN: 0812930371.
The author describe how *Fortune* 500 giants and smaller companies have created e-commerce initiatives that place them well ahead of their competitors.

Vavra, Terry. *Aftermarketing: How to Keep Customers for Life through Relationship Marketing*. Chicago: Irwin Professional Publishing, 1995. ISBN: 0786304057.
Vavra urges organizations to shift their focus from customer conquest to customer retention. He shows how to make customer satisfaction programs more responsive, build formal and informal communication programs, and pursue lost customers to win them back.

SEMINARS

Creating Shareholder Value
University of North Carolina at Chapel Hill,
Kenan-Flagler Business School

This program addresses how companies create value for owners, customers, and employees, and how value creation can be measured.
Length: 2 days
Cost: $1,450
Location: Chapel Hill, NC
Telephone: 800/862-3932
Fax: 919/962-1667
www.bschool.unc.edu

Measuring Customer Satisfaction
California Institute of Technology

This program focuses on customer satisfaction measurement systems, drawing upon examples and lessons learned from organizations that use customer information as a strategic tool.
Length: 2 days
Price: $1,595
Location: Pasadena, CA
Telephone: 626/395-4045
Fax 626/795-7174
www.irc.caltech.edu

Making Corporate Boards More Effective
Harvard University

Topics in this program include: board composition and selection, use of committees, accountability to owners and other stakeholders, the role of the board in strategic planning, and CEO evaluation and compensation.
Length: 4 days
Cost $5,000
Location: Boston, MA
Telephone: 617/495-6555
Fax: 617/495-6999
www.exed.hbs.edu

**Chapter 16
Entrepreneurial
Risk Taking**

Christensen, Clayton M. *The Innovator's Dilemma*. Boston: Harvard Business School Press. 1997. ISBN: 0875845851.
Some organizations let breakthrough innovations languish, because they are initially rejected by customers who cannot currently use them. Instead, they should create new markets and find new customers for their products. This book will help managers see the changes that may be coming their way and show them how to respond for success.

Drucker, Peter F. *Innovation and Entrepreneurship: Practice and Principles*. New York: Harperbusiness, 1993. ISBN: 0887306187.
The first book to present innovation and entrepreneurship as a purposeful and systematic discipline, this classic business title explains and analyzes the challenges and opportunities of America's entrepreneurial economy.

Graham Ehringer, Ann. *Make Up Your Mind: Entrepreneurs Talk About Decision Making*. Santa Monica, CA: Merritt Pub., 1995. ISBN: 1563431017.
Offers readers practical tools for improving their decision-making skills. In-depth interviews with entrepreneurs and businesspeople break down the decision-making process into a few basic models that everyone can use in their own decision-making. Includes flowcharts and templates.

Leonard-Barton, Dorothy. *Wellsprings of Knowledge: Building and Sustaining the Sources of Innovation*. Boston: Harvard Business School Press, 1998. ISBN: 0875848591
Leonard shows that successful innovators are companies that build and manage knowledge effectively. The book outlines lessons for creating, nurturing, and growing the experience and accumulated knowledge of the organization into renewable assets and competitive advantage.

Utterback, James. *Mastering the Dynamics of Innovation*. Boston: Harvard Business School Press, 1996. ISBN: 0875847404.
Utterback offers a pioneering model for how innovation unsettles industries and firms, and features fascinating histories of new product developments and strategies for nurturing innovation.

SEMINARS

The Babson Program on Corporate Entrepreneurship
Babson College
This program explores entrepreneurial mindsets, strategies, and systems (e.g., venture capital standards, business plans) to drive innovation within your organization. You will learn how to capture opportunities as viable business ventures and recognize and assess the markets, trends, and unsatisfied or unserved customer needs.
Length: 3 days
Price: $3,650
Location: Babson Park, MA
Telephone: 781/239-4354
Fax: 781/239-5266
www.babson.edu

Managing the Innovation Process
IMD
This program will broaden senior executives' perspectives on innovation and new product development. It is aimed at executives who are involved in identifying, conceiving, developing, and marketing new products.
Length: 1 week
Cost: Fr9,000
Location: Lausanne, Switzerland
Telephone: (41) 21 618 0342
Fax: (41) 21 618 0715
www.imd.ch/

Managing New Product Development for Strategic Competitive Advantage
Northwestern University, Kellogg Graduate School of Management
This program helps managers identify how they can gain competitive advantage through their product development process.
Length: 4 days
Cost: $3,600
Location: Evanston, IL
Telephone: 847/467-7000
Fax: 847/491-4323
www.kellogg.nwu.edu/

Chapter 17
Mature
Confidence

Bennis, Warren, and Goldsmith, Joan. *Learning to Lead*. Reading, MA: Perseus Press, 1997. ISBN: 0201311402.
The authors assert that leaders are made, not born. They believe that leadership is a function of knowing yourself, having a vision that is well communicated, building trust among colleagues, and taking effective action to realize your own leadership potential. This workbook provides step-by-step, practical advice for developing leadership skills.

Boyett, Joseph H., and Boyett, Jimmie T. *The Guru Guide: The Best Ideas of the Top Management Thinkers*. New York: John Wiley & Sons; 1998. ISBN: 0471182427
This book offers concise explorations of the best of today's thinking on management and leadership. The authors review the thinking of many of today's top business authors, distill the essence of each thinker's core ideas, and use commentaries and case studies to clearly show how each idea has been received and executed in the real world.

Goleman, Daniel. *Working With Emotional Intelligence*. New York: Bantam Books, 1998. ISBN: 0553104624
Goleman provides guidelines for cultivating self-awareness, self-confidence, and self-control; commitment and integrity; the ability to communicate and influence, and the ability to initiate and accept change.

Nierenberg, Gerard I. *Do It Right the First Time: A Short Guide to Learning from Your Most Memorable Errors, Mistakes, and Blunders*. New York: John Wiley & Sons, 1996. ISBN: 047114889X.
Nierenberg raises people's awareness about the way errors are made and provides techniques for substantially decreasing them.

Seligman, Martin E. P. *Learned Optimism*. New York: Pocket Books, 1998. ISBN: 0671019112.
Optimistic people believe they have more control over their lives; as a result, they are healthier, more content, and more successful. Seligman includes a test for measuring one's optimism level and outlines techniques for overcoming a pessimistic "explanatory style."

SEMINARS

Management of Managers: Leadership, Change, and Renewal
Southern Methodist University
This program is designed to help managers become more effective and derive more personal satisfaction from their corporate positions. Participants will review their current level of management proficiency, explore new techniques in managerial leadership, develop plans for renewing those leadership roles, and implement improvements for the betterment of themselves and their organization.
Length: 1 week
Cost: $4,950
Location: Dallas, TX
Telephone: 214/768-3549
Fax: 214/768-2987
www.cox.smu.edu/execdev

Motivation and Behavior
Menninger Management Institute
Participants in this seminar will gain an understanding of human behavior and motivation, take a critical look at their strengths and weaknesses as executives, and devise plans for using this knowledge in their professional and personal lives.
Length: 5 days
Cost: $4,100
Location: Call vendor
Telephone: 800/288-5357
Fax: 913/648-3155
www.menninger.edu

Chapter 18
Adaptability

Brown, Shona, and Eisenhardt, Kathleen. *Competing on the Edge: Strategy as Structured Chaos*. Harvard Business School Press, 1998. ISBN: 0875847544.

Brown and Eisenhardt contend that to prosper in today's fiercely competitive business environments, organizations must follow a new paradigm—competing on the edge. They discuss specific management dilemmas and illustrate effective solutions in a world of change.

Haeckel, Stephan H. *Adaptive Enterprise: Creating and Leading Sense-And-Respond Organizations*. Harvard Business School Press, 1999. ISBN: 0875848745.

Haeckel outlines a sense-and-respond business model that helps companies anticipate, adapt, and respond to continually changing customer needs. He maps out a step-by-step plan that organizations can use to transform themselves into a place where change is not a problem to be solved, but a source of energy, growth, and value.

Tichy, Noel, and Sherman, Stratford. *Control Your Destiny or Someone Else Will: Lessons in Mastering Change—From the Principles Jack Welch Is Using to Revolutionize GE*. New York: Harperbusiness, 1999. ISBN: 0887306705.

Through a chronicle of the GE revolution, the authors present a guide for managers facing intensifying competition and ceaseless change. They draw on their years of work in and around GE and their unprecedented access to CEO Jack Welch and other employees.

Wilson, Paul. *Calm at Work*. New York: Plume, 1999. ISBN: 0452280427. Wilson offers simple, straightforward techniques for overcoming stress on the job and making your life a more tranquil place.

SEMINARS

Managing Individual and Organizational Change
University of Virginia, Darden Executive Education
This program examines the importance of the individual's ability to cope with major change, and sharpens his or her ability to manage personal and organizational change.
Length: 4 days
Cost: $4,000
Location: Charlottesville, VA
Telephone: 804/924-3000
Fax: 804/982-2833
www.darden.virginia.edu/execed/

Leading Organizational Change and Renewal
Columbia University, Graduate School of Business
Participants will learn discovery-driven planning, the latest thinking for coping with fast-paced environments, how to monitor the progress of highly uncertain projects, how to manage cross-cultural and integration issues in change, how to manage disappointments in the change process, and how to avoid the most common pitfalls of change.
Length: 6 days
Price: $5,750
Location: Harriman, NY
Telephone: 212/854-3395
Fax: 212/316-1473
www.gsb.columbia.edu/execed

**Chapter 19
Career and
Self-Direction**

Dotlich, David L., and Noel, James L. *Action Learning: How the World's Top Companies Are Re-Creating Their Leaders and Themselves* (Jossey-Bass Business & Management Series). San Francisco: Jossey-Bass Publishers, 1998. ISBN: 0787903493.

Dotlich and Noel, acknowledged experts in their field, teach readers how to create an executive "gene pool" that will lead companies into the future without the need of expensive and time-consuming off-site training.

Frankel, Lois. *Jump-Start Your Career: How the 'Strengths' That Got You Where You Are Today Can Hold You Back Tomorrow*. New York: Crown Press, 1998. ISBN: 0609801368.

Using self-tests and dozens of examples from the workplace and her own practice, Dr. Frankel helps individuals identify their dominant skills and professional behaviors. She then shows readers how to use these traits to manage people optimally and create innovative solutions to tricky business problems.

Koch, Richard. *The 80/20 Principle: The Secret of Achieving More with Less*. New York: Bantam Doubleday Dell, 1998. ISBN: 0385491700.

The 80/20 Principle—that 80 percent of results flow from just 20 percent of our efforts—is one of the great secrets of highly effective people and organizations. Koch shows how you can achieve much more with much less effort, time, and resources, simply by concentrating on the all-important 20 percent.

Mackenzie, Alec. *The Time Trap*. New York: AMACOM, 1997. ISBN: 081447926X.

Mackenzie has distilled years of studying people's work habits into a book filled with practical, easy-to-use tips and techniques for decision making, organization, delegation, and overcoming procrastination. His suggestions will help readers become more efficient at work and enable them to spend more time on high-priority activities.

McDonald, Bob D., and Hutcheson, Don. *The Lemming Conspiracy: How to Redirect Your Life from Stress to Balance*. Atlanta, GA: Longstreet Press, 1997. ISBN: 1563524236.

This book helps readers examine their talents and skills and use them more effectively by integrating them into career and life vision.

Peterson, David B., and Hicks, Mary Dee. *Development FIRST: Strategies for Self-Development.* Minneapolis: Personnel Decisions International, 1995. ISBN: 0938529137.

Development FIRST outlines practical approaches for individual and team development within the changing corporate environment. Five concise development strategies enable users to plan and execute their own development in a busy, demanding world.

SEMINARS

Organisational and Interpersonal Skills in Management
Cranfield University

This program focuses on attitudes and interpersonal skills. It is aimed at senior-level executives who want to understand themselves and how they relate to others.

Length: 1 week
Cost: £4,345+ VAT
Location: Call vendor
Telephone: 44 (0) 1234 750111
Fax: 44 (0) 1234 751875
www.cranfield.ac.uk

Leadership that Shapes the Future
University of Washington

This program gives leaders an opportunity to focus on their leadership and influencing skills. Each participant creates a personal development plan during the program.

Length: 3 days
Cost: $2,100
Location: Seattle, WA
Telephone: 206/543-8560
Fax: 206/685-9236
www.uwexp.org

**Chapter 20
Cross-Functional
Capability**

Ackoff, Russell. *Re-creating the Corporation: A Design of Organizations for the 21st Century*. New York: Oxford University Press, 1999. ISBN: 0195123875.
While most business and management schools continue to teach the functions of a corporation separately—production, marketing, finance, personnel—the reality is that for a corporation to endure, each division must work with the others to create an effective system. *Re-Creating the Corporation* is Ackoff's blueprint for understanding and creating these model corporate systems.

Harvard Business Review on the Business Value of IT.
Boston: Harvard Business School Press, 1999. ISBN: 0875849121.
Information Technology influences all aspects of business today, and this wide-ranging resource will help managers understand the key concepts and terms and to envision the strategic potential of their IT assets.

Kotler, Philip. *Kotler on Marketing: How to Create, Win, and Dominate Markets*. New York: Free Press, 1999. ISBN: 0684850338.
Kotler's textbooks have sold more than 3 million copies in 20 languages. This is his long-awaited, essential guide to marketing for the new millennium.

Meredith, Jack, and Shafer, Scott. *Operations Management for MBAs.*
New York: John Wiley and Sons, 1998. ISBN: 047129828X.
An introduction to the process and management of transforming inputs into useful outputs. Each chapter contains case studies, questions, and definitions of key terms.

Rothwell, William, et al. *The Strategic Human Resource Leader: How to Prepare Your Organization for the Six Key Trends Shaping the Future.*
Davies-Black Publishing, 1998. ISBN: 0891061223.
This book shows how to align the HR function with organizational objectives, including how to define and measure HR results. It provides guidelines for building new competencies and outlines methods for narrowing the gap between current and future HR roles.

SEMINARS

Driving Flow-Based Operations to a Competitive Advantage
California Institute of Technology

This program provides an advanced view of operations strategies based on flow principles and examines their dramatic impact on manufacturing cycle time, quality, inventory, and order fulfillment. Participants will understand how to develop an effective flow-based strategy, identify the elements required to support the strategy, and plan a successful implementation of flow-based operations.

Length: 2 days
Price: $1,595
Location: Pasadena, CA
Telephone: 626/395-4043
Fax 626/795-7174
www.irc.caltech.edu

Integrated Operations and Marketing Management
Carnegie Mellon, The Graduate School of Industrial Administration

This program gives participants new cross-functional models to enhance marketing and operations decision-making, and create sustainable market and advantage for their companies.

Length: 6 days
Price: $4,950
Location: Pittsburgh, PA
Phone: 412/268-2304
Fax: 412/268-2485
cmu-execnet.gsia.cmu.edu

Managing Critical Resources: Developing a General Management Perspective
University of Virginia, Darden Executive Education

This program is for managers whose positions require an understanding of other areas within the company, so they can coordinate their function with those areas. Participants will also gain an understanding of business practices and policies in an international context.

Length: 2 weeks
Cost: $10,600
Location: Charlottesville, VA
Telephone: 804/924-3000
Fax: 804/982-2833
www.darden.virginia.edu/execed/

Chapter 21
Industry
Knowledge

Davenport, Thomas H., and Prusak, Laurence. *Working Knowledge: How Organizations Manage What They Know.* Boston: Harvard Business School Press, 1997. ISBN: 0875846556.
This primer on knowledge management establishes vocabulary and concepts, and serves as a resource to companies that recognize knowledge as the only sustainable source of competitive advantage.

Fine, Charles. *Clockspeed: Winning Industry Control in the Age of Temporary Advantage.* Reading, MA: Perseus Books, 1998. ISBN: 0738200018.
Drawing from a decade of research at MIT and using examples from the fastest-changing industries, Fine introduces a new vocabulary for analyzing and implementing business strategy. He views managers as "corporate geneticists" who do not react to the forces of change but master them to engineer their company's destiny.

Kahaner, Larry. *Competitive Intelligence: How to Gather, Analyze, and Use Information to Move Your Business to the Top.* New York: Touchstone Books, 1998. ISBN: 0684844044.
Kahaner explains how to turn the raw facts, statistics, and numbers about competitors' activities and market trends into practical guidelines for making the right business decisions.

Mendelson, Haim, and Ziegler, Johannes. *Survival of the Smartest: Managing Information for Rapid Action and World-Class Performance.* New York: John Wiley and Sons, 1999. ISBN: 0471295604.
Two management experts outline a basic framework for measuring and improving your company's "Organizational IQ." Organizational IQ summarizes an organization's capability to process information, make quick and effective decisions, and implement them.

Neff, Thomas J., and Citrin, James M. *Lessons from the Top: The Search for America's Best Business Leaders.* New York: Doubleday, 1999. ISBN: 0385493436.
The authors profile the fifty best business leaders in America, explore how they make their companies great, and outline the lessons we can learn from them.

Porter, Michael E. *Competitive Strategy: Techniques for Analyzing Industries and Competitors.* New York: The Free Press, 1998. ISBN: 0684841487.
Porter's classic book outlines a comprehensive set of analytical techniques for understanding an organization and the behavior of its competitors. He presents techniques to help leaders anticipate and prepare for sudden competitor moves or shifts in industry structure.

SEMINARS

Advanced Management Program
Harvard University
This seminar will provide participants with the insights, tools, and latest management thinking to make their companies more competitive, foster a greater appreciation of the complexities of business, and enhance their ability to lead and change organizations.
Length: 9 weeks
Cost: $44,000
Location: Boston, MA
Telephone: 617/495-6555
Fax: 617/495-6999
www.exed.hbs.edu/

eCommerce: Business Strategies for the New Marketplace
University of Southern California, Marshall School of Business
This program will help participants align their firm's resources to effectively compete in the new marketplace, create new business metrics, and manage the performance of an e-business against them. It will benefit companies new to the e-commerce world as well as experienced companies who want to extend an understanding of e-commerce across the organization.
Length: 3 modules, 4 weeks each
Location: Call vendor
Price: $2,900 (for the entire three-module program)
Telephone: 213/740-8990
Fax: 213/749-3689
www.marshall.usc.edu/execdev

About Personnel Decisions International

Personnel Decisions International (PDI) is a global consulting firm based in organizational psychology. We use our expertise to define, measure, and develop the capabilities needed to make organizations successful by growing the talents of their people, improving customer relationships, and increasing organizational performance.

Founded in 1967, PDI has become an internationally recognized leader in applying behavioral sciences to building successful organizations. PDI delivers services with the highest professional standards to hundreds of corporations and organizations throughout the world, from *Fortune* 500 organizations to emerging companies.

We work closely with our clients to better understand and meet their special needs. PDI's growth has been guided by a firm commitment to maintaining and enhancing the expertise our clients require. As a result, we have won a reputation for both professional excellence and practical results.

There are more than 250 psychologists and consultants at Ph.D. and Masters levels at PDI who specialize in assessment-based development. Our expertise spans many disciplines of psychology, a broad mix of corporate backgrounds, and practical business experience. This diversity of staff experience and professional credentials gives PDI a depth and breadth unique in our field.

Services, products, and consulting from Personnel Decisions International provide solutions to virtually every area of concern in human resources development:

- Assessment—for selection and promotion of the most qualified people for key positions

- Management development—to build the effectiveness and leadership ability of managers and executives

- Organizational effectiveness—to maximize the potential of the entire group

- Career transitions and career development—to strengthen organizations and preserve individual dignity

For information on services and products, call or write Personnel Decisions International, 2000 Plaza VII Tower, 45 South Seventh Street, Minneapolis, Minnesota 55402-1608, USA. Telephone: 800.633.4410 or 920.997.6995. Visit our Web site at **www.personneldecisions.com**.

About the Publisher

ePredix links people to profit by providing a comprehensive and single source for employee and applicant data mining, and in-depth business analyses. Leveraging over 50 years of research and data captured from over 40 million job applicants and employees, ePredix scientifically predicts who will perform effectively.

Fortune 500 companies and government agencies use ePredix's job- and industry-specific hiring, development, promotion, and succession planning products and services. Their scalable, configurable technology solutions streamline employers' access to and tracking of applicant and employee data, reducing cost and time to hire.

Demonstrating return on investment is the keystone of ePredix's business. By collecting job-specific business metrics such as revenue, profitability, turnover, and customer service ratings, ePredix determines the impact their solutions are having on each client's business. This data is then used to continually validate and improve the performance of ePredix's products in each client's environment.

ePredix products and services fall into three key categories:

Hiring

ePredix screening, selection, and interview products match a job candidate's knowledge, skills, experience, cultural fit, and motivations to the demands of the job. Employers get a clear and accurate picture of who will fit, who will perform, and who will stay—for all jobs, at all levels.

Development

Plan2Perform, an online employee development tool, compiles employee performance data from multiple sources to create an individualized development plan. When linked to ePredix assessment and performance solutions, Plan2Perform automatically prescribes a long-term development program for job candidates based on each candidate's strengths and weaknesses.

Promotion & Succession Planning

ePredix promotion and succession planning products accurately identify supervisory and management potential. By identifying hard to measure competencies such as leadership, management, and learning ability, ePredix products ensure that organizations promote individuals who have the ability to be successful leaders.

For more information about ePredix, contact us at 800/447-2266 or visit the Web site at www.ePredix.com

PDI OFFICES

www.personneldecisions.com

NORTH AMERICA

CORPORATE HEADQUARTERS
2000 Plaza VII Tower
45 South Seventh Street
Minneapolis, Minnesota 55402-1608
Phone 800 633 4410 Fax 612 904 7120

ATLANTA
Suite 560
1040 Crown Pointe Parkway
Atlanta, Georgia 30338
Phone 770 668 9908 Fax 770 668 9958

BOSTON
Suite 401
Three Copley Place
Boston, Massachusetts 02116
Phone 617 236 6511 Fax 617 236 6569

CHICAGO
Suite 2270
225 West Wacker Drive
Chicago, Illinois 60606
Phone 312 251 4180 Fax 312 251 4454

DALLAS - AUSTIN
Suite 1700 LB 142
600 East Las Colinas Boulevard
Irving, Texas 75039
Phone 972 401 3190 Fax 972 401 3193

DENVER
Building One DTC, Suite 925
5251 DTC Parkway
Greenwood Village, Colorado 80111
Phone 303 740 1020 Fax 303 740 0390

DETROIT
Suite 390
100 West Big Beaver Road
Troy, Michigan 48084
Phone 248 619 9330 Fax 248 619 9016

HOUSTON
Suite 700
1300 Post Oak Boulevard
Houston, Texas 77056
Phone 713 499 7500 Fax 713 499 7557

LOS ANGELES
Suite 750
2029 Century Park East
Los Angeles, California 90067-2928
Phone 310 556 4860 Fax 310 556 4865

MINNEAPOLIS - ST. PAUL
2000 Plaza VII Tower
45 South Seventh Street
Minneapolis, Minnesota 55402-1608
Phone 612 339 0927 Fax 612 904 7120

NEW YORK
52nd Floor
405 Lexington Avenue
New York, New York 10174-5301
Phone 212 972 6633 Fax 212 692 3300

SAN FRANCISCO
Suite 310
999 Baker Way
San Mateo, California 94404
Phone 650 372 1090 Fax 650 372 1099

WASHINGTON, DC
Suite 1000
1300 Wilson Boulevard
Arlington, Virginia 22209
Phone 703 522 3519 Fax 703 524 6325

EUROPE

BRATISLAVA
WBB Slovensko S.R.O. - a PDI company
Tomásikova 14
SK - 820 09 Bratislava
Slovak Republic
Tel 421 2 4333 9368 Fax 421 2 4341 3977

BRUSSELS
Gulledelle 96
B-1200 Brussels
Belgium
Tel 32 2 777 70 20 Fax 32 2 777 70 30

BUDAPEST
PDI Hungary Ltd.
Victor Hugo utca 11–15
H-1132 Budapest
Hungary
Tel 36 1 350 87 07 Fax 36 1 350 87 09

GENEVA
Immeuble Jean-Baptiste Say
13 Chemin du Levant
01210 Ferney-Voltaire
France
Tel 33 4 50 40 64 11 Fax 33 4 50 40 64 53

GÖTEBORG
Norra Liden 629
411 18 Göteborg
Sweden
Tel 46 31 701 82 12 Fax 46 31 701 82 89

LONDON
80 Wimpole Street
London W1G 9RE
UK
Tel 44 20 7487 5776 Fax 44 20 7487 5356

PARIS
6, square de l'Opéra-Louis-Jouvet
75009 Paris
France
Tel 33 1 43 12 92 92 Fax 33 1 47 42 13 55

STOCKHOLM
Kungsbroplan 3 A
SE-112 27 Stockholm
Sweden
Tel 46 8 402 00 20 Fax 46 8 411 88 30

STUTTGART
PDI Deutschland GmbH
Neue Strasse 7
D-72070 Tübingen
Germany
Tel 49 70 71 55 98 60 Fax 49 70 71 55 98 88

ASIA

HONG KONG
Personnel Decisions International Greater China
Suite 3705-6, 37/F
Tower II, Lippo Center
89 Queensway, Admiralty
Hong Kong
Tel 852 2572 2641 Fax 852 2572 2649

SHANGHAI
Personnel Decisions International Greater China
Room 810, Tomson Financial Building
710 Dong Fang Road, Pudong New Area
Shanghai 200122
China
Tel 86 21 5830 9993 Fax 86 21 5830 0907

SINGAPORE
Personnel Decisions International
#24-08 Orchard Towers
400 Orchard Road
Singapore 238875
Tel 65 6732 2252 Fax 65 6733 2252

TOKYO
Yebisu Garden Place Tower 18F
4-20-3, Ebisu, Shibuya-ku
Tokyo 150-6018
Japan
Phone 813 5798 3400 Fax 813 5798 3410

AUSTRALIA

MELBOURNE
Coyne Didsbury PDI, Pty Ltd
Level 4
398 Lonsdale Street
Melbourne Victoria 3000
Australia
Phone 61 3 9670 3833 Fax 61 3 9600 4001

SYDNEY
Coyne Didsbury PDI, Pty Ltd
Level 2
32 Martin Place
Sydney New South Wales 2000
Australia
Phone 61 2 9235 1516 Fax 61 2 9235 1526

Development Products from PDI

SUCCESSFUL MANAGER'S HANDBOOK

Over 900,000 copies in print, this 700-page reference book provides practical tips, on-the-job activities, and suggestions for improving managerial skills and effectiveness.

ISBN: 0-9725770-1-7 $59.95 U.S.

DEVELOPMENT FIRST: STRATEGIES FOR SELF-DEVELOPMENT

This easy-to-read book walks people through proven, practical steps to development. It helps them assess what they should work on, pick the right approaches and tactics, and learn from their experiences.

ISBN: 0-938529-13-7 $16.95 U.S.

LEADER AS COACH: STRATEGIES FOR COACHING AND DEVELOPING OTHERS

Coaching improves the bottom line because it goes to the heart of what makes people productive. This book discusses five practical coaching strategies that will increase the potential of your people and your organization.

ISBN: 0-938529-14-5 $19.95 U.S.

PRESENTATIONS: HOW TO CALM DOWN, THINK CLEARLY, AND CAPTIVATE YOUR AUDIENCE

This proven approach helps people develop and fine-tune their presentation skills, from crafting a message to delivering it effectively.

ISBN: 0-938529-23-4 $19.95 U.S.

SUCCESSFUL EXECUTIVE'S HANDBOOK

This book is the result of years of work with many successful Fortune 500 executives who lead today's high performance organizations. It is based on the same competency model as The PROFILOR® for Executives from PDI, which identifies the eight factors essential to executive success in every industry.

ISBN: 0-9725770-0-9 $75.00 U.S.

DEVELOPMENT FIRST WORKBOOK

Companion to the *Development FIRST* book, this workbook will help you create and implement a personal learning plan. The workbook comes with fill-in-the-blank templates and a completed sample.

ISBN: 0-938529-21-8 $13.95 U.S.

LEADER AS COACH WORKBOOK

Companion to the *Leader As Coach* book, this workbook offers targeted advice, exercises, and worksheets that will help you develop your coaching capabilities, whether you are a beginner or a seasoned veteran.

ISBN: 0-938529-22-6 $13.95 U.S.

IMPACT WITHOUT AUTHORITY: HOW TO LEVERAGE INTERNAL RESOURCES TO CREATE CUSTOMER VALUE

This book offers a "roadmap" and tools for strategic account managers (SAMs), as well as strategies for executives. SAMs will enhance their ability to influence areas of the organization that impact the customer.

(No volume discounts available.)

ISBN: 0-9728836-9-X $19.95 U.S.

Price Grid for Books Listed	
Quantity	% Discount
1–9	0%
10–24	10%
25–49	20%
50–199	25%
200+	30%
Plus Shipping and Handling Charges	